Aging

Contributing Authors

Ethel Percy Andrus Gerontology Center
University of Southern California

Vern L. Bengtson, Ph.D.
James E. Birren, Ph.D.
Vivian Clayton, M.A.
Neal E. Cutler, Ph.D.
Richard H. Davis, Ph.D.
Paul Denny, Ph.D.
Herbert A. deVries, Ph.D.
David A. Haber, A.B.
Robert A. Harootyan, Ph.D.
Chistopher Hertzog, A.B.
Ira S. Hirschfield, M.A.

Paul A. Kerschner, Ph.D.
Victor Regnier, M. Arch.
K. Warner Schaie, Ph.D.
John R. Schmidhauser, Ph.D.
Arthur N. Schwartz, Ph.D.
Judith Treas, Ph.D.
James Walker, Ph.D.
Robin Jane Walther, Ph.D.
David A. Walsh, Ph.D.
Ruth B. Weg, Ph.D.
Diana S. Woodruff, Ph.D.

AGING

Scientific Perspectives and Social Issues

Edited by
Diana S. Woodruff • James E. Birren
Ethel Percy Andrus Gerontology Center
University of Southern California

D. VAN NOSTRAND COMPANY
New York   Cincinnati   London   Toronto   Melbourne

Acknowledgments

Grateful acknowledgment is made to the following for permission to reprint or adapt tables and figures which are in copyright or of which they are the publishers:

American Sociological Review, Developmental Psychology, Excerpta Medical International Congress, Experimental Cell Research, Journal of Experimental Zoology, Geriatrics, Journal of Gerontology, Psychological Bulletin, Psychological Monographs, Public Opinion Quarterly, Journal of Verbal Learning and Behavior, Academic Press, The Center, The Free Press, University of Michigan Press, Pitman Medical Publishing Co. (London), Plenum Press, and W. B. Saunders Co.

Full source information for all materials is contained within the text.

D. Van Nostrand Company Regional Offices:
New York   Cincinnati   Millbrae

D. Van Nostrand Company International Offices:
London   Toronto   Melbourne

Library of Congress Catalog Card Number: 75-14743

ISBN: 0442-20800-6

Published by D. Van Nostrand Company
450 West 33rd Street, New York, N.Y. 10001

Published simultaneously in Canada by
Van Nostrand Reinhold Ltd.

10   9   8   7   6   5   4

Preface

This book reflects the inspiration of James E. Birren, director of the Ethel Percy Andrus Gerontology Center. Several years ago he originated the idea of a multidisciplinary text in gerontology, and he brought together the scholars who have contributed chapters to this book.

The material in this volume is original. It represents the most up-to-date perspectives on scientific and social issues in aging written by scientists and academicians who specialize in research and training in the field of gerontology. We present this material in a course entitled "Concepts and Issues in Gerontology," which is offered at the University of Southern California during the summer to graduate students and professionals working in the field of aging and during the academic year to upper division undergraduates. Ruth B. Weg had a major role in designing, organizing, and coordinating this course, and her model for teaching this material has been used, for the most part, by those of us who have followed her in coordinating the course.

Aging: Scientific Perspectives and Social Issues is an introductory text written for students interested in the processes and problems of aging and for individuals providing services to the elderly. While we deal with biological, psychological, and sociological concepts, we have not assumed that our readers have had any previous exposure to those disciplines, and thus we have outlined basic concepts underlying each discipline's approach. For those interested in further exploration of any of the topics covered in this volume, we have provided extensive references at the end of each chapter.

The book's organization reflects the pattern we have found to work best with our students. We first provide a broad overview of gerontology, and then gradually narrow the focus from sociological to psychological to biological perspectives. This scientific knowledge-base best prepares the student to deal with the broad social issues of aging which are discussed in the concluding chapters.

The introduction discusses some of the ways the various approaches presented in this volume are related and presents several recurring themes. This overview is followed by a brief history of the field of gerontology. The focus then moves to sociological perspectives of aging; Chapters 3 to 5 include descriptions of the demographic and social aspects of aging and a discussion of aging and the family. The following four chapters (Chapters 6 to 9) are devoted to recent psychological research on the aged individual. Discussion of cognitive processes such as intelligence, learning, and memory are included in this section, along with consideration of the physiological and biochemical substrates of behavior in animals as well as in humans. Chapters 10 to 12 on the biology of aging deal with the simplest levels of organization—aging at molecular, cellular, and physiological levels. From this "microscopic" perspective we turn to a broader view by addressing social and environmental issues and aging. In Chapters 13 and 14, consideration is given to planning residences, institutional settings, and neighborhoods for the elderly. The final section is on certain social issues: the impact of television; the role of economics; the importance of appropriate social policies; the potential of politics and political participation for improving the lives of the aged.

Clearly, this volume has a multidisciplinary approach to aging. At the Andrus Center some of us view the processes of aging through a microscope, others use a stethoscope, still others use a polygraph, or a questionnaire, or become involved as participant-observers. In this volume we attempt to share all of these views of aging, and we also try to apply our various perspectives to demonstrate how this knowledge can help contemporary and future generations of old people.

This book is an Andrus Center "family" project. In addition to the individual authors who all work at the Center, many other people at the Center became involved and earned our deep appreciation. Richard Davis provided the technical support of his publications staff, Eleanor James gave advice and technical assistance and Michael Williams contributed much time. Faith Alexander, Mildred Allyn, Barbara Bennett, Michael Contreras, Claudette Culbreath, Cosandra Douglas, Angie Giammalva, Richard Harpster, Giesla Heiman, Eleanor Hudson, Mary Isaac, Rochelle Smatewitz, Kathie Warren, and Jim Wolverton faithfully worked to put our writing into readable form.

Finally, a special acknowledgment is deserved by the staff at D. Van Nostrand Company. The contributions and encouragement of Sarah Magee paced all of us working in California, and Charity Scott's perspective helped to polish the book. Most of all I wish to thank the company president, Hyung W. Pak, whose belief and personal interest in the project led him to help us make this book a reality.

D.S.W.
April, 1975

Contents

Aging in Broad Perspective

1

Introduction: Multidisciplinary Perspectives of Aging

DIANA S. WOODRUFF

The scientific study of aging is coming of age. Increasing numbers of biological and social scientists are being attracted to this new field of knowledge, as reflected in the logarithmic expansion of the number of research articles and books published in the field of gerontology since 1900. A recent attempt (at the Andrus Gerontology Center) to create a definitive bibliography of the biomedical and social science research and the applied professional aspects of aging for the years 1954–1974 has yielded approximately 50,000 titles. The body of knowledge on aging is becoming so great that researchers specialize in aging not only within their specific disciplines, but also on a particular aspect of aging within the discipline. Thus, in this volume we have psychologists specializing in cognition, learning and memory, and psychophysiology, and we have biologists focusing on cellular mechanisms and physiology. Current information about aging is extensive; we cannot hope to cover all of the scientific perspectives or social issues in aging in one volume. However, by selecting the highlights of the biological, psychological, and sociological perspectives together with some of the social and environmental issues, we feel that the reader will get a representative picture of the field.

In spite of the vast body of knowledge in gerontology, we as investigators feel that we are only beginning to scratch the surface in understanding aging. This feeling is most painfully apparent when we look at the plight of a large percentage of the old people in our society. Aging as a social issue is receiving perhaps even more attention than it is as a scientific question. Both the House of Representatives and the Senate have special committees on aging, and Congress has recently created a National

3

Institute on Aging. The President has a special advisor on aging who heads the Administration on Aging. The judicial branch of federal government is also attending to more cases involving the legal issues of age. Indeed, the aged are recognizing a new means to power and equal rights through legal action. At the state and county levels there are also commissions and area agencies on aging, and city governments, too, are sponsoring conferences and planning programs for the elderly.

Scientific perspectives and social issues in aging are so interrelated that it is difficult to separate the two. Even the most basic of biological research at the molecular level has enormous social implications. If, as discussed in Chapter 10, molecular biologists unlock some of the secrets of DNA and RNA, they may be able to tamper with mechanisms that determine how long we live. When scientists determine some of the biochemical substrates for behavioral phenomena such as learning, memory, and depression as discussed in Chapters 7, 8, and 9, countless aged individuals will be affected. Basic research has already resulted in such practical consequences as estrogen therapy (see Chapter 11), which has affected the lives of hundreds of thousands of middle-aged and aged women. Indeed, basic research is responsible, at least in part, for aging becoming a contemporary social issue. The discovery of antibiotics significantly reduced the infant mortality rate in the early part of this century which led to the survival of greater numbers of people into old age today.

Scientists studying basic mechanisms of aging have in turn been dramatically affected by the social issues of aging. Many owe their training and continued support to the foresight of planners investing in long-term gain through basic research. With the advent of a generation of individuals over the age of 65 comprising fully ten percent of the population in the United States, policy makers have been forced to attend to the social issues of aging.

The Impact of Aging on Society

One of the themes running through this volume is the impact that greater numbers of individuals surviving into old age has on society. There is a greater proportion of aged in our society today than ever before, and the aged population continues to grow. Life expectancy for the average male born today is 67 years, and for the average female it is 75 years. This represents a gain of close to 25 years over what the life expectancy was only 75 years ago.

Birren and Clayton set the stage for this theme in their chapter on the history of gerontology by observing that until the twentieth century only aristocrats, poets, and philosophers thought about longevity. Aging was not a topic of concern to the common man who had to expend all of his energy just to stay alive. As recently as 1900 the average individual was fortunate to survive to the age of 50. The aged in society were few in number and were considered unique and remarkable rather than burdensome. A large proportion of elderly in society is thus a very recent phenomenon.

The changing age structure of our population is detailed in Chapter 3 by Cutler and Harootyan. Declines in the mortality rate, the birth rate, and the immigration rate are presented as the societal forces which have led to an aging of the population. Aging, in turn, affects society, and some of the issues which concern demographers are the impact of increasing numbers of elderly on the dependency ratio (defined as the number of people in the dependent segment divided by the number in the supportive or working population), the effect of large concentrations of elderly in the cities, and the implications of sex difference in longevity. Cutler and Harootyan also present projections suggesting that the number of people over the age of 65 will continue to grow and thus have continued impact on society.

In Chapter 4 on the sociology of aging, Bengtson and Haber develop the notion of continuing change with regard to the aged in society, and they expand on Cutler and Harootyan's discussion of cohort (a group of individuals born in the same five-year period). Since people born around the same time share many common social and historical experiences and hence, perhaps, a common perspective, and since rapid change is characteristic of our society, Bengtson and Haber suggest that new cohorts of aged may be different from previous cohorts. Furthermore, future aged cohorts may retain many of their particular characteristics as younger cohorts. Thus, the radical hippie generation of the late 1960s may be the older radicals of the 2020s.

Cutler and Schmidhauser reemphasize the importance of the increasingly large aged cohort in Chapter 18 on politics and aging as this phenomenon has clear implications for politicians and policy makers. It is essential that programs for the aged be structured flexibly so they can meet the needs of future as well as present cohorts of elderly.

Some of the more positive findings from this cohort analysis are presented by Bengtson and Haber. Future cohorts of elderly will most likely be more fortunate than the contemporary aged. Proportionately fewer individuals in future elderly cohorts will be foreign born and hence they will be more acculturated in American society. Perhaps they will suffer less from culture and future shock and find it easier to be involved in society. Future cohorts of elderly will also be better prepared for retirement, less economically deprived, and better educated. Moreover, as pointed out by Kerschner and Hirschfield in their chapter on social policy, legislators will have had more experience in planning for the elderly and will be able to avoid some of the earlier policy pitfalls.

Schaie was one of the first to recognize the importance of cohort differences, and in Chapter 6 he suggests that to have a sophisticated understanding of human aging one has to be aware of these differences. Since the aged as compared to younger cohorts are educationally deprived, Schaie discusses the need for alleviation of educational obsolescence. While contemporary cohorts of aged need remedial education to bring them to the educational level of younger people, future cohorts of elderly will be better educated. Since people with more education tend to seek out continuing education in greater numbers, future cohorts of aged will have an impact on society as they may demand educational opportunities throughout life. Furthermore, at a time when zero population growth is becoming a reality, schools and colleges will need to fill their enrollments. Classroom space and teachers which might otherwise be unused could serve the needs of the elderly. A life-span approach to education is contrary to the current emphasis on early childhood education, but it would benefit both the educational institutions and the aging if the classrooms were opened to students of all ages.

Treas makes clear the impact of aging on society in Chapter 5 by pointing out the tremendously different experience of contemporary marriage and family life as compared to that experience at the turn of the century. In 1900 one spouse died, on average, before the last child left home. Today, a married couple can expect fifteen to 20 years together after the last child is launched. Treas also dispells the myth of three-generational families and points out that while more and more individuals are surviving to reach grandparenthood, they do not desire nor do they undertake to live with their children and grandchildren.

More of the elderly live in urban than in rural areas. Regnier in his chapter on neighborhood planning suggests that urban areas have the greatest concentration of elderly, and he describes the impact of the urban neighborhoods on the aged and the means for effectively planning facilities to serve the elderly in these neighborhoods. While most elderly live in the community, some are institutionalized or live in housing designed specifically for them. Schwartz describes some considerations for planning and structuring appropriate micro-environments for the aged in Chapter 13.

The increasing population of aged in our society has had significant social impact in politics, in economics, and in the media. Chapters 15, 16,

17, and 18 address themselves to these issues. The importance of the aged as a television audience, their image on television, and most importantly, the potential of television as a means of communication, education, and entertainment for the elderly is discussed in Davis' chapter on television and the aged. Legislative programs for the elderly are considered by Kerschner and Hirschfield in Chapter 17. They are concerned with the manner in which policy makers devise legislation for the elderly. They provide an account of how aging legislation has typically been undertaken in the past and give recommendations for more effective approaches in the present and future. The economic condition of the elderly is explored in detail by Walther in Chapter 16. This discussion of economics and aging points out the economic impact of retirement on the aged and on society and considers the economic implications of some of the social policies described in Chapter 17. The impact of the aged on society is approached from several perspectives in Chapter 18. The aged are a large potential voting bloc, and Cutler and Schmidhauser discuss some of the historical factors which may cause the aged to vote as a bloc along with factors contributing to a diversity of views among the aged. They also approach the significance of age in politics from the perspective of the age of individuals in political power. From this analysis it is clear that selected older individuals do have great prestige and power in the United States.

While the impact of increasing numbers of elderly is discussed directly in many of the chapters, it is not as clear in some of the chapters on psychology and biology. However, the fact that there are greater numbers of aged in society has sensitized academicians to the issues of aging and raised researchers' consciousness of aging as a problem for scientific investigation. As Birren and Clayton point out, one hundred years ago only the aristocrats could afford the luxury of thinking about old age. In a more affluent society where individuals are living longer, scientists are trained and encouraged to undertake, among other things, research on the basic processes in aging. This research, in turn, may have great impact on the future age structure of society. As pointed out in Chapter 3, if cures for cardiovascular disease alone were to be discovered, ten years would be added to the average life expectancy. Cellular level engineering to extend the human life span (Chapter 10) has overwhelming ethical and social implications. Improving the health of the aged through nutrition (Chapter 11) and exercise (Chapter 12) could lead to added vigor in the elderly and perhaps greater participation in social roles. If psychologists devise means to help the aged function as efficiently as the young in learning and memory (Chapter 7), if they discover some of the secrets of brain function and alleviate depression in old age (Chapter 8), or if they aid the elderly in responding as fast as they had in their youth (Chapter 9), aging might become quite a different experience in the future. Clearly, the impact of such discoveries on demography, society, economics, public policy, the media, and politics would be tremendous, and future cohorts of aged would feel and act quite differently than present ones.

Levels of Interaction

The material presented in this volume has been drawn from many disciplines, for aging is a complex phenomenon that can be viewed at a number of levels from a variety of perspectives. Aging has biological, psychological, and social components, and individuals age in all three dimensions. Furthermore, the rates of biological, psychological, and social aging may be different in the same individual. While the biological rate of aging—the efficiency of the biological organism—may contribute to the pace of psychological and social aging, on a psychological level a person may feel and behave somewhat apart from how well his body functions. Social norms prescribe that individuals should "act their age," and again while these prescriptions may be related to biological and psychological phenomena, they can also stand apart from them. Furthermore, social and psychological events can affect the rate of biological aging. We have only to compare pictures of our Presidents when they take the oath of office and when they finish their term to witness the dramatic biological consequences of environmental stress.

We take a multidisciplinary approach to aging in this volume because aging is a multifaceted phenomenon. While aging can occur independently at the various biological, psychological, and social levels, these components generally interact. We often refer in the chapters to other chapters in this volume because, while we recognize the need to examine specific perspectives of aging in depth, we also know that aging at any level occurs against the background of change at all levels from molecular to cultural phenomena.

There are countless examples in this volume of the interactive nature of the aging process. We tend to think of aging as simply a biological process, but in this book it becomes clear that social and psychological factors can affect biological processes at least as profoundly as biology affects behavior, socialized activity, and social policy.

One clear example of a biochemical-psychological-social interaction is alluded to in Chapter 8. Walker and Hertzog suggest that age changes in brain biochemistry may be related to the greater incidence of depression observed in old people; thus, a chemical reaction in the brain has significant psychological consequences. From a sociological perspective we can observe that many of the admissions to mental institutions are old, depressed patients, and also that the suicide rate increases dramatically with age. These phenomena may all be the psychological and social outcomes of age changes in biochemistry.

On the other hand, as pointed out in many of the chapters, the aged suffer a number of losses which might predispose them to be depressed and which might in turn affect brain biochemistry. As discussed in several chapters, retirement leads to loss of role, loss of status, and loss of income. Deaths of friends and spouse are another type of loss faced by the aged. Since in general women outlive their husbands, they are especially likely to face widowhood and the unfortunate psychological and social losses which accompany it (see Chapter 5). The loss of physical vigor discussed by deVries in Chapter 12 and the decline in health described by Weg in Chapter 11 are yet other causes for depression—especially in white males who commit suicide in old age at higher rates than any other group. In many of these cases, suicide occurred as a direct consequence of declining health and vigor.

Thus, there may be independent mechanisms operating in the aged to predispose them to depression. They may be in double or triple jeopardy with regard to depression. Independent biochemical changes may occur to initiate depression in old age, independent physiological losses may cause this mood change, or social and psychological losses may alone serve to depress elderly people. Each of these phenomena might lead to depression, but more likely they interact to present the complex and difficult-to-treat depressions found in the aged. Thus, to intervene and alleviate depression in old age we might prescribe drugs to affect brain biochemistry, we might recommend moderate exercise or a better diet to affect health and vigor, we might suggest psychotherapy to provide emotional support in time of grief, and we might devise new social roles for old people in programs such as Foster Grandparents so that they feel needed in society. Programs such as the latter have the additional benefit of providing financial support to augment economic losses. What the various approaches taken by the authors in this volume suggest is that many of the decrements of aging are the result of multiple causes and are best treated with multifaceted solutions.

Interventions in Aging

Depression is only one of many problems of aging to which interventions at all levels have been directed. Indeed, a major theme recurring through-

out this volume is intervention. What intervention strategies can we devise
on the biological, psychological, social, or policy level to improve the lot
of the aged in society today and of future generations of elderly?

In Chapter 2 Birren and Clayton discussed one intervention which
has already occurred—using antibiotics to cure infectious diseases. The
lowering of the mortality rate, particularly of infants, has been the primary
impact of this medical advance which has made it possible for more individuals to reach old age. In Chapters 9 and 10 there are discussions of the
prospects for future medical advances which could extend still further the
average life expectancy. Concern is also expressed for the need to improve
health in old age and to add life to years rather than merely adding years
to life.

Quality of life and life satisfaction represent one of the sociological
perspectives presented in Chapter 4. Bengtson and Haber discuss the need
to intervene on a social level to affect the vicious cycle of society's attitudes toward the elderly. On a societal level the aged are considered in-
competents to be moved aside to make way for the young. They are
relegated to lower status, they are deprived of their jobs and sources of
income through forced retirement, and they are provided with few alternative roles. Told that they are burdensome and unneeded, the aged themselves begin to believe that they are unfit to take part in society—they
begin to believe that they are incompetent. Incompetence thus becomes a
self-fulfilling prophecy for the elderly. Once they accept the fact that they
are incompetent they fail more frequently and accept failure and defeat as
part of the process of growing old. Surprisingly, the aged themselves are
often the most rigid adherents to negative stereotypes about old age. Be-
lieving they are incompetent, the aged may become less effective in their
actions and confirm the social stereotype. Bengtson and Haber imply the
possibility of intervention at a societal level through the use of mass communication and the potential for intervention with the aged themselves in
terms of changing their self-image. Davis in Chapter 15 points out that
images of aging on television already appear to be changing for the better.

Many chapters in this volume present research findings either suggesting that the old as compared to the young are not incompetent or that
we can intervene to help the aged perform more effectively. Schaie in
Chapter 6 finds few real age changes in intelligence, and Walsh in Chapter
7 presents some cases in which young and old are equal on learning and
memory performance. In Chapter 9 Woodruff discusses the potential of
biofeedback to alter physiological rates in older people and produce a positive effect on their behavior. She also discusses means to stimulate older
individuals who may need to be alerted or aroused to think and act more
efficiently. Schwartz, too, in Chapter 13 discusses environmental prosthetics

as a means to alleviate some of the problems the aged experience as a result of sensory deficits. Additionally, Schwartz presents the negative consequences of bleak institutional environments and provides suggestions as to how these environments can be made more comfortable and stimulating to aged individuals.

The potential for interventions on a neighborhood level are described by Regnier, an architect and planner. In Chapter 14 he discusses the usefulness of social science research to planners in identifying patterns of neighborhood activity. What facilities do the aged use? How do they get access to these facilities? Where are the best locations in the city to provide services for the elderly? How can intervention by means of planning within the neighborhood improve the lives of elderly residents? These are the kinds of questions Regnier considers in an attempt to make urban areas more habitable for the elderly.

The theme of intervening to make societal facilities and supports more accessible to the elderly is also apparent in Chapter 6 on cognition when Schaie stresses the need to provide education for the elderly. The aged are educationally deprived in a relative sense inasmuch as they were in school 50 or more years ago at a time when the knowledge base was considerably smaller than it is today. They are also deprived in an absolute sense as they have received on average four to six years less education than young and middle-aged cohorts. Schaie suggests that much of what we attribute to intellectual decrement in the elderly actually results from educational obsolescence. As an intervention he suggests remedial education to update the elderly. Education can also be viewed as a useful way to open new leisure pursuits to the elderly, and as an end in itself, education can make the lives of the elderly more meaningful.

In Chapter 15 Davis views television as a means of educational intervention for the elderly. Since many elderly have limited mobility and little access to transportation facilities, and since they already tend to view television more frequently than most other age groups, television provides a means of bringing education to the aged in a form with which they are already familiar.

Education is also a means to provide the aged with information about health care and nutrition. Many chapters deal with medical interventions for the elderly, and we do have a great deal of information about how to maximize health in old age. In her chapter on the physiology of aging Weg discusses normal aging processes and disease in old age and presents a number of suggestions about how those of all ages can improve their chances of having a healthy old age and how the already aged can maximize their health. Among the important aspects are the maintenance of a balanced diet (which many old people do not receive due to poverty and/or the fact that when they live alone they do not prepare proper meals) and the avoidance of stress (which leads to pathologies such as strokes, heart attacks, and ulcers). Weg also discusses sexuality and attitudes toward sexuality in old age, the potential intervention of alleviating anxiety about sexuality in old people, and the importance of eliminating some of the negative stereotypes and stigmas we seem to have about sexuality in the aged.

DeVries' chapter on exercise physiology and aging is addressed entirely to the issue of health interventions. He views many of the observed physiological declines as resulting from disuse rather than the aging process, and finds that when old people exercise they not only regain some of their physiological capacity, they also actually feel better.

Chapters 7, 8, and 9 on various aspects of the psychology of aging are all concerned with interventions to help older individuals think better as well as feel better. In describing research on learning and memory, Walsh discusses three models which psychologists have used to explain these phenomena. He uses these models to present a rationale for some of the strategies investigators have used to help older pople learn and remember better. Among these strategies are helping the aged to form associations, making material meaningful to them, presenting material at a slower pace, and making sure the aged are comfortable and relaxed in the learning situation.

Discussing the brain, behavior and aging, Walker and Hertzog extrapolate from work done with animals to its implications for humans. They report the beneficial effect of enriched environments on the regaining of function in surgically impaired animals and draw implications for the care of human stroke victims. Stimulating the patient, talking to him, and providing him with visual and auditory sensory input may help him to recover faster. Woodruff also points out the importance of environmental stimulation for older people as well as stroke victims in the chapter on physiological psychology when she discusses the effects of sensory deficits on the functional capacity of the aged. Since there is a decline with age in the efficiency in most of the sensory modalities, and since the brain seems to require at least a minimal level of sensory input to function efficiently, it is important to ensure adequate illumination levels for the elderly, to speak loudly and clearly, to touch old people, and to maintain a room temperature which makes them comfortable.

Comfortable living for the elderly is addressed from another perspective by Treas in her chapter on aging and the family. She points out the greater longevity of people who are married and considers ways to intervene in what is becoming a growing social problem—widowhood. Women outnumber men in increasing numbers over the life span so that the women who survive to the age of 80 outnumber men by almost two to one. Thus, since living with someone normally enhances life satisfaction and health, Treas considers some alternative living arrangements as an intervention for happiness in old age.

Alternatives to retirement are presented in the chapter on economics. Walther suggests that part-time employment is an intervention which would provide the aged with greater economic independence. She also discusses some of the considerations economists must make when they advise policy makers on the design of programs for the elderly. Programs must be both equitable and efficient, and Walther points out some of the difficulties in structuring intervention programs to meet these constraints.

Interventions on the social policy level are discussed at length by Kerschner and Hirschfield who suggest that legislators have been less than systematic in their attempts to aid the elderly. Health care, housing, and income maintenance are areas in which legislation raising the standards of living for the elderly has been enacted. The authors of Chapter 17 suggest that social policy interventions could have an even greater impact on improving the quality of life for the aged if designed with more foresight and social science input.

The potential of political action as a source of intervention to improve the lot of the aged is presented in Chapter 18. Increased political awareness on the part of the elderly can be used as a powerful force to effect change. Older people tend to vote in greater numbers than do younger cohorts, and they may place themselves in a position to affect their future while younger, more apathetic voters often ignore the political process. Groups like the American Association of Retired Persons and the National Retired Teachers Association, which have a combined membership of over seven million aged, have active lobbyists in Congress and are acknowledged as a political force. More activist-oriented groups such as the Gray Panthers are also forming to demand equal rights for the elderly. Thus, when considering the future of the aged as affected by and affecting politics, Cutler and Schmidhauser predict that age will be a salient factor in the politics of the not too distant future. They base this prediction on five sources of evidence. First, the size and proportion of elderly in the population will continue to grow. Second, as people grow older they tend to participate more and are more interested in politics than the young. Third, people with more education tend to participate more in politics, and future cohorts of aged will have attained higher levels of education. Fourth, future cohorts of elderly are individuals who, in their youth, participated in new forms of political action, and this behavior may continue into old age.

Finally, people are becoming more conscious of old people and of being old, and this consciousness-raising has already begun to lead aged cohorts to become more politically active.

We have traced the theme of intervention through all but one of the chapters in this volume. In that chapter on the cellular biology of aging, Denny presents research which could lead to the most far-reaching of all interventions—the extension of the upper limit to which people have been known to live. We are at a point in gerontological research where this type of genetic intervention is no longer a prospect for science fiction. As biologists begin to break the genetic code of life, we may actually realize the dream expressed through the earliest recorded myths—the dream of conquering or at least postponing death.

Is this the final goal of gerontological research and its social implementation? Most of us working in the field of aging think not. We aim for the most part to affect quality rather than quantity of life, and it is our hope that our work and the material we present in this book will contribute to an understanding of the processes of aging and to improving the quality of life for old people living today and in the future. The quality of life of older Americans has improved dramatically in this century, and as this book is read one begins to perceive the potentials for a better way of life for the aged of the future—a way of life that can offer more options and opportunities.

2

History of Gerontology

JAMES E. BIRREN · VIVIAN CLAYTON

This chapter presents a brief history of gerontology from its emergence as a pattern of thinking and through its evolution to a field for scientific investigation in the twentieth century. Attention will be given to the shifting age structure of our present society and how it is influencing the study of gerontology.

Early Inquiries into Aging

Gerontology is the science of aging. It began as an inquiry into the characteristics or qualities of long-lived people. Indeed, when the average age of life in 1000 B.C. was 18 years, men who lived to be 50, 60, and even 70 were viewed as privileged. Much speculation and many myths attempted to explain why such individuals were favored.

Myths about aging and death in the literature of the past are usually structured around one of three basic themes. The *antediluvian* theme (Gruman, 1966) emerges from myths that are based on the belief that people lived much longer in the past. This theme is exemplified in the book of Genesis, where the life spans of ten Hebrew patriarchs are recorded: Adam lived for 930 years, Seth for 912 years, Noah for 950 years, and so on. Stressing means of avoiding death, legends of the antediluvian type frequently occur in other folklore. The Trobrianders and the Ainu in North Japan, for example, believed their forefathers had been able to rejuvenate themselves by shedding their skins like snakes.

The *hyperborean* theme, originating with the Greeks, arises from the belief that in some distant place there is a culture or society whose people enjoy a remarkably long life. "According to the traditions of ancient Greece, there dwells *hyper* (beyond) Boreas (the north wind) a fortunate people free from all natural ills" (Gruman, 1966, p. 22). "[T]heir hair crowned with gold by-leaves, they hold glad revelry; and neither sickness nor baneful eld mingleth among that chosen people; but, aloof from toil and conflict, they dwell afar" (Pindar quoted in Gruman, 1966, p. 22).

A third theme found in many legends is the *rejuvenation theme,* which is often expressed by a fountain whose waters are purported to rejuvenate. Americans are familiar with the legend of Juan Ponce de Leon whose search for the "fountain of youth" led to the accidental discovery of Florida in 1513. The earliest account of Ponce de Leon's adventure was published in 1535 in the general history of the Indies by Oviedo, who served as a Spanish official in the New World. He wrote that Ponce de Leon was "seeking that fountain of Biminie that the Indians have given it to be understood would renovate or resprout and refresh the age and forces of he who drank or bathed himself in that fountain" (Beauvous quoted in Gruman, 1966, p. 24). Drinking from or bathing in a fountain are not the only expressions of the rejuvenation theme in history. The Chinese, for example, at the time of the Tao Te Ching dynasty (350-250 B.C.) advocated gymnastic techniques for increasing the length of life.

In each of these themes is one principal concern: the quest for prolongation of life. In his monograph *History of Ideas about the Prolongation of Life,* Gruman suggests that the inevitability of dying led mankind to think about ways of extending life. Long-lived individuals were viewed with awe and received respect; undoubtedly it was of some concern to discover whether they possessed magical powers which warded off the demonic spirits thought to be responsible for dying.

Some of the present research pursuits can, in fact, be related to these basic themes. Alexander Leaf, a physician and pathologist, visited many areas where very long lived people are reputed to exist, such as the Peruvian Andes and the Georgian Republic in Russia (Leaf, 1973). Even though he traveled to these regions as a medical investigator and collected empirical data on eating habits, work patterns, and health conditions, his study has a mystical overtone.

Present hopes of rejuvenation extend beyond the fountain. Currently in Switzerland under the auspices of Dr. Paul Niehans, sheep embryos are ground up, homogenized, and injected into an elite circle of his clients. Certain hormones and other substances not present in the adult animal are purported to be in the embryo. Rat embryos that underwent the same procedure were injected into old rats, with the result that the injected rats lived slightly longer. Such efforts often capture the imagination of novelists. The popular *Methuselah Enzyme,* by Fred M. Stuart, is an adaptation of this embryo homogenate theme, and Aldous Huxley develops a closely related theme in *After Many a Summer Dies the Swan.*

The Scientific Era

The advent of the scientific mode of thought in the 1600s caused a break with earlier traditions that relied on magic or speculation to explain naturally occurring phenomena. The scientific method advocated the systematic observation of phenomena in order to discover the underlying laws governing behavior. As Frances Bacon stated, "The end of our foundation is knowledge of causes, and secret motions of things; and the enlargening of the bounds of human empire, to the affecting of all things possible" (Bacon as quoted by Gruman, 1966, p. 80). Bacon's implication for gerontology was that by undertaking a systematic study of the processes of aging one might discover the causes of aging. Bacon thought that poor hygienic practices had the most significant effect on the aging process. His search for a single cause was misleading, however, for there is not one cause of aging. Multiple causation is a more adequate explanation for the aging process.

Early Empirical Period

One of the great American heroes in the early 1700s was Benjamin Franklin. Franklin was a versatile thinker with serious interests in many fields. One of his interests was in science and aging. As had Bacon, he hoped that science would be able to discover the laws governing the aging process and that it might, ultimately, discover a way to rejuvenate people.

> I wish it were possible, from this instance, to invent a method of embalming drowned persons, in such a manner that they may be recalled to life at any period, however distant, for having a very ardent desire to see and observe the state of America a hundred years hence, I should prefer to any ordinary death, the being immersed in a cask of Madeira wine, with a few friends, till that time, to be then recalled to life by the solar warmth of my dear country. But since in all probability we live in an age too early and too near the infancy of science, to hope to see an art brought in our time to its perfection, I must for the present content myself with the treat, which you are so kind as to promise me, of the resurrection of a owl or a turkey cock. (Franklin quoted in Gruman, 1966, p. 84)

Franklin also explored the possibility that lightning might influence the resurrection of deceased animals and people. It was thought at the time that since electricity had a stimulating effect, it would have a direct influence on the life span. A letter from Franklin to a friend reads, "Your observations on the causes of death and the experiments which you propose for recalling to life those who appear to be killed by lightning in this case demonstrate equally your sagacity and humanity" (Franklin quoted in Gruman, 1966, p. 84). Even today some people try to sell static electricity belts under the pretense that they will prolong life.

Although Bacon and Franklin were among those who anticipated the scientific method, a Belgian named Quetelet is considered the first gerontologist (Birren, 1961). Quetelet was born in Ghent in 1796 and received the first doctorate in science from the University of Ghent in 1819 in mathematics. After earning his degree he became interested in probabilities and subsequently developed the concept of the average man around which extremes were distributed. The result of Quetelet's pioneering work was a curve that we now accept as representing a basic distribution of most human traits. The curve indicates that there is an average or central tendency around which are distributed higher and lower measurements. Measurements distribute themselves this way with regard to such characteristics as height, weight, or intelligence. The discovery of the normal distribution is attributed usually to Gauss, but Quetelet anticipated him. (The "Gaussian curve" is often well-known to students, many of whom are graded on the so-called bell-shaped or normal curve.) In his book published in 1835, *On the Nature of Man and the Development of His Faculties,* Quetelet lists the averages and the extremes he measured for various traits, such as hand strength and weight. Quetelet also published records of variations in the death and birth rates, and included some data on the psychology of aging. Specifically, he looked at the age of French and English playwrights and began to analyze their productivity in terms of how old they were. Such notions have been followed up in the more recent work of Lehman (1953), who found that the focus of artistic production changed with the age of the producer. Young poets typically write lyric poems, while many older poets write sagas and epics.

The use of the Gaussian curve to describe human characteristics represented a conceptual revolution. Aristotelian philosophy stated that man was or was not; Quetelet introduced the idea that the traits of man varied in degrees. He had more or less of something, and these differences were measurable. Variations in human traits could also be related to natural causes in keeping with the scientific approach. Quetelet broke with earlier thought and tradition by examining longevity. Before the 1800s longevity belonged to the domain of theology and was not considered fitting matter for natural science. For Quetelet however, little was beyond knowing if one attended to scientific observation and statistical relationships. Although many people are unfamiliar with the work of Quetelet, the many translations of his book show the wide dissemination of his ideas in his time.

Sir Francis Galton was perhaps the next most prominent investigator in the field of aging. Like Quetelet, he was a member of the upper class. He was also a cousin of Charles Darwin. In his own right he was a well-known statistician, responsible for developing the first index of correlation. Galton's fundamental contribution to the study of aging is the data he collected at the International Health Exhibition in London in 1884. Over 9,337 males and females aged 5 to 80 were measured on a number of characteristics, including Quetelet's measure of strength of grip, vital capacity, visual accuracy, and reaction time. The subjects were measured on 17 different abilities altogether. With these data Galton demonstrated that many human characteristics showed differences with age. Hearing for high tones was one of the variables which showed a lower capacity with age. At that time there were no electronic audiometers for measuring hearing, but Galton was a shrewd investigator. He developed a series of whistles to be tuned by varying the volume of the whistles, and he could predict the whistles' frequencies in advance. Galton found that with increasing age the higher-frequency whistles could no longer be heard. The data would seem to confirm English folklore that old farmers could no longer hear the very high frequency sounds of flying bats. The observation of a loss in sensitivity to high tones with age appears to be verified by subsequent research. The causes of this phenomenon are quite another matter, however, and the mechanisms are not understood. (In the earlier, prescientific tradition, such an observation might have been given a magical interpretation rather than an explanation based on possible natural causes.)

Galton later dropped his interests in this area and, becoming more concerned with eugenics, devoted his attention to improving the genetics of society. To this end he founded the Eugenics Society in Britain.

Later Empirical Period

After Galton, a number of individuals began to study various aspects of aging. Minot (*The Problems of Age, Growth and Death,* 1908), Metchnikoff (*The Prolongation of Life,* 1908), Child (*Senescence and Rejuvenescence,* 1915), and Pearl (*Biology of Death,* 1922) were among the major biologists interested in explaining the phenomenon of aging.

Some of the hypotheses of these early scientists were weak or incomplete. Metchnikoff, for example, was impressed by the observation that yogurt eaters of Middle Europe apparently lived long lives. He attributed their longevity to the possibility that yogurt cleansed the gastrointestinal tract of bacteria which he thought caused an increasing toxicity of the organism with age. Metchnikoff's hypothesis was faulty, however, for some of the gastrointestinal bacteria are important. If, for example, a rat's gastrointestinal flora are destroyed, the rat will suffer from vitamin deficiency because the flora synthesize the vitamins needed for normal functioning.

While Metchnikoff's hypothesis was weak, Pearl's hypothesis regarding longevity was incomplete. Pearl was an epidemiologist and biostatistician at Johns Hopkins University. He began to study longevity in families and found that people who had long-lived parents and grandparents tended to live longer than the average of the population. This seemed to be evidence of a genetic factor in longevity. As a result of Pearl's findings, people thought that heredity was the sole key for determining how long we live. If you picked the right grandparents, so to speak, a longer life was guaranteed you. This reasoning, however, represents a violation of one of the major features of the aging process, namely, multiple determination. Getting old is the result of the interplay of biological, social, psychological, and ecological forces. This point can be illustrated by the following example. Imagine that you had grandparents who lived to their eighties. Nevertheless, your personal life style might lead you to be 30 percent overweight, to smoke, and to drink alcohol heavily. These factors could eliminate the genetic advantage of having long-lived grandparents, and you would probably have a shorter life span than the average. In other words, there appears to be no single determinant of longevity, no single gene inherited from our ancestors that predetermines our life spans.

Another book on aging which appeared in 1922 was entitled *Senescence, the Second Half of Life,* by G. Stanley Hall. Hall was a psychologist specializing in childhood and adolescence. He published the first book in this country on the latter topic, and actually coined the word "adolescence." He was president of Clark University and founded one of the first psychology departments in this country at Johns Hopkins University. His concern with his own retirement led him to write *Senescence.* Up to this point, psychologists had regarded old age as but the inverse or regression of development. Hall noted that,

> As a psychologist I am convinced that the psychic states of old people have great significance. Senescence, like adolescence, has its own feelings, thoughts and wills, as well as its own physiology, and their regimen is important as well as that of the body. Individual differences here are probably greater than in youth. (Hall, 1922, p. 100)

One of Hall's innovations was a study of old people's religious beliefs and fears of death by means of a questionnaire. Hall found that people did not necessarily show an increase in religious interest as they grew older; he also discovered that the old in his sample had not become more fearful of death. Gerontologists today keep rediscovering the fact that the aged are afraid of the circumstances of dying, but are not more fearful of death itself. Death, as an abstraction, is more a young person's fear.

A contemporary of G. Stanley Hall was a physician named Osler, an internist at Johns Hopkins University. At that period, medicine had the tradition of looking for a single cause of a disease or disorder. It was thought that the identification of the organism entering the body would lead to the prescription of a specific therapy which in turn would bring the cure. Osler was impressed by a preponderance of arteriosclerosis, or hardening of the arteries, in old individuals. His contribution to gerontology was the discovery that aging was closely related to the state of blood vessels in the body, and he maintained that if the brain did change with age, it was a result of the hardening of the arteries.

While the Americans stressed the relation between calcification of arteries and the cardiovascular system in the aging process in the 1920s. Pavlov and his students in Russia emphasized the importance of the central nervous system. From his now classic conditioning experiments with dogs, Pavlov found that old animals conditioned differently from young ones and that their responses showed a different course of extinction. Pavlov's research and conclusions on the aging process are reflected in the following quotation from a summary of Russian studies on aging:

> On the basis of all the material at our disposal, we can say that the inhibition process is the first to succumb to old age, and after this, it would appear that the mobility of the nervous processes is affected. This is evident from the fact that a large percentage of our aging dogs ceased to tolerate the previous more complex conditioned-reflex system. The responses become chaotic, the effects fluctuate in an entirely irregular fashion, and good results can be obtained only by simplifying the scheme. I think that this can very legitimately be ascribed to the fact that mobility decreases with the years. If we have a distinct effect in a large system, this means that one stimulus does not interfere with another and does not spread its effect to the next nerve process. When a nerve process is delayed, however, the remaining traces of each stimulus become prolonged and influence the succeeding ones, i.e., we have a chaotic state and confusion. (Nikitin, 1958)

The question of whether a perfect nervous system ages only because of external influence such as inadequate blood flow (the focus of early American researchers) or because a "time clock" slows down the functions of the nervous system itself (as the early Russian scientists emphasized) is still being investigated today, and some answers will follow in later chapters. Evidence again suggests the notion of multiple determinants of aging of the nervous system.

In one of his statements, Pavlov presents a fundamental issue of gerontology that has persisted to the present. This issue involves the differentiation between a normal process of senescence and that due to disease. He states, "In our dogs, we were able to observe both *normal physiological and pathological old age*" (italics ours; Nikitin, 1958). Some physicians maintain that only disease or pathology can lead to the demise of an otherwise perfect organism and that it is meaningless to say that someone dies of "old age." Others who oppose this disease model of aging claim that there is a normal pattern of aging, apart from disease. Normal patterns of aging could be the result of genetic or environmental determinants. To distinguish the inevitable from the avoidable through manipulation of the environment is the concern of many researchers today.

Growing Interest in Gerontology

A number of significant publications dealing with the processes of aging appeared in the 1920s. The 1930s laid the groundwork for many of the developments in gerontology that have flourished in the post-World War II period. Medicine became increasingly interested in the degenerative diseases because dramatic progress was being made in controlling the early-life killers, the infectious diseases. Studying chronic disease, however, involves examining the physiological changes of the aging host to that disease. In 1933 *Arteriosclerosis: A Survey of the Problem,* edited by E. V. Cowdry, was published. This volume began to consider the relationship between aging and the blood vessels, of which arteriosclerosis is in part a manifestation. As a result of the activities of the Josiah Macy Jr. Foundation, an interdisciplinary volume was sponsored devoted to the problems of aging. The activities of the Josiah Macy Foundation also led to a conference sponsored by the National Research Council and the Union of American Biological Societies at Woods Hole, Massachusetts, on July 25-26, 1937. The National Research Council further sponsored a conference of its committee on the biological processes of aging on February 5, 1938. The rapid acceptance of another volume edited by Cowdry, entitled *Problems of Ageing,* was evidence that the ideas presented in it were timely. The first edition of 1939 was reprinted in 1940, and a second edition was published in 1942.

Several influential organizations held conferences on aging in 1940 and 1941. Among these were the American Orthopsychiatric Association, the Medical Clinics of North America, the American Chemical Society, and the National Institute of Health. The Josiah Macy Foundation provided a grant to aid the Public Health Service in conducting a conference in Mental Health and Later Maturity, and the National Institute of Health sponsored a conference on this subject on May 23-24, 1941. Many of the topics of that conference are still contemporary concerns, such as the psychiatric significance of aging as a public health problem, intellectual changes with age, psychotherapy in the practice of geriatrics, and industrial aspects of aging personnel. This conference would have had considerably greater impact on the concepts, research, and practice of a variety of sciences and professions had not the United States become involved in World War II before these proceedings could be published.

In opening the Macy Conference, the Surgeon General made the following observations which indicate how many of our current concerns in aging were anticipated and appreciated at that time.

> The aged are people whereas aging is a process. However, in order to solve the urgent clinical and sociologic problems introduced by the greatly increasing numbers of older people in the country, we need to know more of the processes and the consequences of aging. Not the least important of many questions are those concerned with the mental changes introduced by senescence. Without health, the increasing millions past the meridian represent a potential disastrous economic and social menace to the commonwealth. Thus the maintenance of mental and physical health into true senility is an objective worthy of our most conscientious and extensive efforts. . . .
>
> *Senescence is not a disease, nor is it all decline.* Some functional capacities increase with the years as others diminish. This is particularly notable with certain mental activities. It is thus of the greatest importance that far more precise information as to the changes in mental capacities which occur with aging become available if we are to employ wisely and utilize the vast reservoir of elderly persons only too anxious to be of use. There is no greater tragedy for the aged than the unnecessary sense of uselessness which society now imposes upon them prematurely. (USPHS, 1972, p. 2)

Several of the basic concepts of gerontology were developed in the 1930s. One was that problems of aging are complex and are best studied in an interdisciplinary context. A second concept was that aging represented an interactive process of biological predisposition and the environment. As noted earlier, impetus for the study of aging came from the fact that the focus of medicine was shifting from infectious diseases to chronic diseases, which by their nature are involved in the physiology of aging. Another impetus was the fact that the proportion of persons over 65 was expanding during the 1930s. During the 1930s the number of individuals over 65 increased 35 percent, as contrasted with an increase in the general population of only 7.2 percent. There was an increasing realization both of the social consequences of the aggregation of large numbers of older persons and, because of their particular health requirements, of the need for fundamental information on the processes of aging.

By 1940, thinking about problems of aging had become more systematic. Gerontology was receiving recognition as an independent and important field. World War II, however, interrupted research pursuits as many directed their energies to the emergency. Beginning in 1946, a rapid series of developments occurred which merit a characterization of the postwar years as a period of expansion. Laboratories devoted to the study of aging were started, research societies were founded, and many national and international conferences were held.

A detailed description of the growth of the field in this period would be prohibitive, but some examples are appropriate. In 1940 the Surgeon General, Thomas Parran, appointed a National Advisory Committee to assist in the formation of a unit on gerontology within the National Institutes of Health. This culminated in the creation of the National Institute of Aging, which was signed into law in 1974. In 1946 staffing was started at the Gerontological Unit of the National Institute of Health and the Nuffield Unit for Research into Problems of Aging at the University of Cambridge. These units attracted many scientists who are now prominent in the field of aging. An international congress of gerontology was founded and held its first meeting in Liège. The Gerontology Society in America was founded in 1945, and it encouraged discussion among professionals of all disciplines pursuing research in the area of aging.

To illustrate the increase in research output in the postwar years, an examination of the number of publications in aging would be appropriate. In 1835 there was but a mere handful of publications, such as the material by Bacon and Franklin. From about 1835 to the early 1900s, there was not much increase. At the turn of the century there were 5 or 6 books published, and this rate continued until 1949, with some interruption due to World War II. The literature generated between 1950 and 1960 equalled the production of the literature published in the entire preceding 115 years. It appears, then, that research and interest in aging are showing an exponential curve of growth. If this continues, it is expected that between 1970 and 1980 the publication rate will double again.

What is the reason for this awesome growth in gerontological interest and knowledge? Gerontology is really a product of the twentieth century. Historically, old age was certainly not unknown; it was simply uncommon. The average life expectancy at birth in 1000 B.C. is reported to have been about 18 years; in Julius Ceaser's day, approximately 50 B.C., the figure increased to 25 years and stayed about the same until the seventeenth century, when the average life expectancy increased to 32 years. In 1900 life expectancy in the U.S. had increased only to 45 years. However, by 1965 life expectancy had increased to 70.1 years, and the proportion of the U.S. population over 65 had doubled, rising from 4.1 percent in 1900 to 9.4 percent.

It is reasonable to wonder what produced this change in age structure. Perhaps the three most prominent processes responsible for this shift in population structure are mortality, fertility, and migration. These effects on the age structure of the population are described in Chapter 3.

Aging in the Future

We are experiencing a rapid increase in the number of aged persons in our society. What effect will this increase have on the future of gerontology, and how has it already influenced our ideas about aging?

It is apparent that social and economic adjustment will be necessary to meet the needs of the elderly. There is a growing feeling among many old people and psychologists researching the years of later maturity that retirement should not be determined by age alone. Other criteria should be considered, such as ability and motivation to do useful work. With the increasing predominance of females in the older age groups, part-time employment opportunities that would utilize their skills would be ideal. As a result of the decline in birth rates, coupled with the increment in available spare time, oldsters will be coming back for more education at all levels. The materials used in higher education, however, are geared to the young. The skills young people learn might be superfluous to the older individual; conversely, the knowledge and experience the older person brings to the classroom could be utilized. It appears that modification of university curriculum will be necessary.

Some adjustments have already been made in social and economic conditions of older adults; Social Security and pension plans are products of the twentieth century. Planners who design housing for the elderly have been incorporating special features that enable the old to continue living independently and safely. Recreational facilities are expanding their programs to incorporate the old. With more than 20 million individuals over the age of 65, the old represent a significant voting bloc. They have already become politically active, forming such organizations as the National Council of Senior Citizens, American Association of Retired Persons, the Gray Panthers, and others. The goal of these groups has been to bring public attention to their needs as well as to create a new image of the older person as active and interested in continuing his involvement with society.

Is a new type of old person in fact emerging in America? Researchers in many disciplines who study aging have amassed a considerable amount of evidence to indicate that the present generation of old people is different from previous generations of the aged, and perhaps from future aging cohorts (see Cain, 1967; Chapters 3, 4, 6, and 18 in this volume). This makes it very difficult to state with certainty how current trends will influence the future of gerontology. If the growth in the number of people in the older age groups continues, it is possible that men and women will be having second and even third careers. Such a possibility will be created by the accelerated rate of change, making jobs and skills antiquated within a person's life time. Automation, for example, has eliminated a significant number of jobs in the recent past. It has even been said that doctors who receive no postgraduate education after 10 years of practice are out of date; their skills, medications, and techniques have changed too drastically. In the future, it should be possible to elect a new career after concentrated training.

If there is a relation between the increasing number of old people and the growth of knowledge in the field of aging, it is beyond a doubt that the literature reflecting the research in gerontology will continue to increase rapidly. This is perhaps where the most crucial influences on the growth of gerontology will take place. Discovery of prophylaxis or cure of age-related diseases, such as cardiovascular disease and cancer, would significantly alter the expenses and difficulties associated with aging. Unraveling the genetic and the environmental influences on the aging process would enable man to intervene more effectively in modifying some of the less desirable features of getting older.

Though these are great expectations for the future, the importance of the present should not be minimized. Not only has a new kind of old person emerged in America, but a new social movement as well. If our era has been characterized by major upheavals in sexual mores, political standards, and racial equalities, it is clear that the changes brought by the growth and influence of our elderly will be felt for many generations to come in science and in society.

References

Bottig, K. and Grandjeau, E. 1965. The effect of organ extracts on behavior of old rats. In *Behavior, aging, and the nervous system,* ed. A. Welford and J. Birren. Illinois: Charles C. Thomas.

Birren, J. E. 1961. A brief history of the psychology of aging. *Gerontologist* 1:2: 67–77.

Cain, L. 1967. Age states and generation phenomena: the new old people in contemporary America. *Gerontologist* 7:2:82–92.

Child, C. M. 1915. *Senescence and rejuvenescence.* Chicago: University of Chicago Press.

Cowdry, E. V., ed. 1939. *Problems of ageing.* Baltimore: Walhams and Wilkins.

Gruman, G. J. 1966. A history of ideas about the prolongation of life: the evolution of prolongevity hypothesis to 1800. Philadelphia: *American Philosophical Society.*

Hall, G. S. 1922. *Senescence, the second half of life.* New York: Appleton and Co.

Kiser, C., and Whelpton, P. 1956. Social and psychological factors affecting fertility. XXXIII. Summary of chief findings and implications for future studies. *Milbank Memorial Fund Quarterly* 36:3.

Leaf, A. 1973. Every day is a gift when you are over 100. *National Geographic* 143(1): 93–118.

Lehman, H. D. 1953. *Age and achievement.* New Jersey: Princeton University Press.

Metchnikoff, E. 1908. *The prolongation of life.* New York: Putnam and Sons.

Minot, C. 1908. *The problems of age, growth and death.* New York: Putnam and Sons.

Nikitin, V. N. 1958. *Russian studies on age-associated physiology, biochemistry and morphology: historical sketch and bibliography.* Kharkov: A. M. Gorkiy Press.

Pearl, R. 1922. *The biology of death.* Philadelphia: J. P. Lippincott Co.

Rossett, E. 1964. *Aging process of population.* New York: Macmillan.

Thompson, W., and Lewis, D. 1965. *Population problems.* New York: McGraw Hill and Co.

U.S. Public Health Service. 1972. Proceedings of the conference on mental health in later maturity, 23–24 May, 1941. Washington, D.C.: Supplement 168 to U.S. Public Health Reports, Government Printing Office.

Sociological Perspectives

3

Demography of the Aged

NEAL E. CUTLER · ROBERT A. HAROOTYAN

For gerontologists, basic demographic information is of the utmost importance if for no other reason than the demographic changes in the age structure of the population in most modern societies point to a dramatically increasing proportion of older persons. In a very real sense, the trends which have resulted in the dramatic increase in the number and proportion of older persons in the United States are a major reason for the expansion of interest in gerontology.

In this chapter we will present some descriptive demographic data, as such information is useful in understanding the nature and position of older persons in contemporary society. Such descriptive data—typically presented in the form of numerical tables—are useful only to the degree that the concepts which they illustrate are known. Thus, a second purpose of this chapter is to present and briefly explain those basic demographic concepts which are of interest and use to gerontologists. We will, of course, include references to more advanced studies in this field so that more extensive study can be pursued by those who wish to do so.

Before discussing the descriptive demographic data and the concepts underlying this information, it is important to note what demography, the science of population dynamics, can and cannot do. In the first place, it should be remembered throughout this discussion that demography tends to be a macro-level science. That is, it typically focuses at the level of society rather than at the micro-level of the individual which, for example, is the typical focus of psychology. Thus, demography generally focuses on large and broad statistical groups within and across populations.

Sometimes demography deals with "real" groups of individuals, such as the population of Los Angeles or the population of the United States; at other times the subject is an analytic category, such as "all persons age 65 and over." Demographic descriptions of these collectivities or groups are usually given by summary statistical measures such as the mean, the median, or the percentage of a group which has characteristic X or characteristic Y. Thus, it is important to recognize that demographic information represents descriptive statistical generalizations; there will be variations within the group and individual exceptions to the generalizations.

A second major point is that demographic analysis is limited to the kinds of inferences which can legitimately be made from past and present information regarding population dynamics. In this sense it should not be assumed that demography can "predict" the future. What demography can do, however, is "project" the future of a population, given certain data describing past and present population structures and processes and certain assumptions about the likelihood or probability that these structures and processes will continue into the future. Such population projections can be quite accurate when detailed information about a particular population is available.

The population of primary concern for students of gerontology is the category of persons aged 65 and older. Age 65+ has been designated as a useful, if imprecise, identifier of the older population for most demographic and gerontological studies.

The Demography of Aging Past and Present

Historical Trends in Life Expectancy

As noted in Chapter 2, human populations have been improving in average life expectancy since the days of the Babylonian and Roman empires. But these improvements have been slow in coming, at least until the last two centuries. Consider, for example, the change in average life expectancy at birth since 1000 B.C. At that time it was approximately 18 years, but in 1970 the average life expectancy at birth in the United States was 70.9 years. This increase of 52.9 years took almost 3,000

Table 3.1   Average life expectancy at birth and at age 65 in the United States, for various years: 1900-1970

Age	1900	1939	1949	1955	1959	1970
At birth	47.3	63.7	68.0	69.6	69.9	70.9
At age 65	11.9	12.8	12.8	14.2	14.4	15.2

SOURCE: United States Public Health Service, National Center for Health Statistics. *Vital Statistics of the United States: 1970, Vol. II—Mortality*, Part A (Washington, D.C.: U.S. G.P.O.), Tables 5-1 and 5-5, 1974.

years to achieve, but in this century alone average life expectancy at birth in the United States increased by 23.6 years—from 47.3 years in 1900 to 70.9 in 1970, as shown in Table 3.1. Thus, in the United States it took only 70 years to increase average life expectancy by 40 percent of the total gain achieved during the last three millennia of human existence. Note, however, that similar dramatic advances have not been made in average life expectancy at age 65, where there has been a gain of only three years since 1900—from 11.9 to 15.2 in 1970.

Another important fact shown in Table 3.1 is the slower rate of increase in average life expectancy at birth since 1939. The largest increment (16.4 years) occurred between 1900 and 1939. Since then, however, the increase in average life expectancy at birth has only been 7.2 years. The trend is clearly toward a much slower rate of increase in average life expectancy, especially since 1949.

Table 3.2 indicates that other developed countries exhibit similar averages in life expectancy at birth. But the same cannot be said for many of the developing nations, particularly those in Africa and Southeast Asia. In most countries of these regions, the average life expectancy at birth stands in sharp contrast to those of the developed nations. As Table 3.2 clearly shows, average life expectancies in selected African and Asian countries remain below 50 years (some even below 40 years).

The life-expectancy figures presented in Table 3.2 are the best approximations of the aging of individuals within a general population. They represent no one person, however, and must be viewed as averages for the total population. A similar but more specific measure is the probability of survival from one age to another, known as the *age-specific survival rate*. These probabilities of survival at different ages are also averages derived from the experience of a particular population (for example, the 65+ population). Both these measures of aging, life-expectancy and survival rates, are largely a function of changes in mortality rates within the population. Given certain past trends in mortality over time, projections of life-expectancy and survival rates tend to be quite accurate.

Age Composition of the Population

The number of elderly in the United States has increased dramatically since 1900, representing a larger share of the total population for each succeeding decade. The number of persons aged 65 and older in the United States for each decade since 1900 is presented in Table 3.3. Also shown is the percent of the total population age 65 and over and the percentage increase for this older group for each decennial year from

Table 3.2   Life expectancy at birth, by sex and population—age 65 and over for various countries and years

Country	Year	Life expectancy at birth		Population age 65 and over	
		Male	Female	Number (in thousands)	Percent of total
North America					
United States	1970	67	75	20,101	9.9
Canada	1971	68.8	75.2	1,744	8.1
Haiti	1972 (est.)	—44.5—		157	3.1
Mexico	1970	61.0	63.7	1,791	3.7
South America					
Argentina	1972 (est.)	64.1	70.2	1,805	7.5
Brazil	1970	—60.7—		4,760	5.1 (age 60+)
Venezuela	1970 (est.)	—63.8—		252	2.4
Asia					
China	1970 (est.)	—50.0—		—	—
Japan	1970	69.1	74.3	7,330	7.1
Iran	1971 (est.)	—50.0—		940	3.1
Syria	1970 (est.)	—52.8—		193	3.2
USSR	1970	65.0	74.0	28,514	11.8
Europe					
Austria	1970	66.6	73.7	1,047	14.2
Denmark	1969	70.8	75.7	590	12.1
France	1968	68.6	76.1	6,662	13.4
Hungary	1970	66.3	72.0	1,178	11.4
Netherlands	1971 (est.)	71.0	76.7	1,353	10.3
Sweden	1970	71.7	76.5	1,109	13.7
United Kingdom	1971	68.8	75.1	6,397	13.1
Africa					
Ethiopia	1968 (est.)	—38.5—		2,811	11.9 (age 45 |)
Ghana	1970	—46.0—		311	3.6
Kenya	1969	46.9	51.2	391	3.6
S. Africa	1970	—49.0—		870	4.1
Uganda	1969	—47.5—		365	3.8
Zambia	1970	—43.5—		135	4.0 (age 60+)

SOURCE: United Nations. *Demographic Yearbook: 1972* (New York: United Nations), Tables 3 and 6 (1973). Reproduced by permission.

the previous one. For comparison, the corresponding increase of the total population has also been included. Most noticeable from these data is the rapid growth in numbers of the older population, a more than sixfold increase in 70 years. More important for understanding the relevance of these decennial changes is the uninterrupted increase in the *proportion* of the total population represented by the group aged 65 and over since the turn of the century. Not only has the older population of the United States grown from 3.1 million in 1900 to almost 20.2 million in 1970, but their proportion of the total has increased by almost 2.5 times (from 4.1 percent in 1900 to 9.9 percent in 1970).

An efficient way to show this change in the proportion of elderly is to use an age-sex population pyramid, which graphically depicts the composition of the total population by age and sex. For our purposes this distribution is best presented in five-year age intervals (on the vertical axis) expressed as percent of the total population (on the horizontal axis). Figure 3.1 shows the age-sex pyramids for the United States in 1900, 1940, and 1970. Without regard to the absolute numbers, we can graphically see how the age composition of our population has changed during this century. In 1900, when fertility and mortality rates were still quite high (32 births and 17 deaths per 1,000 population), the population pyramid closely approximated a triangle. By 1940, this form was undergoing certain changes, so that the pyramid begins to take on the shape of a pear. This change reflects the effects of lower fertility during the

Table 3.3 Population age 65 and over in the United States, for each decennial year with projections to 2020: 1900-2020

Year	Population age 65 and over		Percent increase from preceding decade	
	Number (in thousands)	Percent of total population	Age 65 and over	Total population
1900	3,099	4.1	—	—
1910	3,986	4.3	28.6	21.0
1920	4,929	4.7	23.7	14.9
1930	6,705	5.4	36.0	16.1
1940	9,031	6.8	34.7	7.3
1950	12,397	8.2	37.3	14.5
1960	16,679	9.2	34.5	18.5
1970	20,177	9.9	21.0	13.3
Projections:		Series B[b] Series E[b]		Series B[b] Series E[b]
1980	24,051[a]	10.2 10.6	19.2	15.6 11.2
1990	27,768[a]	10.0 11.0	15.5	17.7 10.4
2000	28,842[a]	8.9 10.6	3.9	15.7 7.8
2010	30,940	8.1 10.6	7.3	18.3 7.2
2020	40,261	9.1 13.1	30.1	17.3 5.7

[a]Revised data from United States Bureau of the Census. *Current Population Reports,* Series P-25, No. 493, "Projections of the Population of the United States, by Age and Sex: 1972-2020" (December 1972).
[b]Assumptions of completed fertility (average number of births per woman upon completion of childbearing years):
   Series B: 3.10 (high-fertility assumption).
   Series E: 2.10 (low-fertility assumption, which mirrors present replacement level trend in the United States).
SOURCE: United States Bureau of the Census. *Current Population Reports,* Series P-25, No. 470, "Projections of the Population of the United States, by Age and Sex: 1970-2020" (November 1971); Series P-25, No. 38, "Projections of the Population of the United States, by Age, Sex and Color to 1990, with Extensions of Population by Age and Sex to 2015" (December 1967).

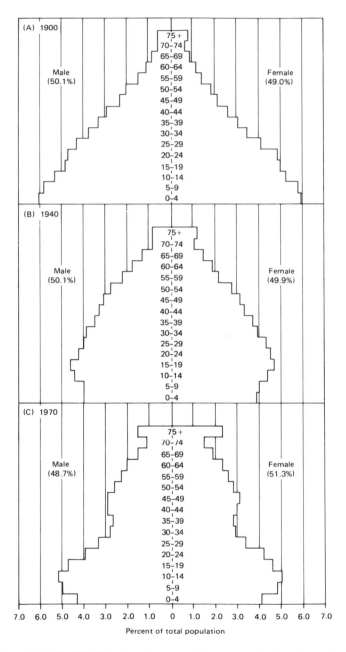

Figure 3.1 (A) (B) (C). Age-sex population pyramids for the United States: 1900, 1940, 1970. (United States Bureau of the Census. *Census of Population: Characteristics of the Population.* 1940, 1970)

post-World War I economic depression years. Further evidence of the effect of changing fertility rates is seen in the 1970 population pyramid and will be discussed in the following section.

The Basic Demographic Processes

There are three demographic processes basic to the understanding of population dynamics which are of particular importance in understanding the demography of aging. These are known as *fertility, mortality,* and *migration.* When one thinks of aging, it is often the case that mortality (or rates of death from various causes) is the only factor considered. Yet if our goal is to understand the dynamics of population changes which have produced a population containing an increasing proportion of older persons, then the complete set of factors must be understood.

The concept of fertility, or the birth rate as it is more popularly known, is strongly related to the "aging of the population." And, theoretically, migration must be considered also. One person can by definition contribute only once to rates of mortality. But a single individual can migrate or change his or her residence many times during the life cycle, and a given woman can give birth to more than one child. Furthermore, since migration and fertility, unlike mortality, represent individual decisions, and can be repeated over time, they add a great deal of variability to the question of population estimates. If the estimation of future population sizes were dependent only upon mortality rates, the task of the demographer would be much simpler. Adding the factors of fertility and migration in considering the "aging" or the "younging" of a population makes the job more complex, but it is crucial to our understanding and projection of changes in the older population.

Fertility

The importance of fertility is seen in how a particular *birth cohort* (all those people born in a particular year or interval of time) will affect a population's age composition throughout the life span of that cohort. Figure 3.2 shows the "crude birth rate" (that is, the number of births per 1,000 population) in the United States since 1900. The variability of these rates over time is important in understanding the population's changing age composition during this century.

The importance of fertility is illustrated by the fact that any age group may be traced back to the size of the group when it was born. Thus, for example, from the population pyramid for 1970 we learn that the 70–74 age group (in 1970) represents 2.6 percent of the total popu-

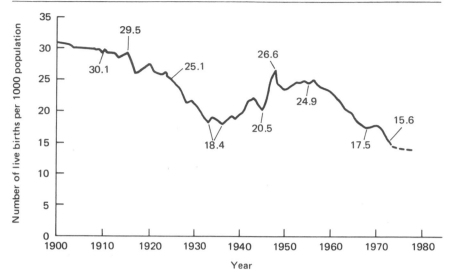

Figure 3.2. Crude birth rates for the United States: 1900–1973. (United States Public Health Service, National Center for Health Statistics, *Vital Statistics of the United States, Volume I—Natality*)

lation. The size of this group, even in 1970, is naturally a function of how big the group was when it was born. From historical data we know that in 1900, when this group was 0–4 years of age, it represented 12.1 percent of the population of 1900. This same birth cohort reached the age of 40–44 in 1940, at which time it represented 7.7 percent of the 1940 population. Thirty years later, the same birth cohort represented 2.6 percent of the population, and, as already indicated, was 70–74 years of age. Of course, the rate of mortality of this cohort, born at the turn of the century, is important in determining just how many members of the cohort survived into the seventh decade of life. Yet, the initial size of the cohort, that is, the fertility information, sets the initial parameter of how large the population group could possibly be; the absolute size of this group, in turn, plays a role in its relative size within the population of 1900, of 1940, and of 1970. Thus, in the first instance, fertility is the process which sets the limiting parameter for the size of the older population 60 or 70 years later.

However, the birth cohorts of every other age group must be considered at the same time to determine the percentage of any age group. Thus, by 1970, the shape of the population pyramid is "pinched" in three areas, making it resemble an hour glass. Note how this shape differs from the pyramids in 1900 and 1940. Without forgetting the influence of changing age-specific mortality rates during this century, we can still see that changes in fertility strongly affect the future older population. To repeat, fertility sets the limits on both the absolute size of any cohort as it ages over time, and its relative size to that of all other age groups in the population.

Because fertility rates have dropped significantly in the United States during the last twenty years (down to 15.6 births per 1,000 population in 1973), the proportion of the total population aged 65 and over in 1970 has increased accordingly. Conversely, although the number of older people is continually increasing, an increase in fertility would yield a smaller proportion of older people in the total population. This latter possibility, however, is less likely to occur, given the lower fertility trends in the United States during the last two decades—a result of such factors as delayed marriage, delayed childbearing, better contraceptive techniques and usage, and an overall decrease in desired family size since 1950.

In sum, the *actual size* of any birth cohort at a given age is a function of the size of that cohort at birth (fertility factors) and the number of individuals within that cohort who survive to that age (mortality factors). The *relative size* of any birth cohort within the population is a function of the size of that cohort and the actual sizes of all other birth cohorts which comprise the total population at a given point in time.

How this relationship works is shown in the population projections to the year 2020 in Table 3.3. Here we see that the older population is expected to double in absolute size within 50 years, yet the proportion of the total population it represents is not expected to increase significantly. How the "baby-boom" birth cohort of the 1950s influences this change is clear. The bulge in the 1970 population pyramid for the cohorts aged 10–14 and 15–19 represents the baby-boom births of the 1950–1960 decade. Following this cohort as it ages, and given certain assumptions regarding the mortality rate for this group, we see that by the 2010–2020 decade there will be a significant increase in the number of people age 65 and over in the United States. This expected 10-year increment of almost 10 million older people is only one million less than the expected *total* increase in the older population for the 40-year period between 1970 and 2010. Thus, the baby boom of the 1950s will mean a "gerontology boom" in the years 2010–2020!

Note also that these numerical projections are dependent only on expected rates of mortality for the different age groups (presently quite accurate in demographic analysis). Fertility has no effect on these calculations because the cohorts involved have already been born. However, under different assumptions about average fertility rates for the next 50 years (i.e., the population under age 50 through 2020), the same *number* of older people can reflect different *proportions* of the total population. Under conditions of high average fertility (3.1 births per woman), the population age 65 and over will be only 9.1 percent of the total in 2020, a figure which is lower than the present one for the older population. But what if average fertility for the next 50 years is only 2.1 births per woman, that is, replacement level fertility, or zero population growth? The number of "new people" will decrease, and the same number of already-born older people will then represent 13.1 percent of the total population. This difference, dependent primarily on fertility, can have distinct ramifications on public policy and the ability of social, economic, and political institutions to serve the needs of the older population.

Mortality

Once fertility has set the stage by imposing certain limits on the size of each new birth cohort, differentials in mortality rates become the major factor in determining a population's composition. Although these two demographic processes are being considered separately, it should be emphasized that they are interdependent factors in population growth and change.

Perhaps the clearest example of this interdependence between fertility and mortality is found in the infant mortality rates. This rate gives the number of deaths to infants under one year of age per 1,000 live births. The decrease in infant mortality has been by far the most significant factor in reducing the general death rate of the United States since early in the century. It is this same reduction which has been the major contributor to increased life expectancy. Referring again to Table 3.1, the improvement in life expectancy *at birth* far outpaces the relatively small gains made in life expectancy *at age 65*.

The reason for this difference is quite clear. The reduction and virtual elimination of infectious diseases in the United States, combined with major improvements in postnatal infant care, have primarily benefitted the youngest age groups. As recently as 1935 the United States had an infant mortality rate of 55.7 (that is, 55.7 deaths under one year of age per 1,000 live births). By 1970 the infant mortality rate had dropped to 19.8, and further reductions have brought this figure down to 18.5 for 1973. The intimate connection between fertility and mortality is demonstrated by this information on the dramatic decrease in infant mortality. The size of the age 65 population in the year 1965 is determined by the number of babies born in 1900. Yet if a substantial number of those born die rather soon from various causes of infant mortality, then the eventual size of this birth cohort 65 years later will be reduced. When infant mortality is substantially reduced, then the effects of fertility can have a greater impact. Thus, of the number of babies born in 1975, a smaller number will die within the first year of life, and a greater number will have the chance to survive into old age, 65 years later. Of course, mortality other than infant mortality will have an impact on the eventual number of individuals who survive to their 65th birthday; yet it is obvious that deaths in the first year of life are the initial mortality phenomenon of importance in this equation.

Indeed, after the first crucial year of life the age-specific death rates for any cohort drop dramatically and only slowly increase over the life of that cohort until it reaches age 65 and over. It is at this later stage in the life cycle that the death rate once again reaches a high level. And it is also at this stage where the least gains have been made in thwarting death. This difference is crucial to understanding the changing age composition of the United States population.

A number of demographic analyses have shown that general declines in mortality rates do not contribute to a rise in the proportion of the population aged 65 and over unless those declines have been concentrated in the older age groups (see Coale, 1956; Hermalin, 1966). *The effect of declining infant mortality rates has primarily been to enhance the effect of fertility,* which, as we have seen, establishes the boundaries for the relative sizes of different age groups at any given point in time.

The dramatic differences in the improvement of life expectancy can be seen by looking at the probability of survival to specified ages in the the United States. This measure is similar to life expectancy, but is expressed as the percent of a birth cohort which is expected to survive from one age to another. In 1900 only 39 percent of those born could be expected to survive to age 64. By 1970, this figure had increased to 72 percent, or a gain of 33 percent. Of the population age 65+ in 1900, the probability of survival to age 80 was 33 percent. By 1970 this proportion had increased to only 49 percent, a much smaller gain than the figures at birth.

Note again that the gains in probability of survival have been far greater at birth than from age 65 onward. The control of infectious diseases during this century has been concentrated in the youngest and oldest age groups, where influenza, tuberculosis, and pneumonia take their greatest tolls. With these diseases now well controlled, it is primarily the aged who remain vulnerable to such degenerative diseases as heart disease, cancers, and strokes.

This fact is seen in Table 3.4, which shows the death rates for the ten leading causes of death in the United States in 1900 and compares these with the rates and ranking for 1970. Influenza, pneumonia, and tuberculosis are no longer major causes of death, while the degenerative diseases have taken their place. And it is this latter group of diseases which is concentrated among the older population (see Chapter 11 for a discussion of the diseases of old age).

For the curious reader we note that the diseases ranked 7th through 10th as causes of death in 1970 were not in the 10 leading causes of death for 1900. These diseases for 1970, listed in rank order from 7 through 10 respectively, were as follows: diabetes mellitus (18.9 deaths per 1,000), arteriosclerosis (15.6), cirrhosis of the liver (15.5), and bronchitis, emphysema, and asthma (15.2).

To further emphasize the relative importance of the degenerative diseases in mortality rates, we can estimate what effect their eradication would have on life expectancy. Given current death rates in the United States, and applying the analytic tool of life-table estimates (Dublin et al., 1949; Barclay, 1958), the elimination of tuberculosis would yield a gain of only 0.1 years in life expectancy at birth and even less than that at age 65. However, if the major cardiovascular-renal diseases (all diseases of the heart, arteries, and strokes) were completely eradicated today, life expec-

Table 3.4   Death rates for the ten leading causes of death in 1900 with comparable rates for 1970 in the United States

Cause of Death[a]	Rate (deaths per 1,000 population)		Rank	
	1900	1970	1900	1970
Influenza and pneumonia	202.2	30.9	1	5
Tuberculosis	194.4	2.6	2	—
Gastroenteritis (diseases of stomach and intestine)	142.7	0.9	3	—
Diseases of the heart	137.4	362.0	4	1
Cerebral hemorrhage and other vascular lesions	106.9	101.9	5	3
Chronic nephritis (kidney diseases)	81.0	3.7	6	—
All accidents	72.3	56.4	7	4
Cancer and other malignant neoplasms	64.0	162.8	8	2
Diseases of early infancy	62.6	21.4	9	6
Diphtheria	40.3	0.0	10	—

[a]Eighth Revision, International Classification of Diseases, Adapted, 1965.
SOURCE: Public Health Service, National Center for Health Statistics. *Vital Statistics of the United States, 1970, Volume II—Mortality*, Part A, Table 1-5; *Monthly Vital Statistics Report*, Volume 22, No. 13 (June 27, 1974), adapted from Tables 7 and 8.

tancy at birth would increase by 10.9 years and by 10.0 years at age 65! For heart disease alone the corresponding gains would be 5.9 and 4.9 years, respectively (United States Public Health Service, Life Tables, 1974).

The hegemony of heart disease, stroke, and cancer is further emphasized by data on the life-time probability of dying from these diseases. For the newborn there is approximately a 61 percent chance of eventually dying from major cardiovascular diseases, a 15 percent chance of eventual death from cancer, and about a 5 percent chance of death due to accidents. Except for accidents, however, the concentration of deaths from these degenerative causes is in the oldest age groups of the population. Note in Table 3.5 that the median age at death in 1970 from influenza and pneumonia was 74.5, indicating their heavier toll on the older rather than the younger population.

Because more people are living to older ages within the total population, health problems associated with the degenerative diseases have become a major concern. By 1969 diseases of the heart, cancers, and stroke together accounted for three out of every four deaths of persons age 65 and over.

Progress in finding early diagnostic methods and effective treatments for these degenerative diseases has been slow. But the extent of the problem has gradually been recognized, in large part because of the increasing number of older people and the visibility of their health problems. One manifestation of this visibility and concern is the current nationwide effort of concentrated research to find the causes and cures for cancer and heart disease. These efforts should provide some gains in reducing future death rates from the degenerative diseases, but we should not expect gains in life expectancy at age 65 on the magnitude of 10 years. Furthermore, it should be remembered that these projected gains are the estimated *maximum* gains to be achieved by complete elimination of particular diseases.

The cause-specific mortality rates of persons in the United States and

Table 3.5 Median age at death from selected causes, United States: 1970

Cause of death	Median age at death
Major cardiovascular-renal disease (heart diseases and stroke)	75.6
Malignant neoplasms (cancers)	67.5
Influenza and pneumonia	74.5
Accidents (all kinds)	39.9

SOURCE: Adapted from United States Public Health Service, National Center for Health Statistics. *Vital Statistics of the United States: 1970, Vol. II—Mortality*, Part A (Washington, D.C.: U.S. G.P.O.), Table 1-26, 1974.

in other relatively developed countries are quite different from those in underdeveloped parts of the world. Those countries with the highest life expectancies in general (illustrated in Table 3.2) are the countries with low infant mortality but relatively high mortality from the degenerative diseases of heart, cancer, and stroke. Data from the *Demographic Yearbook* (1973) show, for example, that in 1970 Sweden had an infant mortality rate of 11.0 (that is, 11 deaths per 1,000 live births), and a heart-disease related mortality rate of 333.9 (per 100,000 population). Mexico, on the other hand, had in 1971 an infant mortality rate of 68.5, but a heart-disease related mortality rate of only 18.9. For the United States in 1970, the corresponding rates were 19.8 and 326.1.

Thus, the increasing contribution of degenerative diseases to death rates in developed countries is, in a sense, an index of the growth of the older population. Nonetheless, what these data illustrate is that actual increases in longevity beyond the age of 65 have not been great. Demographers and others involved in the study of aging (Dublin et al., 1949, Chapter 1) are in fair agreement that even if all disease were controlled, the human life span (the theoretical biological maximum for humans) would remain at about 120 years. Thus, the human is now, and will remain for the forseeable future, mortal.

Immigration

Immigration is the third demographic factor affecting population composition. Throughout this country's history, immigration has served to lower the median age of the population (Hermalin, 1966). Early immigration during the late nineteenth and early twentieth centuries was concentrated among younger males, who were eventually assimilated, married, and had families. During this period, the number of immigrants was high, thereby having a distinct effect on the age and sex composition of our population. From 1881 to 1930, the United States received almost 27.6 million immigrants, most of whom were 15 to 39 years old (United States Immigration and Naturalization Service, various dates). Immigration continues, but the numbers have decreased (from an average annual number of 780,000 during the 1901–1910 period, to only 290,000 yearly for 1961–1965), and the net effect on the total population and its composition is decreasing over time.

With the present annual statutory ceiling of about 400,000 immigrants (with some legal exceptions in times of war or special international crises), *the population projections into the twenty-first century are minimally affected by immigration.* The various sets of age- and sex-specific population projections which are provided by the Census Bureau, based on different fertility-rate assumptions, are further published in terms of whether or not expected immigration occurs. All projections with immigration included assume a net annual influx of 400,000 people distributed by age and sex according to past trends.

Table 3.6 provides two sets of projections. The "Series X projections" are based on a fertility assumption in which completed births will rapidly decline to an average of 2.11 per woman, and remain at that replacement birth rate in the ensuing decades—a birth rate which, after stabilizing over the next 50 years, will represent zero population growth. When there is a higher birth rate (i.e., more children being born), the proportion of older persons and the median age of the population will, of course, be lower than if there were a lower birth rate.

In the context of these population projections we can see the slight effect that immigration will have on the age composition of the future American population. The projections with annual net immigration of 400,000 people yield smaller proportions age 65 and over and a lower median age. With immigration the 65+ age group would constitute 14.5 percent of the population by the year 2025 (and a median age of 36.3). Without such immigration the older group would represent 14.9 percent of the population and would produce a median age of 36.7.

Thus, we *see that immigration alone produces only slight variations in future age composition.* Note, too, that the sex ratios for each of the projected years are virtually identical when projections are made with and without the effects of immigration, ranging from 68 to 73 males per 100 females. In sum, although past immigration has tended to make the population younger and to increase the sex ratio, the recent lower annual number of immigrants indicates that immigration will play a very minor

Table 3.6   Projections of the future older population of the United States, with and without immigration for selected years: 1985-2025 (immigration of 400,000 per year)

Series X fertility assumption[a]	With immigration			Without immigration		
	1985	2000	2025	1985	2000	2025
Percent age 65 and over	10.6	10.6	14.5	10.8	10.9	14.9
Median age (total population)	30.0	33.1	36.3	30.1	33.4	36.7
Sex ratio of older population (males per 100 females)	68	67	72	68	67	73

[a]Series X: assumes decrease in average completed fertility to 2.11 births per woman.
SOURCE: Adapated from United States Bureau of the Census. *Current Population Reports,* Series P-25, No. 480, "Illustrative Population Projections for the United States: The Demographic Effects of Alternative Paths to Zero Growth" (April 1972), Table 7.

role in determining the future age and sex composition of the national population as a whole.

The foregoing discussion has presented a wealth of information to emphasize the important changes in age composition and the growth of the older population in the United States since the turn of the century. We have stressed the past importance of fertility in determining the size and proportion of older people in the American population. While fertility has been the key to setting limits on the potential size of the older population, reduction in mortality, especially in infant mortality, has helped to make the effects of fertility even more pronounced (Sauvy, 1954). Large-scale reductions in already low mortality rates, as we have seen, are unlikely to appreciably change the age composition of the population in the future. But the reduction of deaths from (or at least better treatment for) the major degenerative diseases can provide unmeasurable benefits to the physical and psychological well-being of older people. Attention to both of these basic demographic factors is of utmost concern to anyone interested in gerontological issues.

Three Demographic Indicators

The demographic processes of fertility, mortality, and migration are basic to the understanding of population transitions, and additionally there are three basic demographic indicators which are of particular use to geron- tologists. Each has potentially widespread utility for understanding various facets of the older segment of any population. The first two, *dependency ratio* and *sex ratio,* are quite simple arithmetic representations of relation- ships; the third, *birth cohort,* is crucial in understanding the nature of age changes in social behavior.

The Dependency Ratio

In modern societies, demographic changes have particular signifi- cance for economic arrangements in the society. In the United States, for example, we all recognize that the Social Security system is the basic public pension system. Although Social Security provides other benefits— such as aid to surviving children and aid to the disabled—the major func- tion of the system is to provide at least a minimum income to the older, retired worker. As originally conceived, workers and employers pay into the system, and the workers in turn receive funds during their retirement years. Unfortunately, such factors as inflation and the general increase in the standard of living have severely affected the basic premise of the Social

Security system. Individuals retiring in the 1970s, for example, are likely to take out of the system more than they have put in to it.

The more general issue which this example of the Social Security system raises concerns the relationship between the "dependent" population and the supportive or working population. The measure which demographers use to summarize the relationship between these two classes of individuals is known as the "dependency ratio." Arithmetically, the dependency ratio is quite simple: the number or proportion of individuals in the dependent segment of the population divided by the number or proportion of individuals in the supportive or working population.

The dependent population typically has two components: the young and the old. Babies, children, and most adolescents typically do not support themselves. Thus, at the individual level they are supported by their parents and families; taking a more social system point of view, these youngsters are supported by the working population. Similarly, the retired population is no longer working, but is supported by the working population. Of course, to some extent the recipients of pensions are supported in part by their own contributions to the pension system. In the case of Social Security, however, increased payments or benefits are greater than contributed shares. In such a case, the younger working population is paying its Social Security payments to support the current recipients of benefits.

While there are many economic and even political ramifications of such a situation, demographers employ the dependency ratio to easily summarize the situation. The denominator of the ratio is considered the working population while the numerator is considered the dependent population. Depending on analytic needs, the dependent population could be the younger, the older, or the combination of both populations. For students of gerontology, the old-age dependency ratio indicates the relationship between the "old" population and the "working" population.

Typically the age definitions of "old" and "working" are 65+ and 18–64 respectively. Thus, the old-age dependency ratio is, in simple demographic terms, 65+/18–64. This does not mean to imply that every person over the age of 65 is dependent and that every person in the 18–64 age range is in fact working. But for using the basic census data found in most published sources, and to avoid the detailed process of documenting who is working and who is not, these broad age groupings suffice.

A major utility of the dependency ratio is in noting how it changes over time. We have noted previously that the number and proportion of older persons in the United States have been and still are increasing over time. Equally interesting, however, is the change in the dependency ratio, as given in Table 3.7. Note that in the first decades of the next century, the baby-boom children of the 1940s and 1950s will have reached retirement age, and thus become part of the numerator of the dependency ratio. At the same time, a lowered birth rate, such as we have now, means a relatively smaller work-force population in this same period—comprising the denominator of the dependency ratio. The joint implication of this pair of demographic facts is a continual increase in the dependency ratio.

The dependency ratio can be computed for any nation or for any group within a nation, yielding a quick summary of the relationship between dynamic elements within the population system. To the degree that money represents a scarce resource in any society, and to the degree that the old are to be supported by the society to which they have contributed, the dependency ratio is a useful summary statistic for measuring changes in the population. These changes can have substantial implications for the social, economic, and political systems.

Sex Ratio

A second measure of particular use to students of gerontology is the sex ratio. As usually expressed, the sex ratio is the number of males per 100 females in a population or population group. Thus, if there were an equal number of males and females, the sex ratio would be 1.0. If there were 500 males for every 100 females, the sex ratio would be 5.0. On the other hand, if there were only 50 males for every 100 females, then the sex ratio would be 0.5. In most modern societies, the general sex ratio is less than 1.0, since women tend to outlive men.

The particular importance of the sex-ratio measure is that it allows demographers to describe different population groups. One basic kind of comparison of particular relevance to gerontologists is the changing sex ratio over the life cycle: the later the stage in the life cycle, the smaller the number of males. At the same time, historical projections of sex ratios

Table 3.7   Old-age dependency ratios for the United States: 1930-2050

1930	1940	1950	1960	1970	2000	2020	2050
.097	.118	.133	.167	.177	.177	.213	.257

Dependency ratio = 65+/18-64.
SOURCES: (1930-1940) U.S. Bureau of the Census, *U.S. Census of Population: 1940. Characteristics of the Population,* Table 8, p. 26. (1950-1970) U.S. Bureau of the Census, *Statistical Abstract of the United States: 1972,* Table 37, p. 32. (2000) (based on Series E projections) Herman B. Brotman, "Projections of the Population to the Year 2000", Statistical Memo #25, Administration on Aging. (June 1973) p. 3. (2020, 2050) (based on Series E and Series W respectively) prepared by Dr. David M. Heer, Population Research Laboratory, University of Southern California, February, 1974.

can also indicate the nature of changes in the population system. Table 3.8 indicates the changing sex ratio for different age groups in the current population. As can be seen, the 1970 sex ratio decreases with increasing age. And since 1900 the sex ratio of the older population has continually decreased.

The fact that different age groups within the total population have different and changing sex ratios is closely connected to one of the basic demographic processes described earlier: mortality. Although mortality eventually affects everyone, different causes of mortality are sex-linked; that is, certain causes of mortality are more likely to affect males than females. Consequently, the sex composition of the surviving old-age population is largely influenced by the degree to which the basic causes of mortality in modern society are sex-specific.

An indication of this phenomenon can be seen in Figure 3.3, which portrays the different rates of life expectancy at birth and at age 65 for various time-points in recent American history. Because racial as well as sex factors are strongly associated with differential life-expectancy rates, the data are presented by both categories. As these data indicate, whites have a greater life expectancy than nonwhites; and within both racial groups, females can expect to live longer than males.

While life-expectancy rates and averages are one way to show that females tend to live longer than males, a more direct approach, as indicated above, is to note the differential sex ratios at various ages in the life cycle. A more complete picture of these data is given in Table 3.9, which presents age-based sex ratios for the United States across the period 1900–1970. Various trends can be noted. The first is that across the twentieth

Table 3.8   Sex ratios for the United States, by age groups in 1970 and for the older population in selected years

Sex ratio by age, (males per 100 females)		Changing sex ratios of the 65-and-over age group	
Age group	Sex ratio	Year	Sex ratio
18–24	95	1900	102
25–44	95	1930	101
45–64	92	1950	89
65 and over	72	1960	83
65–74	78	1970	72
75 and over	64	2000	67

SOURCE: Adapted from United States Bureau of the Census. *Census of Population: Characteristics of the Population* (Washington, D.C.: United States Government Printing Office), selected years; Brotman, H. B. "Projections of the Population to the Year 2000", *Statistical Memo #25*, Administration on Aging (June 1973) p. 3.

century the number of males per 100 females in the total population has been steadily decreasing—as can be seen from the "all ages" row in Table 3.9. A second, and perhaps more dramatic, trend is that in both 1960 and 1970 the proportion of men to women among adults over the age of 45 decreased substantially. In both 1960 and 1970 the sex ratio for adults aged 25–44 was 96.9 males per 100 females. However, a substantial increase in mortality among older men during that ten-year period created a situation in which the 1960 sex ratio of 82.6 males per 100 females for the 65+ group dropped sharply to 72.1 by 1970.

A third important trend is seen by comparing the age-specific sex-

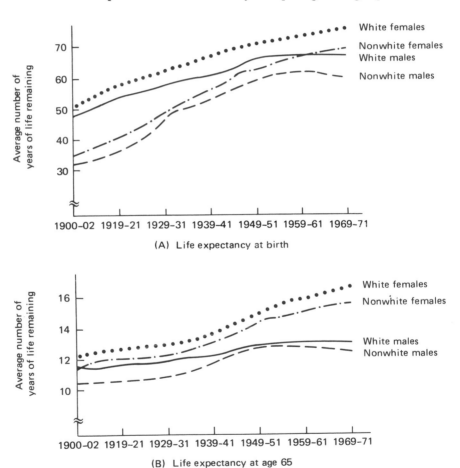

(A) Life expectancy at birth

(B) Life expectancy at age 65

Figure 3.3 (A) (B). Average life expectancy at birth and at age 65 in the United States. (Adapted from United States Public Health Service, National Center for Health Statistics. *Vital Statistics of the United States: 1970, Volume II—Mortality*)

ratio differences within one year with those of another year. Considering these figures for 1900 and 1970, we again see the dramatic change which has occurred in age-specific sex ratios during this century. In 1900 all but one of the age groups had sex ratios over 100 (i.e., more males than females). Notably, the under 15 and the 65+ age groups had identical sex ratios of 102 in 1900. The increasingly strong influence of sex selectivity in mortality at older ages is clearly indicated by the figures for 1970. Note that the sex ratio for the under 15 age groups remains above 100, indicating that infant and childhood mortality rates are not sex-specific. By age 45, however, the burden of higher male mortality rates in contemporary times shows its effect in the declining sex ratios. Most dramatic here is the sex-ratio comparison between 1900 and 1970 for the age 65+ group: from 102 to 72, a drop of 30 males for every 100 females in the older population in just 70 years!

Furthermore, projections to the year 2000 indicate that the sex ratio will drop below 70, and perhaps to as low as 60 males per 100 females. If such is the case, by the year 2000 the gerontology boom of the early twenty-first century is likely to present an even greater degree of widowhood among older women, with attendant social, economic, and housing problems.

Table 3.9   Sex ratios for broad age groups, by race in the United States for various years: 1900-1970 (males per hundred females)

	1900	1930	1960	1970
All races				
All ages	104.4	102.5	97.8	95.8
Under 15	102.1	102.8	103.4	103.8
15–24	98.3	98.1	101.4	102.3
25–44	109.1	101.7	96.9	96.9
45–54	113.9	109.4	97.2	93.2
55–64	106.5	108.3	93.7	89.8
65 and over	102.0	100.4	82.6	72.1
White				
Under 15	102.4	103.2	104.0	104.5
65 and over	101.9	100.1	82.1	71.6
Negro and other races[a]				
Under 15	100.0	99.0	100.0	100.0
65 and over	102.9	105.7	90.1	79.8

[a]"Negro and Other Races" classification is affected by incorrect inclusion of some persons of Spanish surname.
SOURCE: Adapted from United States Bureau of the Census. *Census of Population: 1970, General Population Characteristics* (Washington, D.C.: United States Government Printing Office) Final Report, PC (1)-B1, Table 53.

A final part of this picture, consequently, is to look more carefully at sex ratios in the context of mortality data. If, as the data in previous tables indicate, men are dying at a faster rate than women, then a combination of mortality rates and sex ratios will be able to describe those causes of death most responsible for these differences. Although war deaths have contributed to the proportionately low number of surviving men in older age groups, the sharp decline in the sex ratio since 1930 has been largely due to the increase in male deaths caused by the degenerative diseases. Men have suffered far more from the "major killers" during the last four decades. By 1969 the male death rate for heart disease, cancer, and most other causes was much higher than for females. This is indicated in Table 3.10, which gives the sex ratio for each of a number of major causes of death in the United States in 1969.

The Birth Cohort

The final indicator to be discussed here is one which is central to much demographic analysis, that of the "birth cohort." As indicated earlier, a birth cohort is all of the individuals who are born in a particular period of time (be that period a single month, year, decade, or other unit of time). Thus, all persons born on August 31, 1943 in the United States represent a birth cohort, although this is a much too narrow definition to be useful for any demographic research purposes. All persons born 1940– 1944 is a more useful cohort for purposes of analysis, as might be all persons born in the 1940–1950 decade.

The importance of the concept of the birth cohort can be seen from a number of different (but complementary) points of view. First, by referring to a group or category of individuals as "the cohort of 1940–1944" we recognize the fact that this set of individuals was born in a particular

Table 3.10   Sex ratio by cause of death in the United States: 1969 (male to female ratio)

Cause of death	Ratio (male to female)
All causes	1.350
Diseases of the heart	1.396
Cerebrovascular disease (stroke)	0.876
Malignant neoplasms (cancer)	1.259
Influenza and pneumonia	1.302
Bronchitis, emphysema, and asthma	3.984
Arteriosclerosis	0.807
Accidents (all types)	2.377

SOURCE: Adapted from United States Public Health Service, National Center for Health Statistics. *Vital Statistics of the United States: 1969, Volume II—Mortality,* Part A (Washington, D.C.: United States Government Printing Office) Table 1-8, 1974.

historical time, raised in a particular historical milieu, and from the moment of birth represents a particular configuration of demographic characteristics. Thus, the cohort of 1940–1944 will have different characteristics from the cohort born in 1930–1934. Clearly, the demographic characteristics of these two cohorts as well as the social, economic, and political circumstances of socialization and maturation were quite different.

The consideration of different age groups in a gerontological perspective is strongly affected by a view of age groups in terms of birth cohorts. All people age, and at any particular time-point in history the survivors can be identified as the old people in the population system. Yet the demographic composition of the category of "old people" differs from time to time, and these differences can be traced to the birth cohort of the particular group of old persons. To use the concepts introduced earlier in this chapter, the dynamics of fertility set the initial parameters of a birth cohort as it enters the population and society. Subsequently, factors of differential mortality (such as sex differences in the incidence of degenerative diseases) affect the number and composition of those among the cohort who survive to old age.

Another way of looking at how cohort analysis is important for gerontology follows from the above in that the study of older persons must in some way anticipate the future needs and demands of the older population. Of course, one way to estimate future contributions, problems, and issues of the older population is to observe and study the aging process among today's old people. While much study needs to be done to understand the individual and the societal aspects of aging, we should also be in a position to anticipate future needs as well. And this is where cohort analysis can be useful.

We can describe the old persons who will be alive in the near future, since these persons represent the aging of birth cohorts who are already alive. For example, suppose we are interested in comparing the old people in the year 2000 who will be 65–74 years of age with those in the year 2030 who will similarly be 65–74 years old. By simple subtraction we can determine that the old people in the year 2000 are the survivors of the birth cohort of 1926–1935; similarly, we can determine that the old people in the year 2030 will represent the birth cohort of 1956–65.

Once we have identified the old people for any given year in terms of their birth cohort, the task of "predicting" the future old-age situation becomes substantially easier. In this example, the birth cohorts of 1926–1935 and 1956–1965 have already been born; no new members of these two cohorts can affect the predictions. With fertility completed and immigration a negligible factor, the projection of future cohorts of older people requires "only" two additional kinds of information. The first is a description of the cohort; census data can be used to describe the number of people in each cohort, their geographic distribution, and their economic and various social characteristics. The second factor is the expected survivability of the members of the cohorts; this, of course, is the more tricky part of the problem. While demographic analysis cannot predict with absolute certainty which individuals or types of individuals within a cohort are likely to survive, series of estimates can be made given what is already known about mortality. Thus, the composition of the cohort when it reaches the sixth decade of its own life cycle can be roughly knowable, given such factors as sex and race differentials in mortality, including expected changes over time.

Thus, the concept of a birth cohort and the demographic techniques of cohort analysis can be quite important to gerontological analysis (see Chapters 6 and 18). One can better understand the processes of aging with the realization that old people at any given point in time reflect in part the characteristics of their own particular birth cohort. And a description of the future composition of the older population can be drawn from the fact that many of tomorrow's cohorts of older persons have already been born. When gerontologists consider the various social and economic aspects of the "problems of aging," and how the institutions of society are going to meet those problems, such consideration can be enlightened by an analysis based on the concept of cohort. Indeed, one point of view which has been espoused by social philosophers as well as demographers (for example, Mannheim, 1928; Ryder, 1965) is that history and social change can be viewed as a succession of birth cohorts traveling through society. Each cohort has its own unique set of birth characteristics; its own social, economic, and political life history or collective biography; and for gerontologists, each cohort will represent a different context in which society confronts aging, and in which the aged confront society.

Some Demographic Characteristics of the Present Older Population

Throughout this discussion we have attempted to illustrate the basic demographic processes and useful demographic indicators with descriptive data concerning the past, present, and in some instances future old-age population. In this final section we present additional demographic data to provide a better understanding of the current socioeconomic status and life style of older people in the United States. These data describe such characteristics as the distribution of older persons within the United States in terms of urban vs. rural and in terms of various regions and states within the country. We will also consider the economic and educational status of older persons as well as general patterns of living arrangements found among contemporary older persons. As a final prefatory note to this discussion it should be emphasized that these data are not meant to be a complete description of contemporary older persons. We present only the highlights of available information. Additional data are presented in other chapters in this volume; still additional information can be obtained from the many census documents and other publications cited throughout this chapter.

Residential Distribution

A first part of the description concerns information on where the older population resides. Of the total older population in 1970, the largest number (14.6 million, or 73 percent) lived in urban areas. Of these urban elderly, the majority (55 percent) was located in heavily urbanized areas, with 6.8 million of these in central cities. Only 4.3 million older people lived in suburbs. In this respect the elderly differ from the population as a whole, in which suburbanites outnumber central city residents. Clearly, older people are disproportionately concentrated in central cities—a fact which makes urban problems of congestion, transportation, living costs, crime, and housing of paramount concern to those interested in the health and well-being of older persons.

In terms of the proportion which the elderly represent of an area's total population, however, the highest concentration of elderly is in small rural towns (places of 1,000 to 2,500 total population), in which they are 13.6 percent of the total. Next highest in proportion are the elderly living in urban places of 2,500 to 10,000 population, for which the 65+ group represents 12.2 percent of the population. This residential pattern implies that the smaller the area, the greater the concentration of older people. There is an exception to this pattern, however. Farm areas have one of the lowest proportions of elderly people. This is in part explained by the post-World War II movement of older people from unproductive and burdensome farms to nearby small towns (Youmans, 1967) and by the more recent general migration of older people to cities in the South and West. The other exception to the pattern, suburbia (with only 7.8 percent elderly), is explained by the high cost, excessive size, and transportation necessities of suburban housing relative to the finances and needs of older people (Taeuber, 1972).

Another important distributional characteristic of the older population concerns the states in which they are concentrated. Numerically, the states with the largest populations also have the largest numbers of older people. New York, California, Pennsylvania, and Illinois account for nearly one-third of the total older population of the United States. Ten states account for 56 percent of all older people in 1970, as seen in Table 3.11. Note, however, that these ten states vary widely in the percent increase of their older populations during the 1960–1970 decade. Florida experienced a dramatic increase of 78.9 percent during this decade. Yet some states with high percent increases, such as California, Texas, and New Jersey, still have lower proportions of older people than the national average. This indicates that for some areas (e.g., California) the increase in the 65+ population is part of the area's general population increase, while for other areas (such as Florida), the increase in the 65+ population is a special demographic phenomenon. The explanation of the Florida case is found in the process of migration; it is certainly not the case that Florida has a substantially lower old-age mortality than the rest of the country!

It should be noted that percent change figures can often be misleading when comparing two or more populations, since the denominators (or base population) upon which the percent change is based can vary widely. Thus, California, with its 1960–1970 net increase of 425,000 older persons, represented a 30.9 percent increase, while the net increase of 436,000 older people in Florida represented an increase of 78.9 percent for that state. Conversely, Arizona's similar large increase rate of 79.0 percent in that decade represented only 71,000 additional older people. The percent

Table 3.11   Population age 65 and over: ten leading states in the United States: 1970

Rank	State	Number	Percent increase since 1960	Percent of state total in 1970
1	New York	1,961,000	16.2	10.8
2	California	1,801,000	30.9	9.0
3	Pennsylvania	1,272,000	12.7	10.8
4	Illinois	1,094,000	12.2	9.8
5	Ohio	998,000	11.2	9.4
6	Texas	992,000	33.1	8.9
7	Florida	989,000	78.9	14.6
8	Michigan	753,000	18.0	8.5
9	New Jersey	697,000	24.4	9.7
10	Massachusetts	636,000	11.3	11.2
	United States	20,177,000	21.0	9.9

SOURCE: Adapted from United States Bureau of the Census. *Census of Population: 1970, General Population Characteristics,* (Washington, D.C.: United States Government Printing Office) Final Report, PC (1)-B1, Tables 59 and 62; *Census of Population: 1960, Characteristics of the Population, Volume I,* Part 1 (Washington, D.C.: United States Government Printing Office) United States Summary, Tables 55 and 59.

increase figures may be the same, but the absolute numbers can be quite different.

Given such variations in numbers and percent changes among the states, it is useful to consider estimates of net migration of the 65+ population for a better understanding of where older people are located and where they are going. These estimates are derived from the 1960 and 1970 censuses of population. Simply stated, by applying region-by-region survival ratios (Barclay, 1958) to the population age 55 and over in every region (or state) in 1960, we derive the expected population from this age cohort still alive ten years later in 1970 (the cohort aged 65+). This expected figure can then be compared with the actual older population in the region given by the 1970 census, the difference being the estimated net migration for that cohort during the decade.

Using this method, the net migration figures for the major geographic regions of the United States were derived, and they give us the best picture of the geographic mobility and changing distribution of the older population in the country. It is clear from these data that the South, particularly the South Atlantic, and the West are attracting great numbers of older migrants, while almost all Northeast and East North Central states are losing older people through net out-migration (*Current Population Reports,* 1971).

Underlying these national trends are some interesting state-level differences and contrasts. For example, Florida's net in-migration of over 366,000 older people during the 1960–1970 decade stands in sharp contrast to the net out-migration of almost 203,000 older people from New York. Similarly, where Illinois experienced a net loss of 105,000 older people from 1960–1970, Texas and Arizona had net in-migration of 52,700 and 46,000 older persons, respectively, during the decade. In the same period California had a net gain of almost 143,000 older in-migrants.

Out- and in-migration together affect population. Obviously the net immigration contributes to a state's total increase in population. Also, a state or region can experience a net out-migration of older people despite an increase in its older population. The loss from migration represents the difference between the expected increase and the actual number of older people at the end of the period under consideration. Illinois is a case in point: despite a 12.2 percent increase in its older population during the 1960–1970 decade, it had a net out-migration of 105,000 older people during that time. Its total older population increased, but not by as much as was expected. Out-migration was the reason.

These migration trends, if they continue, will lead to an increasing concentration of older people in the southern and western states. As each state's population composition changes, adjustments in public policy and service delivery systems will be necessary to meet the heavier needs of larger proportions of older people. States such as Florida, Arizona, Texas, and California are particularly challenged to be aware of these trends and to adjust their programs for such needs as adequate housing, health care, leisure activities, and mass transit for the elderly.

Our review of the migration trends of older people must include a note of caution in order to put these trends in proper perspective. Although some states show high rates of in- or out-migration of older people, among all age groups the 65+ group as a whole has the lowest mobility *(Current Population Reports*, April 1972). Table 3.12 presents an interesting portrait of the differences in residential mobility between younger and older persons; the data indicate the rates for moves in the period March 1970 to March 1971 as collected by the Bureau of the Census. Almost half of the age 22–24 population experienced some kind of move in this period—that is, at least living in a different house at the end of the period —as compared with about 9 percent for the 65+ population. Furthermore, the relative distance of old-age residential change is less than for the younger population. Of those who did change residences, two-thirds of the elderly stayed in the same county (6.0 of the 8.7 percent), while the comparable figure for the younger population is slightly over half (25.8 of the 43.8 percent).

Even if we consider only the age 65–74 group of the older population, the migration rates remain low. For the same 1970–1971 period, only 2.9 percent of the age 65–74 population moved to a different county while 5.4 percent moved to a different house in the same county, a total of only 8.3 percent for this age group. But while the migration rates of older persons are relatively small, the point made earlier remains valid: in gen-

Table 3.12   Mobility status and migration rates for selected age groups in the United States, March 1971[a] (percent distribution)

Mobility status	Total population	Age 22–24	Age 65 and over
Same house (nonmovers)	81.3	52.4	91.2
Different house (movers)	17.9	43.8	8.7
Same county	11.4	25.8	6.0
Different county	6.5	18.0	2.7
Within the state	3.1	8.5	1.3
Between states	3.4	9.5	1.4
Total[b]	99.2	96.2	99.9

[a]Mobility occurring between March 1970 and March 1971.
[b]Percentages do not add up to 100 percent because of missing data.
SOURCE: United States Bureau of the Census. *Current Population Reports,* Series P-20, No. 235, "Mobility of the Population of the United States, March 1970 to March 1971" (April 1972), Table 3.

eral, old-age residential migration is selective and is bringing increasing numbers of older persons disproportionately to the southern and western states.

Economic Characteristics

Because Chapter 16 presents a detailed account of the economics of aging in the United States, we will only briefly highlight the demographic aspects of this topic. For example, it should be noted that the participation of white males age 65+ in the labor force has steadily decreased from 45.8 percent in 1950 to 25.5 percent in 1971; the figures for older white females during the same period have remained quite low at approximately 10 percent. The comparable rates for blacks are similar to those for whites.

In line with this low and decreasing labor-force participation among the elderly is the relatively low median income of the older population. In 1971 the median annual income of families in which the head-of-household was 65 or over was $5,453, *about half* the median income for all families in that year ($10,285). Of this older family group, 15.5 percent were below the low-income level of $2,424 (established by the Social Security Administration and updated annually) for a family of two with head-of-household age 65+ in 1971. Indeed, in Tables 3.13-A and 3.13-B we can compare the distribution of incomes for the total population and for the older population. For all types of families among the older population (Table 3.13-B), one-fifth (19.9 percent) had annual incomes of less than $3,000 in 1971 as compared with only 8.3 percent for the population as a whole (Table 3.13-A). Similarly, over 55 percent of all older families had annual incomes of less than $5,000 in comparison to only 24.2 percent for the total population.

The same dramatic age differences exist for unrelated individuals, that is, those persons living alone or with nonrelatives. Median income in 1971 for unrelated individuals aged 65 and over was $2,199, distinctly lower than the national average of $3,316 for the same group. Over 42 percent of this group of elderly people fell below the low-income level of $1,931 designated for elderly individuals. These data emphasize the especially serious economic hardships faced by older people who are living alone.

In Figure 3.4-A, the distribution of low-income status is shown for different groups in the older population. Of all persons aged 65 and over, 4.3 million, or 21.6 percent, fell below the low-income level in 1971. This figure for older people is almost twice the proportion of all persons under age 65 (i.e., 12.5 percent) who were below the low-income level in 1971. Almost 20 percent of older families with female heads of households were

Table 3.13A Type of family and age of head—families and unrelated individuals by total money income in the United States: 1971

Total money income	Total population					
		FAMILIES				
			Male head			
	Total	Total	Married, wife present	Other marital status	Female head	Unrelated individuals
Number (in thousands)	53,296	47,105	752	1,353	6,191	16,311
Percent						
Under $1,000–2,999	8.3	5.5	5.5	12.2	28.1	46.4
$3,000– 5,999	15.9	14.1	13.9	18.5	30.0	24.8
$6,000– 8,999	17.7	17.6	17.4	21.3	19.7	15.1
$9,000–14,999	33.3	35.5	35.6	29.4	15.9	10.6
$15,000 and over	24.8	27.3	27.6	18.6	6.3	3.1
Total	100.0	100.0	100.0	100.0	100.0	100.0
Median income	$10,285	$10,930	$10,999	$8,722	$5,114	$3,316

Table 3.13B Type of family and age of head—families and unrelated individuals by total money income in the United States: 1971

	Population age 65 and over				
	FAMILIES				
		Male head			
Total money income	Total	Total	Married, wife present	Other marital status	Female head	Unrelated individuals
Number (in thousands)	7,478	6,461	6,110	351	1,017	6,060
Percent						
Under $1,000–2,999	19.9	18.8	18.9	15.5	27.2	68.1
$3,000– 5,999	35.6	36.9	37.6	27.6	27.0	21.0
$6,000– 8,999	19.0	19.0	18.7	26.0	18.8	5.7
$9,000–14,999	15.7	15.1	14.8	19.5	19.2	3.7
$15,000 and over	9.8	10.2	10.0	11.4	7.8	1.5
Total	100.0	100.0	100.0	100.0	100.0	100.0
Median income	$5,453	$5,450	$5,394	$6,879	$5,476	$2,199

SOURCE: Adapted from the United States Bureau of the Census, *Current Population Reports*, Series P-60, No. 85, "Money Income in 1971 of Families and Persons in the United States" (December 1972), Table 17.

below the low-income level, but the comparable figure for male heads of households was only 11 percent. The same sex-related differences are seen in the figures for unrelated individuals (i.e., those living alone). Over 45 percent of all women in this category were below the low-income level, but only 33 percent of the men were.

Looking at the distribution within the aged low-income group itself (Figure 3.4-B), we observe that 60 percent were unrelated individuals, with women comprising 83 percent of them. Single or widowed women are clearly bearing the major burden of poverty within the older population. In 1971 older persons as a whole accounted for 17 percent of the generally defined poverty population, although they represent less than 10 percent of the total population in the United States.

The economic situation of older people remains a major problem,

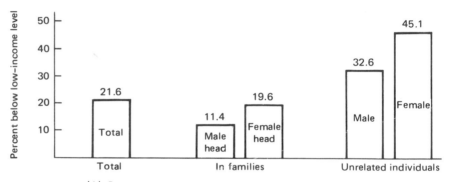

(A) Percent below low–income level within each family status category

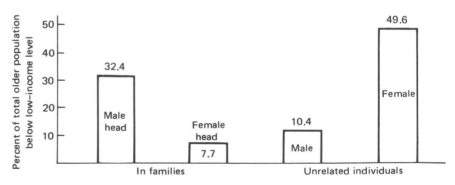

(B) Percent distribution within the total older below low–income level population

Figure 3.4 (A) (B). Characteristics of the age 65+ population below low-income level: 1971. (United States Bureau of the Census. *Current Population Reports*, "Characteristics of the Low-Income Population, 1971")

despite contemporary increases in benefits from Social Security, private pension plans, or the Medicare program. Food, housing, and health care costs are rising far more quickly than are the economic resources of older people, especially those not in the labor force and those located in central cities. Indeed, the combination of relatively fixed incomes and substantial annual inflation has made the economic plight of the older person particularly precarious. As one analyst of the situation has noted, if you're old, you're more than twice as likely to be poor (Brotman, 1971).

Living Arrangements

The characteristics of the older population in terms of marital status and living arrangements reflect the demographic trends of recent decades, especially concerning male-female differentials in mortality rates. As seen in Table 3.14, most elderly men are married and are living with their spouses (70 percent), while only 35 percent of older women fall into this category (see Chapter 5). The increasing prevalence of widowhood among older women (54 percent in 1971) is primarily a function of the current higher death rates for older men. This situation, in turn, helps explain the much higher proportion of older women living alone, 36 percent in 1971, as a significant increase from the 28 percent found in 1960. And for both older men and women there has been an overall decrease since 1960 in

Table 3.14   Percent distribution of the population age 65 and over by marital status and by living arrangement, by sex: 1971

	Male	Female
Marital status		
Single	7.1	7.3
Married, spouse present	70.1	34.5
Married, spouse absent	2.9	1.7
Widowed	17.1	54.2
Divorced	2.7	2.3
Total	99.9	100.0
Living arrangement		
In families	79.7	57.5
Head of family	72.7	8.7
Wife	N/A	33.8
Other relative	7.0	15.0
Living alone	14.7	36.2
Living with unrelated individuals	1.9	1.6
In an institution	3.6	4.6
Total	99.9	99.9

SOURCE: Adapted from United States Bureau of the Census. *Current Population Reports,* Series P-20, No. 225, "Marital Status and Living Arrangements: March 1971", (November 1971), Tables 1, 2, and 6.

the proportion living in families, particularly with relatives other than spouses. Simply stated, the trend toward greater isolation of older people from their families is increasing in our society. This situation, combined with the rising proportion of widows, can only exacerbate the social, economic, and psychological problems of loneliness among older persons, especially women.

Although there has been some recent discussion of a trend toward increasing "pairing" of older unmarried individuals as a way to pool economic resources and to provide companionship, census data do not bear this out. No significant change has occurred since 1960 in the proportion of older persons reported as living with unrelated individuals. To the degree that the census data in Table 3.14 accurately represent changes in living arrangements, the proportion of people living with unrelated individuals remains around 2 percent for both sexes, the same proportion as in 1960.

Educational Attainment

Perhaps one other social characteristic of older persons is important to consider in terms of their future socioeconomic status. Given that education can provide certain occupational, economic, and social advantages, the changing educational attainment of successive groups of older people may indicate life-style improvements in the future years (see Chapters 6 and 18). The present 65+ population compares poorly with the current 25–64 population in educational attainment. Table 3.15 gives a breakdown by years of school completed for these two age groups. These data indicate that the majority of older people in 1970 had some elementary schooling, but that only 28 percent had some high school education, as compared with 55 percent of those age 25 to 64.

Expected changes in educational attainment within the older popula-

Table 3.15 Percent distribution of the population age 25-64 and 65+ by years of school completed for the United States: 1970

	Years of school completed			
Age	No school	Elementary 1–8 years	High school 1–4 years or more	College 1 year or more
25–64	0.7	21.3	55.4	22.6
65 and over	3.1	56.7	28.3	11.9

SOURCE: Adapted from United States Bureau of the Census. *Current Population Reports,* Series P-25, No. 476, "Demographic Projections for the United States," (February 1972), Table 5.

tion are seen in Table 3.16, based upon age-cohort projections through 1990. The change toward an increasingly better educated older population will be gradual through the year 1990, when almost 50 percent of all persons age 65 and over will have had at least some high school education. Also by 1990, the proportion of older people having some college education will have increased to over 17 percent and those with only an elementary school education will have dropped from half to one-third of all older people. Remember that the age 65+ cohort in 1990 represents the age 45+ cohort in 1970. Because most people have completed their education by age 45, these projections can be viewed as minimum figures. Further improvements will continue beyond 1990 as the rather well educated adolescents of the 1960s and 1970s become the old people of the twenty-first century. The 2010–2020 "gerontology boom" will be a well-educated group of people.

Concluding Remarks

In this chapter we have only scratched the surface of possible demographic analysis and data relevant to the concepts and issues of gerontology. Given the expanse of theories and data with which demographers typically work, we have attempted to provide a sampling of the data and a brief introduction to some of the basic concepts.

Thus, we know that the simple fact that there are now more older people in the United States than in previous years is but a small part of the overall story. When we look for the "causes" of increasing numbers of older persons, we must look to the high fertility rates of previous decades coupled with dramatic reductions in infant mortality. Another "cause" of

Table 3.16   Projections of the percent distribution of the 65+ population by years of school completed for the United States: 1975-1990

Year	No school	Elementary 1–8 years	High school 1–4 years or more	College 1 year or more
1975	0.6	52.0	33.8	13.6
1980	0.5	45.9	38.7	14.9
1985	0.4	39.0	44.4	16.2
1990	0.4	32.9	49.2	17.5

SOURCE: Adapted from United States Bureau of the Census. *Current Population Reports,* Series P-25, No. 476, "Demographic Projections for the United States," (February, 1972), Tables 3 and 5.

a growing older population is a declining younger population, one result of a reduction in current fertility and population growth rates. That is, the same absolute number of older persons becomes a larger proportion of the population when fewer babies, children, and adolescents are part of that population.

The "effects" of a growing number and proportion of older persons upon the society are many, and a discussion of the demography of aging is not the place for a full consideration of the social policy implications of aging. Yet some of the demographic facts and indicators discussed here directly suggest the kinds of problems with which the leaders of society must work.

The "dependency ratio" draws our attention to the potential political implications of a changing proportional mix of age groups in society. As long as only a relatively small number of old people are drawing pensions and a large number of younger working people are contributing to those pension systems, the financial problems may be minimal. But the changing population composition, as suggested by the trends in the dependency ratios, predicts a future time when larger number of old people will have to be supported by a society with a decreasing proportion of younger workers. Clearly such a situation has public policy and political implications, as well as social and economic ones.

The combination of fixed incomes, regularized trends in inflation, and a growing older population implies a range of economic security problems and issues. Certainly it is not the case that only the aged are affected by tight economic times. Yet, as our discussion and a number of other analyses have indicated, the old are disproportionately represented among the poor in the United States. Furthermore, old age acts to accentuate other inequalities in the social and economic system, such that when age is combined with minority, racial, and ethnic status, the problems of poverty, disease, labor-force discrimination, and other dislocations become greater for the individuals concerned.

The higher mortality of older males has resulted in a substantially greater preponderance of females in the older population. Thus, a substantial number of old people are widows who live alone; public policy in the domain of housing for the elderly must take into consideration some of the unique demographic aspects indicated by old-age sex ratios. At the same time, this kind of information has implications for medical care, transportation, income maintenance, and tax policy.

Finally, our consideration of the changing educational composition of the population, when combined with the concept of the birth cohort, implies that future cohorts of older persons will be much better educated than past and even contemporary cohorts of older persons. Thus, many of our social and political stereotypes of the elderly, even to the degree that such stereotypes are based on informed observations of old people, will be out of date. (See Chapter 6 for the psychological implications of cohort differences in education.) Tomorrow's cohorts of old people will represent today's cohorts of substantially educated, socially conscious, and politically active and experienced people. While we cannot predict with certainty that the cohorts which were involved in civil rights and student protest activities will be "senior activists" when they reach their 60s and 70s, we should at least seriously consider such a possibility.

Therefore, demographic analysis can provide the descriptive parameters of tomorrow's older population, and some of the economic and social problems which are likely to be precipitated by the predicted age changes in the composition of the population. At the same time, however, demographic analysis predicts that tomorrow's older persons will be, perhaps, in a better position in terms of education, skill, and experience to deal with these problems on the basis of both individual and collective action.

References

Barclay, G. W. 1958. *Techniques of population analysis.* New York: John Wiley & Sons, Inc.

Brotman, H. B. 1971. The older population revisited; first results of the 1970 census. *Facts and figures on older Americans,* Number 2, Administration on Aging, Washington, D.C. SRS-AoA Publication #182.

Brotman, H. B. 1973. Projections of the population to the year 2000. *Statistical Memo #25,* Administration on Aging. Washington, D.C.: U.S. Government Printing Office, June 1973.

Coale, A. J. 1956. The effects of changes in mortality and fertility on age composition. *The Milbank Memorial Fund Quarterly* 34:79–114.

Dublin, L. I.; Lotka, A. J.; and Spiegelman, M. 1949. *Length of life: a study of the life table,* revised edition. New York: The Ronald Press Company.

Hermalin, A. I. 1966. The effect of changes in mortality rates on population growth and age distribution in the United States. *The Milbank Memorial Fund Quarterly* 44:451–469.

Mannheim, K. 1928 (1952). The problem of generations. In *Essays on the sociology of knowledge,* ed. and transl. Paul Kecskemeti, pp. 276–322. London: Routledge and Kegan Paul.

Ryder, N. B. 1965. The cohort as a concept in the study of social change. *American Sociological Review* 30:843–861.

Sauvy, A. 1954. *General theory of population.* Paris: University of France Press.

Taeuber, I. B. 1972. The changing distribution of the population of the United States in the twentieth century. In *Population, distribution, and policy.*

Part 5, ed. S. M. Mazie, pp. 29–107. U.S. Commission on Population Growth and the American Future. Washington, D.C.: U.S. Government Printing Office.

United Nations. 1973. *Demographic yearbook: 1972.* New York: The United Nations, 1973.

United States Bureau of the Census. 1940 and 1970. *Census of population: characteristics of the population.* Washington, D.C.: U.S. Government Printing Office.

United States Bureau of the Census. 1960. *Census of population: 1960, characteristics of the population,* volume I, part 1. Washington, D.C.: U.S. Government Printing Office.

United States Bureau of the Census. 1967 (December). *Current population reports,* Series P-25, No. 38. Projections of the population of the United States, by age, sex and color to 1990, with extension of population by age and sex to 2015. Washington, D.C.: U.S. Government Printing Office.

United States Bureau of the Census. 1970. *Census of population: 1970, general population characteristics,* Final Report, PC(1)-B1. Washington, D.C.: U.S. Government Printing Office.

United States Bureau of the Census. 1971. *Current population reports,* Series P-25, No. 460. Preliminary intercensal estimates of states and components of population change, 1960 to 1970. Washington, D.C.: U.S. Government Printing Office.

United States Bureau of the Census. 1971 (April). *Current population reports,* Series P-20, No. 235. Mobility of the population of the United States, March 1970 to March 1971. Washington, D.C.: U.S. Government Printing Office.

United States Bureau of the Census. 1971 (November). *Current population reports,* Series P-20, No. 225. Marital status and living arrangements: March 1971. Washington, D.C.: U.S. Government Printing Office.

United States Bureau of the Census. 1971 (December). *Current population reports,* Series P-25, No. 470. Projections of the population of the United States by age and sex: 1970–2020. Washington, D.C.: U.S. Government Printing Office.

United States Bureau of the Census. 1972 (February). *Current population reports,* Series P-25, No. 476. Demographic projections for the United States. Washington, D.C.: U.S. Government Printing Office.

United States Bureau of the Census. 1972 (April). *Current population reports,* Series P-25, No. 480. Illustrative population projection for the United States: the demographic effects of alternative paths to zero growth. Washington, D.C.: U.S. Government Printing Office.

United States Bureau of the Census. 1972 (December). *Current population reports,* Series P-25, No. 493. Projections of the population of the United States, by age and sex: 1972–2020. Washington, D.C.: U.S. Government Printing Office.

United States Bureau of the Census. 1972 (December). *Current population reports,* Series P-60, No. 85. Money income in 1971 of families and persons in the United States. Washington, D.C.: U.S. Government Printing Office.

United States Bureau of the Census, 1972 (December). *Current population reports,* Series P-60, No. 86. Characteristics of the low-income population, 1971. Washington, D.C.: U.S. Government Printing Office.

United Stated Bureau of the Census. 1973. *Statistical abstract of the United States: 1972*. Washington, D.C.: U.S. Government Printing Office.

United States Immigration and Nationalization Service. Various. *Annual report,* summarized in United States Bureau of the Census, *Statistical abstract of the United States*. Washington, D.C.: U.S. Government Printing Office.

United States Public Health Service, National Center for Health Statistics. 1974 (June). *Monthly Vital Statistics Report* 22:13. Washington, D.C.: U.S. Government Printing Office.

United States Public Health Service, National Center for Health Statistics. Various. *Vital statistics of the United States, volume I—natality*. Washington, D.C.: U.S. Government Printing Office.

United States Public Health Service, National Center for Health Statistics. 1974. *Vital statistics of the United States: 1970, volume II—mortality, part A*. Washington, D.C.: U.S. Government Printing Office.

United States Public Health Service, National Center for Health Statistics. 1974. *Vital statistics of the United States: 1970, volume II—mortality part A*. Washington, D.C.: U.S. Government Printing Office.

Youmans, E. G. 1967. *Older rural Americans: a sociological perspective*. Lexington: University of Kentucky Press.

4

Sociological Approaches to Aging

VERN L. BENGTSON · DAVID A. HABER

Sociologists and social psychologists in the field of gerontology are concerned with many complex issues regarding change over time. This chapter will focus on three of the basic questions as they pertain to contemporary American society: (1) What are the sociological definitions of aging and time? (2) How can aging and time be analyzed from a sociological and social psychological perspective? (3) Who are today's elderly, and what are their unique social problems?

Sociological Definitions of Aging

Considered sociologically, aging refers to a sequence of events that take place, or are expected to take place, during an individual's life course (Bengtson, 1973). Some of these events are directly linked to specific chronological age by law or other formal definition, such as the age of eligibility to vote, to drink liquor, to marry without parental consent, to retire and to receive Social Security benefits. Other events are less regulated by formal requirements and more influenced by a variety of sociocultural forces, such as an individual's socioeconomic status, the nature of his work, and his ethnicity or subculture membership.

Chronological Age: Definitions of Functions and Events

Chronological age is based on calendar time; to a great extent it reflects a purely arbitrary definition of the passage of certain events in the course of life. Though there is not always a link between chronological age and human behavior, in most societies—and certainly in contemporary

American society—chronological age dominates the structuring of functions and events for approximately the first two decades of an individual's life (Cain, 1964; Neugarten and Moore, 1968). During this early period, the anticipated sequence of interests, skills, and cognitive development is usually more ordered and predictable than in later stages of life, when there are fewer specific expectations and less formalization of events. The predictability of the youthful years is greatly reinforced by the formal system of grade sequence within most public schools.

Chronological age expectations become important again at about age 65, which is frequently the age arbitrarily chosen for compulsory retirement. The selection of 65 as the age marker for the right to receive old-age insurance benefits was a congressional decision of the mid-1930s (Cain, 1974). Legislative provision for retirement came about because of economic and demographic factors: namely, the reduced need for the manpower, skills, and knowledge of the older worker in an increasingly industrialized society. The age marker of 65 has since come into wide, generalized use as the accepted time of retirement from work. Although some latitude does exist, about 70 percent of men and 90 percent of women currently commence their retirement at age 65 or older (Atchley, 1972). This choice of a chronological age rather than performance-capacity indicators or functional age has obvious administrative advantages within a bureaucratic society. The arbitrariness of the decision is the subject of continuing controversy over the restriction of opportunity for well-functioning adults of 65, as well as over the diminished opportunity for income imposed on them (Cain, 1974).

Though arbitrary chronological age markers may be associated with specific events, and though they may be more prevalent in the early and then again in the later stages of life, they nonetheless have broad social and personal significance in our society in all stages of the life cycle. Eight-year-old Johnny is deemed precocious because of his accomplishments compared with other children of his age; some people can't trust anyone over 30; for other people life begins at 40; most people use the age interval around 65 as a general reference point in distinguishing between middle age and old age (Neugarten et al., 1965). An important consideration with chronological age markers is that they do provide social regulation of the aging process, however arbitrary they might be, and no matter how much controversy they generate.

Social Age: Expectations and Status

Not only are the significance and the timing of events chronologically regulated; they are also subject to a complex array of biological, psychological, sociological, and cultural influences (Bengtson, 1973). Three of the sociological influences of an individual's aging are his socioeconomic status, his work context, and his ethnicity.

Several studies (see Neugarten and Moore, 1968) have shown, for instance, that an individual's socioeconomic status can influence the age at which major events occur in his life. In general, the lower his socio-economic class level, the sooner he reaches major events in his life course. Women from lower socioeconomic classes, for example, leave home at a younger age, marry and have a first child sooner, and begin work earlier than their counterparts of the middle and upper socioeconomic class. Working men from lower socioeconomic classes leave school earlier and begin work sooner than men from higher socioeconomic brackets. The careers of unskilled or blue-collar workers may be terminated early as they are replaced by more vigorous younger men or by machine labor. This quicker timing of major events in the lower socio-economic class may also lead to its members perceiving themselves as "old" at earlier chronological ages than members of the middle and upper classes.

Another sociological influence on the aging process is the occupational context in which an individual's work is performed. Caplow and McGee (1958) reported that mathematicians frequently refer to their colleagues as old when they are still in their early 30s. Historians, however, are often considered to be young even in their late 40s. Many analysts of human behavior have observed that careers which require longer education or apprenticeships tend to peak at later ages (Pelz and Andrews, 1966; Dennis, 1966). For example, the profession of medicine requires both a lengthy education and a period of internship, so that a doctor may not reach the highest achievements of his career for another 10 to 15 years. Similarly, in the business world, many years of experience are usually required to produce top executive ability. In some vocations, certain activities may not even be attempted until a later age is reached.

A third sociological factor that has significance in the timing of events and patterns of aging is ethnicity. Although this issue has only recently attracted concerted research effort, it is becoming clear that there are contrasting patterns of needs and adaptations to aging among blacks, Chicanos, and Anglos in contemporary American society (see Ragan and Bengtson, 1975; Cuellar, 1974). As an example, in questions to elderly subjects about the major advantage of being their age, Mexican-American respondents were most negative in their perception of old age, Anglo respondents were most positive, and blacks were intermediate. In the preliminary analysis, Mexican-Americans were most likely to perceive the stigma attached to old age, while blacks tended to respond with a feeling of pride at having survived to such an age. Such results are consistent with the findings of Sterne et al. (1974) on the contrast between ethnic groups in patterns of aging and perception of needs. These studies point to the importance of considering the sociocultural context in assessments of the aging process (Bengtson and Corry, 1974).

A final observation on sociological influences and aging: these influences may be inconsistent from one social institution to another, on an individual or societal level. For example, 50-year-old graduate students with successfully employed adult children may consider themselves young in an occupational career sense, even though their family goals are already accomplished. At the societal level, a familiar example of age-status inconsistency is that young adult males are eligible to lose their lives for their country but are not eligible to drink liquor. Cain (1974) suggests this "age-status asynchronization" is due to the building of law on a case-by-case and statute-by-statute basis rather than from broad, inclusive concepts.

The Aging Individual in a Social Context

The social-psychological perspective examines the complex ways in which individuals internalize the demands of society; that is, how individuals come to accept their social context, including the series of age-related positions they must enter, occupy, and exit. As the social context becomes internalized, it also becomes self-imposed.

A social psychology of the life cycle is built on at least four basic assumptions. First, the age structure within a society is an essential dimension for understanding human behavior. Four decades ago, Linton (1936) noted the universal significance of age structures for the study of social organization. Since that time many studies have supported the idea that all societies provide unique rights and responsibilities for members of different age groups, and that the relations between age groups are governed by sets of rules and expectations (see Riley, Johnson, and Foner, 1972).

Second, biological events and social-psychological processes are not always clearly related to each other. Neugarten and associates (1968), for example, found that menopause is not the major determinant of behavior in the lives of older women, as had once been assumed. Similarly, it has recently become well established that the decreased capacities of age do not necessarily produce depression (Palmore, 1974). Biological models of the life course are inadequate by themselves to account for individual behavior and attitudes because social definition exercises considerable influence.

Third, social-psychological processes are important throughout the life cycle. In recent decades studies have begun to focus on the continuities and changes in social influences over the entire life course, rather than only in childhood. For example, Brim (in Brim and Wheeler, 1966) notes that socialization during childhood works on fundamental motivations and values, such as the controlling of primary drives. After childhood, social influences bear more on overt behavior, such as the acquisition of knowledge and abilities in order to competently perform one's work (see Bengston, 1973, p. 19). In old age neither the motivations nor the behaviors of individuals appear to be subjected to specific and direct socializing influences. While this could be a time of opportunity, an experimentation with alternative patterns of behavior, it often creates social problems for the elderly—an issue we will discuss later.

Fourth, the social-psychological perspective does not view later life as merely a variation of earlier years. Strauss (1969, pp. 89–93), for instance, views the developmental process as a "transformation of identity," a radical change of behavior and identity from earlier times. For example, entering the role of "boss" for the first time requires dealing with new sets of problems and developing new perspectives. Attitudes toward such things as production schedules, company policies, worker efficiency, labor unions, and authority must be changed in relation to the person's new position in the company. After 65 many individuals again undergo a transformation of identity. Some of today's elderly must reluctantly give up their life's work and, in its place, are expected to substitute less important activities, including card playing, bingo, and other games which contribute little in the way of a positive self-image. The awareness of a new constellation of expectations and behaviors occurs with each new role or status, producing a distinctive reconstruction, or transformation, of one's identity (see Bengtson, 1973, pp. 19, 36).

The ultimate test of these basic social-psychological assumptions will be the significance of the research emanating from them.

Age-Status Systems

Researchers in social psychology have found the concepts of age-status systems and age norms to be important to a social perspective on aging. An age-status system is the sequence of roles available to an individual—such as son, daughter, brother, sister, friend, student, husband, wife, intern, father, mother, neighbor, professional colleague—through the life course. It is "the system developed by a culture to give order and predictability to the course followed by individuals" (Cain, 1964, p. 278).

Every new role or status may signal the beginning or ending of a major stage of an individual's life. The most significant characteristic of an age-status system is that major stages or periods of the life course emerge, contract, or elongate, and eventually terminate. Studies over the last several decades in America, for example, reveal trends toward a longer period of postparenthood (Neugarten and Moore, 1968; see also Chapter 5), or "the empty nest," as sociologists often call it. Aries (1962) reminds us that childhood did not always exist as a major period of the life cycle. This acceptance of the idea of an early stage of life with its own distinctive needs and unique characteristics appeared only after the growth of industrialization reduced the need for child labor, causing the child to remain longer in a sheltered status. The stage of adolescence appeared in the early part of this century, as middle- and upper-class young people were encouraged to remain in school for at least 12 years, and even longer, in order to prepare for increasingly complex kinds of work.

The end of the life cycle is increasingly emerging as another distinctive period of life. In addition, as more people reach old age (Brotman, 1973) and as longevity slowly increases (Sachuk, 1970), demographers are starting to distinguish between the old and the very old (Neugarten, 1974).

Age Norms

The distinctive sets of norms associated with particular periods of the life course are assigned to specific age ranges not only by social scientists, but also by a vast majority of people. A sample of middle-class, middle-aged people, for instance, achieved a high degree of consensus regarding the appropriate or expected age for retirement (Neugarten et al., 1965). A wide variety of other age-related characteristics in adulthood are located with an identifiable range by a large percentage of people (see Table 4.1).

It is not so much the age norms characterized by a high degree of consensus, but the systematic deviation from norms that has entranced generations of sociologists. Three such intriguing variations found in Neugarten's study are pertinent to our subject: (1) norms are perceived as more binding for others than they are for oneself; (2) as people grow old, they ascribe more importance to age norms; and (3) the discrepancy between the binding force of norms for oneself versus others is considerably greater for the young person than the old person.

Turk's study (1965) appears to be directly applicable to the finding that all norms are more binding for others than for oneself. He rejects the prevalent definition of norms as ideas on how one should personally behave. Instead he finds norms to be expectations about how others should behave. This interpretation is consistent with Neugarten's data: all age groups regard norms as a more coercive force for others than for themselves. However, Turk's study does not address the issue of why aging people ascribe increasing importance to the personally binding force of age norms. The concept of adult socialization is useful in this regard (Neugarten et al., 1965). As people grow old they are more likely to experience the consequences of not having fulfilled previous age-related expectations. They may feel a stigma from not having married during the appropriate time span. They may be disappointed at feeling it is too late to begin study for a profession they wish they had pursued. The personal belief in the relevance and validity of age norms, therefore, increases over the life course.

None of these ideas, however, appear to be adequate for explaining why the young are likely to minimize the coercive nature of age norms for themselves, while the old are likely to maximize the validity of norms for all age strata. One useful possibility for explaining this discrepancy is the *generational stake:* the expectations that one generation has of

Table 4.1   Consensus in a middle-class, middle-aged sample regarding various age-related characteristics

	Age range designated as appropri- ate or expected	Percent who concur	
		Men (N=50)	Women (N=43)
Best age for a man to marry	20–25	80	90
Best age for a woman to marry	19–24	85	90
When most people should become grandparents	45–50	84	79
Best age for most people to finish school and go to work	20–22	86	82
When most men should be settled on a career	24–26	74	64
When most men hold their top jobs	45–50	71	58
When most people should be ready to retire	60–65	83	86
A young man	18–22	84	83
A middle-aged man	40–50	86	75
An old man	65–75	75	57
A young woman	18–24	89	88
A middle-aged woman	40–50	87	77
An old woman	60–75	83	87
When a man has the most responsibilities	35–50	79	75
When a man accomplishes most	40–50	82	71
The prime of life for a man	35–50	86	80
When a woman has the most responsibilities	25–40	93	91
When a woman accomplishes most	30–45	94	92
A good-looking woman	20–35	92	82

SOURCE: Neugarten, Moore and Lowe. Age norms, age constraints and adult socialization. *American Journal of Sociology.* © 1965. Used by permission of University of Chicago Press.

another (Bengtson and Kuypers, 1971). While the parental expectation for the young is continuity and similarity, the personal goal of the young is frequently the freedom to experience, create, and re-create—to divest oneself of the parental "stake," or investment, in the younger generation. The young are likely, therefore, to see age norms as much less constraining and relevant for themselves than for older people. Old people, however, have a stake in continuing that which has been found desirable or deemed appropriate. They are more likely, therefore, to maximize the validity and relevancy of norms.

A final attribute of age norms to be mentioned here is the sanctions—rewards and penalties—for approved and disapproved behavior that are applied to major stages of the life cycle. An example of internalizing a sanction is the man who engages in a period of job experimentation until he feels that "it's time" to settle into a particular career. Age norms can "operate as prods and brakes upon behavior, in some instances hastening an event, in others delaying it" (Neugarten et al., 1965, pp. 22–23). Individuals who feel that their timing is early or late for a particular major event may "move back toward the norm on the next event" (Neugarten and Datan, 1973). For example, a man who postpones marriage until the completion of a long preparatory period of education may wish to have children shortly thereafter. Age-related activity can be controlled by external sanctions as well. Perhaps the most common example of how other people informally enforce conformity to age norms is the sharp rebuke, "Act your age!"

Sociological Perspectives on Time

Time is not merely the steady accumulation of equal units as measured on clocks and calendars. Time can also be interpreted as a sequence of socially defined and regulated experiences through history. Modern sociologists employ the terms *cohort* and *generation* to express concepts of sociological time. A cohort refers to those who are born during the same period of specific calendar time or who enter into a specific social institution, such as school or work, during the same precisely demarcated intervals. A generation refers to a group of people who are conscious of having shared similar sociocultural experiences, sometimes regardless of chronological boundaries.

Cohort analysis was devised by demographers in order to compare groups of people born during specific intervals of calendar time, usually consisting of five- or ten-year intervals. Those who are born in each period of time share the experience of particular cultural and historical events, as well as membership in a cohort of a particular size and composition. For instance, the cohort of people born between 1945 and 1955 was the first to experience living under the threat of nuclear destruction, followed by forced participation in an unpopular Asian war. It is often observed that these historical conditions have had an effect on the consciousness and behavior of many members of this cohort (Kenniston, 1968).

Not only are cohorts affected by the events occurring around them, but demographic characteristics of cohorts can influence the social institutions with which they came into contact. The sheer size of the 1945–55 cohort (the so-called baby boom) compared with those of previous decades resulted in the opening or expanding of maternity wards, the construction of new schools, increased demands for housing, and an expansion of the labor supply. Similarly, the decline in birth rate that characterized the succeeding cohorts has just recently begun to create its own dislocations: the slowing down or closing of maternity or pediatric wards as well as the dwindling occupancy of nursery and elementary schools. Furthermore, some demographers predict that as the trends toward zero population growth and increased longevity continue, the relative size of future cohorts of elderly may force institutional changes at least as great as the ones caused by the baby-boom cohort.

Demography describes an age cohort quantitatively, and includes such facts as size, geographical distribution, socioeconomic distribution, average age at marriage, and death rate. Cultural and historical events —such as the threat of nuclear war, racial upheaval, the advent of space exploration, and economic depression—are qualitative aspects of an age cohort, and they are most important when considered from the perspective of generational analysis.

Generational analysis is useful in studying the contributions of age groups to social change. Although the concept of generation has to be described in various ways by social analysts over a long period of time, Mannheim (1952) was one of the first to write systematically about generations. A generation consists of a group of individuals in a generalized period of historical time who share experiences of the same qualitative nature, and, most importantly, who share an awareness or consciousness of themselves as distinctive because of such experiences. Mannheim also conceived of generational units, subunits that can arise within a generation that may be contrary to the dominant cultural trends. Generational analysis employs the concept of age cohorts and historical experience in constructing the base information for more far-reaching implications in terms of social change.

Leonard Cain's (1967) analysis illustrates the interlocking use of both cohort and generational analyses. Cain compares the cohort born during the decade just before the turn of the century with the cohort born during the decade just afterwards. His data reveal cohort differences on such characteristics as labor-force participation, fertility rates, education, and sexual attitudes. He also made comparisons of sociocultural factors existing during the two decades and used them in a more far-reaching, generational analysis. The generation born just after the turn of the century was a more favored generation than those born just ahead of them. This advantaged generation had less to cope with in the way of crises and more to benefit it in terms of economic, technological, and educational resources. Specifically, this generation did not have to fight in World War I, fared well through the depression, and, beginning with the high-paying defense positions during World War II, has enjoyed an exceptional period of prosperity. Furthermore, they had fewer children to support, spent less time at work and more time in school. Cain implies there were differences in certain ideological stances or value systems between the two groups. In general, the more favored group followed a trend away from institutionalized religion and the Protestant Ethic and toward greater affluence and leisure time and a certain loosening of sexual attitudes. Since these and other differences emanated from the two groups, Cain suggests that a distinctive generation may be identified with each cohort. In order to examine intriguing questions such as whether the elderly constitute a potential generation unit, see Ragan and Dowd (1974) and Laufer and Bengtson (1974).

The New Old People in American Society

Although some sociologists and social psychologists of aging focus their attention on growing old over the life cycle or on the relationships between generations and cohorts, much of the current research in social gerontology restricts its scope to the state of being old. From a scientific standpoint this perspective can be helpful for counteracting the long-standing bias of social scientists and sources of funding that human behavior ceases to be interesting after childhood. However, from a purely pragmatic standpoint, the current focus on the state of old age is practically guaranteed to continue because of a very dramatic, extrascientific phenomenon: the tremendous population growth of the elderly. The remaining pages, therefore, will focus not on the individual as he ages, but on the characteristics of those who are already considered old. (References to the old, the aged, or the elderly are to the population of people age 65 or over, in accordance with the common parlance and practice of population experts.)

Between 1900 and 1970 the elderly population in America increased from 3.1 to 21 million people. This sevenfold increase among the aged during this century is significant even when compared to the upsurge in numbers of those under age 65. One way to compare the dramatic population changes of the old with the young is to note that the proportion of the entire population which is over 65 rose from 4 percent in 1900 to just under 10 percent in 1970. If the birthrate decline of the past two decades continues, the percentage of older people will rise significantly in the next century as well (see Table 4.2).

Life expectancy at birth has increased more than 20 years since the turn of the century. Most of this increase is attributable to a reduction in infant and childhood mortality. Life expectancy for those already 65 has increased less than 3 years during the same period. Those who turn age 65 in the future, however, could have a longevity increase by 10 years if major cardiovascular-renal diseases are eliminated (Brotman, 1968).

Life expectancy also appears to be sex-linked. In 1900 women were outliving men by 3 years, while by 1965 the difference had widened to 7 years. If this trend continues, some demographers predict that 2 out of 3 aged persons in the year 2000 will be women (Atchley, 1972). It is not likely that the current trend toward equal working roles for men and women will offset this discrepancy in longevity; there is a tendency for females to outlive males within equivalent sociocultural settings, such as exist in monastic life, as well as under controlled experiment with animal species.

A rough, broad sketch of the contemporary American population reveals a variety of differences between the elderly and people under the age of 65. Old people are most likely to live in the city, as are younger people, but more likely to live in the central city rather than the urban fringe or suburbs, where more younger people are found (Brotman, 1972). Older people are slightly more likely to live in small towns and rural areas than are younger people. The aged are considerably more likely to be functionally illiterate. Not only are they more likely to have stopped before completing high school, but more likely to be without much education at all. Old people are twice as likely to be poor. They are also

Table 4.2   Population percentages for the United States: 1900-2050

	1900	1930	1940	1950	1960	1970	2000	2020	2050
Young (under 18)		38.8	34.4	31.1	35.8	34.3	27.4	25.6	24.7
Work force (18–64)		55.8	58.7	60.8	55.0	55.9	61.7	61.3	59.9
Old (65+)	4.0	5.4	6.9	8.1	9.2	9.9	10.9	13.1	15.4

SOURCES: U.S. Bureau of the Census, *Statistical Abstract of the United States: 1972;* Brotman, H. B., Statistical Memo #25, Department of H. E. W., Administration on Aging, June 1973.

twice as likely to have one or more chronic physical conditions than are people in the age strata between 15 and 44. The aged spend three and one-half times as much on health care as do those under age 65 (Brotman, 1973). More older women are widows than wives. The eight percent of the older population who are black are likely to be even worse off than their aged colleagues in terms of income level, education, and health. And perhaps most pervasive of all, the elderly population almost categorically suffer from diminished resources of all kinds, particularly finances, health, physical ability, and even their eligibility to work.

The contemporary older American can also be differentiated from the elderly of other epochs. Though we have less information about older persons in 1900 than we do about the aged today, a rough comparison can still be made. Around the turn of the century older people were considerably more rare, both in absolute numbers and in proportion to the rest of the population. The elderly did not go into retirement; the majority were expected to continue whatever work and life style they had been following. In this respect the elderly of 1900 were not as likely to be differentiated from the remainder of the population as are older people today. The elders in a rural multigenerational family were respected for their useful information and skills. As rapid industrialization drew families into the city, the shortage of existing housing led to similar three-generational households and comparable respect in an urban context; the elderly served as a source of valuable information within a stable environment (Brotman, 1972, 1973). The older urban person was appreciated in a time when the community itself was an important and satisfying social resource. Today's more mobile society tends to build relationships according to work-related or interest-related activities, not necessarily restricted to the home community.

Accumulating facts about the future elderly does not guarantee clearcut predictions about their relative position in tomorrow's society. For example, we know that old people of the future will be better educated than today's aged population, because an inceasingly larger percentage of America's young people—the future elderly—are entering school. Yet, we are also aware that the educational level of those under age 65 increases even more rapidly than does each new cohort of old people. This means that either the educational disparity between young and old will continue to widen for some time to come or, in a society that requires constant renewal of knowledge, the growing numbers of older people taking advantage of continuing educational opportunities over their life course will reduce this gap.

We also know that reduced birthrate, a slight increase in longevity, greater numbers of people reaching traditional retirement age, and the recent advent of plans calling for retirement earlier than 65, all contribute to what demographers call an increasing *dependency ratio,* as discussed in Chapter 3. This demographic tool reveals the proportion of people who are economically dependent on the work-force population. From 1930 through 2050, the dependency ratio for the older population is expected to follow a general linear trend upward, with increasing proportions of people dependent (Cutler et al., 1974). If this forecast is accurate, some demographers predict that within the next half-century, for every 2.2 employed persons there will be one dependent person on social security.

We also know that the sex ratio is expected to increase dramatically. As noted earlier, if the tendency for women to outlive men increases over the life span (see Table 4.3), and if the age median for women over 65 continues to rise as it has during the past several decades, the ratio of elderly women to elderly men may increase to 2 to 1 by the year 2000. If the social tradition of women's marrying men older than themselves persists, the percentage of elderly women widowed and living alone will be startling. Alternatives to this prospect might be to reverse the social custom of men's marrying women younger than themselves or to adopt new forms of social institutions, such as communal or polygamous living arrangements in which women can find companionship with each other as well as share the more scarce resource of the older man.

Aging as a Social Problem

The identification and interpretation of social problems are in large measure shaped by the particular sociocultural context in which they are made. The identification of the aged as a social problem is a product of such factors

Table 4.3   Population of females per 100 males, United States: 1970

Age	Females per 100 males
All ages	103.7
Under 45	98.7
45–64	108.7
65+	134.7
65–74	126.0
75–84	147.4
85+	163.1

SOURCE: From Brotman, 1970.

as rapid industrialization, its resulting social changes, and twentieth-century American values (Kuypers and Bengtson, 1973). Even the existence of the American Gerontological Society, which has identified old age as a social problem, contributes to this bias. All factors considered, however, there is an enormous amount of evidence to document that modern society is singularly unprepared to meet the basic needs of its rapidly expanding older citizenry. Some of that evidence follows, demonstrating three ways in which the aged can be viewed as a social problem.

Poor Health

As gerontologists are wont to observe, the popular portrayal of the decrepit oldster is grossly misleading. Major contributions to art, music, literature, and science are made by people in their 70s and 80s or beyond (Lehman, 1953). Bertrand Russell was writing important philosophical ideas until his death at nearly 100. Painter and sculptor Pablo Picasso continued his contributions to the artistic world well past his 90th year. Investigations of more everyday types of work reveal that nonagenarians are active in the Foster Grandparent program and Operation Green Thumb (Brotman, 1969). A more general view of the capabilities of those 65 and over discloses that less than 4 percent require institutionalized care and of those who are noninstitutionalized, 80 percent are mobile (Brotman, 1972). If a more flexible and imaginative labor market existed there would undoubtedly be many" more elderly, even up to advanced ages, contributing their personal resources to their communities.

Yet, although most older people are unlike the stereotypical image of a superannuated human being, they are not likely to be as healthy as people under 65. Though poor health is not necessarily associated with old age, older people in general suffer from a greater prevalence of chronic conditions. Such serious conditions as arthritis, rheumatism, high blood pressure, and heart disease tend to increase with age after 50 (Atchley, 1972). Though the majority of older persons do not have serious chronic conditions, 7 out of 8 have one or more chronic conditions (Brotman, 1969); 4 in 10 suffer restrictions on their ability to perform major activities, such as simple tasks of personal care; and nearly 1 in 10 are both housebound and bedridden (Shanas, 1965).

Older persons are not only more physically disadvantaged by their health, they are also likely to spend more on their health care. Those over 65 spend more on drugs, usually for their chronic impairments, are more likely to see a physician, and tend to have more and longer hospital stays (Brotman, 1973). In 1970, 25 percent of the country's hospital beds were occupied by the elderly, though they constitute only 10 percent of the American population. Health-care expenditures of the elderly are three and one-half times greater than those of the under-65 age group, and only two-thirds of the cost is paid for by public programs (Brotman, 1971, 1973), the rest of the burden being borne by the resources of the elderly themselves or by their relatives or friends.

While the general older population is clearly more physically disadvantaged than younger people, the health status of the very old is more impaired than that of those under the age of 75. For example, 40 percent between 65 and 74 have some type of impairment, while 60 percent of those over 75 have similar difficulty. Nearly 25 percent of the very old are totally disabled. In 1963, less than 1 percent of the 65–74 age group, but nearly 14 percent of those over 85, were residents of nursing and personal-care homes (Atchley, 1972).

In addition to the increasing prevalence and severity of health problems with age, the numbers of very old are increasing as well. During the decade of the 1960s, the very old increased their numbers at three times the rate of those between the ages of 65 and 74, and this trend is expected to continue (Brotman, 1968). The obvious consequence of dramatic increases in the numbers of the very old will be a heightened demand for an improved health delivery system for the aged as well as a health-care plan to cover the spiraling costs.

Poverty

Many people experience a rising level of income over their life course, with a peak shortly before age 65 (Riley, 1968), followed by a 50 percent reduction of income on their first day of retirement (Morgan and Barfield, 1969). While earnings and economic productivity have increased steadily since the turn of the century, the income levels provided by retirement programs have lagged considerably behind. Retirement income is not only based on lower wage earnings of the past, but is also especially vulnerable to the higher prices that accompany inflation. In addition to private programs, public programs are a major source of retirement income, providing half of the aggregate income of elderly persons (Brotman, 1970). Public programs, unfortunately, suffer from the same problems of comparatively low, fixed payment levels. The magnitude of the discrepancy between income and need makes the aged poor an identifiable social problem.

The percentage of the elderly who are poor varies considerably, depending on the source of the definition. According to the measure of adequate income provided by the Bureau of Labor Statistics, 75 percent of the aged live below standard (Binstock, 1971); Atchley suggests that 60 percent of the aged are poor (1972, p. 148); in an overall view of the various living situations of the American population, the U.S. Bureau of Census reports that 20 percent, or 5 million, of the elderly are impoverished (Brotman, 1971). This more conservative estimate of poverty still means that every fifth older American is poor. An example of this poverty is the 1971 median income of families with heads of households 65 or over ($5,453), compared with median income for all families in that year ($10,285). Elderly Americans living alone or with nonrelatives, as well as the nonwhite elderly, are even worse off (Brotman, 1970). Regardless of the definition of poverty, the aged are more likely to be poor, and the proportion of aged poor has been rising. During the 1960s, for example, the indigent elderly increased from 15 percent to 20 percent of the total poor in this country, though they represented not quite 10 percent of the total population by the end of that decade (Brotman, 1971).

The sharply reduced income levels that beset individuals at retirement are not compensated for by a diminished economic need nor by a decrease in the motivation to consume. In fact, the consumption pattern of the affluent elderly is markedly similar to that of affluent youth. It is only the less fortunate members of the older age stratum that must spend up to 75 percent of their income on such staple items as food, housing, household operations, and medical care (Brotman, 1972). Their resources must be spread out to meet transportation costs, clothing, household furnishings, and recreation. When the income cannot be stretched sufficiently to meet all of these needs, psychological needs are sacrificed first. Despite the prevalence of leisure time during retirement, for example, the aged person spends less on recreation than the job-oriented young person. Stringent financial conditions force a shift in the consumption patterns of the elderly population that would appear to be detrimental to their psychological well-being.

There is an obvious reciprocal relationship between the economic plight of the aged and their health problems. The reduced economic resources of the aged encourages both a crisis-oriented approach to health care (Suchman, 1966) and an inadequate diet (Guthrie et al., 1972). The neglect of preventative health care increases the already higher probabilities of disabling illness. Poor health, in turn, aggravates the economic strains associated with old age. These related problems too often have pathetic consequences for an aged individual.

Social Loss

Even those older persons with adequate physical and financial resources are inevitably faced with the problem of social loss. Essentially every older adult loses some rights and responsibilities attached to social roles, that is, specialized positions within social groups. Men and women retire from work, losing such roles as coworker, union member, manager, fund chairman. By the time of retirement, most people have already shed such parenthood roles as cook, confidant, disciplinarian, school visitor, committee member. The deeper losses are those brought about as friends and spouses and other family members die, sometimes leaving the aged individual entirely alone. With every loss of role and relationship, the number of contacts diminishes (see Table 4.4). Often, financial and physical restraints make it increasingly difficult to continue other social roles such as club or political membership, or substitute activities that might fill the expanding amount of free time.

Elderly people also experience a reduction in normative control; that is, the norms available to govern their behavior become increasingly less well defined or disappear altogether (Kuypers and Bengtson, 1973). For

Table 4.4   Rates of interaction by age and sex

| | | Percent of numbers interviewed | |
| | | Large number of roles | High daily interaction |
Sex and age	Number interviewed	(I)	(II)
Both sexes	*211*	*41.7*	*47.9*
50–54	36	61.1	72.2
55–59	34	61.8	58.8
60–64	34	58.8	58.8
65–69	31	38.7	45.2
70–74	50	22.0	34.0
75 and over	26	7.7	15.4
Males	*107*	*42.0*	*46.7*
50–54	19	68.4	78.9
55–59	18	61.1	50.0
60–64	19	47.4	52.6
65–69	12	50.0	50.0
70–74	25	20.0	32.0
75 and over	14	7.1	14.3
Females	*104*	*41.3*	*49.0*
50–54	17	52.9	64.7
55–59	16	62.5	68.8
60–64	15	73.3	66.7
65–69	19	31.6	42.1
70–74	25	24.0	36.0
75 and over	12	8.3	16.7

SOURCE: From *Growing Old: The Process of Disengagement* by Elaine Cumming and William E. Henry. © 1961 by Basic Books, Inc., Publishing Co., N.Y.

example, people in careers lose much of their social identity and patterns of interaction when they retire from work. Many women lose their social function and source of emotional support when their children are launched and their husbands are outlived. The expectations that do exist for the elderly are general, vague, and often inappropriate. Havighurst and Albrecht (1953), for example, found little evidence of explicit norms for old age. Instead, the prescriptions for this period of life are rather general and vague standards about family, social and religious activities, characterized by a tapering off in intensity over time. Clark (1967) observed that older people often resort to norms of middle age, such as independence and providing for one's own needs.

The consequences of this reduction in normative control for the elderly person are subject to some disagreement. Advocates of the *disengagement* perspective, for instance, argue that since man inevitably declines in both economic productivity and social interaction, the weakening of the pressures of normative constraint is not only consonant with this natural process, but beneficial as well. Devotees of the *activity* perspective, on the other hand, claim that active middle-age roles and norms are still appropriate in old age, although to a lesser degree (for succinct and more detailed summaries of both these frameworks, see Bengtson, 1973, and Atchley, 1972). There is some evidence, however, that if either orientation became accepted to the exclusion of the other, there might be deleterious effects on many older people. For example, if an aged individual maintains the expectations of middle age (activity orientation) in the face of biological decline, he or she may be a likely candidate for psychiatric problems (Clark, 1967). On the other hand, if compulsory retirement leads to a reduction of normative constraint (disengagement orientation) for an unwilling 65 year old, the probable result will be uncertainty and alienation (Martin, Bengtson, and Acock, 1973). This potential for diversity among the aged poses the question of whether explicit and specific norms for old age will develop. If so, they will likely develop within reference groups, of which the elderly were members in their earlier years.

A reference group is the group whose perspective is used by an individual as a source of social identity and standard for behavior. During an individual's life, his reference group may be either a present or an anticipated one, either real or symbolic. The rhetoric that older people constitute a subculture with a sense of group consciousness and political awareness—and therefore a potential reference group for its members—seems premature (Rose, 1965; Ragan and Dowd, 1974). The reference group for older people, regardless of whether functional or chronological criteria are used to define old age, so far continues to be that of the former years. As Binstock cogently states:

Even if the disadvantaged aged see their problems as age-related problems, they see them in other contexts as well. A full life cycle of socialization, experiences and attachments—family, schooling, ethnicity, occupation, income, residence, peer and other associations—presents a multitude of sources for group identification and perceptions of special interest. (Binstock, 1971, p. 15)

Perhaps a prerequisite to determining whether the reference groups of older people are other older people would be to assess general attitudes toward old age, particularly those endorsed by old people themselves. More than a decade ago, Kogan and Wallach (1961) questioned 268 male and female subjects on their attitudes toward various life-stage concepts. Half of the subjects were university students; the other half were adults with a mean age of 71. The study found a generally negative evaluation of the elderly, old age, and death, although old people were less negative than young people. What changes in the image and self-image of the elderly have taken place since then? In the continued presence of health and economic losses, how likely are the aged to adopt negative stereotypes of themselves? How likely are they, consequently, to eliminate being elderly as a desirable source of social identity and standard for behavior? These are only a few of the many questions with far-reaching implications for the future of the elderly in America.

There is no question that the elderly often have a difficult position in American life. Some are able to maintain a positive self-image and to adapt well to the changes of age; many are not. A great deal of human talent and energy is now being wasted, and a great deal of unnecessary suffering exists. Even if we did not each have a vested interest in the issues of aging and old age, there are important implications to the denial of benefits to a sizable and increasing number of elderly. For as de Beauvoir (1973) has written, "By the way in which a society behaves towards its old people, it uncovers the naked, and often carefully hidden, truth about its real principles and aims" (1973, p. 131).

References

Aries, Philippe. 1962. *Centuries of childhood*. New York: Random House.
Atchley, Robert C. 1972. *The social forces in later life*. California: Wadsworth.
Bart, P. 1968. Social structure and vocabularies of discomfort: what happened to female hysteria? *Journal of Health and Social Behavior*. 9:188–193.
Beauvoir, Simone de. 1973. *The coming of age*. New York: G. P. Putnam's Sons.
Bengtson, V. L. 1973. *The social psychology of aging*. New York: Bobbs-Merrill Company, Inc.

Bengtson, V. L. and Corry, E. M. 1974. Academic research and social concern. Paper presented at the 27th Annual Meeting of the Gerontology Society, Portland, Oregon.

Bengtson, V. L. and Cutler, N. 1975. Generational analysis in gerontology. In *Handbook on Aging in the social sciences,* eds. E. Shanas and R. Binstock. New York: Van Nostrand, in press.

Bengtson, V. L. and Kuypers, J. A. 1971. Generational differences and the developmental stake. *Aging and human development,* vol. 2.

Berger, B. 1960. How long is a generation? *British Journal of Sociology,* 2:10–23.

Binstock, R. and Lohmann, R. 1971. Identity and power: the case of the aged. Unpublished paper presented at American Political Science Association, 1971.

Brim, O. 1965. Socialization after childhood. *Socialization through the life cycle,* ed. O. Brim and S. Wheeler. New York: John Wiley.

Brotman, H. 1968. Who are the aged: a demographic view. U.S. Administration on Aging, *Useful facts #42,* August 1968.

Brotman, H. 1969. Who are the aged: a demographic view. *Geriatrics Digest,* March 1969.

Brotman, H. 1970. The older population—some facts we should know. U.S. Department of H. E. W. Social and Rehabilitation Service, Administration on Aging, April 1970.

Brotman, H. 1971. Facts and figures on older americans; measuring the adequacy of income. U.S. department of H. E. W. Social and Rehabilitation service, Administration on Aging, March 1971.

Brotman, H. 1972. The fastest growing minority: the aging. National Agricultural Outlook Conference, 24 February 1972.

Brotman, H. 1973. The fastest growing minority: the aging. A talk to the Institute on Gerontology, Fordham University, New York, March 1973.

Cain, Leonard. 1964. Life course and social structure. In *Handbook of modern sociology,* ed. R. E. L. Faris. Chicago: Rand McNally.

Cain, Leonard. 1967. Age status and generational phenomena: the new old people in contemporary America. *The Gerontologist* 2:2.

Cain, Leonard. 1974. The growing importance of legal age in determining the status of the elderly. *The Gerontologist* 14:167–174.

Caplow, Theodore and McGee, Reece. 1958. *The academic marketplace.* New York: Basic Books, Inc.

Clark, Margaret. 1967. The anthropology of aging, a new area for studies of culture and personality. *The Gerontologist* 7:55–64.

Cuellar, J. 1974. Ethnographic methods: studying aging in an urban Mexican-American community. Paper presented at the annual meeting of the Gerontological Society, Portland, Oregon, 30 October 1974.

Cumming, E. and Henry, W. 1961. *Growing old.* New York: Basic Books.

Cutler, N. et al. 1974. Number and needs: the changing population structure of Los Angeles. Unpublished manuscript. April 1974.

Dennis, Wayne. 1966. Creative productivity between the ages of 20 and 80. *Journal of Gerontology* 21:1–8.

Fendrich, James. 1974. Activists ten years later: a test of generational unit continuity. 1971. *The Journal of Social Issues* 30:2, part 2.

Flacks, R. 1971. Youth and social change. Chicago: Martham.

Guthrie, Helen, et al. 1972. Nutritional practices of elderly citizens in rural Pennsylvania. *The Gerontologist* 12:330–335.

Havighurst, R. and Albrecht, R. 1953. *Older people.* New York: Longmans, Green.

Kenniston, Kenneth. 1968. Young radicals: notes on committed youth. New York: Harvest Books.

Kogan, Nathan and Wallach, Michael. 1961. Age changes in values and attitudes. *Journal of Gerontology* 16:272–280.

Kuypers, J. A. and Bengtson, V. L. 1973. Social breakdown and competence. *Human Development* 16:181–201.

Laufer, R. 1972. Sources of generational conflict and consciousness. In *The new pilgrims: youth protest in transition,* ed. P. Altbach and R. Laufer. New York: David McKay.

Laufer, R. and Bengtson, V. 1974. New perspectives on the problem of generations. *The Journal of Social Issues* 30:part 2.

Lehman, Harvey. 1953. *Age and achievement.* New Jersey: Princeton University Press.

Linton, Ralph. 1936. *The study of man.* New York: Appleton-Century-Crofts, Inc.

Mannheim, Karl. 1952. The problems of generations. In *Essays on the sociology of knowledge,* ed. Paul Kesskemeti. London: Routledge and Kegan Paul, Ltd.

Martin, W. C. et al., 1973. Alienation and age: a context-specific approach. *Social Forces* 53:266–274.

Morgan, James and Barfield, Richard. 1969. *Early retirement: the decision and the experience.* Michigan: Braun-Blumfield.

Neugarten, Bernice. 1974. Age groups in american society and the rise of the young-old. *The Annals of the American Academy of Political and Social Science.* September 1974.

Neugarten, Bernice. ed., 1968. *Middle age and aging.* Chicago: The University of Chicago Press.

Neugarten, Bernice. 1968. The awareness of middle age. In *Middle age and aging.* Chicago: The University of Chicago Press.

Neugarten, Bernice et al. 1968. Women's attitudes toward the menopause. In *Middle age and aging.* Chicago: The University of Chicago Press.

Neugarten, Bernice and Moore, Joan. 1968. The changing age-status system. In *Middle age and aging.* Chicago: The University of Chicago Press.

Neugarten, Bernice et al. 1965. Age norms, age constraints and adult socialization. *American Journal of Sociology* 70:710–717.

Neugarten, Bernice and Datan, Nancy. 1973. Sociological perspectives on the life cycle. In *Life span developmental psychology: personality and socialization,* ed. Paul Baltes and K. Warner Schaie. New York: Academic Press.

Palmore, E., ed. 1974. *Normal aging: II.* North Carolina: Duke University Press.

Pelz, Donald and Andrews, Frank. 1966. *Scientists in organizations.* New York: John Wiley and Sons, Inc.

Ragan, Pauline and Bengtson, Vern. 1975. Perceptions of quality of life among aging blacks, chicanos and anglos. Paper submitted to the Annual Meeting of the Pacific Sociological Association, Victoria, British Columbia, 17–19 April 1975.

Ragan, Pauline and Dowd, James. 1974. The emerging political consciousness of the aged: a generational interpretation. *The Journal of Social Issues,* 30:2, part 2.

Riley, M. W. et al. 1968. *Aging and society, vol I: an inventory of research findings.* New York: Russell Sage Foundation.

Riley, M. W., et al. 1972. *Aging and society, vol. III: a sociology of age stratification.* New York: Russell Sage Foundation.

Rose, A. M. 1965. The subculture of the aging. *Older people and their social world,* ed. A. M. Rose and W. A. Davis. Pennsylvania: F. A. Davis.

Sachuk, N. M. 1970. Population longevity study: sources and indices. *Journal of Gerontology* 25:262–264.

Shanas, Ethel. 1965. Health care and health services for the aged. *The Gerontologist* 5:240.

Suchman, Edward. 1966. Health orientation and medical care. *American Journal of Public Health* 56:97–105.

Sterne, R. S.; Phillips, J. E.; Rabushka, A. 1974. *The urban elder poor: racial and bureaucratic conflict.* Lexington, Mass.: D. C. Heath.

Strauss, A. L. 1969. *Mirrors and masks: the search for identity.* San Francisco: The Sociology Press.

Szasz, T. S. 1960. The myth of mental illness. *American Psychologist* 15:113–118.

Troll. L. 1970. Issues in the study of generations. *Aging and Human Development.* 7:199–218.

Turk, Herman. 1965. An inquiry into the undersocialized conception of man. *Social Forces,* pp. 518–521.

Zuckerman, Harriett and Merton, Robert. 1968. Age, aging and age structure in science. In *Aging and society, vol. III: a sociology of age stratification,* ed. M. W. Riley et al. New York: Russell Sage Foundation.

5

Aging and the Family*

JUDITH TREAS

Few people, lay or professional, will quarrel with the notion that family ties are particularly salient for the aged. Indeed, we rely, rightly or wrongly, on the family bonds of affection and obligation to make up for the shortcomings in society's provisions for the well-being of our older citizens. Kin can function as important resources for the elderly, meeting health or financial needs with services, gifts, and monetary contributions. They can provide affection and companionship at a time when the older person's social network may be circumscribed by infirmities and budget restrictions. While we recognize friendships to be transient—dependent on common interests and geographic proximity—we tend to view familial relationships as enduring and hence suited to sustaining the individual throughout the life cycle.

In this chapter, we focus on family relations in the second half of life. First, we will consider the extended kin network, that is, the relationships of older persons to their children, grandchildren, aged parents, siblings, cousins, inlaws, and other peripheral kin by blood or marriage. While sometimes characterized by infrequent interaction or low affect, extended kin display cohesiveness transcending generational, geographical, and socioeconomic differences. Second, we will turn to the family centered on husband and wife: the conjugal family of parents and dependent children sharing a common household, life style, and social status. Predictable changes accompany the maturation of the family—notably, a contraction in household size. Marital relations and individual adjustments in middle and old age will be examined from a family life-cycle perspective, one which stresses the family alterations typically experienced in the course of aging.

*Support for the preparation of this chapter was derived from NICHD grant HD 157.

Living Arrangements of Older People

There are critics who argue that historical changes in the family are responsible for many of the problems faced by the aged today. They point to a mythic past when grandparents were contributing members of three-generation households, enjoying the fortunes and company of kin, respected by all as repositories of acquired wisdom. Today, media are replete with accounts of lonely and destitute old people, abandoned by kin in rest homes or downtown hotels and stripped of their feelings of personal worth and usefulness. Actually, historians and demographers now doubt that multigenerational households have ever been the norm, if only because in the past so few people survived to old age (P. Laslett, 1974). Social researchers find little evidence that the lot of older people today would be substantially improved by their incorporation into extended households.

As Table 5.1 demonstrates, most older people do not live alone or even with nonrelatives. Most live in families, although such families typically consist of only an aged husband and wife. Since they usually have a surviving spouse, older men enjoy family living more often than their female counterparts. Because more women are widowed, they live alone more often. Admittedly, few older people live in multigenerational households. A 1961 survey found less than a quarter of older people to be sharing households with offspring (Shanas et al., 1968 pp. 156–7). Not even three percent of households encompassed parents, children, *and* grandchildren (U.S. Bureau of the Census, 1973b, Table 17).

Those older people who share housing with offspring may be either heading their own households or living as guests in their children's homes.

Table 5.1   Living arrangements of those 65 and older by race and sex: 1970

Living arrangement	Male		Female	
	White	Black	White	Black
In families	79.1	69.6	58.2	62.2
Primary individual[a]	15.1	21.6	33.7	31.2
Other[b]	2.1	5.5	2.1	3.3
Institutionalized	3.8	3.2	5.9	3.2
Total[c]	100.0	100.0	100.0	100.0

[a]A household head living alone or with nonrelatives only.
[b]Includes lodgers, resident employees, and those living in group quarters such as convents or rooming houses.
[c]Totals do not add to 100 due to rounding error.
SOURCE: U.S. Bureau of the Census. *Census of Population: 1970.* Subject Reports. Final Report PC (2). 4B. Persons by Family Characteristics. Table 2.

The latter option is exercised largely by those who are unmarried, ill, impoverished, and/or very old. Contrary to common belief, the widow is not much more likely to move in with kin than is the widower, and only a third of those whose spouses have died live with relatives (U.S. Bureau of the Census, 1973a, Table 2). The rarity of residentially dependent parents is suggested by the fact that less than five percent of households in 1970 contained a parent or parent-in-law of the head (U.S. Bureau of the Census, 1973b, Table 2).

Neither is it common for the aged to head households containing younger generations. Only 3.3 percent of all household heads 65 and older have dependent offspring under 18 in their homes, although the figure is closer to 10 percent in black and Spanish-surname homes where late childbearing is more usual. Occasionally grown children who are single or just starting married life live with their parents so that, of older husbands heading households, one-in-six has offspring in residence. However, grandchildren seldom live in their grandparent's home. Only three percent of families headed by older people include grandchildren. Again, subcultural variations exist, for 13 percent of black families with older heads contain grandchildren (U.S. Bureau of the Census, 1973b, Table 17).

It would be wrong to conclude from the living arrangements of older people that they have been spurned by kin. Most older people have chosen to live apart, that is, alone or with their spouse. This preference for privacy is not limited to the aged: the young, single or married, are also less likely to share housing with their middle-aged parents today than was the case forty years ago (Beresford and Rivlin, 1966). The independent living arrangement of the aged couple or widow is but one aspect of a broader trend toward smaller and more private households; in 1870 the average household had 5.7 persons (Glick, 1957), but a century later the average is just over three persons (U.S. Bureau of the Census, 1973b, Table 3). This trend may owe less to the demise of the extended family than to declines in fertility, servants, and boarders (B. Laslett, 1973).

There is nothing to indicate that the morale of older people suffers from such private living arrangements. A survey of 11,153 individuals 58 to 63 years of age found that those married men and single women living with kin were actually less likely to report themselves happy (Murray, 1973, p. 18). Another study of married couples in retirement revealed the morale of both husbands and wives to be inversely related to the propinquity of offspring (Kerckhoff, 1966a). Widows have been shown readily to identify sources of potential friction in intergenerational living; they point to life-style differences, conflicts over authority or household division of labor, and the irritating boisterousness of grandchildren (Lopata, 1973, pp. 114–23).

Intergenerational Relations

Many older people manage to maintain both their own homes and involvement with kin—a pattern aptly characterized as "intimacy at a distance." For example, 90 percent of respondents aged 65 and over report having seen one of their children in the last month (Shanas et al., 1968, p. 196). This reflects the accessibility of kin, with three-quarters of older people having a child who lives less than thirty minutes away (Shanas et al., 1968, p. 193).[1] Of course, not all children are in close contact with parents. It seems daughters keep in touch more than do sons, unmarried offspring more than married ones, own children more than sons- and daughters-in-law, and nearby children more than distant ones.

Clearly, interaction with aging parents depends not merely on bonds of affection, but also on financial constraints to visiting, other responsibilities, and competing social or recreational interests. Visiting with relatives is more common in the working class. If distance is taken into account, however, it is the middle class who visit most—both because they have the economic wherewithal and because they typically move away to pursue economic opportunities, not to escape from kin (Adams, 1968). Retirement sometimes permits middle-class parents to move nearer to their children (Litwak, 1960), and parents in ill health seem more likely to have children residing nearby (Shanas, 1962, p. 119).

In addition to socializing together, families typically exchange help along generational lines, and most people turn to their kin with their troubles. Help may take the form of financial assistance, gifts, services, or advice and counseling. Some help is routinely given (for example, child care, chauffeuring, shopping, housekeeping), while other aid may be extended periodically on ceremonial occasions or during crises. For instance, relatives may make funeral arrangements, help pay a hospital bill, or attend sick kin.

There is little support for any stereotype of the aged as abjectly dependent on or brazenly demanding of the resources of the kin network. Older people endorse self-reliance: they are more likely to feel older folks should provide for themselves after retirement and less likely to assign responsibility to children than is the general public or the offspring of the elderly (Shanas, 1962, pp. 133–4). Either older people represent a more independent generation or they come to hold such views only with age—

---

1. Only three percent of the noninstitutionalized population over 65 are without kin (Riley, 1968) although the proportion is doubtless higher among the five percent requiring institutional care. About 18 percent of those over 65 have no living children.

as they measure their own capacities, their potential as an economic burden, and the willingness and ability of others to help. Data from the Cornell Study of Occupational Retirement suggests that while four-fifths of older people expect their children to keep in touch by visiting or writing, fewer believe that children are obliged to take care of them; only a minority feel children should live nearby or frequently entertain parents (Streib and Thompson, 1965, p. 478). It seems, then, that older people value personal affection and respect from children above concrete aid, but that they are loathe to intrude on their children's lives. An accounting of help received by the grandparent generation of a three-generation sample showed that while a third of the older people acknowledged economic assistance, they were more likely to report getting help during illness (61 percent), help running their households (52 percent), or emotional gratification (62 percent) (Hill, 1970, p. 67).

Instead of being passive recipients in the family aid network, older people commonly contribute to relatives, especially children. While declining health and finances may sometimes make the aged dependent on kin for support and services, older family members seem to give to the limits of their resources. Sons are apt to receive monetary aid while daughters get services such as child care (Sussman, 1953). Parents are also more likely to furnish housing for married daughters than for married sons, perhaps because of the legendary antagonism between wives and mothers-in-law. In general, the working class may rely more on an exchange of services; middle-class kin are better able to provide financial help, a form of assistance transcending geographic separation (Adams, 1968).

Adjacent generations maintain the closest relations. Visiting and mutual assistance occur infrequently between grandparents and grandchildren (Hill, 1970), and nearly half of Chicago widows feel close to none of their grandchildren (Lopata, 1973, p. 170). By and large, it is the middle-aged, not the aged, person who has young grandchildren. Involvement with this youngest generation is so varied that Neugarten and Weinstein (1964) can distinguish five styles of grandparenting: formal, fun-seeker, distant figure, substitute parent, and reservoir of family wisdom. The latter two styles are rare, for few grandparents assume motherly care of or patriarchal authority over grandchildren. Although some grandparents, especially younger ones, foster playful relations, most exercise greater reserve, maintaining a benevolent concern, but perhaps only fleeting contact. Grandparenting is not universally enjoyed, and a third of grandparents interviewed by Neugarten and Weinstein found the role uncomfortable, disappointing, or unrewarding.

Siblings also evidence less solidarity than do parents and children.

Indeed, a principal link between adult siblings is often the aged parent. Apparently, siblings assume greater importance in the lives of the never married and the childless widowed (Shanas et al., 1968, p. 166), and sisters form stronger attachments to one another than do brothers (Adams, 1968).

In reviewing all the evidence on contemporary kin relations, Peterson (1970, p. 516) finds considerable support for the thesis that family "relations do not offer substantial intimacy or emotional support to aging persons." For many older people, contact with kin is too infrequent to provide companionship. Money and services may be exchanged with only minimal affect and interaction. While families may fall short of providing day-to-day social sustenance to the aged, younger kin are sources of generative gratification and vicarious accomplishment. As Bengtson and Kuypers (1971) point out, parents view offspring as social heirs who extend their personal histories and validate their lives. Given this involvement, it is not surprising that older people feel their children should move away from them if better economic opportunities beckon (Peterson 1970; Streib 1958). This "developmental stake" in descendents encourages parents to minimize generational differences and to perceive greater closeness, understanding, and communication between family members than do their young (Bengtson and Kuypers, 1971). Clearly, family satisfaction and solidarity survive even in a mobile and rapidly changing society such as ours.

The Later Family Life Cycle

Thus far our discussion has focused on the influence of extended kin in the lives of older people. It is worth noting, however, that the conjugal family undergoes predictable changes in composition, organization, and function as its members age. These changes, under the rubric of the family life cycle, represent a modal pattern of family experience. Deviations from this pattern or variations in timing of experience are important determinants of the social context of aging for the individual.

From an historical perspective, the most striking feature of family life in later years is the prolonged period which a couple may expect to spend together after their children have left home. It is estimated that mothers born in 1920 will average 52 years at the marriage of their last child as compared with 56 years for those women born in 1880—a decline due to the mothers' early conclusion of childbearing and their offsprings' propensity to marry young (Glick and Parke, 1965). More noteworthy is the fact that eight-in-ten mothers will share this final launching with their husbands while among the earlier generation only half of couples survived to see their last child wed. Declines in mortality have meant couples may anticipate a decade or two together without children in the home.

While we recognize that family life-cycle schema are inapplicable to some (for example, the never married, the childless, and the divorced), it is useful to consider those family situations which are customarily experienced by the majority of middle-aged and aged. These include a child-launching phase during which offspring assume economic independence, a childless preretirement period, a retirement stage, and ultimately widowhood. Despite the association of stage and age, there is considerable diversity in the timing and duration of each phase of the family life cycle (Neugarten and Moore, 1968), and the impact of any stage on the individual may depend on the scheduling of family events.

Consider childbearing patterns. Couples who complete their families at young ages will still be in the prime of life when the last child leaves home; the parents of "change of life" babies may have a dependent child in the household when they are ready to retire. Adolescent children are expensive to support, and increasingly parents are called on to subsidize the prolonged schooling or early marriages of offspring. If heightened economic responsibilities coincide with peak earnings of the breadwinner, there is no threat of a deterioration in family living standard. However, as Valerie Oppenheimer (1974) has noted, the father whose earning power declines as family needs rise faces a serious problem, and this pattern of "life-cycle squeeze" unfortunately typifies the lower-paying occupations. A crisis of the family exchequer may be averted by moonlighting, overtime, or the wife's return to work, just as an earlier generation met rising expenses by taking in boarders (see Modell and Hareven, 1963). Those couples who in their late 50s or 60s must still support children, especially when the breadwinner's income fails to keep pace, have little opportunity to save for retirement.

A considerable body of research evidence suggests that sudden life changes (a residential move, divorce, or a financial windfall, for example) can precipitate declines in health and morale. Chance creates a staggering accumulation of change in the lives of a few individuals. (Most of us have known someone beset like Job with a rapid succession of calamaties). The intersection of physical, economic, social, and family life cycles assures that most older people experience patterned (and possibly disconcerting) episodes of heightened change. Retirement, for instance, usually is accompanied by a drop in income, sometimes involves relocating in a retirement community, and may result from a disability.

The child-launching stage brings a welcome reduction in economic responsibilities and a release from household chores and child supervision.

While this postparental period presents opportunities for increased marital intimacy, travel, and new leisure activities, it is thought to be a troubled time, particularly for women. Recently, the "empty nest" phenomenon gained national attention with well-publicized accounts of First Lady Betty Ford's own bout with depression, a demoralization associated with grown children and a busy husband. Many women seem to experience a crisis of purposelessness when their days of active mothering are behind them. Pauline Bart (1971) reports that maternal role loss is characteristic of middle-aged women hospitalized for depression and that emotional illness serves to reinvolve children in mother's life. Physiological aging compounds the "empty nest syndrome." Youth, beauty, and sex appeal, qualities so valued in women, are regarded as virtually synonymous in our culture; it is hardly surprising that to middle-aged women wrinkles and sagging flesh represent the loss of important assets. Menopause, so shrouded in myth, also signals the end of youth. Husbands, for whom the middle years may mean the zenith of a career, are sometimes too involved in work to be very supportive. In fact, some husbands may be preoccupied with crises of their own—crises instigated by declining sexual potency or the realization that they must reconcile youthful ambition with their more modest accomplishments.

The usual prescription for the problems of the empty nest is the substitution of new roles for lost ones. Women are encouraged to find a job, return to school, get involved in community affairs, or take up a hobby. Of course, these tend to be middle-class solutions to what may be largely a middle-class problem. Perhaps the lower-class housewife is more satisfied with her lot since there are fewer expectations that she establish a separate identity, keep pace with her husband's intellectual growth, and so on. She is not as likely to expect intimacy with her husband, and she may maintain closer relations with grown children through socializing together, providing housing for young marrieds, or caring for grandchildren.

Actually, few mothers wait until the nest is empty to reenter the labor force. Family economic need is greater when the children are still at home, and as they get older, children qualify for day-care centers, go to school, assist with chores, and require less care and supervision. By working after the children are launched, a woman may be contributing to retirement savings, demonstrating career commitment, or just keeping busy. Women workers, however, tend to retire earlier than do men, in response to reduced economic need, younger qualifying ages for pensions, husband's retirement, or declines in health and energy, making it more difficult to keep house while holding a job.

As we might anticipate, household changes (such as the children's dispersal or the husband's retirement) are associated with changes in marital interaction. Unfortunately, researchers have achieved no consensus on the question of whether the last half of marriage affords couples more or less satisfaction than earlier years; some have discerned growing marital disenchantment (for example, see Pineo, 1968), while other find an upswing in contentment among middle-aged and older couples (Rollins and Common, 1974; Stinnett, Carter, and Montgomery, 1972). However people may view their own marriages, the later years are not considered the best time in most marriages; only eight percent of respondents in a 1972 Gallup poll believed married couples are happiest after the children have left home (Blake, 1974, p. 38).

Available evidence contradicts the notion that couples grow apart; middle-aged husbands and wives were found to be more alike in personality than were newlyweds (Murstein, 1961). Nevertheless, qualitative changes in marital interaction are apparent. For one thing, companionship seems to replace romance and passion (Feldman, 1964). Although an end to sexual activity is not inevitable, coital frequency decreases after the middle years. When marital sex ends, it is usually due to the husband's wishes or declining capacities (Pfeiffer et al., 1970), but, as Masters and Johnson (1966, 1970) have pointed out, boredom, fatigue, overeating, preoccupations, illness, or heavy drinking may cause temporary impotence which is reversible if not compounded by grave anxieties about declining virility. The physical changes of menopause need not hamper sexual pleasure either, although some women benefit from hormone therapy. For both men and women, sexual capacity in old age depends on previous adjustment and continuing sexual stimulation; long periods of abstinence in old age are associated with declining sexual prowess. Despite physiological changes lengthening necessary arousal time or reducing orgasmic intensity, the greatest obstacle to full sexual enjoyment may well be the widely held misbelief that sexuality is not a normal aspect of old age.

Older couples focus conversations on different topics than do their younger counterparts. They discuss children less often, for example, than those whose offspring remain at home. The talk of elderly marrieds has been found to be limited to conventional topics: church, home upkeep, and particularly health (Feldman, 1964). To be sure, aging may reorder the conversational concerns of older couples. Some interactional differences between middle-aged and aged couples, however, may reflect cohort differences in preoccupations. Unfortunately, there is a lack of longitudinal data following couples over time—data which could clarify many issues of aging and marital adjustment.

Relatively little is known about interpersonal adaptations demanded by retirement of the family's principal breadwinner. Incorporating a newly idle husband into the daily household routine is commonly thought to be stressful for a wife. In fact, several studies suggest wives may become increasingly disillusioned with their spouse's retirement. For one thing, retirement often fails to fulfill women's expectations of more time in which to pursue their interests (Kerckhoff, 1966b). Retirement typically requires a downward adjustment of living standard due to the decline in income, but it may take some time before any inadequacies of retirement provisions are recognized. Also, the longer a man is retired, the more likely he and his wife are to suffer poor health. For whatever reason, women with husbands retired five or more years are more likely to wish for later retirement on the part of their spouses than are wives of more recently retired men (Kerckhoff, 1966b). A positive relation was also found between the length of husband's retirement and the proportion of wives saying they were sorry their husbands stopped working (Heyman and Jeffers, 1968).

A husband's retirement may occasion change in task allocation as he helps more around the house. Infirmities sometimes require major shifts in household division of labor as couples work out ways to accomplish basic housekeeping (and perhaps new nursing) responsibilities. There is some evidence that women acquire more power with age. In Hill's (1965) study of three generations, interviewers reported grandmothers to dominate the interview more often than did wives in the two younger generations, despite the fact that the grandfather was more often reported to have the final word in decision-making. Neugarten and Gutmann (1968) report the results of a Thematic Apperception Test in which respondents were asked to fantasize a story based on the picture of a conventional group consisting of an old man, an old woman, a young man, and a young woman. Interestingly, passivity and familial attachment were often attributed to the old man while the old woman was commonly described as aggressive and demanding. These age-sex role descriptions were reported most frequently by older respondents; since T.A.T. results are often interpreted as projections of respondents own needs and traits, it seems age may well bring a convergence (or even a reversal) of gender-linked personality characteristics.

Widowhood

The conclusion of the family life cycle involves marital dissolution and the new role of widowhood for the surviving partner, usually the wife. The increase in the percent widowed, shown graphically in Figure 5.1, illus-

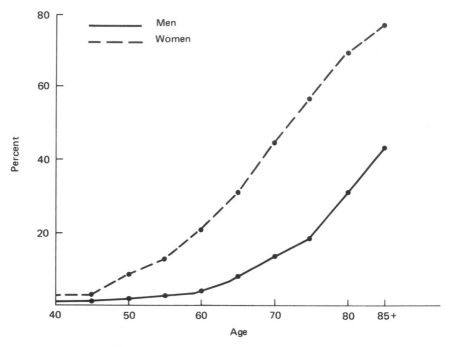

Figure 5.1. Widowed as a percentage of the population by age and sex, 1970. (United States Bureau of the Census. *Census of Population: 1970.* "Marital Status," Table 2.)

trates the gradual attrition from the married population. After age 65, less than half of women are living with a spouse. Because widowhood touches most aging families and demands such dramatic adaptations in the lives of survivors, this last stage of the family life cycle warrants special consideration.

Some psychological preparation for widowhood usually occurs before bereavement. The death of friends' spouses may precipitate mental rehearsals for one's own potential loss, as does the declining health or terminal illness of one's mate. As we have suggested before, timing may influence the impact of a life-cycle event (such as widowhood) on the individual. The young widow, whose loss is typically sudden and unanticipated, is thought to be more shaken by the death of a spouse than is the older woman who has had more ample time to ready herself psychologically and economically (Heyman and Gianturco, 1974).

Despite anticipatory socialization, bereavement is typically a trying time of numbness, with subsequent uncontrolled episodes of longing and sorrow interspersed with depression; weight loss, insomnia, and irritability are common conditions (Parkes, 1965). While symptoms usually abate in a few months, one-in-five widows reports that she has never gotten over her grief (Lopata, 1973, p. 51). Indeed, the widowed are more likely to report themselves unhappy than are the married (Gurin et al., 1960). As we might expect given the known association of life change and illness, the widowed represent a population of high health risk, with higher rates of mental illness (Gove, 1972), mortality (Gove, 1973), and suicide (Bock, 1972).

Exactly what life changes occur with the death of one's spouse? Helena Lopata's (1973) study of Chicago-area widows represents a pioneering effort to provide some answers to this question. Clearly, widowhood means the loss, reorganization, and acquisition of social roles. In ceasing to be a wife, a woman can no longer function as her husband's nurse, confidant, sex partner, or housekeeper, but she may have to assume unfamiliar roles like financial manager, handyman, or worker. Other social relations may also be disrupted. Intimacy with inlaws seems not to survive the husband's death; only a quarter of Chicago widows saw their husband's relatives with any frequency (Lopata, 1973, p. 57). The widow may find that she is avoided by friends who are discomforted at her grief, that she is a "fifth wheel" in couple-oriented interaction, and that she can no longer maintain old social contacts because her entertainment budget is limited or she doesn't drive. New activity patterns, friends, and gratifications may eventually supplant old ones; half of Lopata's (1973, p. 75) widows had so adjusted to their new life style as to see compensations in widowhood (for example, independence or a reduction in work load).

Those who would undertake to help the newly widowed adjust would be well informed by Lopata's (1973, p. 270–4) suggestions. Companions who can listen sympathetically to the widow's grief, relieve loneliness, and share activities are most valuable. Building the widow's competence and confidence at problem-solving is top priority; while help with immediate crises is desirable, well-meaning advice which encourages dependency is not. Major decisions (such as investments or change of residence) are best postponed for a year or so, until the widow's outlook and life style adjusts to the change in her status.

Children may facilitate the mother's adjustment in three ways: by assuming responsibilities previously borne by the father, by replacing the father as a focus of the mother's attention and ministration, and by maintaining supportive interpersonal relations. While sons are reportedly most helpful at overseeing funeral arrangements and finances, daughters (who give services and visit frequently) are regarded as emotionally closer to the mother. Apparently, oldest and youngest children are especially obliged to help, for first and last children who shirk filial responsibilities are subject to the most maternal criticism (Lopata, 1973, pp. 101–3).

New Marriages and Marital Alternatives

Although loneliness is reportedly the greatest difficulty faced by widows (Lopata, 1973, pp. 66–72), remarriage is not a commonly employed recourse. Marriage rates for older people are low, despite variations by sex and previous marital status. Many senior citizens seem to view remarriage as improper; about a third of those over 60 in a rural sample frowned on such matches, although younger respondents were more tolerant of these older unions (Britton and Britton, 1967, p. 67). The much higher nuptiality rates of the nonwhite aged suggest subcultural differences in support for marriage late in life (National Center for Health Statistics, 1960, Table 1M). Nevertheless, children's opposition or Social Security penalization of widows who remarry may discourage many from seeking new partners. Happily, late marriages seem to enjoy considerable success, especially when buttressed by motivations of love or companionship, adequate income, and offspring's approval (McKain, 1969).

Older people encounter some difficulties in finding new mates. Since limited mobility, energy, and budgets restrict courtship activities, it is not surprising older people tend to marry long-time acquaintances (McKain, 1969). Men are six times more likely to marry after 65 than are women. Due to sex differences in mortality and widowhood, there are three single women for every unmarried man in the population over 65 (U.S. Bureau of the Census, 1972, Table 1). Older men, however, are not restricted by social norms to marrying older women: 20 percent of grooms over 65 attract brides under 45, while only 3 percent of older brides wed men under 45 (National Center for Health Statistics, 1969, Table 1-18). Certainly, this behavioral evidence buttresses survey findings that women are seen as "old" sooner than are men (Neugarten, Moore, and Lowe 1965).

Although older men have an easier time finding partners, they also may have more to gain from marriage than do older women. Widowhood may be a more devastating experience for men: because so few husbands can expect to survive their partners, they may not undergo the mental rehearsals for life alone which are typical of older wives. Widowers seem to suffer from greater social isolation than do widows, a condition leading us to predict the higher suicide rates of widowed men (Bock, 1972). Not only do widowers lose a companion, they also experience a greater decline in kin interaction (Bernardo, 1967), presumably because the wife typically maintains contact with relatives. We know husbands tend to be more enthusiastic than wives about their marriage—reporting greater happiness, fewer marital problems, and less blaming of spouse (Gurin et al., 1960, pp. 84–116); it follows that men may be more favorably disposed toward remarriage, given their more satisfactory experiences within the institution. At least among women, Lopata (1973, pp. 90–1) found widows satisfied with previous unions to be more receptive to the notion of remarrying.

Despite the benefits which married living confers, there are obvious demographic constraints on the numbers of older people who can pair off in traditional unions. Alternatives to conventional marriage may offer solutions to the unmet needs of some older people, just as foster grandparent programs can furnish affectionate intergenerational contacts. Recently, a retirement magazine featured an article entitled, "Should Retired Women Live Together?" On the basis of her own experience, the author answered "yes," pointing out the economy and companionship in sharing a home (Conklin, 1974). Cavan (1973) speculates that many marital innovations (heretofore limited largely to bohemian youth) could work for the aged if their disapproval could be overcome. Nonmarital cohabitation, polygyny, group marriage, communes, and homosexual companionships are examples. As Gebhard (1970, p. 94) reports, a sizable minority of older women already acknowledge unconventional liaisons; of those 51–60, 40 percent of divorcees and 25 percent of widows reported postmarital coitus.

Conclusion

The family is the locus of many of the life changes associated with aging, such as the dispersal of offspring and the loss of a spouse. While the family is a source of life change, it is also a resource for change. The kinship aid network, the intergenerational investments of emotion, and the reciprocal support of marital relations all may mitigate the stressful personal disorganization which can accompany life's transitions. The family may fall short of meeting the needs of some older people, and its inadequacies may be even more apparent if the broader society fails to provide adequately for older citizens. Nevertheless, the American family shows remarkable solidarity in the face of a mobile and changing world. Mutual affection and concern seem here to stay.

References

Adams, Bert N. 1968. *Kinship in an urban setting.* Chicago: Markham Publishing Co.

Bart, Pauline. 1971. Depression in middle-aged women. In *Women in sexist society,* ed. Vivian Gornick and Barbara K. Moran. New York: New American Library.

Bengtson, Vern L. and Kuypers, Joseph A. 1971. Generational difference and the developmental stake. *Aging and human development* 2:249–60.

Beresford, John C. and Rivlin, Alice M. 1966. Privacy, poverty, and old age. *Demography* 3:1:247–58.

Bernardo, Felix M. 1967. Social adaptation to widowhood among a rural-urban aged population. Washington Agricultural Experimental Station Bulletin 689 (December).

Blake, Judith. 1974. Can we believe recent data on birth expectations in the United States? *Demography* 11:1 (February):25–44.

Bock, E. Wilbur. 1972. Aging and suicide: the significance of marital, kinship, and alternative relations. *The Family Coordinator* 21:1 (January):71–9.

Britton, Joseph H. and Britton, Jean O. 1967. The middle aged and older rural person and his family. *Older rural Americans,* ed. E. Grant Youmans. Lexington, Ky.: University of Kentucky Press.

Cavan, Ruth Shonle. 1973. Speculations on innovations to conventional marriage in old age. *The Gerontologist* 13:4:409–11.

Conklin, Faith. 1974. Should retired woman live together? *NRTA Journal* No. 25 (November–December): 19–20.

Cumming, Elaine and Henry, William. 1961. *Growing old.* New York: Basic Books.

Feldman, Harold. 1964. Development of the husband-wife relationship. Preliminary report. *Cornell studies of marital development: study in the transition to parenthood.* Department of Child Development and Family Relationships. New York State College of Home Economics, Cornell University.

Gebhard, Paul. 1970. Post-marital coitus among widows and divorcees. In *Divorce and after,* ed. Paul Bohannan. Garden City, N.Y.: Doubleday.

Glick, Paul C. and Parke, Jr., Robert. 1965. New approaches in studying the life cycle of the family. *Demography* 2:187–202.

Glick, Paul C. 1957. *American families.* New York: John Wiley and Sons.

Gove, Walter R. 1972. The relationship between sex roles, marital roles, and mental illness. *Social Forces* 51:34–44.

Gove, Walter R. 1973. Sex, marital status, and mortality. *American Journal of Sociology* 79:1:45–67.

Gurin, Gerald; Veroff, Joseph; and Feld, Sheila. 1960. *Americans view their mental health.* New York: Basic Books.

Heyman, Dorothy K. and Gianturco, Daniel T. 1974. Long term adaptation by the elderly to bereavement. In *Normal aging II,* ed. Erdman Palmore. Durham, N.C.: Duke University Press.

Heyman, Dorothy K. and Jeffers, Frances G. 1968. Wives and retirement: pilot study. *Journal of Gerontology* 23:4:488–96.

Hill, Reuben. 1965. Decision making and the family life cycle. In *Social structure and the family: generational relations,* ed. Ethel Shanas and Gordon F. Streib. Englewood Cliffs, N.J.: Prentice-Hall.

Hill, Reuben. 1970. *Family development in three generations.* Cambridge, Mass.: Schenkman.

Holmes, Thomas H. and Masuda, Minoru. Life change and illness susceptibility. In *Personality and socialization,* ed. David L. Heise. New York: Random House.

Kerckhoff, Alan C. 1966a. Family patterns and morale in retirement. In

Social aspects of aging, ed. Ida Harper Simpson and John C. McKinney. Durham, N.C.: Duke University Press.

Kerckhoff, Alan C. 1966b. Husband-wife expectations and reactions to retirement. In Social Aspects of aging, eds. Ida Harper Simpson and John C. McKinney. Durham, N.C.: Duke University Press.

Laslett, Barbara. 1973. The family as a public and private institution: an historical perspective. *Journal of Marriage and the Family* 35:3:480–92.

Laslett, Peter. 1971. *The world we have lost.* London: University Paperbacks.

Litwak, Eugene. 1960. Geographic mobility and extended family cohesion. *American Sociological Review* 25:385–394.

Lopata, Helena Z. 1973. *Widowhood in an American city.* Cambridge, Mass.: Schenkman.

McKain, Walter C. 1972. A new look at old marriages. *The Family Coordinator* 21:61–69.

Masters, William H. and Johnson, Virginia E. 1966. *Human sexual response.* Boston: Little, Brown.

Masters, William H. and Johnson, Virginia E. 1970. *Human sexual inadequacy.* Boston: Little, Brown.

Modell, John, and Hareven, Tamara K. 1973. Urbanization and the malleable household: an examination of boarding and lodging in american families. *Journal of Marriage and the Family* 35:3:467–79.

Murray, Janet. 1973. Family structure in the preretirement years. *Retirement history study report No. 4.* U.S. Department of Health, Education, and Welfare.

Murstein, B. I. 1961. The complementary need hypothesis in newlyweds and middle-aged married couples. *Journal of Abnormal and Social Psychology* 63:194–7.

National Center for Health Statistics. 1960. *Vital statistics of the United States, vol. 3: divorce and marriage.*

National Center for Health Statistics. 1969. *Vital statistics of the United States, vol. 3: divorce and marriage.*

Neugarten, Bernice L. and Gutmann, David L. 1968. Age-sex roles and personality in middle-age: a thematic apperception test. In *Middle age and aging,* ed. Bernice L. Neugarten. Chicago: University of Chicago Press.

Neugarten, Bernice L. and Moore, Joan W. 1968. The changing age-status system. In *Middle age and aging,* ed. Bernice L. Neugarten. Chicago: University of Chicago Press.

Neugarten, Bernice L.; Moore, Joan W.; and Lowe, John C. 1965. Age norms, age constraints, and adult socialization. In *Middle age and aging,* ed. Bernice L. Neugarten. Chicago: University of Chicago Press.

Neugarten, Bernice and Weinstein, Karol. 1964. The changing American grandparent. *Journal of Marriage and the Family* 26:199–204.

Oppenheimer, Valerie. 1974. The life-cycle squeeze: the interaction of men's occupational and family life cycles. *Demography* 11:2:227–46.

Parkes, C. Murray. 1965. Bereavement and mental illness: a clinical study. *British Journal of Medical Psychology* 28:1–26.

Peterson, James A. 1970. A developmental view of the aging family. In *Contemporary Gerontology: Concepts and Issues,* ed. James E. Birren. Los Angeles: University of Southern California Gerontology Center.

Pfeiffer, Eric; Verwoerdt, Adriann; and Wang, Hsoih-Shan. 1970. Sexual behavior in aged men and women. In *Normal aging,* ed. Erdman Palmore. Durham, N.C.: Duke University Press.

Pineo, Peter. 1968. Disenchantment in the later years of marriage. In *Middle age and aging,* ed. Bernice Neugarten. Chicago: University of Chicago Press.

Riley, Matilda, et al. 1968. *Aging and society, vol. 1: an inventory of research findings.* New York: Russell Sage Foundation.

Rollins, Boyd C. and Cannon, Kenneth L. 1974. Marital satisfaction over the family life cycle: a reevaluation. *Journal of Marriage and the Family* 36:2:271–82.

Shanas, Ethel. 1962. *The health of older people: a social survey.* Cambridge, Mass.: Harvard University Press.

Shanas, Ethel, et al. 1968. *Old people in three industrial societies.* New York: Atherton Press.

Stinnett, Nick; Carter, Linda Mittelstedt, and Montgomery, James E. 1972. Older person's perceptions of their marriages. *Journal of Marriage and the Family* 34:4:667–72.

Streib, Gordon. 1958. Family patterns in retirement. *Journal of Social Issues* 14:2:35–45.

Streib, Gordon F. and Thompson, Wayne E. 1965. The older person in a family context. In *Social structure and family intergenerational relations,* ed. Ethel Shanas and Gordon F. Streib. Englewood Cliffs, N.J.: Prentice-Hall.

Sussman, Marvin B. 1953. The help pattern in the middle class family. *American Sociological Review* 43:22–28.

Sussman, Marvin B. 1965. Relationships of adult children with their parents. In *Social structure and the family intergenerational relations,* ed. Ethel Shanas and Gordon Streib. Englewood Cliffs, N.J.: Prentice-Hall.

U.S. Bureau of the Census. 1972. *Census of population: 1970.* Marital status. Final Report PC(2)-4C. Washington, D.C.: Government Printing Office.

U.S. Bureau of the Census. 1973a. *Census of population: 1970.* Persons by family characteristics. Final Report PC(2)-4B. Washington, D.C.: Government Printing Office.

U.S. Bureau of the Census. 1973b. *Census of population: 1970.* Family composition. Final Report PC(2)-4A. Washington, D.C.: Government Printing Office.

Psychological
Perspectives

6

Age Changes in Adult Intelligence

K. WARNER SCHAIE

The intelligence-quotient concept has been widely criticized in many educational and other contexts. Nevertheless, the observations made by the student of behavior when he looks at the performance of young and old people on a variety of measures of intelligence may still be very useful since many other socially significant behaviors can be predicted thereby.

But any discussion of intellectual functioning in adulthood requires attention, at least in passing, to some of the methodological issues which are involved in judging whether or not there is acceptable evidence on changes in intelligence from maturity to old age.

We often make the observation that older people tend to function systematically less well than do younger people. It is not surprising that one might, therefore, draw the conclusion that in the development of intelligence we reach our maximum peak as young adults; from then on, we go downhill, slowly at first, more rapidly later. The life course of intelligence may be no different, then, than the life course of some other biological phenomena.

If one takes this point of view, it is still interesting to ask whether developmental change in intelligence is a uniform phenomenon. Intelligence is not something tangible. It is a construct, and as such is not different in its nature from other constructs. We make it more tangible by defining certain ways of measuring it through what we usually call an intelligence test. But a measure of intelligence, or I.Q., is no more than a summary statistic; by summing over various dimensions that may be important for effective mental functioning, we can arrive at an index number by which we characterize the behavior of an individual. It is obvious,

111

however, that when we try to measure intelligence, we are measuring many different things. And while it is conceivable that the life course of the summary index may indeed show growth and decline, it does not necessarily follow that such life course would also be true for the components of intelligence.

We must keep in mind that there is not necessarily a direct isomorphic relationship between biological and psychological changes in the organism. Many aspects of psychological developments depend very much on the interaction of the individual with the culture that he lives in, and changes in the behavior of an individual over his life course may be much more affected by changes in the culture he lives in than by changes in his body. Granted, there are some constraints. Only living organisms can answer questionnaires or take intelligence tests. If you are about to die, it is reasonable to assume that just as your other life functions dramatically decline, so will your intelligence. But there is no necessary reason why we have to accept the age decrement model for intelligence without first subjecting it to a number of serious questions. This chapter will examine two principal issues: (1) Is there any reason to suggest that the life courses of different intellectual functions are identical? (2) Is there any reason to accept inevitable decrement in the life course of intelligence?

Studies of Intelligence in Adulthood

All of the early studies on intellectual development in adulthood have made use of what is known as the cross-sectional method. That is, in these studies the same intelligence test was given to a number of groups of people of different ages at the same point in time. For example, the Army-Alpha intelligence test was administered by Jones and Conrad in a New England community in the early 1930s. These investigators examined practically all persons in this small community from age 16 to 90, divided them up into subgroups by age, and were able to show that on many tests there was a peak in young adulthood and a drop thereafter. Similar findings were reported by David Wechsler when he first reported age-related data with the Wechsler-Bellevue, an intelligence test whose revisions represent the standard measurement instrument used in clinical practice. Wechsler had to provide different norms for different age groups to adjust for these age differences.

Let us now examine the methodological issues raised by such an approach. Whenever we consider the results of a cross-sectional study, we cannot assume *a priori* that differences between age groups have been caused by physiological age changes. People who differ by age frequently also differ by other characteristics. Most notably, they must belong to different generations; obviously there are no two individuals, say one age 20 and one age 30, who were born at the same time. Differences in age imply differences in life experience for which there cannot be overlap.

If we wish to understand the behavior of the aged, we must understand the particular kind of life experiences they have had. Different age groups must have had different life experiences, and it is frequently more plausible to argue that people of different ages differ on a given characteristic because they belong to a different generation, rather than because they differ in age. In fact, for many psychological variables it is much more plausible to argue that group differences are heavily affected by the particular circumstances of the environment that have changed. One of the major characteristics of our society is that it is in extremely rapid transition. In primitive agricultural societies, change might not be an issue of concern, but it cannot be ignored in our case.

In order to solve the question of whether observed age differences are due to age or to generations, we would have to conduct some *longitudinal studies,* in which we followed the same individuals over their life courses to find out if there are indeed age changes within the individual. Such studies are difficult to conduct, and few longitudinal studies may be found in the literature. Some of the more interesting longitudinal studies of intelligence include the Berkeley Guidance and Growth studies (Bayley, 1968), follow-up studies of Lewis Terman's *Study of Genius* in the late 1930s (Bayley and Oden, 1955), a study by William Owens (1963) who retested men who were ROTC members at Iowa State University during World War I, and Blum and Jarviks' study of aged twins (Blum et al., 1970).

Yet there is a problem also with the interpretation of data from longitudinal studies. We do not know to what extent observed changes in the behavior of individuals are due strictly to age and to what extent they were caused by some environmental event which occurred during the interval between our measurement points. Examples of such intervening events are transitory changes in nutritional levels due to war, depressions, and the like, and the dramatic changes in information transmission because of the introduction of TV. The latter event would affect one generation very much and another generation not at all, because they had either lived before the era of TV or within the era of TV. In other words, we need to differentiate between what change in function is due to age, and is thus characteristic of all members of a species, and what change is a transitory effect due to particular environmental events which occurred during the time period being examined. (For further elaboration of the distinction between age changes and age differences, see Schaie, 1967.)

Another issue is raised by the question of why we should expect that the course of different intellectual abilities should be the same. For example, Raymond Cattell and John Horn (Horn, 1972) have proposed a model of intelligence that distinguishes between certain kinds of abilities which they call "crystallized" and others which they call "fluid." Crystallized abilities depend upon the acquisition of certain kinds of information and skills transmitted by the culture which are not available to the individual simply by virtue of his characteristics as a human being. Horn and Cattell argue that there is no reason to believe significant decrement should occur in such abilities, assuming that there is continued access to the content of our culture. But the second kind of ability, which they call "fluid ability," seems to be related to the physiological characteristics of the organism. If we accept the concept of a biological clock or of systematic age changes in the biological system, particularly with such variables as speed and reaction time, it would then seem reasonable that many abilities should indeed have a life course with an adult peak and some decrement thereafter. There should certainly be a significant difference in the life course of these two kinds of intelligence.

Some Research Evidence

Some research studies on the course of adult intelligence which I and my associates have conducted over the past twenty years or so shed light on these issues. (Also see Schaie, 1974.)

In our first study we addressed ourselves to the issue that there might be differences in intellectual functioning in the aged for different abilities. I had felt in talking to some older people that one of their problems seemed to be that they did not respond as quickly as they once had. Instead of giving the traditional kind of speeded intelligence test, I administered a test known as a Primary Mental Abilities Test, developed from the work of Louis Thurstone (1941), to a group of older subjects. The test was administered under nonspeeded conditions in order to maximize differences between functions if they were present (see Figure 6.1). For numerical skills, with no speed limit, our subjects performed virtually at the top of the adolescent group. For verbal meaning they also performed at a very high level. But on other variables, such as spatial visualization and abstract reasoning, people in their 50s still did well, while in the high 60s or 70s there appeared to be a substantial drop. The peculiar upturn for the oldest group may simply reflect that my few very old people were probably highly selected and not representative of their age group. (But see Schaie and Strother, 1968b.) The results of this study suggest that if there was decrement in the several functions, it certainly was not a uniform phenomenon.

The same study was repeated later (Schaie, 1958) with a more care-

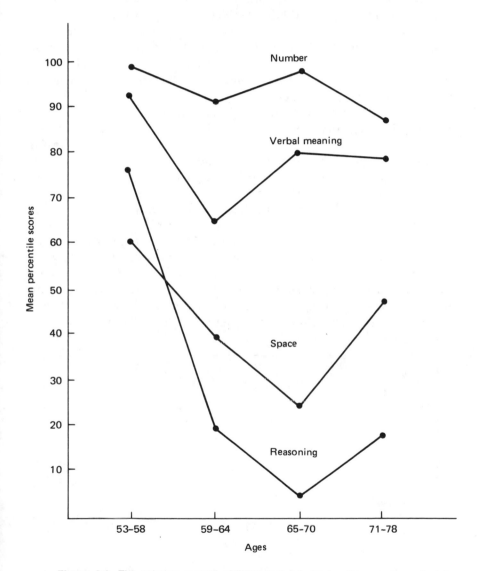

Figure 6.1. The primary mental abilities test administered as a power test to older persons. (From Schaie, Rosenthal, and Perlman, 1953. Used by permission.)

fully selected sample of 25 men and women in each five-year age interval from 21 to 70 years. As shown in Figure 6.2, we again find peaks in young adulthood and differential decrement gradients for the different abilities thereafter.

Both of the above studies are, of course, cross-sectional in nature and consequently have the validity problems outlined earlier in this chapter. I became seriously concerned about these problems when I reviewed data on some of the longitudinal studies on adult development. The latter studies, in contrast to my own findings and those by Jones and Conrad and by Wechsler, indicated the absence of age decrement in intelligence, especially in the verbal abilities.

In fact, Owens (1963) reported some increment over a 30-year period and showed that his subjects now in their 50s scored higher than they had in their 20s. Similarly, the follow-up of the Berkeley Growth study (Bayley, 1968) showed that in mid-life adults performed better than they had as adolescents. I then took another look at some cross-sectional studies and found that the so-called peak age seemed to be less than constant. When Lewis Terman standardized the original Stanford-Binet back in 1916, he assumed arbitrarily that adult intelligence peaks at age 16. It turns out that already in the 1930 study of Owens and Conrad, the average peak occurs at about 20. When Wechsler standardized the Wechsler-Bellevue the first time around, his reference group was age 20 to 24; when he restandardized for the newer WAIS version of his tests some 10 years later, all of a sudden it appeared that the optimal level for some of them now was at ages 25 to 30. My own data collected in the mid-1950s sug-

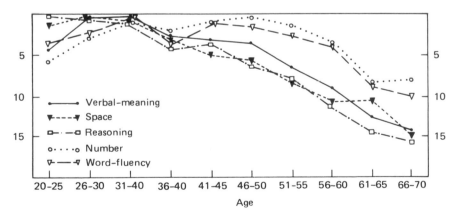

Figure 6.2. Performance differences on the primary mental abilities test from young adulthood to old age. (From Schaie, 1958)

gested an average peak at ages 25 and 35. Curiously, the peak age of performance appeared to keep increasing.

Obviously, there is a discrepancy of findings here which requires explanation. We can approach the problem systematically by noting that different kinds of information are obtained in cross-sectional and longitudinal studies. Furthermore, if one compares results from different tests on different populations, one may be looking at some very special artifacts. It occurred to me, therefore, that one way in which one might solve the problem was to convert a cross-sectional study into a longitudinal one. And that is precisely what we did. In 1963 we conducted a follow-up study and retested about 60 percent of the sample I had first examined in 1956. This gave me a series of seven-year longitudinal studies (Schaie and Strother, 1968a). The advantage of this kind of design is that both cross-sectional and longitudinal data are obtained on the same subjects with the same measurement variables. Another concern is that in any study over time, peculiar test and retest effects may occur. Also, loss of subjects in longitudinal studies is not necessarily random. To handle this problem we also obtained a new sample from the same population and age range, seven years later, which we thought would be instructive with respect to the issue of shift in peak age of performance.

Our joint analysis of the cross-sectional and longitudinal data showed that scientists who from their cross-sectional studies argued that there was age decrement were right; but so were the other scientists who denied age decrement on the basis of longitudinal data. That is, in my studies we found that the cross-sectional data indeed showed apparent age decrement. But what we found wasn't really decrement; rather, we were talking about age differences. What I had shown was that different generations performed at different levels of ability. My longitudinal gradient within the generations looked quite level and showed only very mild decrement. Obviously, as it grows older, any given sample has a larger proportion of members who have some kind of pathology which interferes with their ability to respond; even on items such as inadequate visual correction there would be a higher incidence in older people.

On the basis of our longitudinal studies we next constructed some composite age gradients. To show what happens when the appropriate cross-sectional and longitudinal data are compared, Figure 6.3 shows the age gradient for the Verbal Meaning task on the Primary Mental Abilities test. In this test the subject is given a stimulus word, say, "old." He then gets a list of four other words, say, "new, young, bad, ancient," and is required to identify the one word which is most like "old." This is a recognition vocabulary test. If we examine the longitudinal data and compose the appropriate composite age gradient within generations, it turns out the peak is not at age 35, but at age 55. Even at age 70 the estimated performance is still of higher ability than it would have been at age 25.

Some of the results of our 1963 study were criticized because we had pieced together longitudinal gradients by considering data collected over a single 7-year period, which may have been an atypical period. In 1970 we were fortunate enough to be able to do another follow-up study of the same population (Schaie and Labouvie-Vief, 1974). We now have data for some people over a 14-year period, and data for many people for two distinct 7-year periods. We were now able to construct families of age gradients over a 14-year period. An example of our comparative cross-sectional and longitudinal data is shown in Figure 6.4. This figure shows data for the PMA variable of spatial visualization. This is a particularly interesting test because it measures one of the abilities for which we are now fairly certain that there are reliable sex differences of a genetic origin. This test consists of geometric figures, some of which have been rotated clockwise and others counterclockwise. The subject must pick the ones that have been rotated clockwise. It is a novel and complex task for most people and is a good measure of spatial visualization.

The left side of Figure 6.4 shows three cross-sectional gradients:

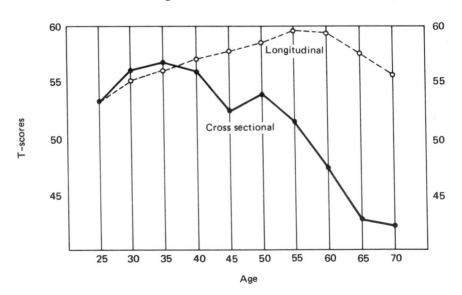

Figure 6.3. Comparable cross-sectional and longitudinal age gradients for the verbal meaning test. (From Schaie and Strother, 1968a)

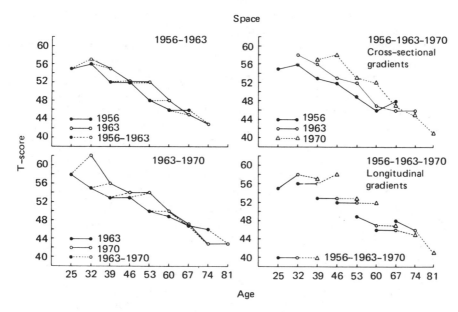

Figure 6.4. Cross-sectional and longitudinal age gradients for the space test from the primary mental abilities. The two graphs on the left depict changes over two different 7-year time periods for two different samples of subjects. The graphs on the right provide comparable cross-sectional and longitudinal gradients for a single sample followed over a 14-year period. (From Schaie and Labouvie-Vief, 1974)

the bottom one for data collected in 1956, the second one for 1963 data, and the third one for 1970 data. The shapes of these gradients are quite identical. But note the systematic displacement. That is, at each age, for consecutive 7-year periods, the later-born cohorts perform at a higher level than the earlier-born and, consequently, the peak ages keep increasing. This type of evidence can only be accounted for by generation differences; it confirms what some of us have suggested intuitively, namely, that we are smarter than our parents were, and that our children, in turn, are likely to be smarter than we are.

Now consider longitudinal data on the right of Figure 6.4. These are not estimates, but the actual data on the same people measured at three points in time, seven years apart. For the two youngest cohorts, ranging from about 20 to 40, spatial ability seemed to keep going up within these generations. For the next two cohorts, up to age 63, there is no change at all. The next gradient, which goes to about age 70, shows a minor decrement, and only for the very oldest cohort is there a significant drop. Even this drop must be viewed with caution because it could be a characteristic of that particular generation. That is, it may be characteristic only for individuals who are now in this age range and who have had a history of infectious childhood diseases, which would be quite atypical for later cohorts.

From these studies we can now conclude that on the crystallized abilities there is very little change in intellectual function for an individual throughout adulthood. However, there are certainly marked differences between levels of function for successive generations. These differences are not just a matter of level but may also affect the rate of change. It is at this time reasonable to suggest that the present generation of old people, from age 70 on, experienced some intellectual decrement, although much less than we had previously suspected. But it is not at all clear whether such decrement will be found in future generations of old people. For one thing, many of the people whom we have looked at thus far are individuals who are about to die. We probably happened to test them about three or four years before their death, and they may already be in the stage, before death, when a general decline of all functions is typically experienced (Riegel and Riegel, 1972). If we were able to examine persons who live until 90 or 95, we might at age 80 observe no decrement either. (For a more detailed popular discussion of these issues, see Baltes and Schaie, 1974.)

Although it is apparent from our studies that there is very little age decrement in intelligence, in functions that do not require speeded response or are affected by the slowing of reaction time within the individual, there are nevertheless marked differences in performance level between successive generations. For practical purpose this means that although many older people are functioning at least as well as they did when they were young, still the young of today function at a much higher level than those who were young 50 years ago. The implications of this conclusion for the practitioner, however, are dramatically different from those that would follow acceptance of the fact of intellectual decrement in the old.

Our studies strongly suggest that in the areas of intellectual abilities and skills, old people, in general, if they are reasonably healthy, have not declined, but rather have become obsolete. This conclusion might be viewed as a rather negative value judgment. That is not true at all, because obsolescence can be remedied by retraining, while deterioration would be irreversible. Indeed, if it can be shown that the real intellectual problem for older people is the fact that they are functioning at the level they attained in their younger days, but which is no longer appropriate for successful performance in contemporary society, it follows that we may be able to do something about this situation, rather than conclude that such individuals are simply deteriorated and bound to get worse. In such instances, the logical approach might be the development of compensatory education programs at about the time of retirement, perhaps comparable to the "operation headstart" programs attempted with culturally disadvantaged children.

Individual Differences in Changes in Intellectual Function with Age

All of the material presented above, of course, refers to findings on groups of people. What about the range of individual differences? While it does not follow that all old people have declined intellectually, some indeed have, but so have some people at age 30. Our longitudinal studies of individuals show that we have some remarkable individuals who gained in level of performance from age 70 to age 84; others have declined from age 20 to age 30. What can account for these individual differences? Two major classes of variables may be important. First, we suspect the role of cumulative health trauma which may vary widely across individuals. In other words, individuals who have had significant and accumulative physical illness may be at a disadvantage. Secondly, we know that young children function at the upper limits of their intellectual capability in terms of intelligence if they have been raised in a rich and complex environment. It is not unlikely that the maintenance and growth of intelligence of an adult may also have much to do with the complexity of his environment. We are currently examining a series of field interviews in which we looked at the complexity of adult life in terms of such variables as the nature of activities, the kind of books and newspapers read, the characteristics of a person's friends, daily patterns of activities, extensiveness of travel, and so on. We suspect that it will be possible to show that people who live in a varied environment are often the ones who show continued growth throughout life, while those who live in a static environment may be the ones who most likely show some decrement.

How important are the differences in intellectual performance between young and old? Scientists are often impressed by a difference that is "statistically significant." But what does statistical significance of a difference mean? All that is implied by the term is that the difference is reliable; if the same experiment were done again, we would expect again to find the same difference or one of similar magnitude. It does not mean that the difference needs to be great. In fact, if one has large enough samples, practically any difference will be statistically significant. Some of the differences shown in the graphs in this chapter are so small as not to make much of a practical difference. If, at age 30, an individual is able to produce 40 different words in a three-minute period but at age 70 can produce only 36 words, it is doubtful whether this "decrement" is going to make a lot of difference in his life. All it means is that it takes a little more time for him to come up with the required answers or that he may have to refresh his memory by taking more notes. Other differences are of a large enough magnitude to have some implications. For example, the generational differences in spatial visualization are of enough significance to cause the Federal Aviation Authority to change repeatedly their age limits for pilots. This age limit has gone up successively because successive generations have been functioning at higher levels. Generational differences may be significant enough so that by comparison with younger people, older people may indeed be at a disadvantage and compensatory procedures may be indicated. But often such data are simply used as rationalizations to deny the elderly societal roles they could well handle if they were allowed to do so. (Also see Schaie, 1973.)

Another reason to question the practical significance of some of the previous findings on age changes in the elderly is related to the validity of using the same tasks to measure intelligence at all ages. For example, some of the subtests on the Wechsler-Bellevue intelligence test measure different aspects of intelligence in young adulthood than in old age, simply because the skills required to solve the particular problems on these tests tend to change with age.

Some investigators have in fact prepared tests on which older people do better by using materials which are more meaningful for the mature adult (cf. Demming and Pressey, 1957). Especially in the area of verbal behavior it can be shown that tests can be designed deliberately to favor different cohorts by maximizing item contents of terms that were fashionable when the particular cohort was at the young adult age level. Thus, the same arguments which have been used to claim discrimination when tests built for middle-class white children have been applied to minority group members can also be applied when tests built for young adults are applied to work with the aged.

A final matter of concern when viewing the significance of lower test performance by the aged is the tendency toward cautiousness found in the elderly (Botwinick, 1973). Consequently, many elderly are less willing to guess test items about which they are uncertain, unless tests are set up in such a way that it is clearly to the old person's advantage to guess (Birkhill and Schaie, 1975). Young people in most test situations tend to make many more errors of commission than omission, but the reverse is true for the elderly. Perhaps the old are more cautious because they have been discouraged often for doing the wrong thing. Cautiousness may often be adaptive, but in this instance it may make the elderly appear less able than they actually are.

References

Baltes, P. B., and Schaie, K. W. 1974. Aging and IQ: The myth of the twilight years. *Psychology Today* 7:10:35–40.

Bayley, N., and Oden, M. M. 1955. The maintenance of intellectual ability in gifted adults. *Journal of Gerontology* 10:91–107..

Bayley, N. Cognition and aging. 1968. In *Theory and methods of research on aging*, ed. K. W. Schaie. Morgantown, W.Va.: West Virginia University.

Birkhill, W. R., and Schaie, K. W. 1975. The effect of differential reinforcement of cautiousness in intellectual performance among the elderly. *Journal of Gerontology,* in press.

Botwinick, J. 1973. *Aging and behavior.* New York: Springer.

Blum, J. E.; Jarvik, L. F.; and Clark, E. T. 1970. Rate of change on selective tests of intelligence: A twenty-year longitudinal study of aging. *Journal of Gerontology* 25:171–176.

Demming, J. A., and Pressey, S. L. 1957. Tests "indigenous" to the adult and older years. *Journal of Counseling Psychology* 4:144–148.

Horn, J. L. 1972. Intelligence: Why it grows, why it declines. In *Human intelligence,* ed. J. M. Hunt. New Brunswick, N.J.: Transaction Books.

Jones, H. E., and Conrad, H. S. 1933. The growth and decline of intelligence: a study of a homogenous group between the ages of ten and sixty. *Genetic Psychology Monographs* 13:223–294.

Owens, W. A. 1963. Age and mental abilities: a longitudinal study. *Genetic Psychology Monographs* 48:3–54

Riegel, K. F., and Riegel, R. M. 1972. Development, drop and death. *Developmental Psychology* 6:309–319.

Schaie, K. W. 1958. Rigidity-flexibility and intelligence: a cross-sectional study of the adult life span from 20–70. *Psychological Monographs* 72:9.

Schaie, K. W. 1967. Age changes and age differences. *Gerontologist* 7:128–132.

Schaie, K. W. 1970. A reinterpretation of age related changes in cognitive structure and functioning. In *Life-span developmental psychology: research and theory,* ed L. R. Goulet and P. B. Baltes. New York: Academic Press.

Schaie, K. W. 1973. Reflections on papers by Looft, Peterson and Sparks: toward an ageless society. *Gerontologist* 13:31–35.

Schaie, K. W. 1974. Translations in Gerontology—from lab to life: intellectual functioning. *American Psychologist* 29:802–807.

Schaie, K. W., and Labouvie-Vief, G. 1974. Generational versus ontogenetic components of change in adult cognitive functioning: a fourteen-year cross-sequential study. *Developmental Psychology* 10:305–320.

Schaie, K. W.; Rosenthal, F.; and Perlman, R. M. 1953. Differential mental deterioration of factorially "pure" functions in later maturity. *Journal of Gerontology* 8:191–196.

Schaie, K. W., and Strother, C. R. 1968a. A cross-sequential study of age changes in cognitive behavior. *Psychological Bulletin* 70:671–680.

Schaie, K. W., and Strother, C. R. 1968b. Cognitive and personality variables in college graduates of advanced age. In *Human aging and behavior: recent advances in research and theory,* ed. G. A. Talland. New York: Academic Press.

Thurstone, L. L. 1941. *Multiple factor analysis.* Chicago: University of Chicago Press.

7

Age Differences in Learning and Memory

DAVID A. WALSH

Three different theoretical views of learning and memory have guided research in geropsychology. Research by theorists holding these separate views has frequently used different procedures, different materials, and emphasized and ignored different problems. A direct comparison of research growing out of these different theoretical positions is impossible. Furthermore, selecting the correct view to present is no simple problem since one's theoretical bias will necessarily determine correctness. Choosing the "correct view" thus appears to be as straightforward as choosing the "correct religion"! The present chapter will characterize each of these theoretical views and review some of the research they have produced. Space limitations prohibit an exhaustive cataloging of all research, so only the most relevant investigations which best characterize conceptual problems, approaches and findings of each will be considered.

Stimulus—Response Associationism

Experimental investigations of higher mental processes were begun by Herman Ebbinghaus in the 1870s. His theoretical and methodological decisions for investigating these phenomena have guided much of the research carried out since his work. Ebbinghaus' conception of learning and memory was taken directly from the British Associationists. Memory, it was held, consisted of associations between ideas or events. These associations are, of course, the product of experiences that are contiguous in time. To study learning, he only needed to give a subject a series of experiences. If he counted how many times the subject had to be exposed to a series before he could recall it completely, he would have a measure of learning difficulty. The measurement of memory was more problematic. If you learn something to a given criterion of one correct recitation but the next day can recall none of it or only bits and pieces, how can an experimenter get a measure of memory? Ebbinghaus' insight was that he could require the subject to relearn the material on the next day and see how many rehearsals it took him to reach the same criterion he reached the day before. That is, he would measure memory by calculating how much savings there had been in relearning.

Another problem for Ebbinghaus was to find suitable material. Prose, poetry and other meaningful material seemed too unequal in difficulty to use in studies that required careful measurement. Ebbinghaus' solution was to develop his own materials, nonsense syllables. These syllables consisted of consonant-vowel-consonant combinations—such as SEB, WUC, LUP—and, for Ebbinghaus, had the virtue of not meaning anything.

The procedure used by Ebbinghaus was to have his subject (himself) carefully read each syllable in the list to a ticking metronome. The reading was repeated until he felt he had completely learned the list. His procedure has been modified by contemporary psychologists to *serial anticipation learning*. Now material is exposed to a subject one item at a time on a fixed time schedule. The subject reads each item and tries to anticipate the next. The learning is complete when the subject successfully anticipates every item. A more popular method of studying verbal learning today is *paired-associate anticipation learning*. Here, the subject is presented with pairs of words or nonsense syllables to learn instead of a list. One member of the pair (the stimulus) is first presented alone. Then it is followed at some fixed interval (usually two seconds) by the other member of the pair (the response). The subject is required to anticipate the response before it appears. Between trials the order of the pairs is usually changed, but not the items paired together. The subject is considered to have learned the list when he gives the correct response to each stimulus item as it appears before the response item is exposed.

Age Differences in Paired-Associate and Serial Learning

These procedures have been used to generate a sizable body of research comparing aged persons to the young. Gilbert (1941) found a decline in performance with age on a variety of learning and memory tasks with the greatest decrement appearing in a paired-associate learning task. Many times since Gilbert's study, the paired-associate task has been found to be especially difficult for older persons to learn. Such findings were originally taken as evidence that the effectiveness of the associative machinery of learning declines with age. Arguments about the relation between observable performance on paired-associate tasks and learning ability have suggested other explanations of these findings.

Botwinick (1973) draws a distinction between learning as an internal process and performance as an external act. The observer can see only the act and not the process; he must infer that learning ability is poor when he observes little or no improvement in performance after training. It is possible this conclusion is wrong, because the poor performance may be a result of factors other than the associative machinery, such as poor motivation, lack of confidence, or unfavorable conditions of training. If information about such noncognitive factors is available, more correct inferences about learning can be drawn.

Noncognitive factors are especially important to the S-R associationist when he tries to infer learning ability from changes in performance with age. What in the past was regarded as exclusively a deficiency in the associative machinery of learning is now seen by some researchers as a problem in the noncognitive performance factors. In other words, it may be the case that older people learn as well as young persons but for noncognitive reasons are unable or unwilling to demonstrate what they have learned. With the cognitive/noncognitive distinction in mind, we can proceed to consider those findings which suggest that some, but not all, of the performance deficits found in the aged are attributable to noncognitive factors.

Canestrari (1963) argued that most studies of paired-associate learning use a rapid rate of stimulus pacing that is not fair to older persons. Canestrari compared old and young (17–35 years and 60–69 years) persons across three pacing rates. The old persons showed the greatest deficit compared to the young with the fastest pacing (1.5 seconds), less deficit with medium pacing (3.0 seconds), and the least deficit with self-pacing. The self-pacing allowed subjects to take as much time as they wished both to study the paired-associates and to respond. Canestrari reported that both old and young subjects utilized the time in making responses to stimulus words but did not increase the time spent studying the pairs. Since the old show the least deficit in the self-pacing condition, it may be that what older people need is more time than is usually allowed to produce newly learned information.

The idea that older people perform poorly in quickly paced experimental tasks because of insufficient time to respond, rather than as a result of impaired learning ability, also receives some support from studies involving serial learning tasks. Eisdorfer (1965) varied both the exposure duration of the stimulus words (the time available to study the word) and the interval between the stimulus words (the time available to respond by anticipating the next word). Older subjects benefited both from the longer inspection times and the longer response times. These findings show that while some of the performance deficits of older persons result from noncognitive factors, such as response speed, older adults have less of a deficit when they are allowed more time to study the stimulus materials. This suggests that the old may need more time to learn in the first place. Additional research, such as the work of Arenberg (1965), also supports the idea that performance deficits found with older people are attributable to both cognitive and noncognitive factors.

Thus the performance deficits found for older persons in laboratory investigations of verbal learning are not explainable by either cognitive or noncognitive processes alone. When noncognitive factors, such as response time, are made more favorable to older persons, they show a definite improvement in performance. However, older persons further benefit from longer study time and still show poorer performance than young subjects.

Other Noncognitive Causes of Performance Deficits

While many of the performance deficits seen in older people may be the result of insufficient response time, researchers with associative theories have identified two other noncognitive factors that cause performance deficits.

Overarousal.   Powell, Eisdorfer, and Bogdonoff (1964) used the level of free fatty acids (FFA) as an index of autonomic nervous system (ANS) arousal during a serial learning task and concluded that older persons were more aroused than young persons in this situation. Furthermore, FFA levels in the aged continued to rise even after the termination of the serial learning task. Powell et al. suggest that old people have a performance deficit in new learning situations because they are too aroused or too motivated. Performance deficits from over-motivation are not a new finding in psychology. Yerkes and Dodson (1908), in a classic study, found that many learning situations have an optimal level of motivation which when exceeded impairs performance. Further investigation of the ANS overarousal hypothesis was undertaken by Eisdorfer, Nowlin, and Wilkie (1970) who administered either a drug (Propranolol), believed to suppress autonomic and organ activity, or a placebo, to old people engaged in a serial learning task. Their hypothesis, that excess autonomic arousal was the cause of performance decrements in the elderly, was supported. In another experiment, Eisdorfer (1968) had considered the possibility that situational anxiety may also result in performance decrements. He reasoned that rapid pacing in serial learning and the insertion of a needle when blood was sampled for FFA determination worked together to decrease performance through situational anxiety. He tested this hypothesis with a group of aged performing serial learning with both a four second and a ten second exposure duration, first without and then with the insertion of the needle. Results indicated that both the rapid rate of presentation and the anxiety caused by needle insertion resulted in a performance decrement.

A very recent attempt to replicate Eisdorfer's work on ANS over-arousal and serial learning performance presents a different perspective. Comparing the effect of propranolol and a placebo drug on ANS arousal and performance in serial learning in the same subjects, Froehling (1974) was unable to replicate Eisdorfer, Nowlin, and Wilkie (1970). Old subjects in Froehling's study did not appear to be anxious in the learning situation, and their FFA levels and performance on the learning task did not show the deficits or improvements evident in the Eisdorfer work. It may be that anxiety and overarousal is a transitory state occurring only in the older subjects' first few visits to the laboratory. Since Froehling trained her subjects and had them visit the laboratory and practice the serial learning task several times before actual testing, FFA level evaluation, and drug administration occurred, she may have obviated the occurrence of overarousal in the laboratory.

Meaningfulness. Task relevance is another factor which can affect motivation and thus be a noncognitive aspect of learning performance. Laboratory studies of learning have often been criticized for using tasks that are meaningless and trivial—tasks which have little or no interest for older people. Shmavonian and Busse (1963) studied task involvement in young and old subjects. They found that when the young were presented with simple tones they showed significantly greater amounts of responsiveness (as measured by galvanic skin response) than did the old people. However, when the stimuli were changed to meaningful spoken phrases, the differences between young and old subjects' responsivity diminished.

Although this study did not involve learning, it did suggest that older people were less involved in the laboratory task when it was less meaningful to them. A clearer example of the same effect in learning situations has been reported by Hulicka (1967). She tried to teach a paired-associate learning task in which response words such as "insane" were paired with stimulus letters such as "TL." Hulicka reported an extremely high rate of attrition with elderly subjects (aged 65–80 years), reaching 80 percent. Many of these older subjects refused to exert themselves to learn "such nonsense." When Hulicka changed the task and made it more meaningful (substituting occupation names and personal surnames for the letters and words respectively), the older subjects carried out the task willingly, although their performance was still inferior to that of a young comparison group.

Associational Mediators

A number of procedures have been found to optimize learning of paired-associate and serial learning tasks, apparently because they increase the efficiency of the associative learning machinery. Canestrari (1968) surveyed the research literature involving these mediational techniques and found evidence suggesting that excellent performance in paired-associate learning occurs when subjects are told to form linkages between each word-pair associate. Such linkages or mediators may take the form of syntactical or verbal characteristics (sentences) or of visual imagery (mental pictures). Hulicka and Grossman (1967) believed that part of the learning deficit observed in old subjects might be due to the failure to use mediational techniques spontaneously. This conclusion was drawn from an investigation in which they found that older persons did not use mediators spontaneously as did young people, but that older people showed a greater improvement than young people when both groups were specifically instructed to use mediators. However, even with the greater improvement found for elderly subjects with mediator instructions, their performance was still poorer than that of the young.

A speculation by Hulicka and Grossman, that elderly persons use more verbal than visual image mediators as compared to the young and that verbal mediators are less beneficial, was investigated by Canestrari (1968). He provided subjects with both kinds of mediators and predicted that the visual mediators would help older subjects more than the verbal mediators. Contrary to his expectations, Canestrari did not find better learning with visual mediators than with verbal mediators for either young or old subjects. He did find, however, that both visual and verbal mediators resulted in a doubling of correct responses for the old subjects with no reliable change in the performance of the young. Despite this dramatic improvement for old subjects using mediators, absolute performance in the elderly was still poorer than that for young subjects.

Information Processing Models of Memory

The development of modern computers required many engineering advances for the storage of information. For example, a computer must hold the first columns of information punched on an IBM card in a buffer register while successive columns are read. Once the information on a card has been read the contents of the record buffer can be stored in the computer and the buffer itself cleared to hold the next card in sequence. The storage of the buffer's contents into the more permanent core memory of the computer usually involves an intermediate step. The buffer contents are loaded into a central processing unit register which then assigns them to an address specified location in core memory. Thus three memory functions can be identified in modern computers: peripheral buffer memory which holds items being read until appropriate size chunks have collected, working memory registers used to hold information actively being processed by the computer, and core memory which holds large amounts of inactive but addressable information. The impressive performance of computers that these storage functions allow has not gone unnoticed by psychologists. These concepts have been adapted as a theoretical framework in which to view human memory.

Murdock's (1967) modal model characterizes the work of theorists who developed computer analogy models (Atkinson and Shiffrin 1968, 1971; Waugh and Norman, 1965). The model has three human storage capacities that parallel the storage functions of modern computers. Table 7.1 represents in outline these three components and their hypothesized characteristics (see Craik and Lockhart, 1972 for a more complete discussion). Sensory memory is the first component and corresponds to buffer memory of computers. Sensory memory is further differentiated as to the sense modality of incoming information. It is called iconic memory when the sense modality is vision (Neisser, 1967) and echoic memory when auditory (Crowder and Morton, 1969).

Investigations of iconic memory began in the early 1960s (Sperling,

Table 7.1   An outline of information-processing theories of memory

Features	Sensory memory	Short-term memory	Long-term memory
1. Entry of information	1. Preattentive	1. Requires attention	1. Rehearsal
2. Maintenance	2. Not possible	2. Continued attention (rehearsal)	2. Repetition-organization
3. Form of information	3. Literal copy of input	3. Phonemic	3. Semantic
4. Capacity	4. Large	4. Small (4-7 items)	4. Unlimited
5. Information loss	5. Decay	5. Displacement	5. Loss of accessiblity
6. Trace duration	6. ¼ - 2 sec.	6. Up to 30 sec.	6. Minutes to years
7. Retrieval	7. Readout	7. Items in consciousness	7. Retrieval cues

SOURCE: Adapted from Craik and Lockhart, 1972.

1960; Averback and Coriell, 1961) with a tachistoscope presentation which briefly exposed visual information. Averback and Coriell (1961) presented subjects with 50 msec. exposures of arrays of letters aligned in two rows of eight items. A marker pointing to one item in the array was presented simultaneously. Under these conditions subjects reported the marked letter with high accuracy. The marker was then delayed for various durations and the accuracy of reporting the marked letter was observed. A high accuracy of partial report was maintained with delays of the marker as long as 250 msec. This performance contrasts sharply with the observation that subjects can report only four letters from the total 16-item array. Together these observations suggest that all of the visual information in tachistoscopic presentations is maintained in a brief sensory memory that decays rapidly. While the duration of visual sensory memory (iconic) has been found to be about 250 msec, auditory sensory memory (echoic) appears to last for durations as long as two seconds (Haber and Standing, 1969, 1970; Crowder and Morton, 1969).

As shown in Table 7.1, entry of information into sensory memory occurs in the absence of attention (preattentive). The contact of physical energy with the appropriate sensory system appears to be sufficient for the entrance of that information into sensory memory. No operations have been found for prolonging the duration of sensory memory. The format of information in sensory memory is a literal copy of the physical input and is assumed to contain all of the information presented. The information presented decays at a rapid rate and this decay begins with the initiation of the physical stimulus (Haber and Standing, 1969, 1970). Information is retrieved from sensory memory by attending to it and thus bringing it under direct processing (consciousness).

Attention to the material in sensory memory is equivalent to reading it out and transfering it to short-term memory. Here, verbal items are coded in some phonemic fashion (Shulman, 1971) or in auditory-verbal-linguistic terms (Atkinson and Shiffrin, 1968). Short-term memory is further distinguished from sensory memories by virtue of its limited capacity (Miller, 1956; Broadbent, 1958) and by the finding that information is lost principally by a process of displacement (Waugh and Norman, 1965). The rate of forgetting is much slower for short-term memory; estimates range from 5 to 20 seconds as compared to 250 msec to 2 seconds for sensory memories. The duration of short-term memory can be extended by an active process of rehearsal.

One of the major distinctions between short-term memory and long-term memory is the storage capacity. Whereas short-term memory has a limited capacity, long-term memory has no known limit. The coding characteristics of long-term memory serve as a second distinction: whereas verbal items are usually coded phonemically in short-term memory, they are largely coded in terms of their semantic content in long-term memory (Baddelcy, 1966). Long-term memory also differs from short-term memory in rate of forgetting; while loss from short-term memory is usually complete in 30 seconds or less (following the termination of rehearsal) forgetting from long-term memory may not occur or proceeds very slowly (Shiffrin and Atkinson, 1967).

The three-box model of memory is attractively easy to understand, but it has not gone without criticism. While detailed criticism will be considered later in this chapter it is useful to consider here the questions raised by Melton (1963). Melton has argued that the distinction between long-term and short-term memory is unnecessary: both show the same characteristics in that information is acquired gradually and forgetting results from interference by preceding and following items. These arguments have been questioned by Waugh and Norman (1965) who draw a distinction between the temporal duration of a retention period and the processes by which information is maintained. They introduce the terms primary memory and secondary memory to correspond to what is here called short-term and long-term memory. Primary memory, or short-term memory, involves the active process of information rehearsal whereas secondary memory, or long-term memory, is a structured and organized store of semantic content. Waugh and Norman (1965) contend that the findings leading to Melton's criticism reflect storage and loss of information from secondary memory only. Waugh and Norman argue he is confusing short and long retention periods with primary and secondary memory processes respectively.

With this outline of information processing views of human memory in mind we can proceed to consider some of the research investigating age differences in these memory functions. The reader should be clear on the incompatibility of these views with those of S-R associationists. The questions to be investigated are not about the conditions required to form associations between stimuli and responses. Rather it is assumed that the organism is designed to process the information presented. Thus the research focuses on how efficiently information presented once is maintained over time.

Sensory Memory

Few studies of age differences in sensory memory have been reported. Botwinick (1973) cites an investigation by Abel (1972) that attempted to look at age differences in iconic memory. Abel used the procedure employed by Sperling (1960) which shares many features with the procedure of Averback and Coriell (1961) reported above. Arrays of letters arranged in three rows of three items were presented tachistoscopically. Subjects reported only a single row of three letters; the row to be reported was designated by a tone presented either simultaneously with the letters or delayed for various durations after the letters. As with the Averback and Coriell procedure changes in the accuracy of partial reports were measured with increasing delays of the tone signaling the items to be reported.

Abel found only marginally significant age differences in accuracy of report. Furthermore, no age differences were found in the rate of decline of partial report accuracy. Figure 7.1 presents these findings. An important point in Figure 7.1 is the equivalent difference between old and young groups at all delay periods from 0 to 1200 msec. This finding might suggest that the storage capacity of sensory memory declines with age, while the rate of decay remains unchanged. The latter conclusion is supported by the finding of equal rates of decline in accuracy with increasing delay periods for all age groups. The conclusion of decreases in storage capacity with age follows from the finding that older adults report fewer items than young even when the tone indicating which row to report occurs without delay. However, for methodological reasons, it is questionable that Abel's investigation really deals with iconic memory.

Abel's investigation is interesting, however, in that it shows older adults report fewer items than the young when both age groups have available equal durations of information. After Neisser (1967) we can conceptualize human pattern recognition as proceeding in sequential stages of preattentive segregation of wholistic entities followed by focal attention and constructive recognition. Iconic memory is hypothesized to be a storage buffer for the preattentive step of object segregation. The limit of four items that can be reported from large tachistoscopic arrays is explained by the time requirements of shifts in focal attention and constructive recognition of separate letters: the time required to perform these processes on five letters equals or exceeds the duration of iconic memory for the segregated wholistic but unidentified objects. Abel's use of 500 msec. stimulus probably equates the duration of preattentive information for all age groups. The differences between age groups at a 0 msec. delay is, therefore, explained by age differences in the speed of focusing attention on segregated objects and/or recognizing the patterns they represent.

This interpretation is supported by preliminary findings in an investigation being conducted by Larry W. Thompson and David Walsh. Age differences in iconic memory are being investigated using a procedure similar to that of Averback and Coriell (1961) in which letter arrays are presented for 50 msec. and followed by a marker (50 msec.) designating one of the items to be reported. Subjects are presented with 128 different arrays containing two rows of four letters each. Eight arrays and eight markers, exhausting letter position, are presented in random order at each of 16 delay periods (0 to 700 msec.). Before these experimental trials begin subjects are rehearsed until they can report six out of eight items correctly when there is no delay between the array and marker.

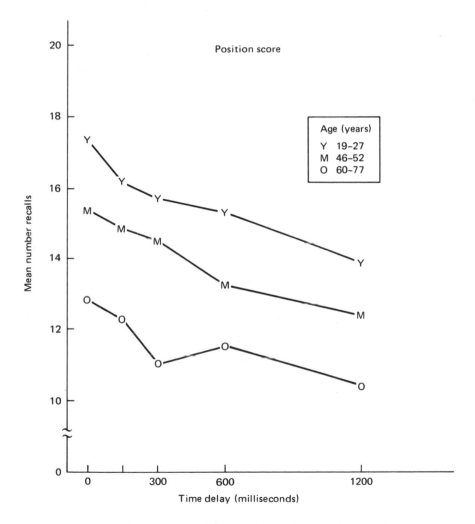

Figure 7.1. The number of letters reported from tachistoscope arrays as a function of time-delay of a signal indicating what to report. Items were scored as correct only if their spatial position was known. (Data from Table 1 of Abel 1972).

To date, nine young (18–31 years) and ten old (60–72 years) subjects have participated in this experiment. The difference between old and young subjects is dramatic. Young subjects typically report the first 8 practice items presented correctly. The task at 0 msec. delay is extremely simple for the young subjects tested thus far. Following the successful completion of this preliminary criterion, which is reached immediately by the young, the rest of the experiment requires only 20 minutes. This performance contrasts sharply with that of older adults. Eight out of ten subjects tested have found the task impossible to perform even with no delay. After two hours of practice (in spaced sessions) these older subjects have been unable to report more than four out of eight items correctly. The two older subjects who have reached criterion did so immediately, much as all nine young subjects. The data collected from these two unique subjects is presented in Figure 7.2 along with the performance of the nine young subjects.

Inspection of Figure 7.2 shows that the performance of the young declines gradually from 96 percent at 0 msec. delay of the marker to 49 percent at 350 msec. Although no tests of significance have been con-

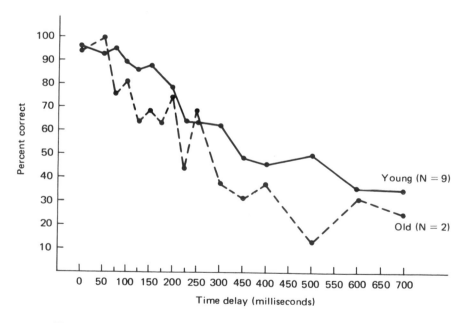

Figure 7.2. Percentage of letters reported correctly from tachistoscope arrays as a function of the time-delay of a marker indicating which letter to report. The data of two exceptional old subjects, who did not find the task impossible, are compared to nine representative young subjects.

ducted and the mean data based on the two older subjects "who were able to perform the task" does not produce a very smooth curve, it would appear that their performance is not dramatically different from the young. What is of relevance here, however, is the nonperformance of the other eight old subjects. Three possible explanations suggest themselves.

One possibility is that these subjects have no iconic memory: they must have the physical stimulus continually present until successful pattern recognition has occurred. This possibility seems extremely unlikely given other screening data available on these subjects. The target duration required to recognize single letters with 100 percent accuracy was determined for both eyes of each subject. The duration was 3.5 msec., a finding that rules out the absence of iconic memory unless we are willing to make the untenable assumption that successful pattern recognition for single items is completed in less than 3.5 msec. (see Turvey, 1973). These data also rule out the likelihood that pattern-recognition processing time exceeds the duration of iconic memory for older adults, since all of the subjects failing to reach criterion for iconic memory testing succeeded in recognizing single letters under these short stimulus presentations.

The most likely explanation of this nonperformance is the shift in focal attention required by the Averback and Coriell (1961) procedure. Subjects are required to focus attention on a single item designated by the marker in the preattentively segregated iconic store. Only the focusing of attention to a specific item separates the cognitive processing under this procedure from that required with single letter presentations; in both cases the pattern presented must be held in iconic memory while recognition processing operates. Thus it would seem that more direct measures of iconic memory not requiring shifts in focal attention are more appropriate for assessing age differences in iconic memory (Haber and Standing, 1969).

Short-Term Memory

Atkinson and Shiffrin (1971) conceptualize short-term memory as an important control system for all thinking and remembering. It is a holding system for the conscious processing of information. A number of different experimental paradigms produce data relevant to short-term memory functions. One source of data is the recency effect observed in free recall studies. The experimental procedure involves reading a list of items (usually English words) to subjects who know they will be required to remember them. Immediately after the list is presented subjects are allowed to recall the items in any order they wish. The classic finding is that subjects recall the last few items from the list first and that they are more likely to be remembered than other items. These data are usually attributed to subjects still having the last few items in short-term memory —an active rehearsal memory. Using this experimental paradigm, age differences in short-term memory have been investigated by Craik (1968b) and Raymond (1971). Specifically, they compared the recency effect of young subjects to that of old. They found no difference as a function of age: Older subjects were just as likely as young subjects to recall the last two or three items of a free recall list. These findings suggest that short-term memory functions remain stable and efficient with increasing age.

A second procedure used to assess age differences in short-term memory is the digit span test. Subjects are read strings of digits immediately. The number of digits a subject can reliably repeat in correct sequence is taken as a measure of the storage capacity of his short-term memory. Investigations of age differences in short-term memory using the digit span test provide reasonable consensus in showing that there is little (Botwinick and Storandt, 1974; Friedman, 1974; Gilbert, 1941) or no decline with age in short-term memory storage capacity (Bromley, 1958; Craik, 1968a; Drachman and Leavitt, 1972).

A number of investigators have increased the difficulty of the digit span procedure by adding to the cognitive processing load placed on the subject. One modification requires the subject to repeat the digits in backward order. For example the string "9, 3, 1, 6, 5" must be repeated as "5, 6, 1, 3, 9." The reorganization of the string requires active processing involving further use of short-term memory "holding" the original string. Thus this task most likely reflects flexibility of processing and some component of long-term memory as well. It is not inconsistent with other findings, therefore, that backward span declines with age (Bromley, 1958; and Botwinick and Storandt, 1974).

While it seems clear that the storage capacity of short-term memory does not decline with age, an investigation by Anders, Fozard and Hillyquist (1972) shows that the rate at which information can be retrieved from short-term memory does decline. Anders et al. used a procedure developed by Sternberg (1966). They presented subjects with lists of 1, 3, 5, and 7 digits and asked them (yes or no) if a single test digit appeared in the list. The time required to respond yes or no was measured. The rationale of this procedure assumes that subjects hold the list presented in short-term memory and retrieve it item by item to compare against the test digit. By increasing the number of items in the list, and observing increases in time to reach a decision, the rate of retrieving items from short-term memory can be determined. Figure 7.3 presents the findings of Anders et al. (1972) in their investigation comparing three age groups: 19–21 years, 33–43 years, and 58–85 years. The differences in response time between age groups with one-item lists reflect overall response speed including such factors as motor speed and encoding speed of the test digit. The differences in response speed between the longer and shorter lists reflect the rate at which items are retrieved from short-term memory. Figure 7.3 shows that the curves of the older groups were steeper in slope than that of the younger group, and are thus thought to indicate that the older groups retrieve information at a slower rate from short-term memory.

Long-Term Memory

An important distinction between short and long-term memory, as shown in Table 7.1, is storage capacity. Watkins (1974) estimates the capacity of short-term memory to be 2.6 to 3.4 words. Baddeley (1970) and Murdock (1972) have made estimates that closely agree—two to four words. Crannell and Parrish (1957), however, have reported that the ca-

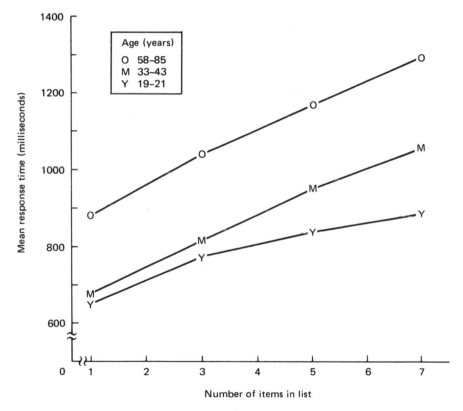

Figure 7.3. Mean recognition response time as a function of the number of digits in a list. (From Botwinick, 1973, as adapted from Anders et al., 1972).

pacity varies between five and nine items depending on whether the items in question are words, letters, or digits. Whatever the precise values (if they exist) the previous section shows that little or no changes in capacity occur with age. Presumably when the capacity of short-term memory is exceeded by incoming information the information held must be transfered to long-term memory so that short-term memory is free to accept new inputs from sensory memory.

A number of researchers have investigated age differences in memory where the capacity of short-term memory is exceeded. Friedman (1966) presented two age groups with lists varying from four to twelve items and observed performance in serial recall. He found that the older group (60 to 81 years) performed more poorly than did the young group (20 to 34 years). Craik (1968a) presented subjects in their 20s and 70s with lists varying from four to nine digits. The older subjects performed more poorly on the longer lists although the interaction was not significant.

Craik (1968a) also investigated age differences in free recall when both the number of items presented and the size of the pool from which they were selected was varied. The number of items in the lists were varied from five to twenty and the size of the pool was manipulated by selecting the items from English county names, animal names, or unrelated words. Craik found that older subjects recalled fewer items than the young from longer lists and also that the older subjects recalled fewer items as the size of the pool of alternatives increased. Craik interprets these findings as evidence for a decline in long-term memory with age and argues that some part of the decline is attributable to inability to retrieve information, since the old show poorer performance when the pool of alternatives is large.

A retrieval explanation of age differences in long-term memory has received support from a number of investigations. Laurence (1967a) compared the free recall performance of young and old subjects on word lists chosen from a single conceptual category (animal names) and from multiple categories. It was found that older subjects showed only minimal differences on single category lists but significant decrements with multiple category lists. A second investigation by Laurence (1967b) used a cued recall procedure designed to facilitate the retrieval of information from long-term memory. When the names of the conceptual categories composing the multiple category lists were used as cues, the age decrement in free recall was eliminated. This finding suggests that some of the age differences observed are attributable to the inability of older subjects to retrieve information that is stored in long-term memory.

An investigation by Schonfield and Robertson (1966) provides further support for the hypothesis that older adults have difficulty in retrieving information stored in long-term memory. These researchers presented old and young subjects with a list of 24 English words and required both age groups to first recall the items and then recoginze, out of sets of four items, which word was presented in the acquisition list. The recall task requires subjects to retrieve information stored in long-term memory, whereas the recognition test does not require retrieval. Schonfield and Robertson found a large age decrement on the free recall test but no age differences in recognition. Figure 7.4 presents these data suggesting older adults are less able to retrieve information from long-term memory. This finding of no age differences in recognition has been replicated by Craik (1971), although other researchers have found a significant age difference in recognition memory (Botwinick and Storandt, 1974; Erber, 1974). These latter studies, however, also support the idea that a portion of the age differences seen in long-term memory result from retrieval difficulties in that they found the differences between old and young subjects are considerably less in recognition than in free recall.

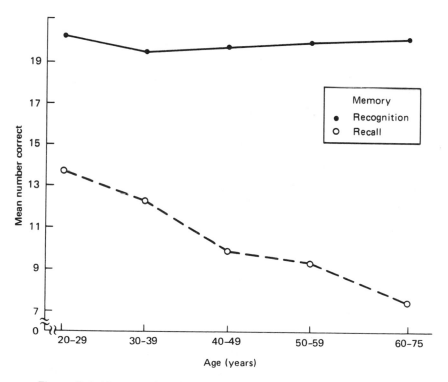

Figure 7.4. Mean recall and recognition scores as a function of age. (From Botwinick, 1973, as adapted from Schonfield, 1965.)

While the above investigations have looked at age differences in retrieval from long-term memory, other investigators have assessed age differences in the entry of information into long-term memory. A number of investigators have found no age differences in free recall of word lists from long-term memory when initial acquisition is equated (Wimer and Wigdor, 1958; Hulicka and Weiss, 1965; Moenster, 1972). Procedures equating initial acquisition usually require that all subjects reach a fixed criterion of 100 percent immediate recall. Age differences in recall from long-term memory are then assessed at a later point in time. The finding that old subjects require more trials to reach the fixed criterion but then remember as well as young subjects suggests that older adults are less efficient in entering information into long-term memory.

Mandler (1967) has equated the process of organization with entry of information into long-term memory. According to Mandler, to organize information is to store it in long-term memory. The experimental procedure used by Mandler requires subjects to sort reliably a list of words into categories. The words are printed on cards and subjects are seated in front of sorting boxes. They repeatedly sort the list until they reach a criterion of two successive identical sorts. Then they are given pencils and paper and asked to remember the words. Mandler has found over a series of seven investigations that recall is a positive function of the number of categories used to sort the stimulus list (median correlation = .70) and that word recall is unrelated to the number of trials it requires subjects to reach the criterion of two successive identical sorts.

Hultsch (1969, 1971, 1974) has investigated the hypothesis that age differences in organizational efficiency explain the poor free-recall performance of older adults. Hultsch (1971) had three age groups of adults sort a set of stimulus words using Mandler's procedure. Three control groups were paired with experimental subjects of the same age and asked to inspect the word list, without sorting, for the same number of trials required by experimental subjects to reach the sorting criterion. Hultsch found that, without sorting, the two older groups of subjects (40–49 and 60–69 years) recalled fewer words than the younger subjects (20–29 years). The sorting task, however, had a positive effect on the recall of the older subjects: both of the older groups showed an improvement in recall with the sorting task. However, the oldest sorting group was still poorer than the younger group without sorting. While this finding does not show that all age decrements in recall from long-term memory result from poor organizational ability, it does show that some of these deficiencies are attributable to organizational factors. Another investigation of the effect of age differences in organization on free recall supports this conclusion. Hultsch (1969) presented three age groups of subjects with a free-recall task. Each age group was further divided into three subgroups that were given different organizing instructions. One group was given no specific instructions, a second group was told to "organize" the words and a third group was told to "organize the words based on the alphabetical position of their first letter." Hultsch found that, for people of low verbal ability, the oldest age group and the middle age group were poorer than the young with the first two types of instructions. However with the third type of instructions, those most helpful in organizing the list, no age differences in free recall performance were found. These findings support the idea that older adults enter less information into long-term memory than the young because they are less likely to organize the information.

Depth of Processing

The attractiveness of separate storage components in information processing theories is easy to understand. They provide a clear and simple metaphor for conceptualizing human theory. However, as research motivated by these storage concepts has collected, the independence and clarity of these separate storage functions has been lost (Craik and Lockhart, 1972). For example, estimates of the storage capacity of short-term memory now disagree. Researchers using words arrive at estimates of twenty items (Craik and Masani, 1969) as compared to estimates of four or five items when letters and digits serve as material. This finding suggests a flexible capacity that varies as a function of type of material used—a complication that removes a previously important defining characteristic of short-term memory.

Research by Shulman (1970) calls into question a second characteristic of short-term memory. He found evidence to support the idea that information in short-term memory can be coded semantically. Semantic coding has been an important criterion in information processing theory for distinguishing long-term memory from short-term memory. The loss of the criterion of coding characteristics along with that of storage capacity upset the attractive simplicity of the three-storage function model. Also the turn in more recent formulations of information processing theory (Atkinson & Shiffrin, 1971) to control processes, unspecified executive functions responsible for moving items between short- and long-term memory, detracts from the once simple clarity of the model.

An alternative conceptualization of human memory has been outlined by Craik and Lockhardt (1972). They suggest that information processing explanations which explain the duration of memory as a function of the box information is stored in can be replaced by one which focuses on the perceptual processes carried out. Craik and Lockhardt (1972) conceptualize perceptual processes as involving at least 3 steps: the analysis of sensory features, the matching of constellations of features against stored abstractions collected from previous learning, and the elaboration and/or enrichment of the meaning of the items recognized. They believe the result of perceptual processing is a memory trace. The duration of a memory trace is believed to be a direct function of the "depth" at which it was processed. The deeper, or more meaningful, the perceptual processes carried out on information the more persistent the memory trace. The coding characteristics of information are also determined by the level at which it was processed. Thus items processed at the deepest (meaningful) level of perceptual analysis would be coded semantically, whereas items processed to less deep levels would be coded phonemically. These hypothesized operations lead to predictions compatible with existing findings: semantically coded items persist for longer duration while phonemically coded items are more ephemeral.

The theoretical proposal of Craik and Lockhardt distinguishes between two types of memory functions. Type I processes involve the processing of information to deeper and deeper levels. For example, a visual stimulus flashed for a brief duration is first processed at a primitive level as contours, shadows, lines and other simple features. A deeper level of processing interrelates these features to synthesize a global object which in turn may be processed at a still deeper level of pattern recognition. This level of processing might categorize the stimulus as a picture of a cat. The recognized pattern may be processed at successively deeper levels involving the verbal labeling of the object as a "cat" and relating it to other felines, shredded furniture, and veterinarian's bills. As each successively deeper level is arrived at, the coding characteristics of the stimulus change and the duration of memory trace produced increases.

Type II processes involve "recirculation" at a given level of processing. For example, the verbal labeling of the visual stimulus might be repeated producing what information-processing theories describe as verbal or articulatory rehearsal. Type II processing maintains a memory trace indefinitely as long as active recirculation continues; once it stops the trace decays at a rate normal for information processed to that level. The ability to recirculate, or reactivate, the processes at a level varies directly with the depth of the processes. The shallowest levels are seen as incapable of being reactivated, providing an explanation compatible with the inability to maintain iconic memory.

The theoretical proposal of Craik and Lockhardt was motivated by findings from an incidental learning paradigm adapted by Jenkins and his colleagues to the study of memory (Hyde and Jenkins, 1969; Johnston and Jenkins, 1973; Till and Jenkins, 1973 and Hyde and Jenkins, 1973). The study by Walsh and Jenkins (1973) is representative of the procedures and findings of these investigations. They presented young subjects with a free-recall task in an incidental-learning situation. To disguise the memory requirements of the study and to direct the type of processes subjects would use, a number of different orienting tasks were assigned. One task, hypothesized to be facilitative of memory because it required the stimulus words to be processed as meaningful elements, involved the evaluation of the meaning of words as pleasant or unpleasant. A second task, hypothesized to be inefficient for memory because it required stimulus words to be processed as nonmeaningful collections of elements, involved the search for either the letter E or G in the spelling of each word. When undertaking these tasks, subjects were not informed that they should learn the words or that they would be asked to recall them. On the other hand, subjects in a control condition performed no orienting task but were told, as is typical in free-recall tasks, that they should remember the list of words. The hypothesis is that meaningful processing would facilitate learning was supported. Subjects who processed words as meaningful elements recalled twice as many as subjects who processed the words as nonmeaningful elements. The control group that performed no orienting task but knew of the learning requirements, recalled slightly fewer words than the meaningful processing group.

Thus in the incidental learning, paradigm-orienting tasks are used to control the cognitive processes of the subject. Tasks which involve the subject with phonemic or orthographic characteristics hold perceptual processing at shallow levels, while tasks involving the meaning of words force processing to deeper levels. These experimental and theoretical paradigms offer interesting possible ways to conceptualize the study of age changes in memory. One explanation of the finding of poorer free recall for older subjects is that they process materials to less deep levels. We need not assume that they are unable to process to deeper levels, only that they do not. Typical laboratory studies of age differences in memory have made no effort to control the processes subjects use on materials. Thus older adults may choose to process experimental materials at less deep levels than the young and their poorer recall may reflect this shallow processing rather than any decline in memory processes per se. A test of this hypothesis is afforded by the orienting task methodology.

A pilot study in Walsh's laboratory replicated the Walsh and Jenkins (1973) study introducing age as a variable. Three groups of old subjects (60–70 years) were compared to three groups of young subjects (18–25 years). One group of each age performed an orienting task requiring meaningful processing; a second pair of groups performed an orienting task involving nonmeaningful processing; and the final groups listened to the materials with knowledge of the recall requirements without an orienting task. Contrary to prediction, old subjects were found not to remember as well as the young when the processes they used were equated with orienting tasks. The data from this preliminary investigation show the old were particularly poor at recall, as compared to the young, when meaningful processing was required. The recall differences between old and young were twice as large following meaningful tasks than after nonmeaningful ones, although both age groups showed better recall performance with meaningful orienting tasks. These findings suggest that older adults may be less able than the young to process at deep levels, or alternatively that the memory traces resulting from processing at deep levels are less durable for the old.

A study by Eysenck (1974) collaborates these findings. Old and young subjects were tested in free recall after performing one of four orienting tasks. Two meaningful processing tasks were used and required subjects to write meaningful adjectives and form an image of the words. Two nonmeaningful processing tasks required subjects to count the number of letters in the spelling and to write a word that rhymed. Eysenck found no difference in the recall of old and young in the nonmeaningful orienting task conditions. However, the old recalled significantly fewer words than the young when both groups had performed meaningful orienting tasks. These findings are suggested by Eysenck as support for a processing-deficit explanation of age differences in memory. Another investigation (White and Craik, in preparation) using the orienting task methodology, however, suggests that the observed age decrement in recall under meaningful processing conditions may be explained by retrieval rather than processing deficits.

White and Craik had old and young subjects perform four tasks on 64 words—each subject performed each of the four tasks on 16 words. Subjects determined whether the word was capitalized (the presentation was visual), whether it rhymed, what semantic category (animal, vegetable, mineral) the word belonged to or they tried to remember it for later recall. In free recall White and Craik found the same pattern of age differences reported in the above two experiments—the old show substantially poorer recall, as compared to the young, under conditions of meaningful processing.

White and Craik argue, however, that this finding may reflect age differences in retrieval rather than processing deficits in the old. They reason that the old may have processed the words to as deep a level as the young producing a memory trace of equivalent duration, but that the old are less able to retrieve the stored trace. They tested this hypothesis

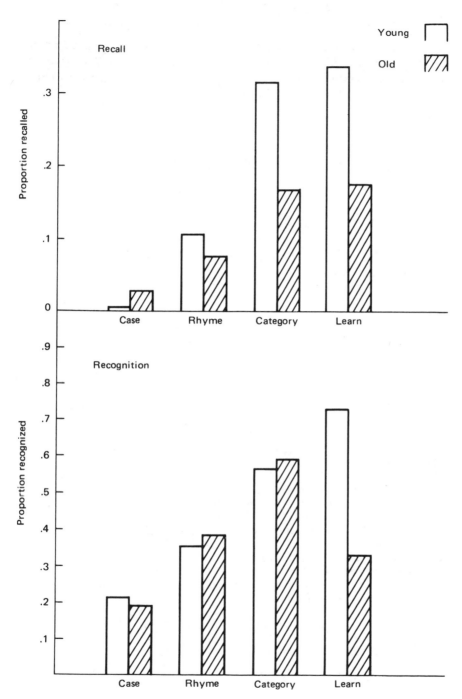

Figure 7.5. Proportion of words recalled and recognized following four different orienting task conditions. (From White and Craik, in preparation)

by measuring recognition memory following the orienting task and free recall procedures. Their findings are presented in Figure 7.5. When the retrieval step was minimized with recognition procedures the old subjects performed as well as the young, in all but the learning condition. This latter condition does not control the processes used by subjects and the finding of poorer recognition memory for the old is support for the idea that older adults do not, on their own, process laboratory tasks as deeply as the young. This pattern of recognition performance for young and old suggests two loci of explanation for age deficits in memory. First the improved performance of old subjects using tasks requiring meaningful processing suggest that some of the memory deficit of older adults is attributable to how deeply they process. With intentions only to learn, older adults apparently process at less deep levels. Second, the differences between recall and recognition performance for the young and old on the meaningful category classification task suggest that older adults are less able to retrieve memory traces even when durable traces have been built with deep levels of processing.

References

Abel, M. 1972. The visual trace in relation to aging. Unpublished doctoral dissertation. St. Louis, Mo.: Washington University.

Anders, T. R.; Fozard, J. L.; and Hillyquist, T. D. 1972. The effects of age upon retrieval from short-term memory. *Developmental Psychology* 6:214–217.

Atkinson, R. C., and Shiffrin, R. M. 1971. The control of short-term memory. *Scientific American* 224:82–89.

Atkinson, R. C., and Shiffrin, R. M. 1968. Human memory: A proposed system and its control processes. In *The psychology of learning and motivation: advances in research and theory*, Vol II., eds., K. W. Spence and J. T. Spence, pp. 89–195. New York: Academic Press.

Arenberg, D. 1965. Anticipation interval and age differences in verbal learning. *Journal of Abnormal Psychology* 70:419–425.

Averback, E., and Coriell, A. S. 1961. Short-term memory in vision. *Bell Systems Technical Journal* 40:309–328.

Baddeley, A. D. 1970. Estimating the short-term component in free recall. *British Journal of Psychology* 61:13–15.

Baddeley, A. D. 1966. Short-term memory for word sequences as a function of acoustic, semantic, and formal similarity. *Quarterly Journal of Experimental Psychology* 18:362–365.

Botwinick, J. 1973. *Aging and behavior.* New York: Springer Publishing Co., Inc.

Botwinick, J. and Storandt, M. 1974. *Memory related to age.* Springfield: C. C. Thomas.

Bromley, D. C. 1958. Some effects of age on short-term learning and remembering. *Journal of Gerontology* 13:398–406.

Broadbent, D. E. 1958. *Perception and communication.* New York: Pergamon Press.

Canestrari, Jr., R. E. 1968. Age changes in acquisition. In *Human aging and behavior,* ed. G. A. Talland, pp. 169–188. New York: Academic Press.

Canestrari, Jr., R. E. 1963. Paced and self-paced learning in young and elderly adults. *Journal of Gerontology* 18:165–168.

Craik, F. I. M. and Lockhart, R. S. 1972. Level of processing: a framework for memory research. *Journal of Verbal Learning and Verbal Behavior* 11:671–684.

Craik, F. I. M. 1971. Age differences in recognition memory. *Quarterly Journal of Experimental Psychology* 23:316–323.

Craik, F. I. M. 1968a. Short-term memory and the aging process. In *Human Aging and Behavior,* ed. G. A. Talland, pp. 131–168. New York: Academic Press.

Craik, F. I. M. 1962b. Two components in free recall. *Journal of Verbal Learning and Verbal Behavior* 7:996–1004.

Craik, F. I. M. and Masani, P. A. 1969. Age and intelligence differences in coding and retrieval of word lists. *British Journal of Psychology* 60:315–319.

Crannell, C. W. and Parrish, J. M. 1957. A comparison of immediate memory span for digits, letters, and words. *Journal of Psychology* 44:319–327.

Crowder, R. G. and Morton, J. 1969. Precategorical acoustic storage. *Perception and Psychophysics* 5:365–373.

Drachman, D. A. and Leavitt, J. 1972. Memory impairment in the aged: storage versus retrieval deficit. *Journal of Experimental Psychology* 93:302–308.

Eisdorfer, C.; Nowlin, J. and Wilkie, F. 1970. Improvement of learning in the aged by modification of autonomic nervous system activity. *Science* 170:1327–1329.

Eisdorfer, C. 1968. Arousal and performance: experiment in verbal learning and a tentative theory. In *Human aging and behavior,* ed. G. A. Talland, pp. 189–216. New York: Academic Press.

Eisdorfer, C. 1965. Verbal learning and response time in the aged. *Journal of Genetic Psychology* 107:15–22.

Erber, J. T. 1974. Age differences in recognition memory. *Journal of Gerontology* 29:177–181.

Eysenck, M. W. 1974. Age differences in incidental learning. *Developmental Psychology* 10:936–941.

Friedman, H. 1966. Memory organization in the aged. *Journal of Genetic Psychology* 109:3–8.

Froehling, S. 1974. Effects of propranolol on behavioral and physiological measures of elderly males. Unpublished doctoral dissertation. Duke University.

Gilbert, J. G. 1941. Memory loss in senescence. *Journal of Abnormal and Social Psychology* 36:73–86.

Haber, R. N. and Standing, L. 1970. Direct estimates of apparent duration of a flash. *Canadian Journal of Psychology* 24:216–229.

Haber, R. N. and Standing, L. G. 1969. Direct measures of short-term visual storage. *Quarterly Journal of Experimental Psychology* 21:43–54.

Hulicka, I. M. 1967. Age differences in retention as a function of interference. *Journal of Gerontology* 22:180–184.

Hulicka, I. M. and Grossman, J. L. 1967. Age-group comparisons for the use of mediators in paired-associate learning. *Journal of Gerontology* 22:46–51.

Hulicka, I. M. and Weiss, R. L. 1965. Age differences in retention as a function of learning. *Journal of Consulting Psychology* 29:125–129.

Hultsch, D. F. 1974. Hearing to learn in adulthood. *Journal of Gerontology* 29:302–308.

Hultsch, D. 1971. Adult age differences in free classification on free recall. *Developmental Psychology* 4:338–342.

Hultsch, D. 1969. Adult age differences in the organization of free recall. *Developmental Psychology* 1:673–678.

Hyde, T. S. and Jenkins, J. J. 1973. Recall for words as a functional of semantic, graphic, and syntactic orienting tasks. *Journal of Verbal Learning and Verbal Behavior* 12:471–480.

Hyde, T. S. and Jenkins, J. J. 1969. The differential effects of incidental tasks on the organization of recall of a list of highly associated words. *Journal of Experimental Psychology* 82:472–481.

Johnston, C. D. and Jenkins, J. J. 1971. Two more incidental tasks that differentially affect associative clustering in recall. *Journal of Experimental Psychology* 89:92–95.

Laurence, M. W. 1967a. Memory loss with age: a test of two strategies for its retardation. *Psychomomic Science* 9:209–210.

Laurence, M. W. 1967b. A developmental look at the usefulness of list categorization as an aid to free recall. *Canadian Journal of Psychology* 21:153–165.

Mandler, G. 1967. Organization and Memory. In *The psychology of learning and motivation. Advances in research and theory*, Vol. 1, eds. K. W. Spence and J. T. Spence, pp. 328–372. New York: Academic Press.

Melton, A. W. 1963. Implications of short-term memory for a general theory of memory. *Journal of Verbal Learning and Verbal Behavior* 2:1–21.

Miller, G. A. 1956. The magical number seven, plus or minus two: some limits on our capacity for processing information. *Psychological Review* 63:81–97.

Moenster, P. A. 1972. Learning and memory in relation to age. *Journal of Gerontology* 27:361–363.

Murdock, B. B. Jr. 1967. Recent developments in short-term memory. *British Journal of Psychology* 58:421–433.

Neisser, U. 1967. *Cognitive psychology*. New York: Appleton-Century-Crofts.

Powell, A. H. Jr.; Eisdorfer, C.; and Bogdonoff, M. D. 1964. Physiologic response patterns observed in a learning task. *Archives of General Psychiatry* 10:192–195.

Raymond, B. J. 1971. Free recall among the aged. *Psychological Reports* 29:1179–1182.

Schonfield, D. and Robertson, E. H. 1966. Memory storage and aging. *Canadian Journal of Psychology* 20:228–236.

Shmavonian, B. M. and Busse, E. W. 1963. The utilization of psychophysiological techniques in the study of the aged. In *Process of aging—social and psychological perspectives, eds.* R. H. Williams, C. Tibbets, and Wilma Donohue, pp. 235–258. New York: Atherton Press.

Schulman, A. I. 1971. Recognition memory for targets from a scanned word list. *British Journal of Psychology* 62:335–346.

Shiffrin, R. M. and Atkinson, R. C. 1967. Storage and retrieval processes in long-term memory. *Psychological Review* 76:179–193.

Shulman, H. G. 1970. Encoding and retention of semantic and phonemic information in short-term memory. *Journal of Verbal Learning and Verbal Behavior* 9:499–508.

Sperling, G. 1960. The information available in brief visual presentations. *Psychological Monographs: General and Applied* 74:(II)1–28.

Sternberg, S. 1966. High-speed scanning in human memory. *Science* 153:652–654.

Till, R. E. and Jenkins, J. J. 1973. The effects of cued orienting tasks on the free recall of words. *Journal of Verbal Learning and Verbal Behavior*.

Turvey, M. T. 1973. On peripheral and central processes in vision: inferences from an information-processing analysis of masking with patterned stimuli. *Psychological Review* 80:1–52.

Walsh, D. A. and Jenkins, J. J. 1973. Effects of orienting tasks on free recall in incidental learning: "difficulty," "effort," and "process" explanations. *Journal of Verbal Learning and Verbal Behavior* 12:481–488.

Watkins, J. 1974. A review of short-term memory. *Psychological Bulletin* 81:695–711.

Waugh, N. C. and Norman, D. A. 1965. Primary memory. *Psychological Review* 72:89–104.

White, S. and Craik, F. I. M. Effects of orienting task on recall and recognition-memory of the aged. In *Handbook of aging*, J. E. Birren. New York: Van Nostrand, in press.

Wimer, R. E. and Wigdor, B. T. 1958. Age differences in retention of learning. *Journal of Gerontology* 13:291–295.

Yerkes, R. M. and Dodson, J. D. 1908. The relation of strength of stimulus to rapidity of habit formation. *Journal of Comparative Neurological Psychology* 18:459–482.

8

Aging, Brain Function, and Behavior

JAMES WALKER · CHRISTOPHER HERTZOG

This chapter discusses how the relationship between brain function and behavior may be affected by the aging process. The goal of scientists interested in this field of inquiry is first to know how brain function organizes behavior in general. Only then can they know how aging alters the structure and function of the brain and how these alterations will affect the observable behavior of an organism.

At this time no definitive theories can be advanced to explain how aging affects the brain and behavior. The scientific discipline which studies brain-behavior relationships, physiological psychology, is still in its infancy in that the function of the brain and its relationship to behavior is still poorly understood. However, even the work done on the relationship between the brain and behavior is extensive when compared with the amount of work done on how aging affects this relationship.

A scientific approach to this question of aging, brain function, and behavior involves the experimental manipulation of behavior and brain function in organisms of different ages. To date, a mere handful of behavioral studies involving the aging process have combined experimental manipulation of the brain with behavioral observations in order to examine patterns of change or stability in the brain-behavior relationship during advancing age. Thus, in order to discuss brain-behavior relationships under the rubric of aging, we are forced either to extrapolate brain status from the behavioral patterns of aged organisms, based upon the available knowledge of brain-behavior relationships in young adult organisms, or to estimate behavioral changes from brain changes reported in the biological literature on aging. Either of these approaches is at best a poor substitute for the direct experimental studies which are desperately needed in this field.

Obviously, an experimental approach to this topic requires that much of the research be carried out with animals. Scientists interested in the role of a certain region of the brain in behavior will usually attempt to manipulate the function of that region by one of several available methods. They then observe the behavioral changes caused by such manipulation. They might interfere with brain function by using a chemical agent to disrupt it, or they might surgically remove an area, thus creating a permanent brain lesion. Whatever the method used, such experiments must generally be carried out in animals, and the implications for humans inferred.

The use of animals has one major advantage aside from the ethical issue: it is much easier to control for the effect of variables the experimenter is not interested in studying. For example, if the experimenter is not interested in motivation, all he need do to ensure that his animals will be equally motivated to perform on a task where the reward is a pellet of food is to deprive the animals of a percentage of their normal food supply. Similarly, the experimenter can control for the effects of different genetic make-up by purchasing inbred animals known to have a similar genetic background. Such control of variables peripheral to the interest of the investigator is difficult to achieve in human studies.

One major drawback in using animals as experimental subjects is that the results obtained relating brain function to behavior in animals may not accurately reflect the results that would be obtained in an experiment with human subjects. This is a particular problem when the animals being studied are relatively far down the evolutionary scale—rodents, for example. In a study of aging, we are forced to assume that the aging process is similar in all mammalian species if we wish to generalize from animal studies to human aging. The short life span of lower mammals (rats usually do not live longer than three years) makes them good candidates for aging studies. It is generally assumed that, within the limits implicit in evolutionary change, results obtained from animal studies are generalizable to human brain-behavior relationships; however, it is useful to remember that this is an assumption and not a proven fact.

As stated above, research in this area is typically limited to biological studies of the brain with no behavioral measurement, or to animal behavior studies with no investigation of concomitant brain function. Thus, the ways in which aging affects the brain-behavior relationship are largely unknown, a fact which makes a review of brain function and aging difficult. Therefore, this chapter will concentrate on three major topics of interest: (1) a review of the information available on age changes in animal behavior; (2) a discussion of the implications of such research for the status of the brain-behavior relationship during aging, in light of the evidence available on age changes in the brain; and (3) a discussion of psychological stress, an example in which the research on age changes in animal-behavior relationships may have direct impact upon theories of how aging in humans affects their behavior.

Animal Behavior and Aging

In general, the experiments which have examined the effects of aging upon the behavior of animals have found some age-related decrements in a wide range of behaviors, although the magnitude of these deficits is not overwhelming. (See Jakubczak, 1973, for a comprehensive review.) Older animals tend to be less active than younger animals, whether they are engaged in exploratory activity (Goodrick, 1965, 1971) or exercising on a running wheel (Jakubczak, 1967b, 1970). Older animals, however, tend a habituate more quickly to a novel environment than younger animals, as indicated by the amount of exploratory activity (Parsons et al., 1973). Nevertheless, the decline in exploratory activity can be overestimated if the older animals are compared to very young animals, since there is a decline in exploratory activity and an increase in habituation from birth to maturity (Williams et al., 1966).

In terms of drive-related behaviors, such as feeding and sex, older animals also seem to undergo decremental changes. Food and water deprivation are less effective in increasing eating and drinking in old rats (Jakubczak, 1969; Goodrick, 1969). Amphetamine inhibits feeding more easily in old rats than in young rats (Farner, 1961). In reviewing these experiments, Jakubczak (1973) stated that with increasing age, the consumption of food and water are more difficult to activate and easier to inhibit.

Sexual behavior in the male rat is impaired with advancing age; the aged male engages in normal precopulatory approach behavior, mounts the female normally, but takes longer to achieve his first ejaculation.[1] However, once the older rat achieves his first ejaculation of sperm, subsequent intercourse is facilitated and the old rat achieves as many ejaculations as young rats (Larsson, 1963). Old male guinea pigs exhibit a normal level of precopulatory arousal but lower intromission (insertion

---

1. Female sexual behavior has not been studied in old age in subhuman mammals.

of penis) and ejaculation scores (Jakubczak, 1964). These changes occurred without any detectable pathological changes in the male gonads. Such deficits in male sexual behavior may be related to a reduced level of sensory-produced arousal during intercourse, since Larsson and Essberg (1962) found that nonspecific arousal (handling in between sexual acts) improved the performance of aged male rats. In review of the evidence regarding male sexual behavior and aging, Jakubczak (1967b) suggested that there may be age-related changes in the brain mechanisms which control the timing of sexual arousal leading to ejaculation. He also emphasized that gonadal dysfunction may play a significant role in the decline in sexual behavior in senescent male animals, but that the decrement in sexual behavior appears prior to any change in the gonads, so that gonadal changes probably augment rather than initiate the decrement.

A large number of studies have examined learning and memory in older animals. Changes in learning ability with age are not always detected in studies using animal subjects. Experiments which utilize relatively simple tasks have usually found no age decrement in performance at all. An excellent example is the study by Kay and Sime (1962). These investigators taught male rats to discriminate between a circle and a triangle for food reward. The animals learned to approach the geometric design that had been designated correct. After a series of trials, the other, heretofore incorrect, figure was designated as the correct design. Kay and Sime found that both young and old male rats had difficulty with the discrimination task in the beginning and improved at the same rate. There was no evidence that the older group was in any way inferior to the younger group (see Figure 8.1).

Several other studies have failed to find age-related deficits on a simple discrimination task (Dye, 1969; Lisensby, 1968), on a slightly more complex discrimination task (Oldfield-Box, 1969), or on a simple maze learning task (Botwinick et al., 1962).

Goodrick has shown, however, that as the complexity of the maze task to be learned increases, the aged animal begins to show a learning deficit. In an initial study, Goodrick (1968) found that older rats were inferior to "young-mature" rats in learning a 14-choice maze for a milk and sucrose reward. The poorer performance of the old group as a whole was in large part due to the fact that several of the older rats had failed to learn the maze to criterion after 40 trial runs in the maze. Goodrick, in examining the performance of these "senescent slow learners," found that they tended to perseverate errors, that is, they continued to enter specific, incorrect cul-de-sacs in the maze on every trial. Subsequent to his initial testing, he also found that with drastically increased numbers of learning trials (112 trials per day instead of the normal 4 trials per day) he was able to bring the senescent slow learners to the criterion of learning. These results suggested to Goodrick that the slow learning in the aged group might be due to some kind of age-related, short-term memory deficit, since increased daily practice enabled the slow learners finally to learn the maze. He found no evidence for a long-term retention deficit in the older animals, given an equivalent level of original learning.

Goodrick (1972) replicated and extended the findings of his earlier study by directly comparing old and young animals on a straight alley, T-maze, 4-choice maze, and 14-choice maze. There were no age differences whatsoever in learning the straight alley maze or the simple T-maze. On the 4-choice problem, a slight but noticeable age difference was detected; the older animals made more errors on the first trial of a new series, but learned the maze as well as young rats by the end of the series. Goodrick used four different 4-choice mazes to begin each new series of tests. Apparently, the change of maze which occurred at the beginning of each new series had interfered more with the performance of the older ani-

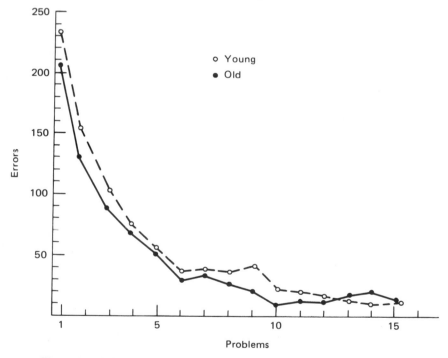

Figure 8.1. Mean errors in learning each pair of problems to criterion. No age differences are seen in the performance of this simple visual discrimination task; old rats performed slightly better during most of the task. (Kay and Sime, 1962. Used by permission.)

mals. Still, this initial slowness following the switching of mazes did not represent a major learning deficit.

Goodrick found a more substantial learning deficit in the performance of the aged animals on the 14-choice T-maze. Old and young rats were tested on the maze for 20 trials on the first day, and on 1 trial a day for the following 20 days. While the animals did not differ on the initial trials of the first day, by the last five trials (16–20), the young-mature rats made fewer errors and had lower time scores than the aged rats. The older made more perseverate errors in the subsequent trials, as in Goodrick's earlier study. The 14-choice T-maze represented a sufficient level of complexity to demonstrate a learning deficit in the senescent rats.

Another type of learning task that has been used to test old and young animals is an avoidance task, a behavioral paradigm in which the animals must perform some kind of task in order to avoid being shocked. Doty (1966a, b) demonstrated that there is an age difference in learning the avoidance response if the task is relatively difficult. In two separate studies she reported that rats of different age groups could all learn a discriminated avoidance (responding to an appropriate geometric design to avoid shock), but that the senescent animals were inferior to all but the youngest (25–30 days old) in the acquisition of the discriminated avoidance when a delay was introduced into the paradigm. All the age groups of rats found the delayed task more difficult than the simple discrimination task, but the performance of the senescent rats dropped off more sharply than that of the other groups.

This finding seems closely akin to the results of Goodrick on maze complexity, since the more complicated avoidance task produced an age deficit, when the simpler task did not. The mechanisms involved do not seem to be entirely the same, however, since massed practice aided Goodrick's aged rats to acquire the maze learning (Goodrick, 1968), but the massing of trials interfered with the performance of Doty's rats on the avoidance task (Doty, 1966a). Doty's finding that frequent trials inhibited avoidance learning may be related to the heightened arousal or emotionality of animals being shocked. While recognizing that a performance variable, such as differential motivation produced by electric shock, might account for age differences, Doty preferred to interpret the data as suggesting an "immediate memory" deficit in the older animals which is manifested in the delayed condition.

Ray and Barrett (1973) explored the possibility that old rats could actually learn an avoidance task, but that some other variable prevented them from translating their learning into performance. They developed a Y-maze avoidance problem, where the animal had to learn when and where to run to avoid the shock. (The animals had to learn to run to the correct arm of the maze after an appropriate delay period.) In this task, the older animals of two different rat strains were significantly inferior to the younger animals in learning the avoidance task, but they made close to the same number of correct discriminations as to which arm of the Y-maze to enter. In other words, they had learned where to run, but had not responded at the appropriate time (Figure 8.2). Ray and Barrett interpreted these results as demonstrating that there is no memory retrieval problem or loss of learning in the aged rats—there was only a decline in performance. However, this is not the only possible interpretation. It is conceivable that the older animals were able to learn a simple Y-maze quite adequately, as in Goodrick's studies, so that they knew which arm was safe from shock, but never learned the timing of the escape from shock in the start box. They may have learned one aspect of the task but not the other, rather than knowing the task but not being able to perform it as well.

Both Ray and Barrett (1973) and Doty (1966b) found that the deficit of the older animals on the avoidance task could be ameliorated by

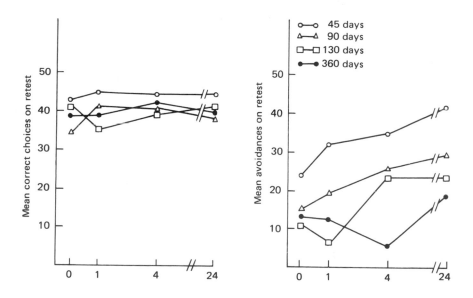

Figure 8.2. Data from avoidance task of Ray and Barrett, run with animals of different ages (45, 90, 130, 360 days). Results show animals of each age group learned which arm to choose to avoid shock (left graph), but that there were age differences in the ability to wait for the appropriate amount of time before entering the arm, resulting in differences in correct avoidances (right graph). (From Ray and Barrett, 1973)

doses of amphetamine, with Ray and Barrett suggesting that amphetamine-induced improvement was due to a reduction in "shock-induced behavioral suppression" or the tendency of the animal to freeze upon being introduced into the shock-eliciting arena. These findings may support some sort of differential arousal as related to the performance deficit (see Woodruff, Chapter 9 on the issue of overarousal in human studies on aging), but other interpretations are possible. Whether or not Ray and Barrett have enough supporting evidence to lend weight to their performance-deficit hypothesis, their approach (examining the data to determine whether a nonlearning variable could be responsible for "learning deficit") is an important one which we will discuss in greater detail below.

Learning and memory studies done with primates are needed in order to establish whether deficits reported for rodent samples can be replicated with a mammalian species phylogenetically closer to human beings. Only two reliable studies have been executed, both from the same laboratory. Medin (1969) tested old and middle-aged rhesus monkeys on a form perception and pattern reproduction task in a test apparatus commonly used in primate learning experiments. Patterns of on and off lights in a 4' x 4' matrix of lighted cells were presented to the monkeys, and they were required to punch the light panels which had been lit (thereby reproducing the panels) after various intervals of delay. Medin found that old monkeys performed as well or better than the middle-aged monkeys on the short delay intervals, but were inferior to middle-aged animals on the long delays. Medin dismissed the possibility that older monkeys were less motivated by reporting that the older monkeys would work as hard as the younger monkeys for a food reward in a lever-pulling task.

Medin et al. (1973) utilized a slightly different visual discrimination task to test learning in old and middle-aged rhesus monkeys. The monkeys were presented with 20 pairs of complex visual stimuli constructed on checkboard-like black and white squares four times a day for four days of testing. Within each pair of designs, one design was designated correct, so that the monkey would receive a food reward if he chose it. Several different correct and incorrect designs were used in each block of 20 pairs. On the first day of testing the two age groups were comparable in performance, but on subsequent test days the old monkeys displayed substantially poorer learning performance, leading the investigators to report that the older monkeys displayed much more forgetting than did middle-aged monkeys. These findings suggest that a deficit on learning and memory tasks may be generalized across species if a delay factor or other aspect of higher complexity is present in the task.

Thus, preliminary evidence in animal studies suggests that there may be behavioral changes during the aging process, but that they are not gross, universally observable changes. Some slowing of activity and of male sexual behavior has been observed; in addition, subtle changes in the motivational mechanisms involved in consummatory behavior have been noted. Learning and memory deficits have been reported in several studies, but only with tasks of relative complexity. Such deficits are not a total inability to learn, but a slower rate of learning which can be ameliorated under certain conditions.

The fact that the behavioral changes during aging are not of a staggering magnitude lends further importance to the question of whether these behavioral changes are due to the process of aging or are merely manifestations of other factors. This question cannot yet be adequately answered, but there is some evidence that confounding variables exist which can mislead an investigator who does not control for them. One such variable, differential levels of arousal in young and old animals, was addressed by Ray and Barrett (1973), as discussed above. Two possible confounding variables that have not been adequately controlled for by behavioral scientists interested in aging are disease and environment.

An excellent example of how an animal's performance can be disrupted by age-related pathology rather than normal age change was given by Fletcher and Mowbray (1962). A 34-year-old rhesus monkey donated to the Primate Laboratory at the University of Wisconsin was tested on 10 simple object discrimination problems. He exhibited a severe deficit accentuated by a physical handicap on these simple tasks. The animal died shortly afterwards, indicating that he probably had been experiencing some disease process at the time of testing, a possibility that could account for the deficits. The possibility that disease, including diseases directly related to growing old, may be responsible for behavioral differences between different age groups has rarely been carefully monitored. Few experimenters have reported the physical health of their animals, or even performed post-mortem autopsies to screen out those animals suffering from gross pathologies. (For a discussion of age-related pathology versus normal aging, see Chapter 11.)

Another potentially important intervening variable which could account for performance deficits in older animals is the environment in which they live. It is well known that brain changes can be induced in neonatal rodents by environmental manipulation. Several studies (see Rosenzweig et al. 1970 for a review) have shown that exposing a neonatal rat to a complex, stimulating environment causes structural and biochemical changes in the brain. These changes include changes in cerebral dimensions, increased enzyme production, increased glial proliferation, and the like. Greenough et al. (1973), and Greenough and Volkman (1973) have reported an increase in dendritic branching, and by inference an increase in the number of synapses, in certain cortical regions after exposure to an enriched environment. Conversely, Fifkova (1968) and Riesen (1966) have reported studies in which environmental deprivation, such as confinement to a totally dark cage, during development leads to substandard brain development.

Until recently, it was felt that such environmental manipulation was only effective in producing alterations in the brains of very young animals. However, Riege (1971) reported that the brains of adult rats (1 year old) were also susceptible to environmental manipulation. The effect was specific to certain brain regions; increased environmental complexity induced a proliferative response in the cortical regions, including the hippocampus, but not in the subcortical regions of the diencephalon, brain stem, and cerebellum (see Figure 8.3). These findings were extended by Cummins et al. (1973), who showed that the proliferative response of the brain to an enriched environment could still be observed in animals approaching senescence (over 600 days old). They found that the overall brain weight increased in those animals exposed to enriched environments, and that this increase was due to an increase in forebrain weight (primarily including cortex and structures such as the septum and hippocompus), thus confirming the findings of Riege (1971).

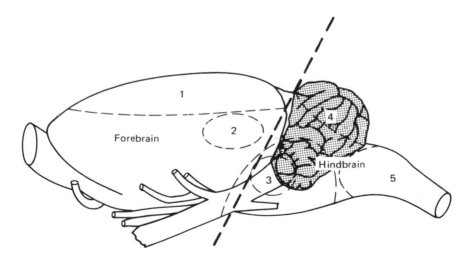

Figure 8.3. Diagram of rat brain. Changes in cerebral dimensions and in brain anatomy and chemistry are often seen in the forebrain following environmental enrichment, but not in the hindbrain. Numbers indicate regions explored by Riege. He found enriched environment responses in cortex (1) and hippocampus (2), but not in the diencephalon (3), cerebellum (4), or brain stem (5).

Both Riege (1971) and Cummins et al. (1973) found that exposure to enriched environments in adult rats led to improvements in learning performance. Cummins and coworkers provided an additional insight into the process of brain plasticity by showing that those animals which had been kept in an isolated home-cage environment performed more poorly than enriched environment animals on their learning task, but that exposure to the task itself had triggered a proliferative response in the brains of the isolated animals. This was discovered by comparing the brain weights of animals which had been isolated and then tested on the learning tasks with the brain weights of isolated animals which had not been tested. The implication of this finding is that the brains of isolated animals maintained the ability to respond in a plastic manner despite two years of environmental isolation.

These investigations have important implications for behavioral research with aged animals. The findings reported above as age changes may not be due to aging alone, but also to the cumulative effects of the animals' isolation in the relatively deprived environment, that is, standard laboratory housing. This possibility was underscored by Doty (1972), who also found that enriched environment caging resulted in an improvement in learning performance in aged rats. She took 300-day-old rats and randomly assigned them to enriched or normal environments for one year. Animals in the enriched environment were significantly better at learning a response-reversal task and a passive avoidance task.

The unfortunate fact is that until further experimental studies which repeat previously used paradigms are performed on animals housed in enriched environments, and on animals whose health is properly monitored, we will be unable to state precisely the nature of the behavioral changes which accompany aging.

An Experimental Study

One study which has utilized experimental manipulation of the brain to examine behavioral changes in animals of different age groups is the work of Dru et al. (1975b). They examined age changes in rats' ability to recover performance in a visual discrimination task after an area of the brain known to be crucial for that task, the primary visual cortex, was removed.

The phenomenon of a recovery of function following brain damage is quite complex. In general, a recovery of behavioral function is *most* likely: (1) if damage is sustained to the neocortex, rather than subcortical structures, (2) if the brain lesions are executed in stages, rather than all at once, (3) if there are certain kinds of nonspecific stimulation and activity following the operation (for a review, see Dru et al., 1975c). Other factors are also involved. A recovery of behavioral function by noncortical regions is not usually seen after total destruction or complete removal of these brain areas. However, an operation which merely severs the neural connections between these regions, but leaves the brain cells themselves undamaged, leaves the brain in a state from which it can recover. Axons, the "electrical wiring" of the brain which connects brain cells with each other, tend to group in large bundles, or tracts, analogous to an electrical cord which contains many small copper wires within it. Severing the tracts which come from a functionally distinct brain nucleus deprives the rest of the brain of communications from that nucleus, but apparently does not prevent some kind of repair or reorganization process to occur which restores the behavioral capacity of the organism. For example, Dawson et al. (1973) and Levere and Weiss (1973) were unable to observe a recovery of function following serial removal of the hippocampus, but Greene et al. (1972) found a recovery of function in the rat when the main input/output fiber tract of the hippocampus, the fornix, was transected in two stages.

Another salient variable in recovery of function is the age of the animal. Lesions performed on neonatal animals are likely to produce less debilitation than lesions in adult animals. A likely explanation is that a developing brain can undergo more structural reorganization than a fully developed brain. Dru's work dealt with the other end of the age continuum—senescence. Is there a decreased ability of the aged animal to recover function after a brain lesion?

Dru et al. (1975a) trained rats to discriminate horizontal bars from vertical bars and required them to perform a discrimination avoidance task, choosing the appropriate stimulus in order to avoid shock. As one might expect from our previous discussion of avoidance learning, the older animals were fully capable of learning this simple avoidance task— they were even slightly better at it than mature rats.

After the animals had learned the task to criterion, they received ablation lesions on one side of their visual cortices (Krieg's area) and were then placed in various environments for an interoperative period of eleven days, after which the other half of the visual cortices was removed. One quarter of the rats from each age group were randomly assigned to the following interoperative environments: (1) total darkness for the interoperative period; (2) cages with diffuse light for four hours a day each day and total darkness the rest of the day; (3) a patterned visual environment containing horizontal bars, stripes, and triangles through which the animals were passively transported (see Figure 8.4) for four hours a day each day, with the rest of the day spent in darkness; and (4) access to the same patterned environment described above for four hours, but with no restrictions on the animals' ability to move around. These various environmental treatments were inspired by the work of Held and coworkers (see Held and Hein, 1963), who demonstrated that, in normal neonatal rats, normal visual development was dependent upon unrestricted movement through a visual field, some kind of visuo-motor integration being crucial to normal perceptual development.

The results of Dru et al. with the mature animals were consistent with the previous literature. All animals who had been placed in darkness, diffuse light cages, or passively transported through the patterned environment failed to relearn the task. Only those animals allowed free movement in the patterned environment recovered the avoidance task. Apparently, as in the normally developing brain, voluntary coordination between the visual system and the motor system are necessary for the neural reorganization needed to recover the behavioral function.

Figure 8.4. Rat being passively transported through patterned visual environment (condition 3 in text). Only those rats allowed unrestricted movement in this environment recovered the ability to discriminate between geometrical figures following lesion of the visual cortex.

The crucial aspect of the experiment is the effect of the lesions on the aged animals. The older group performed almost identically to the mature group, in that the older animals with free movement in the patterned environment recovered the task. They relearned the task significantly more slowly than did the younger animals, yet they did recover the function. These results strongly suggest that the aged brain has not declined to the point where it cannot undergo functional reorganization following injury. Further, the age decrement noted in the speed of recovery may be a function of a greater amount of time in the deprived environment of standard laboratory housing before the experiment, rather than a function of aging itself. These results imply that a generalized decremental view of brain status with age is inaccurate.

Of course, in order to understand what a slightly impaired ability to recover from brain damage in old age means we need to know the mechanisms which make recovery of function possible, and these mechanisms are not well understood. There is a reasonable amount of evidence available to suggest that axonal sprouting, the growth of new axons, may mediate the recovery (Guth and Windle, 1973). Selective destruction of fiber input to several brain regions has been shown to cause collateral axon sprouting and, in some cases, a reinnervation of synaptic sites left vacant by those axons which had been destroyed (Raisman, 1969; Lynch et al., 1973). However, no studies have attempted directly to observe axonal sprouting during a recovery-of-function study. If synaptic reorganization is the basis for recovery of function, then the study of Dru et al. implies that the aged brain is capable of axonal sprouting and synaptic reorganization.

Implications of Behavioral and Biological Studies

If the changes seen in the behavior of older animals are an accurate reflection of the effects of aging (certainly a big "if"), what are the implications of the behavioral experiments done on aged animals for the status of brain function and the brain-behavior relationship during senescence? The major implication seems to be that the brain does not normally undergo gross, widespread deterioration, since the behavioral changes seen in senescence are subtle and tend to involve slight impairments in function. The most general effect of aging seems to be a behavioral slowing in exploratory behavior. Such an age-related change is not likely to be due to gross deterioration of the central nervous systems (CNS). In those human beings who have had gross physical deterioration of the brain as in organic disease, the behavioral deficits are far more acute.

Another implication seems to be that different brain regions and different brain functions age at different rates. To explain the rationale for this statement, we must discuss some aspects of brain function and behavior.

In terms of the organization of behavior, certain neural subsystems seem to be crucial to the execution of certain behaviors. The limbic system is shown in Figure 8.5 and for the purposes of this discussion will include: (1) the phylogenetically old regions of the forebrain, the hippocampus cingulate cortex, septum, amygdala; (2) the hypothalamus; and (3) certain portion of the midbrain tegmentum (for a discussion of limbic system anatomy, see Nauta, 1972). The limbic system seems to be particularly important in the organization of basic and complex behaviors (Adey and Tokizane, 1967). One of the most important connections between limbic brain areas is the medial forebrain bundle (MFB), which runs from the base of the frontal cortex through the lateral hypothalamus into the midbrain area and receives axonal input from most major limbic system structures. Lesions of the MFB have been shown to cause specific

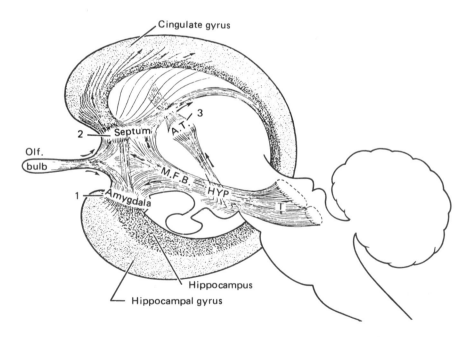

Figure 8.5. The limbic system comprises the limbic cortex and structures of the brainstem with which it has primary connections. The diagram shows the ring of limbic cortex in light and dark stipple and focuses on three pathways (1, 2 and 3) that link three main subdivisions of the limbic system. *Abbreviations:* A.T., anterior thalamic nuclei; HYP, hypothalamus; M.F.B., medial forebrain bundle; OLF, olfactory; T, tegmentum. (Adapted from McClean, 1958, 1967)

behavioral impairments. MFB lesions at the level of the lateral hypothalamus produce disruption of consummatory behaviors; male animals
with MFB lesions fail to copulate normally because of a difficulty in
initiating the sexual act, will not eat normally (aphagia) and do not drink
normally (adipsia) (Teitelbaum and Epstein, 1962; Paxinos and Bindra,
1973). While not all fiber connections crucial to these basic kinds of behavior traverse the MFB, it is probably the single most important group
of connections for these behaviors.

Damage to the MFB as a whole during aging seems highly unlikely.
The kind of decrement seen in male sexual behavior with MFB lesions
involves the initiation of copulation (Cagguila et al., 1973). Male animals
with MFB damage are as behaviorally aroused as normal males, but do
not mount the females. Old males, on the other hand, approach and
mount females normally but take longer to achieve ejaculation. MFB-
lesioned animals show no deficit in time to ejaculation if they do manage
to achieve intromission. Age changes in male sexual behavior do not
seem to be due to age changes in the function of the MFB as a whole.

Aging may, however, affect certain portions of the MFB and not
others. Two of the main transmitter substances (chemicals which are
responsible for the transmission of nerve impulses across synapses) utilized
by nerve cells in the MFB are acetylcholine (ACH) and norepinephrine
(NE). There is some evidence that a system of neurons involving the
MFB, which uses ACH as a transmitter, may be involved in regulating

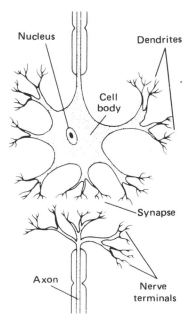

Figure 8.6. A representative nerve cell.

drinking behavior, while a system of neurons whose axons traverse the MFB and are crucial to feeding behavior probably use NE as a transmitter (Grossman, 1962). Since no age differences have been found in drinking behavior, and some age differences have been found in feeding behavior, it is possible that aging affects the NE system within the MFB and not the ACH system. Further, Liebowitz (1973) has evidence which suggests that NE can inhibit or excite feeding behavior depending upon the type of NE synapse involved, that is, the type of receptor present in the postsynaptic region. Since feeding behavior is easier to inhibit, and harder to facilitate, in old age, it is also possible that the different elements of the NE system are affected differentially by the aging process.

Preliminary neurobiological investigations have hinted that there may be changes in the efficiency of norepinephrine synapses in the hypothalamic-MFB region. Finch (1973) has reported a slowed turnover of tyrosine, an amino acid which is made into NE in the hypothalamus of aged mice. Bondareff (1973) has reported changes in the extracellular space in the brains of aged rats which may have effects on the reuptake of transmitter substances after they have been released. Reuptake is felt to be more important for synapses using catecholamines such as norepinephrine than for synapses mediated by acetylcholine. Obviously, such evidence is far from conclusive and more intensive study of changes in neurotransmitter function in the brain, and in the MFB region in particular, is needed.

Naturally, our discussion on norepinephrine synapses in the MFB needs to be labelled for what it is—speculative. It may be completely inaccurate, especially since it is based on findings in behavioral aging and brain function which have not been extensively replicated and accepted as hard scientific fact. The major value of such speculation is that it illustrates the concept of *differential aging*.

Differential aging implies that the process of aging may affect different physical and chemical systems of the organism in different ways. We know, for example, that the liver and the heart show different patterns of aging, probably because of the different types of cells which make up each organ. Differences in the effects of aging may also exist within the brain. We know that, in the early stages of development, certain brain areas mature more rapidly than others, and certain kinds of brain cells migrate from their place of origin to their final locations before other types of brain cells are formed. There is no reason to think that such distinctions may not carry over into the final stages of development as well.

At this time, there is little agreement as to which neural systems may be involved in learning and memory, or even if any area of the brain is more important than any other for learning (John, 1972); thus it is much more difficult to discuss the implications of the behavioral changes seen in older animals during the acquisition and retention of a task for the status of the brain-behavior relationship with age. Two brain regions which have been most often discussed and investigated as being involved in mediating the delayed learning tasks (which seem particularly difficult for older animals) are the prefrontal cortex (and its associated thalamic nucleus, the dorsomedial thalamic nucleus) and the hippocampus (including other temporal lobe cortex regions functionally associated with the hippocampus). Age-related changes in the ability to perform on a delayed response task, as in the studies of Medin and coworkers, may involve age changes in these areas. In the human clinical literature, damage to the hippocampal gyrus and the hippocampus results in memory impairments (Milner, 1970). However, experimental studies on animals have not supported the notion of the hippocampus as a "memory machine," even though it may be crucial to the learning and remembering of certain tasks (Douglas, 1967; Drachman and Ommaya, 1964; Gaffan, 1974). Lesions in the dorsolateral prefrontal cortex impaired delayed responding in monkeys (Warren and Akert, 1964).[2]

To date, only one study has examined age changes in the hippocampus, and none has examined age changes in the prefrontal cortex (other than studies of cell loss and lipofuscin accumulation; see below). Hasan and Glees (1973) prepared hippocampal tissue from rats for electron miscroscope examination. They discovered a fairly complete loss of axosomatic synapses (synapses terminating on the cell bodies) on the hippocampal pyramidal cells, and substantial loss of axodendritic synapses (synapses terminating on the dendritic tree of the pyramidal cells). These synaptic changes in the hippocampus should have far-reaching effects on its ability to function normally.

The preliminary work of electrophysiologists studying the responses of the aged hippocampus to stimulation point to the importance of the investigation of changes in synaptic events during aging (Cameron, personal communication). The axosomatic synapses, reported by Hasan and Glees (1973) to be greatly reduced in number during aging, are known to inhibit the pyramidal cells from "firing" (sending an impulse down the axon to communicate with other nerve cells). Cameron has found that the pyramidal cells of aged rats seem to be largely released from inhibi-

---

2. It is impossible to discuss this complex and sometimes controversial area of brain research fully in the limited space available. A more detailed description of the research is available in most physiological psychology textbooks.

tory influences, as evidenced by a substantial increase in their firing frequency. Other aspects of hippocampal activity, too complicated to be discussed here also change with age. These changes in hippocampal activity can be expected to alter the efficacy of hippocampus in the aged animal.

The studies of Hasan and Glees (1973) and Cameron et al. are significant aside from their potential importance for the status of the hippocampus in senescence, because they represent experiments examining the integrity of synaptic connections with age. In spite of the importance of synaptic events in brain function, few studies in aging have examined the aging synapse. If we are to relate research on the aging brain to studies with normal animals, a greater emphasis on the synaptic activity of specific brain regions is needed. Unfortunately, the preponderance of the remaining neurobiological studies on the aging brain is of little help in indicating what kinds of behavioral changes might accompany age changes in the brain. Most of the studies in this area have examined the issue of cell loss in the brain with advancing age, or the accumulation of the so-called "aging pigment," lipofuscin, in brain cells. As far as cell loss is concerned, it is still a matter of debate whether significant cell loss occurs in the absence of cardiovascular disease or other brain pathology (Tomasch, 1971; Howard, 1973). The severe cell loss and other neural degeneration that accompanies certain CNS diseases and acute brain arteriosclerosis are known to have behavioral concomitants—senile psychoses and dementia. However, it is not easy to predict what kinds of behavioral changes, if any, would accompany a 10 percent to 15 percent loss of cortical neurons, a figure often estimated as average for the aging brain (Brody, 1973). The physiological and behavioral significance of brain lipofuscin accumulation remains a mystery.

Of the remaining neurobiological studies, the most significant may be those which examine age changes in the hypothalamus as they relate to alterations in hypothalamic control of endocrine function. One of the most important functions of the hypothalamus, particularly the medial portions of the hypothalamus which lie above the pituitary gland, is the regulation of the endocrine glands in the body. This regulation is accomplished by the hypothalamic production of "releasing factors," hormones which regulate the release of the major hormones of the body.

Age changes in the hypothalamus could be expected to have profound effects on many hormonal systems. The possibility of age changes in the function of the pituitary-adrenal system is of particular interest to behavioral scientists since adrenocorticotropic hormone (ACTH), produced by the pituitary, and the adrenal hormones, especially the cortical steroids (corticosterone, cortisol, etc.), are known to have effects on behavior. For example, ACTH (DeWied, 1974) and corticosterone (Endroczi, 1972) are known to facilitate the acquisition of avoidance learning in rats.

The study by Finch (1973) which showed a slowed turnover of tyrosine (converted into NE in the brain) is of particular relevance in the discussion of hypothalamic regulation of the pituitary-adrenal system in senescence, since NE is believed to be involved in the hypothalamic mechanisms which regulate ACTH (Ganong, 1974; Scapagini, 1974). According to these authors, NE synapses in the medial hypothalamus are involved in the inhibition of ACTH secretion. A decline in the efficacy of NE synapses in the hypothalamus could be expected to alter ACTH secretion.

Other elements of the system controlling ACTH secretion have been found to change with age. Corticosterone is known to enter the brain and be selectively taken up by cells involved in monitoring blood corticosterone levels in order to regulate ACTH synthesis. The feedback of hormones like corticosterone to the brain is a common feature of all the hormones of the organism, for this feedback information enables the brain to maintain endocrine secretion at the proper level. McEwen (1969) has reported that corticosterone receptors are present in the hippocampus, septum, amygdala, and hypothalamus of rats with the highest concentration in the hippocampus. Latham (1974) investigated the hippocampal corticosterone receptors in mice and found that the number of cystoplasmic receptor proteins which bind corticosterone declined with age in the hippocampus. Latham's findings tend to support the view of Dilman (1971) that hypothalamic threshold of response to feedback control via circulating hormones increases with age, making the hypothalamus less responsive to hormonal feedback.

These changes in feedback sensitivity would probably affect hormonal output. Everitt (1973) has suggested that decreased sensitivity to hypothalamic feedback may primarily affect the suppression of further hormone secretion, causing an overproduction of hormones, including ACTH and the adrenal steroids. According to Everitt, such an overproduction of certain hormones (the adrenal steroids and ACTH among them) may accelerate the aging process.

Psychological Stress and Aging

Apparently, increases in psychological stress, which activate adrenal hormone production, further accelerate the aging process. Henry and his associates (1971, 1972) have demonstrated that housing mice in an environment conducive to the establishment of dominant-subordinate social hierarchies among the males accelerates the aging process by substantially increasing pathological processes. The male mice, which have been reared apart from each other, are introduced into an environment with access to a nest of female mice and various housing areas. The males immediately begin fighting among themselves to establish which mouse will become dominant and "rule the roost," a social position which has as one of its advantages sexual access to the female mice. The mouse that emerges as dominant expresses his dominance by patrolling the enclosed environment in an attempt to confine the subordinate males to their own living areas, thereby denying them access to the female nesting area. (Interestingly, male mice reared together as siblings will not engage in the formation of a dominant-subordinate hierarchy).

Obviously, such social behavior is stressful to both the dominant mouse and his subordinates. The effect of this stressful environment is to increase drastically the incidence of severe pathology in the mice, especially arteriosclerosis, heart disease, and kidney disease. The increase in pathology is probably directly attributable to increased stress hormone output. Axelrod et al (1970) reported that the stressful environments caused marked elevation in the levels of enzymes in the adrenal glands which produce epinephrine (adrenalin) and norepinephrine. (Norepinephrine acts as a neurotransmitter in the brain and as an arousal-producing hormone in the body.) Epinephrine and norepinephrine, along with the adrenal steroids, are the major "stress hormones" in the body.

Wexler (1964) has demonstrated that the stress of frequent breeding markedly increases the incidence and severity of arteriosclerosis in male and female rats. These animals showed evidence of hyperactivity in the pituitary and adrenal glands. These results, and the findings of Henry and coworkers, suggest that an overproduction of stress-related hormones may indeed accelerate the aging process, as hypothesized by Everitt.

These animal studies are directly analogous to medical findings which demonstrate that tense, anxious "on-the-go" people are more susceptible to high blood pressure, heart disease, and cardiovascular disease. Rahe (1969) reported that the amount of stress one endures during life is directly related to the incidence and severity of illness. While some of the stress-producing factors are outside personal control (for example, the death of a spouse), many of the stressful incidents are self-produced, particularly in the "on-the-go" type of person, who is constantly putting himself under stress in order to achieve his goals. The physiological consequences of the high-stress life style have their effects on intellectual functioning towards the end of the life span. Wilkie and Eisdorfer (1973) have reported that aged people with high blood pressure are more susceptible to intellectual decline and have shorter life expectancies than people with normal or slightly elevated blood pressure. Obrist (1972) has discussed how brain arteriosclerosis and its resultant reduction in cerebral blood flow may lead to brain damage and intellectual and behavioral impairment. Thus we have an interesting phenomenon in which a behavioral disposition, a high-stress life style, may ultimately lead to an acceleration of the normal aging process (due in part to changes in endocrine function) and the onset of life-threatening pathology. We have devoted much of the chapter to discussing the age changes in the brain which might lead to behavioral changes, but here is an example of how behavior may alter physiology and ultimately lead to changes in the brain.

These findings on stress and the aging process are also important examples of the implications of animal experiments for the benefit of humanity. The similarity of stress-produced pathology between rodents and man enables scientists interested in this phenomenon to manipulate stressful conditions experimentally (as in the work of Henry and co-workers) and to explore the physical results of stressful environments and behaviors. It is hoped this work will lead us to an understanding of how to prevent the stress-related pathology which seems to be on the rise in our technological, "future shock" society.

Conclusions

The neuropsychology of aging is a field of study which has yet to emerge within the broader field of aging. Experimental studies manipulating the brain-behavior relationship are badly needed. However, it is apparent that within the literature already extant which deals with animal behavior and the physiology of aging in the brain, inadequate attention has been paid to crucial issues such as the presence of disease in animals and the life history (environmental conditions) of the laboratory animals. Thus, future studies on the brain-behavior relationships should involve the control of health and experience of the animals to a degree sufficient to insure that any differences observed are indeed due to the aging process.

Given adequate attention to these concerns, we can expect a great expansion of our knowledge about age changes in the brain-behavior relationship. Such an expansion of knowledge will be best facilitated by studies which seek to expand current knowledge about brain-behavior relationships in mature animals into a developmental perspective. Such an expansion demands the implementation of a "systems" viewpoint of different areas comprised of chemically and anatomically distinct sub-groups. Research can then proceed to search for the effects of aging upon different aspects of brain control over different behaviors.

In this chapter we have briefly discussed the limbic regions of the brain from this viewpoint, and offered a few hypotheses about age changes in limbic mechanisms which might account for the behavioral changes observed in the aged animal. These kinds of hypotheses emphasize the anatomical and chemical relationships among nerve cells as a primary focus for investigation into the brain-behavior relationship in the aging animal. Their emphasis is upon the integrity of synaptic connections between nerve cells. It is thus encouraging to notice an increasing number of studies investigating the efficacy in synaptic transmission in the nervous system, such as the studies on the hippocampus discussed above. Ultimately, such studies should also involve an investigation of the integrity of behaviors known to be related to the function of the brain area involved.

This functionally specific approach to the investigation of the brain-behavior relationship and aging is demanded, in a sense, by the subtlty of the age changes in behavior. The changes are not great in magnitude; therefore, we should not expect extremely large decrements in brain physiology or function as a whole. Our review of the literature leads us to conclude that age changes in the brain are not as universal as would be predicted by a generalized decremental view of brain function during aging. Thus, a viewpoint which entertains the notion of differential effects of aging upon discrete brain areas may hold more promise for explaining the brain-behavior relationship during aging.

In summary, it is our hope that the future of this field will not involve merely an increase in the number of experiments involving the brain, behavior, and the relationship between them, but that we will also observe an increased awareness of the intricate tangle of relationships among variables that lead to the aging process, and an increased effort on the part of investigators in this field to deal coherently with these variables.

References

Adey, W. R. and Tokizane, eds. 1967. *Structure and function of the limbic system; progress in brain research,* Vol. 27. Amsterdam: Elsevier.

Axelrod, J.; Mueller, R. A.; Henry, J. P.; and Stephens, P. M. 1970. Changes in enzymes involved in the biosynthesis and metabolism of noradrenaline and adrenaline after psychosocial stimulation. *Nature* 225:1059–1060.

Bondareff, W. 1973. Age changes in the neuronal microenvironment. In *Development and aging in the nervous system,* ed. M. Rockstein, pp. 1–17. New York and London: Academic Press.

Botwinick, J.; Brinley, J. F.; and Robbin, J. S. 1962. Learning a position discrimination and position reversal task by Sprague-Dawley rats of different
ages. *Journal of Gerontology* 17:315–319.

Brody, H. 1973. Aging of the vertebrate brain. In *Development and aging in the
nervous system,* ed. M. Rockstein, pp. 121–133. New York and London:
Academic Press.

Cagguila, A. R.; Antelman, S. M.; and Zigmond, M. J. 1973. Disruption of
copulation in male rats after hypothalamic lesion; a behavioral, anatomical
and neurochemical analysis. *Brain Research* 59:273–287.

Cummins, R. A.; Walsh, R. N.; Budtz-Olsen, O. E.; Konstantinos, T.; and
Horsfall, C. R. 1973. Environmentally induced changes in the brains of
elderly rats. *Nature* 243:516–518.

Dawson, R. G.; Conrad L.; and Lynch, G. 1973. Single and two-stage
hippocampal lesions: a similar syndrome. *Experimental Neurology* 40:
263–277.

De Wied, D. 1974. Pituitary-adrenal system hormones and behavior, In *The
neurosciences, third study program,* ed. F. O. Schmitt and F. G. Worden,
pp. 653–665. Cambridge and London: MIT Press.

Dilman, V. M. 1971. Age associated elevation of hypothalamic threshold to
feedback control, and its role in development, aging, and disease. *Lancet*
1:1211–1233.

Doty, B. A. 1966a. Age differences in avoidance conditioning as a function of
distribution of trials and task difficulty. *Journal of Genetic Psychology*
109:249–254.

Doty, B. A. 1966b. Age and avoidance conditioning in rats. *Journal of Gerontology* 21:287–290.

Doty, B. A. 1972. The effects of cage environment upon avoidance responding
of aged rats. *Journal of Gerontology* 27:358–360.

Douglas, R. J. 1967. The hippocampus and behavior. *Psychological Bulletin*
67:416–422.

Drachman, D. A. and Ommaya, A. K. 1964. Memory and the hippocampal
complex. *Archives of Neurology* 10:411–425.

Dru, D.; Walker, J. P.; and Walker, J. B. 1975a. Self-produced locomotion restores visual capacity after striate lesions. *Science* 187:265–266.

Dru, D.; Walker, J. B.; and Walker, J. P. 1975b. Recovery of visual function
in aged rats after striate lesions. In preparation.

Dru, D.; Walker, J. B.; and Walker, J. P. 1975c. Recovery of function: serial
lesion effects. *Recent Advances in Psychobiology, Vol.* 111, ed. A. Riesen.
New York and London: Plenum Press.

Dye, C. J. 1969. Effects of interruption of initial learning upon retention in
young, mature, and old rats. *Journal of Gerontology* 24:12–17.

Endroczi, E. 1972. *Limbic system, learning, and pituitary adrenal function.*
Budapest: Akademiai Kiado.

Everitt, A. V. 1973. The hypothalamic pituitary control of aging and age-
related pathology. *Experimental Gerontology* 8:265–277.

Farner, D. 1961. Untersuchungen iiber die Wikung Von Pharmaka auf Tiere
Verschiedene Alters. *Gerontologia* 5:45–54.

Fifkova, E. 1968. Changes in the visual cortex of rats after unilateral deprivation. *Nature* 220:379–381.

Finch, C. E. 1973. Monoamine metabolism in the aging male mouse. In *Development and aging in the nervous system,* ed. M. Rockstein, pp. 199–218. London: Academic Press.

Fletcher, H. J. and Mowbray, J. B. 1962. Note on learning in an aged monkey. *Psychology Reports* 10:11–13.

Ganong, W. F. 1974. Brain mechanisms regulating the secretion of the pituitary gland. In *The neurosciences: third study program,* ed. F. O. Schmitt and F. G. Worden, pp. 549–563. Cambridge and London: MIT Press.

Gaffan, D. 1974. Recognition impaired and association intact in the memory of monkeys after transection of the fornix. *Journal of Comparative Physiological Psychology* 86:1100–1109.

Goodrick, C. L. 1965. Social interactions and exploration of young, mature, and senescent male albino rats. *Journal of Gerontology* 20:215–218.

Goodrick, C. L. 1968. Learning, retention, and extinction of a complex maze habit for mature-young and senescent Wistar albino rats. *Journal of Gerontology* 23:298–304.

Goodrick, C. L. 1969. Taste discrimination and fluid ingestion of male albino rats as a function of age. *Journal of Genetic Psychology* 115:121–131.

Goodrick, C. L. 1971. Free exploration and adaptation within an open field as a function of trials and between-trial interval for mature-young, mature-old, and senescent Wistar rats. *Journal of Gerontology* 26:58–62.

Goodrick, C. L. 1972. Learning by mature-young and aged Wistar albino rats as a function of test complexity. *Journal of Gerontology* 27:353–357.

Greene E.; Stauff, C.; and Walters, J. 1972. Recovery of function with two stage lesions of the fornix. *Experimental Neurology* 37:1–22.

Greenough, W. T. and Volkman, F. R. 1973. Pattern of dendritic branching in occipital cortex of rats reared in complex environments. *Experimental Neurology* 40:491–504.

Greenough, W. T.; Volkman, F. R.; and Juraska, J. M. 1973. Effects of rearing complexity on dendritic branching in front, lateral, and temportal cortex of the rat. *Experimental Neurology* 41:371–378.

Grossman, S. P. 1962. Direct adrenergic and cholinergic stimulation of hypothalamic mechanisms. *American Journal of Physiology* 202:872–882.

Guth, L. and Windle, W. F. 1973. Physiological molecular and genetic aspects of central nervous system regeneration. *Experimental Neurology* 39:iii–xvi.

Hasan, M. and Glees, P. 1973. Ultrastructural age changes in hippocampal neurons, synapses, and neuroglia. *Experimental Gerontology* 8:75–83.

Held, R., and Hein, A. 1963. Movement produced stimulation in the development of visually guided behavior. *Journal of Comparative Physiological Psychology* 56:872–876.

Henry, J. P.; Ely, D. L.; Stephens, P. M.; Ratcliffe, H. L.; Santisteban, G. A.; and Shapiro, A. P. 1971. The role of psychosocial factors in the development of arteriosclerosis in CBA mice. *Atherosclerosis* 14:203–218.

Henry, J. P.; Ely, D. L.; and Stephens, P. M. 1972. Blood pressure, catecholamines, and social role in relation to the development of cardiovascular disease in mice. *Neural and psychological mechanisms in cardio-vascular disease,* ed. A. Zanchetti, pp. 211–223. Milan: Il Ponte.

Howard, E. 1973. DNA content of rodent brains during maturation and aging, and autoradiography of postnatal DNA synthesis in monkey brain. In

Neurobiological aspects of maturation and aging; progress in brain research, ed. D. H. Ford. 40:91–114. Amsterdam: Elsevier.

Jakubczak, L. F. 1964. Effects of testosterone propionate on age differences in mating behavior. *Journal of Gerontology* 19:458–461.

Jakubczak, L. F. 1967a. Age differences in the effects of terminal food deprivation (starvation) on activity, weight loss, and survival of rats. *Journal of Gerontology* 22:421–426.

Jakubczak, L. F. 1967b. Age, endocrines, and behavior. In *Endocrines and aging,* ed. L. Gitman, pp. 321–345. Springfield, Ill.: Charles C. Thomas.

Jakubczak, L. F. 1969. Effects of injection of glucose on food intake of mature and old food-deprived rats. *Proceedings of the 77th Annual Convention of the American Psychological Association* 4:723–724.

Jakubczak, L. F. 1970. Age differences in the effects of water deprivation on activity, weight loss, and survival of rats. *Life Sciences* 9:771–780.

Jakubczak, L. F. 1973. Age and animal behavior. In *The psychology of adult development and aging,* eds. C. Eisdorfer and M. P. Lawton, pp. 98–111. Washington, D.C.: American Psychological Association.

John, E. R. 1972. Switchboard versus statistical theories of learning and memory. *Science* 177:580–864.

Kay, H. and Sime, M. E. 1962. Discrimination learning with old and young rats. *Journal of Gerontology* 17:75–80.

Larsson, K. and Essberg, L. 1962. Effects of age on the sexual behavior of the male rat. *Gerontologia* 6:133–143.

Larsson, K. 1963. Nonspecific stimulation and sexual behavior in the male rat. *Behavior* 20:110–114.

Latham, K. R. 1974. Aging and glucocorticoid binding proteins in the liver and brain of C57 B1/6J mice. Unpublished doctoral dissertation. University of Southern California.

Leibowitz, S. F. 1974. Adrenergic receptor mechanisms in eating and drinking. In *The neurosciences, third study program,* eds. F. O. Schmitt and F. G. Worden, pp. 713–719. Cambridge and London: MIT Press.

Levere, T. E. and Weiss, J. 1973. Failure of seriatum dorsal hippocampal lesions to spare spatial reversal behavior in rats. *Journal of Comparative Physiological Psychology* 82:205–210.

Lisensby, D. D. 1968. Chronological age, physiological change, and performance, the mature ginean pig. Unpublished doctoral dissertation. Washington University.

Lynch, G.; Deadwyler, S.; and Cotman, C. 1973. Post-lesion axonal growth produces permanent functional connection. *Science* 180:1364–1366.

McClean, P. D. 1958. Contrasting functions of limbic and neocortical systems of the brain and their relevance to psychophysiological aspects of medicine. *American Journal of Medicine* 25:611–626.

McEwen, B.; Weiss, J. M.; Schwartz, L. 1969. Uptake of corticosterone by rat brain and its concentration by certain limbic structures. *Brain Research* 16:227–241.

Medin, D. L. 1969. Form perception and pattern reproduction by monkeys. *JCPP* 68:412–419.

Medin, D. L.; O'Neil, P.; Smeltz, E.; and Davis, R. T. 1973. Age differences in retention of concurrent discrimination problems in monkeys. *Journal of Gerontology* 28:63–67.

Milner, B. 1970. Memory and the medial temporal regions of the brain. In *Biology of Memory*, eds. K. Pribram and D. Broadbent, pp. 29–50. New York: Aacdemic Press.

Nauta, W. J. H. 1972. The central visceromotor system: a general survey. In *Limbic System Mechanisms and Autonomic Function*, ed. C. H. Hockman, pp. 21–38. Springfield: Charles C. Thomas.

Obrist, W. D. 1972. Cerebral physiology of the aged: influence of circulatory disorders. *Aging and the Brain*, ed. C. M. Gaitz, pp. 117–133. New York and London: Plenum Press.

Oldfield-Box, H. 1969. On analysing the formation of learning-sets in young and old rats. *Gerontologia* 15:302–307.

Parsons, P. J.; Fagan, T.; and Spear, N. E. 1973. Short-term retention of habituation in the rat: a developmental study from infancy to old age. *Journal of Comparative Physiological Psychology* 84:545–553.

Paxinos, G. and Bindra, D. 1973. Hypothalamic and midbrain neural pathways involved in eating, drinking, irritability, aggression, and copulation in rats. *Journal of Comparative Physiological Psychology* 82:1–14.

Raisman, G. 1969. Neuronal plasticity in the septal nuclei of the adult rat. *Brain Research* 14:25–48.

Rahe, R. H. 1969. Life crisis and health change. In *Psychotropic drug response: advances in prediction*, eds. P. R. H. May and J. R. Wittenborn, p. 92. Springfield: Charles C. Thomas.

Ray, O. S. and Barrett, R. J. 1973. Interaction of learning and memory with age in the rat. In *Psychopharmacology and aging*, eds. C. Eisdorfer and W. E. Fann, pp. 17–19. New York & London: Plenum Press.

Riege, W. H. 1971. Environmental influences on brain and behavior of year old rats. *Developmental Psychobiology* 4:157–167.

Riesen, A. H. 1966. Sensory deprivation. In *Progress in Physiological Psychology*, Vol 1, eds. E. Stellar and J. M. Sprague, pp. 117–147. New York: Academic Press.

Rosenzweig, M. R.; Bennett, E. L.; and Diamond, M. C. 1970. Chemical and anatomical plasticity of brain; replications and extensions. In *Macromolecules and behavior*, 2nd edition, ed. J. Gaito. New York: Appleton, Century, Crofts.

Scapagini, U. 1974. Pharmacological studies of brain control over ACTH secretion. In *The neurosciences, third study program*, eds. F. O. Schmitt and F. G. Worden, pp. 565–569. Cambridge and London: MIT Press.

Teitelbaum, P. and Epstein, A. N. 1962. The lateral hypothalamic syndrome; recovery of feeding and drinking after lateral hypothalamic lesions. *Psychological Review* 69:74–90.

Tomasch, J. 1971. Comments on neuromythology. *Nature* 233:60–61.

Warren, J. M. and Akert, K., eds. 1964. *The frontal granular cortex and behavior*. New York: McGraw-Hill.

Wexler, B. C. 1964. Spontaneous arteriosclerosis in repeatedly bred male and female rats. *Journal of Atherosclerosis Research* 4:57–80.

Wilkie, F. L. and Eisdorfer, C. 1973. Systemic disease and behavioral correlates. In *Intellectual Functioning in Adults*, eds. L. Jarvik, C. Eisdorfer, and J. E. Blum, pp. 83–93. New York: Springer.

Williams, C. D.; Carr, R. M.; and Peterson, H. W. 1966. Maze exploration in young rats of four ages. *Journal of Genetic Psychology* 109:241–247.

9

A Physiological Perspective of the Psychology of Aging

DIANA S. WOODRUFF

Identifying and explaining relationships between physiology and behavior is the goal of physiological psychology. Psychophysiologists concern themselves with examining how systems, such as the cardiovascular, pulmonary, and nervous systems, affect the way we act, and conversely, how our feelings and actions affect these physiological systems. The application of psychophysiological techniques is especially pertinent in the field of aging as it is clear that physiological functions change with age (see Chapters 10–12 on the biology of aging). Indeed, geropsychologists have tended to be so preoccupied with physiological age changes and how they affect behavior that they have often ignored behavioral influences on physiology.

Behavior has all too frequently been interpreted in terms of the biological decremental model of aging which stipulates that aging is represented by decline in all physiological systems (Woodruff, 1973). This leaves psychologists in the unfortunate position of merely describing behavioral decrements, and, for the most part, this is the main perspective reflected in psychological studies of aging. If, on the other hand, geropsychologists more carefully viewed the *interactive* nature of physiology-behavior relationships, we would be in a better position to attempt to modify age changes in behavior and even age changes in physiology.

A major portion of this chapter will be devoted to the interactive perspective in the psychophysiology of aging along with the implications of this research for the elderly. Also to be examined are some of the models used to explain behavioral aging. This information will then be used to guide us toward a realistic perspective of the behavioral capacities of the aged.

Behavior-Physiology Interactions

The gerontological literature abounds with references to behavior-physiology relationships. One very striking example of the interactive nature of physiology and behavior is in the dramatically increased incidence of depression in old age. Indeed, depression appears to be one of the major psychological problems of the aged (Busse, 1959; Butler, 1963; Lowenthal, 1964). At both a biochemical level and an environmental level the elderly may be predisposed toward depression. The environmental effects of significant losses—loss of income, loss of loved ones, loss of employment, and so forth—are tangible factors which cause older individuals to feel depressed. Losses in physical capacity and energy level also undoubtedly play a role. Additionally, however, there is some evidence that on a biochemical level, production of certain neurotransmitters in the aging brain may be altered which may also predispose old people to feel depressed (see Chapter 8 for a discussion of neurotransmitters and the aging brain). Thus, with regard to depression, the aged may be in a state of double jeopardy. Biochemically and physiologically, they may be predisposed to depression, and, in addition, the environment is stressful as life at the point of old age is full of losses undoubtedly contributing to depression. Whether biological changes are caused by these environmental stresses, whether the biological and physiological changes are completely independent, or whether they exacerbate one another has not clearly been determined. Perhaps if we examine aging animals with some of the techniques described in Chapter 8, we will find that biologically older organisms are more predisposed towards depression without any environmental stresses. This is all the more reason to alleviate the environmental stresses which plague contemporary aged cohorts. While we may not be able to eliminate losses due to deaths of friends and spouse, we can alter problems of inadequate income, housing, health care, and transportation. The point here is that we can take a behavioral or environmental approach toward improving the lives of the elderly which might affect the mood state of depression on a physiological or biochemical level.

In Chapter 6 Warner Schaie points out the flaws in our thinking about intelligence and aging in terms of the biological decremental model. He suggests that we simply assume that there is organic deterioration in the older brain when we note that the aged score lower on intelligence tests. This may not be the case at all, for the aged may score lower on intelligence tests as a result of educational obsolescence (Baltes and Schaie, 1974; Birren and Woodruff, 1973; Schaie, 1970) or as a result of other noncognitive factors (see Chapter 6). A number of gerontologists have suggested the environmental intervention of education to reduce this obsolescence. Others have suggested a restructuring of the intelligence test so that it would not discriminate against the aged person.

Schaie also suggests in this volume that much of what we attribute to biological decline may be environmental influence, and he further suggests that the environment probably affects behavior in old age more than does biology. This implies that while some of the biological changes in old age are irreversible, the environment is more salient than biology in behavior. The clear implication is that environmental interventions can successfully alleviate most of the behavioral deficits in old age. While environmental influences and interventions are certainly critical in reversing decline in old age, it has not yet been conclusively demonstrated that even the biological decline is inevitable or irreversible. Biological decline is being identified in descriptive studies of aging in animals and man, but few attempts have been made to manipulate biological variables to determine if biological decline can be reversed. We are only beginning to undertake experimental studies to determine if biological changes are really inevitable in old age, and when we do try to affect physiological functioning in the aged, we are surprising ourselves at how often we can observe beneficial results of the kind reported by deVries in Chapter 12.

DeVries has found physiological reversals—that is, improvement in physiological functioning in the aged—as a result of moderate exercise. It is not age itself which causes individuals to decline physiologically. Other factors, some of which it may be possible to alter, are associated with declining physiological capacity in the aged. DeVries demonstrated that one of the factors associated with physiological decline is disuse, the lack of exercise in contemporary sedentary life styles. With a modified exercise program, even very old individuals can regain some of the physiological efficiency they had lost with advancing years.

If we are searching for new approaches and new information in the psychology of aging, and in gerontology generally, we must reexamine some of the changes that we have long thought to be irreversible. This is being done in a number of biology and psychobiology laboratories where investigations of aging are being carried out. In Caleb Finch's laboratory at the University of Southern California, investigations are being undertaken to examine how hormonal changes in aging rats might be reversed. Estrogen-replacement therapy has been one of the outcomes of this type of research, and progress in this area may lead to the maintenance of optimal hormonal levels in postmenopausal women. Such research has clear implications for sexual behavior in older women who sometimes abstain from sex because of pain in the genital region, which has atrophied in the absence of normal hormone levels (see Chapter 11).

Why is it only now that we are beginning to take a new look in our studies of aging to see how much capacity is left? Why have we failed to believe that we could reshape behavior in the elderly? Why have we believed that it is only the brains and behavior of children and young animals that are plastic? One of the major contributions to our thinking about brain plasticity comes from studies of accidents and language behavior. It has been demonstrated that if damage is caused to a specific area (located in the left cerebral cortex of right-handed individuals; for left-handed individuals it may be either in the right or left cortex) before a child reaches adolescence, the child will lose language function for a period of time and then be able to regain it. The same damage in an adult will render him mute for the rest of his life. He will never again have language capacities. The young brain appears to be plastic, able to compensate for damage in one area by relegating function to another area. Thus, we believed that the youthful brain is malleable to a point, but after a certain age brain function ceases to be plastic. On the basis of these accident studies we accepted as fact that the older brain could not regain function, and investigators did not even include older animals in their brain plasticity studies because they thought it was useless even to test plasticity in older brains. This reluctance to experiment with older organisms in studies of brain plasticity attests to the degree to which scientists and physicians believed there could be no recovery of function in older brains. It was thus extremely unorthodox for Denise Dru and her colleagues (Dru, Walker, and Walker, 1975) to include a group of old rats in their study of recovery of function in the visual cortical areas. This work is described in detail in Chapter 8 and represents a pioneering study demonstrating plasticity in older as well as younger brains.

Can Physiological Decline Be Reversed?

The most important point to be made in this chapter is that physiological age functions may not be fixed and inevitable, and there may be behavioral intervention strategies and biological intervention strategies which may reverse some of the deleterious performance observed in old people.

EEG Changes with Age

The brain is composed of billions of nerve cells called neurons. The electrical activity of hundreds of thousands of neurons can be recorded by attaching electrodes to an individual's scalp and amplifying the tiny electrical signals roughly a million times. The characteristic oscillating pattern of electrical activity recorded in this manner is called the electroencephalogram (EEG), and it has been used as a clinical tool to identify abnormal brain activity and as an experimental tool to examine brain-behavior relationships. Since it is not feasible to invade the brain with recording techniques, the EEG is one of the few means available to measure human brain activity.

There are at least four identified rhythms in the EEG. The alpha rhythm is in the 8 to 13 cycle per second (cps) range and is the dominant or modal brain wave rhythm. Behaviorally, it is associated with a relaxed but alert state and is most prominent in the back parts of the head, especially when the eyes are closed. Beta activity is a faster rhythm, above 13 cps, and is associated with an alert, thinking state of consciousness. Theta activity is in the 4 to 7 cps range and is associated with day-dreaming and drowsiness. Activity in the 1 to 3 cps range is called delta and occurs during sleep. Thus, faster brain waves are associated with alertness and arousal, while slower rhythmic patterns are related to drowsiness and sleep. Clinical uses of the EEG include the identification of tumors and areas of pathology in the brain, which manifest themselves as areas of localized slowing of EEG activity. Thus, slowing is associated with drowsiness, sleep, and brain pathology.

The dominant brain wave rhythm of young adults is 10.2 to 10.5 cps (Brazier and Finesinger, 1944). One of the best-documented findings in the psychophysiological literature is that this dominant brain wave rhythm slows with age (see Obrist and Busse, 1965; Thompson and Marsh, 1973 for reviews). By the time an individual reaches the age of 60 to 65, his dominant brain wave rhythm is probably around 9 cps. Although some eighty year olds have brain wave patterns similar to those of twenty year olds, the normal pattern in even the healthiest of aging individuals is for EEG slowing to occur with age. Figure 9.1, taken from the work of Walter Obrist, illustrates slowing in the same individual over a ten-year period.

Obrist, Henry, and Justiss (1961) demonstrated that the slowing of the EEG alpha rhythm is a reliable phenomenon occurring in longitudinal as well as cross-sectional studies. In the ten-year period of Obrist's longitudinal study, two-thirds of the subjects manifested slowing of the dominant rhythm. Since this slowing has been related to pathology, the subjects may have had some kind of disease, such as cerebral arteriosclerosis, which would cause a slower metabolic rate in the brain and lead to slower brain wave rhythms. It has been demonstrated that senile patients, patients with arteriosclerosis or severe brain atrophy, have very slow brain wave rhythms. One of the studies which convincingly demonstrates that alpha slowing occurs in even the healthiest of aged individuals was reported in a monograph by Birren et al. (1963). An extensive study was undertaken to examine biological and behavioral changes in 47 old men chosen because they were in optimal health. Obrist examined the EEGs of these men and found that even in these healthy old men, there was a slowing of the EEG alpha rhythm to 9 cps. Thus, alpha slowing is a phenomenon associated with normal aging and is not necessarily the result of disease.

The slowing of the dominant EEG rhythm is part of the legacy of descriptive studies of aging, and this finding is cited, along with numerous others, to support the biological decremental model of aging. While there are at least 20 studies documenting deleterious age changes in the EEG, there have been no attempts until one quite recent study (Woodruff, 1975) to determine if these age changes in EEG are reversible.

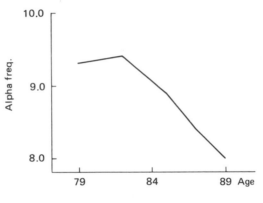

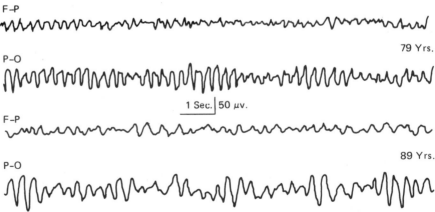

Figure 9.1. Alpha frequency plotted as a function of age for a mentally "normal" old man over a ten year period. The top tracing was recorded at age 79, the bottom tracing at age 89. The latter EEG was associated with mild signs of intellectual impairment. F-P = Fronto-Parietal: P-O = Parieto-Occipital. (From Obrist, Henry, and Justiss, 1961)

Changes in Reaction Time with Age

Another clear finding in the geropsychology research literature is the slowing of reaction time (RT) with age. In Chapter 2 on the history of gerontology, Birren and Clayton mention the work of Sir Francis Galton who set up a health exposition in London in 1877 and collected RT data. In 1923 two investigators, Koga and Morant (1923), analyzed some of Galton's data and found that both visual and auditory reaction time was slower in the old than in the young subjects in this sample. This is one of the first studies in the literature on the psychology of aging, and there are hundreds of studies that have substantiated it. Birren, Riegel, and Morrison (1962) undertook an interesting study in which they factor-analyzed a large group of tasks in young and old subjects and found that one major factor that appeared in the old that was different in the young was speed. The speed factor could account for about three or four times as much of the variance in performance in old people as in the young. In a more recent study in which he factor-analyzed scores on tests of intellectual performance, Cunningham (1974) also found a factor involving speed of performance which was present in the data for the old subjects but which did not emerge from the data of the young subjects.

Reaction time slows in other species as well. Chapter 8 in this volume documents psychomotor slowing in animals, and observing such data led Birren (1965) to state that slowing will occur in any individual who survives beyond young adulthoood. This age change in RT, like the age change in EEG, is what we call a normal aging phenomenon. It occurs uniformly without regard to disease.

Again in the very healthy old men in the Birren et al. (1963) study cited previously, there was slowed RT. People who are sick, who have some of the chronic diseases (and most old people have at least one chronic disease), have more psychomotor slowing. Nevertheless, even in the most fit of old people, there is still behavioral slowing. There is such a wide range of studies on slowing of behavior that Hicks and Birren (1970) compared all the literature and found that studies reporting slowing in old people found slowing ranging from 20 percent to 110 percent. It depends on the task, on the investigator, and on a number of variables, but older people perform more slowly than young.

Some investigators have used behavioral intervention strategies to determine if psychomotor slowing was reversible. Murrell (1970) and Hoyer, Labouvie, and Baltes (1973) used extensive practice and found that the aged could improve their speed and close some of the gap between their performance and the performance of young subjects. To alter motivation in old subjects, Botwinick (1959) has used the tactic of shocking subjects mildly when they responded more slowly than their normal responding time, and he found some improvement in performance under certain conditions. While these strategies indicated that some of the behavioral slowing was reversible, the age differences could not be completely erased.

Brain Waves and Reaction Time

Since scientists first began thinking about the EEG, the EEG alpha rhythm has been associated with speed and timing in the nervous system. The possibility that the alpha rhythm reflected periodicity in the activity of the central nervous system was first considered by Bishop (1933, 1936) and by Jasper (1936) who speculated that the alpha rhythm reflects cyclic fluctuations in brain excitability. Lindsley (1952) summarized a variety of psychological and neuropsychological research in support of this proposition and suggested that the waxing and waning in the alpha cycle may arise from synchronous and rhythmic metabolic or respiratory activities in large aggregates of neurons. Subsequent research (e.g., Andersen and Andersson, 1968; Callaway, 1962; Dustman and Beck, 1965; Frost, 1968) consistently has supported the general notion that the alpha cycle reflects underlying modulations in brain responsiveness. So it is perhaps a basic property of the nervous system that at some times it is more excitable than at other times. This relates to the timing of behavior in that if a signal is received at a time when the nervous system is most excitable, it will be responded to more quickly than when the system is not excitable.

Walter Surwillo attempted to determine if the slowing of RT with age could be accounted for by the slowing of the EEG alpha rhythm. In 1961 Surwillo reported a study in which he had simultaneously recorded RT and EEG in 13 subjects ranging in age from 18 to 72. In this study Surwillo found a rank-order correlation of .81 between the period of the alpha rhythm (inverse of alpha frequency) and simple RT to auditory stimuli. Surwillo (1963a) replicated these results with a sample of 100 subjects, and he also demonstrated (1963b, 1964a) that the alpha period was related to RT variability and to the latency of choice RTs (and hence presumably to central decision time). On the basis of these results Surwillo hypothesized that the alpha period represents a fundamental unit of time in the programming of events in the central nervous system.

Surwillo's hypothesis implies a causal relationship between alpha period and RT, but correlational evidence does not provide unequivocal support for this hypothesis. More convincing evidence for the hypothesis that alpha frequency determines RT could be derived from a demonstration that experimental alterations in alpha frequency lead to changes in RT. One such experiment was reported by Surwillo (1964b) who attempted to modify alpha frequency by flashing bright lights at subjects at rates of 6–15 flashes per second. This technique proved ineffective as only 5 of the 48 subjects showed evidence of alpha synchronization over more than a restrictively narrow range of photic frequencies. Consequently, the limited results of this study do not convincingly test Surwillo's hypothesis.

Until recently, alternative techniques for manipulating the alpha frequency, and hence for experimentally testing the relationship between alpha frequency and RT, were not available. The newly emergent biofeedback technique, however, provided another means by which alpha frequency could be manipulated. The work of Kamiya (1968) and others has demonstrated that subjects can increase and decrease the abundance of activity in the EEG band encompassing the alpha rhythm. Furthermore, it has been established that individuals can selectively increase the abundance of EEG activity in narrow frequency bandwidths (Green, Green and Walters, 1970a, 1970b; Kamiya, 1969).

Biofeedback as an Intervention

Biofeedback is a technique that involves providing individuals with information about the activity of bodily processes of which they are unaware. When a person becomes aware that he is producing a certain type of brain wave rhythm, that his heart is beating at a certain rate, or that his blood pressure is at a certain level, he can learn to alter or maintain that physiological rate. Connecting an individual to an electronic system which amplifies physiological signals and then activates signals which provide him with information about his internal states makes it possible for him to control those internal states. The electronic system provides the individual with information about bodily activity (such as blood pressure, heart rate, or EEG frequency) of which he is normally unaware.

It appears that once a person knows or becomes aware of an internal state, he can alter it. Thus, the electronic system—the biofeedback system—provides the individual with knowledge about the activity of his internal organs, and when people have this awareness they become capable of consciously regulating to some extent the function of the organ. For example, in the case of the EEG alpha rhythm, a person typically is not aware of whether he is producing brain waves in the 8–13 cps (alpha) range. If, however, he is placed in a situation in which his brain waves are measured and the information is "fed back" to him in the form of a tone or light which signals to him that he is or is not producing alpha activity, he can learn to increase or suppress that brain wave activity.

With biofeedback it became possible to determine if the slowing of the dominant brain wave frequency in older people could be reversed. That is, it was possible to determine if old subjects could increase the time they spent producing alpha waves in the frequency bandwidths of young subjects. This biofeedback technique also made it possible to test Surwillo's hypothesis regarding the relationship between brain wave frequency and RT.

We designed an experiment in which young and old subjects learned to increase the abundance of EEG alpha activity at the modal frequency and at frequencies two cps faster and slower than the mode. Old subjects were just as capable of manipulating brain wave frequency in this manner as were young subjects, suggesting that some of the alpha slowing may be reversible. It was also determined that when the subjects produced fast brain wave frequencies, their RT was faster than when they produced slow brain wave frequencies. Thus, biofeedback provides a means to help older individuals to produce faster brain waves and possibly to speed their RT (Woodruff, 1975).

A series of studies is being undertaken to determine the significance of alpha slowing for more complex behavior such as attention and intelligence. We will use biofeedback to help older subjects alter brain wave frequencies to see if we can improve performance. If such work proves successful, it might be possible to train subjects to be aware of internal processes to a degree where they could control these processes without the additional aid of the biofeedback device. Alternatively, it might be possible to design miniature biofeedback units which could be worn by subjects and which would sound an alarm when brain wave frequency reached a degree of slowing associated with behavioral impairment. While such applications sound like science fiction today, physicians, psychiatrists, and clinical psychologists are looking to experimental psychologists for advances in biofeedback techniques and are beginning to adopt biofeedback procedures to treat their patients.

Biofeedback is currently being used on a limited basis to treat migraine headaches, a procedure which involves training patients to relax the frontalis muscle in the forehead (Budzynski, Stoyva, and Adler, 1970). Some forms of epilepsy not amenable to drug treatment are being controlled with brain wave biofeedback (Sterman and Friar, 1972), and hypertension has been reduced in some patients with biofeedback of blood pressure (Shapiro, Tursky and Schwartz, 1970).

As a behavioral intervention to affect physiological decline in the elderly, biofeedback has great potential (Woodruff, 1971). With this technique we may be able to demonstrate that there is residual capacity in the older organism which we would have never believed existed.

Models in the Psychophysiology of Aging

What are some of the psychological models of aging? What has some of the descriptive research told us? What are some of the hypotheses in the psychophysiology of aging? We have been carrying out psychophysiological studies in psychology for about 30 to 40 years now, and there is a relatively large body of descriptive literature that can be drawn on to derive more general principles about behavior and aging. These models are useful as they organize and draw together a number of divergent studies and lead us to devise research to test the models.

The Discontinuity Hypothesis

From his extensive work with old individuals, Birren (1963) developed the discontinuity hypothesis which states that it is only when a physiological function becomes abnormal that the physiological variable affects behavioral variables. When a physiological variable goes into an abnormal range, then and only then may it affect behavior. In other words, physiological variables which do not affect behavior when they are in a normal range in young subjects may affect behavior in old subjects when the physiological function reaches an abnormal level.

A few examples may help to illustrate the discontinuity hypothesis. In the study of 47 healthy old men mentioned previously (Birren et al., 1963), the investigators used a sophisticated battery of clinical tests. This testing procedure was more intensive than a normal physical examination, and while the investigators had selected a group of what they thought were 47 extremely healthy men, they found that even among these healthiest of aged individuals, there was a group of about half who had some subclinical forms of disease, that is, disease that would not be detected by a physician in a routine examination. In the healthiest group, there were only five statistically significant correlations between all of the physiological variables and all of the behavioral variables. In the less healthy, subclinical pathology group, 26 of the physiology-behavior relationships were statistically significant. This suggests that only when we start getting into poor health or start shading in the range of poorer health does physiology affect behavior.

Another study supporting the discontinuity hypothesis was undertaken at Duke University. Wilkie and Eisdorfer (1972) found in a longitudinal study relating blood pressure to behavioral variables, such as memory and intelligence, that only when blood pressure was elevated did it relate to or affect the behavioral variables. Blood pressure in the normal range does not appear to be related to behavior. So again, only when there was pathology was there a behavior-physiology relationship.

What kind of implications does this have in daily life? For one thing, it stresses the incredible adaptability of old people and the hope that although some physiological functions decline, the life styles of the elderly may not have to change dramatically.

Old people are extremely adaptable. Birren tells a story about an experience he had while doing research on visual perception. To be in contact with elderly subjects he set up his experiment at a local nursing home, and a part of the experiment involved giving the subjects a visual acuity test. One of the volunteers for the project was a man of around 85 years old who was active in the home and a leader in the activities there. One of the programs at this nursing home involved the production of plays, and this old man had the leading role in the production. He was well known by most of the residents and well liked. When Birren tested this man for visual acuity he found that the old man was functionally blind. Birren went to the nursing-home administrator and asked if the administrator knew that Mr. X was blind. The administrator couldn't believe Birren. Observing the old man's behavior very carefully, Birren found that the man was always accompanied by his wife, and she very subtly guided him and gave him cues so that, although this man was functionally blind, not even the nursing-home staff were aware of it. This remarkable example stresses the adaptability of old people.

Arousal Level

Another model in the psychophysiology of aging involves the concept of arousal. Psychologists have been exploring the relationship between level of arousal and efficiency of performance for years, and in its simplest form, the arousal hypothesis states that there is a U-shaped relationship between level of arousal and efficiency of performance. On a conceptual level this means that if you are underaroused—tired or drowsy, for example—you will not be at your most efficient level for performance. As you become more alerted and aroused you perform more efficiently until you reach an optimal level of performance. If you exceed that optimal level by, for example, becoming anxious, this will cause interference with performance and you will not do as well. Investigators have speculated about the arousal level of older individuals and have interpreted some evidence to suggest that old people are underaroused and other evidence suggesting that the aged are overaroused. Still other investigators have attempted to integrate and explain these seemingly contradictory results, and we will examine the evidence for both positions and try to find some resolution to the controversy.

Support for the notion that older individuals are underaroused comes from a number of psychophysiological studies where EEG measures of central nervous system (CNS) activity have been used. (The CNS includes the brain and the spinal cord. The EEG measures CNS activity inasmuch as EEG recordings reflect electrical activity generated in the brain.) Slower brain wave frequencies which occur in older people have been related to underarousal in young subjects, and more complex EEG measures, such as the Averaged Evoked Potential (AEP), also suggest underarousal in the aged (Schenkenberg, 1970). Other evidence for underarousal comes from tasks such as critical flicker fusion (CFF). If you flash a strobe light at around 40 cycles per second, people are unable to perceive that there are individual flashes. The threshold for critical flicker fusion is higher in old age than it is in young. In other words, the old will perceive a continuous signal at fewer flashes per second than the young. This is related to arousal in that Fuster (1958) found that if you stimulate in the brain stem in the reticular formation, which seems to be the brain site that is related to activation and arousal, you get lower CFF thresholds. Since the aged have higher CFF thresholds, this is a sign that perhaps older people are less aroused.

Of course, the reaction time data also indicate that the old are less aroused. People who are less alert, less aroused, also perform more slowly on reaction time tests. It is also true, however, that people who are overaroused perform more slowly on reaction time tests.

Data from the laboratory of Carl Eisdorfer suggest that on serial learning performance tests, old people, according to autonomic nervous system (ANS) measures of arousal, are actually more aroused than are young subjects. The autonomic nervous system is part of the central nervous system, but it is the part of the central nervous system that innervates the glands and the viscera, all of the organs that supposedly are autonomous—the organs over which an individual supposedly has no conscious control. (Biofeedback research has demonstrated that this is probably inaccurate. The term autonomic was used as if some functions were autonomous—neither consciously controlled nor subject to conscious control. With biofeedback, ANS functions can come under conscious control.) Using biochemical measures of autonomic nervous system function, it has been suggested that older people are overaroused. This means that during certain stresses such as performing a serial learning task, older subjects had a higher level of ANS activity than did younger subjects.

How do we integrate these data? Thompson and Marsh (1973) have suggested that perhaps both the notion of underarousal and overarousal are true; that old people are both overaroused and underaroused depending on what aspect of the nervous system is measured. In the case of central nervous system measures (measures of brain function such as EEG and evoked potentials), the older organism may be underaroused. But, on the other hand, some parts of the autonomic nervous system may not be integrated as well in the functioning of the central nervous system in old people as in young. Thus, by these autonomic measures, the old may be overaroused. What Thompson and Marsh have suggested is a desynchronization hypothesis. With age, the total integration of the nervous system, the integration between central nervous system and autonomic nervous system functioning, may deteriorate.

There are some data supporting this notion of ANS-CNS desynchronization. Using an autonomic nervous system measure (heart rate) and a central nervous system measure (contingent negative variation), Thompson and Nowlin (1973) reported a disparity between the two. Contingent negative variation (CNV) is another EEG averaged measure. It has been determined that when you expect a stimulus (for example, when you are given a warning signal and told that a second later you are going to get a second signal) there is a slow build-up of negative brain wave activity which is maximal just before you press the reaction time button. After you press it, there is a rapid return to positivity. The important thing to remember is that the CNV is a measure of central nervous system excitability. Thompson and Nowlin (1973) measured CNV and heart-rate deceleration. In a warned reaction time task, Lacey and his colleagues have shown that as the time for the imperative signal approaches, heart rate slows. In young subjects the deceleration is about four beats per second and the faster the reaction time, the more the heart beat slows. Old people do not respond as efficiently in this way. They have significant slowing of their heartbeat, but the slowing is less than one heart beat per second. Thus, Thompson and Nowlin (1973) found big differences between old and young in an autonomic nervous system correlate of RT performance. At the same time that they were measuring the heart rate, Thompson and Nowlin were measuring CNV, the central nervous system measure. They found that the CNV's between the old and the young were not different. While there was a big differnce betweeen young and old subjects on an autonomic nervous system measure, there was no difference on a central nervous system measure. This suggests that the integration, the relationship between the central nervous system and autonomic nervous system, may not be as efficient in the old as in the young. This is a tentative hypothesis, and it is currently being examined in greater detail in our laboratories.

What does this mean in terms of practical applications? If old people are underaroused, then they should be stimulated. Levels of illumination should be increased, old people should be spoken to more loudly, and input to all of their sensory systems should be increased. On the other hand, if old people seem to be overaroused, they should be relaxed.

One of the characteristics of the studies in which overarousal has been demonstrated has been that the subjects are threatened. They are forced to learn a list of word pairs in a limited time. Such a task may be especially threatening to old people. Froehling (1974) demonstrated, however, that once older people are exposed to this task several times they no longer respond in terms of biochemical overarousal. The practical lesson for educators from this research is to familiarize older learners with the classroom and allow them to learn at their own pace in a relaxed atmosphere so that they will not suffer from anxiety and hence biochemical overarousal.

Sensory Deprivation

The old, relative to the young, have been considered to be in a state of sensory deprivation. It has been determined, and this again is the biological, decremental perspective, that sensory acuity declines due to deficits in the peripheral sensory systems. In the visual system at a peripheral level the lens thickens, the pupil aperture narrows, and the muscles in the eye function less well so that accommodation is not as efficient. Generally, it takes more light energy to have the same effect on the older eye as on the younger eye. Some studies have indicated that there is no way that you can compensate for the difference between the old and the young eye. There are physical changes in the eye that makes it less responsive to light. The hearing apparatus also changes. Ability to hear high tones declines with age. So again there is less auditory information available to the older ear. In terms of the skin, receptors for touch and pain are lost. The skin loses its elasticity, and generally, touch is a sense that declines in old age. About two-thirds of the taste buds in the mouth die by the time an individual is 70. (Taste, however, is also clearly a learned ability to some extent. Most gourmets are old. This means that there is compensation that takes place even though taste buds are lost.) The sense of smell also declines. A large percentage of the sensory receptors in the nose die with age. Generally, then, there is a picture that less sensory information is getting in to the older brain.

Studies on sensory deprivation have indicated that when an individual is deprived of sensory information he experiences some difficulty. The brain appears to need a certain level of stimulation, a certain amount of sensory input, to function optimally. The old relative to the young may be in a state of sensory deprivation and for this reason they may function less efficiently. A study was undertaken by Kemp (1970), who tried to get at this issue by putting both young and old subjects in a sensory deprivation chamber to see if the old were selectively more affected than the young by this procedure. There were no age differences, so the hypothesis that the old are in a state of sensory deprivation is at this point relatively unproven.

The sensory deprivation model again suggests that old people need stimulation. Stroke patients who receive additional stimulation seem to recover faster. At the hospital where Kemp carried out his research, a very interesting thing happened as a result of sensory deprivation studies. Sensory deprivation research was underway, and the researchers talked to some of the therapists and explained theoretical issues in the area of sensory deprivation. One of the therapists got the notion that if sensory deprivation does affect people in a negative way, then patients in comas who are unstimulated are perhaps being mistreated. So at this hospital they decided to institute a program in which they started talking to patients in comas even though the patients could not respond. As a result of this treatment there seemed to be some improvement in recovery time.

Toward a Realistic Perspective of Aging

Up to now it may be that the way we have undertaken research in aging has been rather negative. We always look for decline. A colleague working with schizophrenics decided that the best way to learn about schizophrenia was to find behavioral variables on which schizophrenics performed better than normals. In other words, he was attempting to maximize performance in schizophrenics, and he felt that if he got good performance from them, he would be able to learn more from that behavior than from random abnormal responses. This notion is relevant for old age as well. Why not look for some behaviors that are better in old people than in young people? Maybe this tactic would give us more answers about old age than we are getting now.

There are a number of behaviors we might explore in this way. In one biofeedback study it was observed that the older subjects actually learned a little more quickly than the young to perform the alpha conditioning tasks (Woodruff, 1972). This was amazing, for there had been some speculation that it would not be possible to train the old people at all. But, on second thought, a person who has been living in his body for 65 years probably knows a lot more about it than someone who has only been in it for 20 years. Maybe old people are more perceptive of their own physiological functioning. Neugarten (1967) suggests that the middle aged and old are more internally aware, and perhaps old people are more sensitive to bodily function and more able to control it than are the young.

Birren (1969) studied decision making in middle-aged executives and found that they accumulate information in chunks rather than processing information in little bits as younger people tend to do. Another behavior that is being investigated by Clayton (1974) is wisdom. We always talk about old people as wiser. Are they? Can we identify some intellectual capacities that in old age are superior? These are the kind of studies that we need to undertake.

Are we overreacting to the negative stereotype of old age and currently adopting an overly positive approach? Gerontologists writing in this volume have stated that future cohorts of old people will be better off than earlier cohorts. For example, fewer of them will be foreign born, thus leaving the majority more adapted to the American society. They will be economically less disadvantaged and are going to live longer. They will be healthier and better educated (see Chapters 3, 6, and 18). Schaie, in Chapter 6, stated that most of the declines in intelligence with age are really a myth. Until people are ready to die, they appear to perform intellectually as well as when they are young. It has been suggested that even the biological decrements described in Chapters 10, 11, and 12 may be reversible.

Is all of this optimism appropriate? Those working daily with old people are aware that age differences are not entirely a myth. While gerontologists speak about normal aging as if there were not disease, it is clear that most old people suffer from one chronic disease and many are affected with three or four chronic diseases. Why do gerontologists present such a positive perspective? One reason is to dispel the negative myths about aging which have arisen in a youth-oriented culture.

While it is important to look at old age positively, it is also essential that we be realistic. Hopefully, scientists and laymen will come together and agree on a realistic perspective of aging that will help us to aid old people and to improve the quality of life in old age. Hopefully, too, such a perspective will help us all to be able to age with dignity rather than with despair.

References

Andersen, P. and Andersson, A. 1968. *Physiological basis of the alpha rhythm.* New York: Appleton-Century-Crofts.

Baltes, P. B. and Schaie, K. W. 1974. Aging and IQ: the myth of the twilight years. *Psychology Today* 7:35–40.

Birren, J. E. 1963. Psychophysiological relations. In *Human Aging: A Biological and Behavioral Study,* eds. J. E. Birren, R. N. Butler, S. W. Greenhouse, L. Sokoloff, and M. R. Yarrow. Washington: United States Government Printing Office, 1963.

Birren, J. E. 1965. Age changes in speed of behavior: its central nature and physiological correlates. In *Behavior, aging and the nervous system,* ed. A. T. Welford and J. E. Birren, pp. 191–216. Springfield, Illinois: Charles C. Thomas.

Birren, J. E. 1969. Age and decision strategies. In *Decision making and age,* eds. A. T. Welford and J. E. Birren, pp. 23–36. Basel/New York: S. Krager.

Birren, J. E.; Butler, R. N.; Greenhouse, S. W.; Sokoloff, L.; and Yarrow, M., eds. 1963. *Human aging: a biological and behavioral study.* Washington, D.C.: United States Government Printing Office.

Birren, J. E.; Riegel, K. F.; and Morrison, D. F. 1962. Age differences in response speed as a function of controlled variations of stimulus conditions: evidence for a general speed factor. *Gerontologia* 6:1–18.

Birren, J. E. and Woodruff, D. S. 1973. Human development over the life span through education. In *Life span developmental psychology: personality and socialization,* eds. P. B. Baltes and K. W. Schaie. New York: Academic Press.

Bishop, G. H. 1933. Cyclic changes in excitability of the optic pathway of the rabbit. *American Journal of Physiology* 103:213–224.

Bishop, G. H. 1936. The interpretation of cortical potentials. *Cold Spring Harbor Symposium on Quantitative Biology* 4:305–319.

Botwinick, J. 1959. Drives, expectancies and emotions. In *Handbook of aging and the individual: psychological and biological aspects,* ed. J. E. Birren, pp. 739–768. Chicago: University of Chicago Press.

Brazier, Mary A. B. and Finesinger, J. E. 1944. Characteristics of the normal electro-encephalogram. I. A study of the occipital-cortical potentials in 500 normal adults. *Journal of Clinical Investigation* 23:303–311.

Budzynski, T.; Stoyva, J.; and Adler, C. 1970. Feedback-induced muscle relaxation: application to tension headache. *Journal of Behavior Therapy and Experimental Psychiatry* 1:205–211.

Busse, E. L. 1959. Psychopathology. In *Handbook of aging and the individual,* ed. J. E. Birren. Chicago, Illinois: University of Chicago Press.

Butler, R. N. 1963. The facade of chronological age: an interpretive summary. *American Journal of Psychiatry* 119:721–728.

Callaway, E. 1962. Factors influencing the relationship between alpha activity and visual reaction time. *Electroencephalography and Clinical Neurophysiology:* 14:674–682.

Clayton, V. 1974. An exploratory analysis of the concept of wisdom. Unpublished manuscript. Andrus Gerontology Center, University of Southern California.

Cunningham, W. R. 1974. Age changes in the factor structure of intellectual abilities in adulthood and old age. Unpublished doctoral dissertation. University of Southern California.

Dustman, R. E. and Beck, E. C. 1965. Phase of alpha brain waves, reaction time, and visually evoked potentials. *Electroencephalography and Clinical Neurophysiology* 18:433–440.

Dru, D.; Walker, J. P.; and Walker, J. B. 1975. Self-produced locomotion restores visual capacity after striate lesions. *Science* 187:265–266.

Froehling, S. 1974. Effects of propranolol on behavioral and physiological measures of elderly males. Unpublished doctoral dissertation, Duke University.

Frost, J. D. 1968. EEG-intracellular potential relationships in isolated cerebral cortex. *Electroencephalography and Clinical Neurophysiology* 24:434–443.

Fuster, J. M. 1958. Effects of stimulation of brain stem on tachistoscopic perception. *Science* 127:150.

Green, E. E.; Green, A. M.; and Walters, E. D. 1970a. Self-regulation of internal states. In *Progress of Cybernetics: Proceedings of the International Congress of Cybernetics, London, 1969*, ed. J. Rose. London: Gordon & Breach.

Green, E. E.; Green, A. M.; and Walters, E. D. 1970b. Voluntary control of internal states: psychological and physiological. *Transpersonal Psychology* 2:1–26.

Hicks, L. H. and Birren, J. E. 1970. Aging, brain damage, and psychomotor slowing. *Psychological Bulletin* 74:377–396.

Hoyer, W. J.; Labouvie, G. V.; and Baltes, P. B. 1973. Modification of response speed and intellectual performance in the elderly. *Human Development* 16:233–242.

Jasper, H. H. 1936. Cortical excitatory state and synchronism in the control of bioelectric autonomous rhythms. *Cold Spring Harbor Symposium on Quantitative Biology* 4:320–338.

Kamiya, J. 1968. Conscious control of brain waves. *Psychology Today* 1:56–60.

Kamiya, J. 1969. Operant control of EEG alpha rhythm and some of its reported effects on consciousness. In *Altered States of Consciousness*, ed. C. T. Tart, pp. 507–517. New York: Wiley.

Kemp, B. J. 1971. Simple auditory reaction time of young adult and elderly subjects in relation to perceptual deprivation and signal-on versus signal-off conditions. Unpublished doctoral dissertation. University of Southern California.

Koga, Y. and Morant, G. M. 1923. On the degree of association between reaction times in the case of different senses. *Biometrika* 15:346–371.

Lindsley, D. B. 1952. Psychological phenomena and the electroencephalogram. *Electroencephalography and Clinical Neurophysiology* 4:443–456.

Lowenthal, M. F. 1964. Social isolation and mental illness in old age. *American Sociological Review* 29:54–70.

Murrell, F. H. 1970. The effect of extensive practice on age differences in reaction time. *Journal of Gerontology* 25:268–274.

Neugarten, B. L. 1967. The awareness of middle age. In *Middle age,* ed. R. Owen. London: British Broadcasting Corporation.

Obrist, W. D.; Henry, C. E.; and Justiss, W. A. 1961. Longitudinal study of EEG in old age. *Excerpta Medical International Congress,* Serial No. 37: 180–181.

Obrist, W. D. and Busse, E. W. 1965. The electroencephalogram in old age. In *Applications of electroencephalography to psychiatry: a symposium,* ed. W. P. Wilson. Durham, North Carolina: Duke University Press.

Schaie, K. W. 1970. A reinterpretation of age related changes in cognitive structure and functioning. In *Life-span developmental psychology: research and theory,* eds. L. R. Goulet and P. B. Baltes. New York: Academic Press.

Schenkenberg, T. 1970. Visual, auditory, and somatosensory evoked responses of normal subjects from childhood to senescence. Unpublished doctoral dissertation. University of Utah.

Shapiro, D.; Tursky, B.; and Schwartz, G. E. 1970. Control of blood pressure in man by operant conditioning. *Circulation Research,* Suppl. 1:26–27, 27–41.

Sterman, M. B. and Friar, L. 1972. Suppression of seizures in an epileptic following sensorimotor EEG feedback training. *Electroencephalography and Clinical Neurophysiology* 33:89–95.

Surwillo, W. W. 1963a. The relation of simple response time to brain wave frequency and the effects of age. *Electroencephalography and Clinical Neurophysiology,* 15:105:114.

Surwillo, W. W. 1963b. The relation of response time variability to age and the influence of brain wave frequency. *Electroencephalography and Clinical Neurophysiology* 15:1029–1032.

Surwillo, W. W. 1964a. The relation of decision time to brain wave frequency and to age. *Electroencephalography and Clinical Neurophysiology* 16:510–514.

Surwillo, W. W. 1964b. Some observations on the relation of response speed to frequency of photic stimulation under conditions of EEG synchronization. *Electroencephalography and Clinical Neurophysiology* 17:194–198.

Thompson, L. W. and Marsh, G. R. 1973. Psychophysiological studies of aging. In *The psychology of adult development and aging,* eds. C. Eisdorfer and M. Powell Lawton, pp. 112–148. Washington, D.C.: American Psychological Association Press.

Thompson, L. W. and Nowlin, J. B. 1973. Relation of increased attention to central and autonomic nervous system states. In *Intellectual functioning in adults: psychological and biological influences,* eds. Lissy R. Jarvik, C. Eisdorfer and J. E. Blum, pp. 107–123. New York: Springer Publishing Co.

Wilkie, F. and Eisdorfer, C. 1971. Intelligence and blood pressure in the aged. *Science* 172:959–962.

Woodruff, D. S. 1971. Biofeedback—implications for gerontology. In Design strategies and hypotheses of psychobiological research in aging, ch. D. S. Woodruff. Mini-symposium presented at the 24th annual meeting of the Gerontological Society, Houston, October 1971.

Woodruff, D. S. 1972. Biofeedback control of the EEG alpha rhythm and its effect on reaction time in the young and old. Unpublished doctoral dissertation. University of Southern California, 1972.

Woodruff, D. S. 1973. The usefulness of the life-span approach for the psychophysiology of aging. *Gerontologist* 13:467–472.

Woodruff, D. S. 1975. Relationships between EEG alpha frequency, reaction time, and age: a biofeedback study. *Psychophysiology,* in press.

Biological
Perspectives

10

Cellular Biology of Aging

PAUL DENNY

This chapter explores age-associated cellular changes within the organism. While the process of aging is very complex and does not uniformly result in decreased functional capacity, this survey will be limited to the assumption that the loss of vitality with the passage of time is due to the decline of functions within the organism.

The first part of this chapter presents a brief overview of relevant principles of cell biology. Following this, we will survey the nature and extent of cellular changes associated with aging. Then, based primarily upon experimental manipulations, the question whether cellular aging is due to intrinsic or extrinsic factors will be confronted and evidence that cellular aging is related to organismic aging and longevity presented. Finally, some popular explanations for the aging phenomenon will be evaluated and some possibilities for future research and areas of development will be discussed.

Principles of Cell Biology

The central theorem of cell biology is that cells are the fundamental units of structure and function of all living creatures. Although many important parts of the organism are essentially noncellular, such as bone and connective tissue, even their formation and functions are dependent upon cell-mediated processes. Furthermore, the complex functions of the organism—such as sensory perception, movement, and communication—are the results of organized efforts of individual cells or groups of cells. The coordinators of these high-level functions, such as hormones or nerve impulses, are themselves of cellular origin or manufacture. Hence, the conclusion that the function and well-being of the organism are intimately dependent upon cellular activities is inescapable.

As we look more closely at what constitutes a cell, it should be borne in mind that this review is by no means comprehensive but emphasizes those cellular activities which can be associated with or implicated in the aging process. The three main divisions of the cell are the plasma membrane, the cytoplasm, and the nucleus (see Figure 10.1). The plasma membrane serves as the interface between the living cell and its surrounding environment. This membrane is composed of proteins and lipids (fats) having both polar and non-polar (water soluble and non-soluble) portions arranged in such a way that the cell's integrity is maintained while allowing selected nutrients to pass into and waste products to pass out of the cell. The cell whose plasma membrane has ceased to function is or soon will be dead.

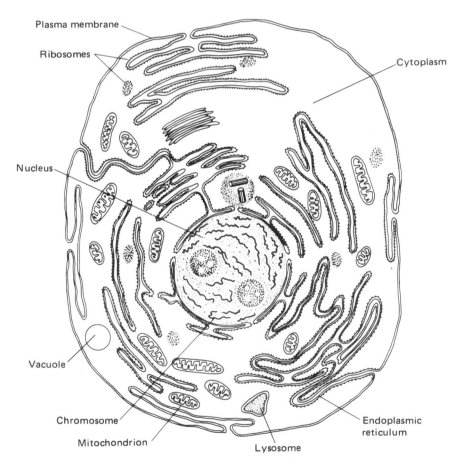

Figure 10.1. The cell and its organelles.

The nucleus plays one of the most central roles in the cell as it contains within the chromosomes the genetic material, DNA. DNA not only contains the blueprint for the organization and development of the entire organism, but also is the source for most of the information, in the form of RNA, required for the everyday maintenance of cellular integrity and function. Thus if the DNA becomes defective or in some way the flow of information from RNA to the rest of the cell is impaired, cellular function will be affected.

The cytoplasm is a highly ordered mixture of organelles (literally, the organs of the cell) and compounds, demonstrating many different functions. One of these functions is respiration which provides the energy-rich compound ATP and is performed by the mitochondria. The mitochondria are self-contained and show a highly characteristic pattern of membrane organization (Figure 10.1). Since ATP is required for many other cellular functions and syntheses, the efficiency of mitochondria in converting nutrients to ATP is a major factor in determining the efficiency of cellular activities.

Another process which occurs in the cytoplasm is protein synthesis. This not only requires ATP but also three different types of RNA—ribosomal, messenger, and transfer—which are derived from the DNA of the nucleus. Protein synthesis provides the cell with many of its structural components, and with the enzymes necessary to catalyze crucial reactions. Without these enzymes the synthesis of other important compounds, including carbohydrates, lipids (fats), DNA and RNA, would not be possible. It also provides, either directly or indirectly, such compounds as hormones, antibodies, and digestive enzymes, which operate outside of cells to benefit the entire organism. Protein synthesis occurs on structures (polyribosomes) which may be attached to cytoplasmic membranes (called endoplasmic reticulum) or may be free in the cytoplasm. The products are qualitatively different; that is, the membrane-associated synthesis is directed towards cellular export and the free polyribosome output is for use by the cell itself.

The cytoplasm also contains organelles which are responsible for intracellular digestion as might be required when a white blood cell ingests a pathogen or when a cell dies. These membrane-enclosed vesicles, called lysosomes, are smaller than mitochrondria and contain, among others, enzymes for breaking down DNA, RNA, proteins, and lipids. As will be discussed later, these structures have been implicated in the aging process.

From this brief survey of cellular components and processes it can be seen how defects in or abnormal outputs of any of the cell's component parts could impair the functional capacity of the entire cell which might, in turn, lead to organism-wide secondary effects. Because of the interrelated nature of cellular processes it is often difficult to identify the primary or first cause of reduced cellular activity. This is one of the major problems faced by investigators of cellular aging phenomena.

Do Cells Age *In Vivo?*

Having seen the critical role of the cell within the organism, we can now consider the fundamental question whether cells age or are affected by the organismic aging phenomenon. Based upon many different examples there is no doubt that cells do show age-related changes, but as will become apparent, the direct relationships of these changes to aging and death are not yet clear.

The most striking change which can be observed in cells with increasing age is the appearance of "age pigment," called lipofuscin. The pigment is contained in granules which are round to oblong in shape with a diameter between one and three microns and have a color range of yellow to brown. They do not accumulate in all tissues but are found most commonly in neural, muscle, liver, spleen, adrenal, pancreas, thymus, epididymus, and seminal vesical cells. Deposition of lipofuscin in some of these cells begins relatively early and increases in a linear fashion during the life span (Figure 10.2).

The granules are found in organisms throughout the animal kingdom, protozoa to mammals, and it is quite clear that their appearance is a function of the animal's "age" relative to its life span rather than to the passage of time. For instance, nematodes (a kind of simple worm) show the same pattern and extent of lipofuscin accumulation over their 28-day life span as do mice over a period of three years and humans over a period of one hundred years.

Though the etiology of the granules is not yet conclusive, there is good evidence that it involves a chemical reaction (peroxidation) of a lipid-protein complex. From a variety of observations, it also appears that lysosomes are the source of the granules and that the inability of lysosomal enzymes to metabolize efficiently certain lipid by-products is responsible. Consistent with this explanation are the dietary observations that vitamin E deficient old rats show an increased rate of pigment granule accumulation (Wünscher and Küstner, 1967) and more recently that high dosages of vitamin E inhibit the accumulation of granules in nematodes (Epstein, Himmelhoch, and Gershon, 1972). In these cases, vitamin E, which is a known biological antioxidant, could be expected to act in preventing the formation of peroxides. Another corroborating observation is that diets high in polyunsaturated fats tend to increase the rate of lipofuscin formation (Strehler, 1962); while this class of fats is essential to good nutrition, under certain conditions they are prone to form peroxides. Thus these observations support, at least indirectly, the idea that lipofuscin formation is due to inadequate mobilization of lipid oxidation by-products.

One of the major questions remaining about the "age pigment" is how it might contribute to age-related impairment of function. So far, there has been no demonstration of a positive correlation between lipofuscin accumulation and reductions in heart tissue capabilities in humans, rats, or mice. On the other hand, observations of exceptionally large accumulations in neurons have been associated with degenerative changes but even here there is no evidence for a causal relationship (Timiras, 1972a). Thus though the possible sources of lipofuscin formation have

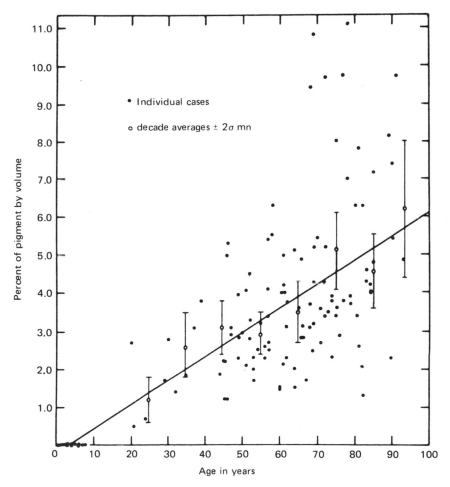

Figure 10.2. The relationship between age and lipofuscin content in the human myocardium. (Strehler, et al., 1959. Used by permission.)

been indicated, there is as yet no evidence of the effects of lipofuscin accumulation on the whole organism.

It has been reported that kidney, liver, and cardiac muscle cells show age-related changes in their mitochondria, endoplasmic reticulum, and pattern of lipid metabolism (Timiras, 1972b). The mitochondria tend to become swollen and the endoplasmic reticulum, instead of maintaining its usual thin bilayer configuration, becomes more vesicular. Both of these changes are probably due to a decline in the membrane function which controls osmotic balance in these organelles. Whether this decline is due to reductions in the availability of ATP or due to intrinsic membrane changes is not known. A possible stress factor may also contribute and will be discussed later. In addition, there is a tendency for these cells to accumulate fats either in the form of small, dispersed droplets or as a single large vacuole. This observation lends support to the idea that old cells tend to be less effective in processing lipids than young cells.

Examination of other cellular functions has not singled out any primary aging stimulus. DNA content remains the same throughout the life span, although there is some evidence for the higher incidence of DNA strand breaks and chromosomal aberrations in cells from older animals (Curtis, 1963; Price, Modak, and Makinodan, 1971). RNA content may vary in different cell types but is apparently correlated with a general cytoplasmic volume reduction rather than a specific change. Enzyme activities can change with age but do so in no clear pattern. For instance in the liver, some fifty percent of the enzymes show no change and approximately twenty-five percent show decreases and twenty-five percent increases. There is a suggestion that the increase tends to favor the degradative enzymes. The tenuousness of these studies is emphasized by the fact that a survey of the literature indicates that variation may be due not only to age differences but to the tissue, species, strain, and methodology. As with enzyme activities, rates of protein synthesis appear to vary somewhat in different tissues with age. The question of changes in the rates of RNA synthesis has been clouded with conflicting observations and as yet no definite conclusions can be drawn. Lysosome enzyme activities appear to increase only during the later stages of cellular degeneration and do not show a close correlation with the normal aging phenomenon.

Respiration is reduced with the advance of organismic age in some cell types (Barrows, Falzone, and Shock, 1960). However, measurements of respiration by mitochondrial preparations from young and old tissues failed to indicate any loss of normal function. What might be a very significant exception is that under conditions of stress, such as low-oxygen tension, mitochondria in cardiac muscle and autonomic nerve cells from old rats swelled and became fragmented, whereas in young rats under similar conditions no changes were observed (see Figures 10.3 and 10.4) (Sulkin and Sulkin, 1967). The cells from older animals also tended to accumulate lipid droplets under these conditions (Figure 10.5).

A decreased ability to adapt to environmental stress is also evidenced biochemically in studies of the cold-temperature-induced liver enzyme, tyrosine aminotransferase (Finch, Foster, and Mirsky, 1969). In these experiments, young, adult, and senescent mice were subjected to 9°C for two hours then returned to 24°C. Enzyme activities in the younger groups of mice began to increase immediately, whereas in old mice there was a delay of nearly two hours. Since the induction of this enzyme is based on higher-order regulatory functions, the delay causing lesion may be associated either with hormone production or with the responding liver cells. Regardless of whether this age-related impairment is at the level of signal reception or product synthesis, it is most probably cellularly based. A similar decline in stress response with age has been demonstrated with the rat liver enzyme, glucokinase, following glucose feedings (Adelman, 1970). These observations strongly suggest that while many, if not all, cellular functions normally can be performed at non-limiting rates throughout the life span, the ability of cells to respond and

Figure 10.3. Cardiac muscle from 118-day-old rat in the anoxic chamber for 28 days at final oxygen level of 5.5%. Muscle appears normal. X32,600. (Sulkin and Sulkin, 1967. Used by permission.)

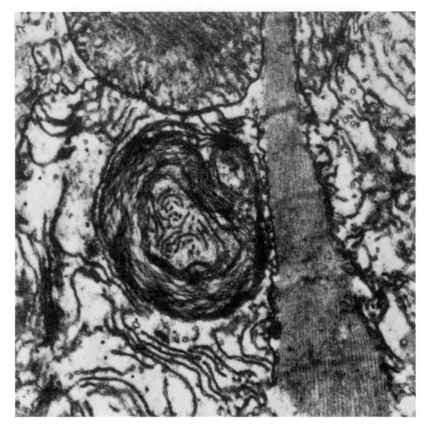

Figure 10.4. Cardiac muscle from 1032-day-old rat in anoxic chamber for 28 days at final oxygen level of 5.5%. Mitochondria markedly swollen with severe alterations of the cristate. Myofibrils show alterations in striation. X32,600. (Sulkin and Sulkin, 1967. Used by permission.)

adapt to environmental stress declines with age. The mechanisms and extent of this phenomenon have not been explored extensively at the cellular level. Knowledge of such mechanisms could provide key insights into the aging process.

Cell Renewal

The process of cell replacement is central to the maintenance of many functions in the organism and on theoretical grounds could be a key to longevity. On examination it can be seen that cell renewal occurs in most tissues but at different rates (Cameron, 1971). Two notable exceptions are all neurons and cardiac muscle cells. In fact, the number of neurons shows a substantial decline over the period from birth to maturity in humans and additionally there may be a gradual loss with aging. This latter finding is not, however, borne out in studies of animals grown under controlled conditions and may be a reflection of the medical history of human sample populations rather than of aging (Buetow, 1971). While there is some evidence for a decline in the functional capacity of heart muscle cells, their number does not appear to change appreciably throughout the life span.

Tissues undergoing some degree of renewal may be classified in three main groups: (1) those which show a complete cellular turnover in less than thirty days, (2) more than thirty days but still within the life span of the animal, and (3) those which show some cell division activity but probably do not renew all of the cells within the life span (Cameron, 1971). These groupings are used primarily for reference to the steady-

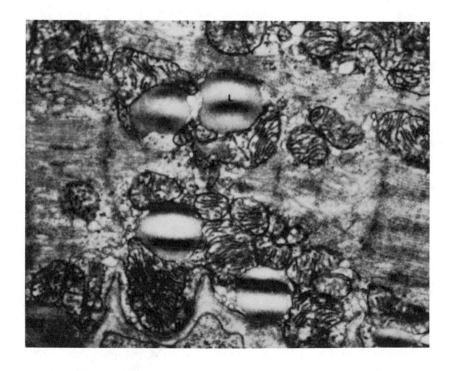

Figure 10.5. Cardiac muscle from 1032-day-old rat in anoxic chamber for 28 days at final oxygen level of 5.5%. Note accumulation of numerous lipid bodies. *L*, lipid body. X 21,000. (Sulkin and Sulkin, 1967. Used by permission.)

state condition of the mature adult and not to the expanding cell populations observed during development.

The first class is composed of those cell types whose life span is necessarily limited for reasons of mechanical wear and/or specialized function such as the lining of the gastro-intestinal tract, skin (epidermis), red (hemopoietic) and white (lymphopoietic) blood cells. The second category includes cell populations in the lining of the respiratory tract (epithelium), certain glandular cells (pancreas, salivary and adrenal cortex), liver cells (hepatocytes) and connective tissue of the skin (dermis). The group demonstrating the lowest index of cell division includes smooth muscle cells, bone cells (osteocytes), glial cells of the brain and tubule cells of the kidney. Most of these observations have been made on animal rather than human tissues, and a yet unresolved question is whether the cell division time intervals remain the same or get longer with the longer life span.

In most of the tissues which have been examined, the percentage of cells in division at any given time decreases with age (Buetow, 1971). In the case of the stem cells responsible for maintaining the lining of the small intestine, a thorough analysis of the phenomenon in mice (Thrasher and Gruelich, 1965) indicated that there was a decline in the number of cells exhibiting DNA synthesis (DNA synthetic index) which was interpreted as an increase in the length of time between division (generation cycle) (Table 10.1). These data are quite clear in suggesting that with this increased cell generation-cycle time the rate of cell renewal declines with age. Assuming that the amount of wear and tear on cells remains the same, or at least does not decrease with age of the individual, one can understand why certain tissues show an age-related decrease in the total cell number (Buetow, 1971).

Cell Replicative Potentials *In Vivo*

Having focused on some of the more obvious changes occurring in cells with age, one must turn to model animal systems in order to experimentally approach the questions which have been raised. The use of animals other than humans has many advantages, not the least of which is working with short life spans. For instance, one group of animals which is becoming popular for the study of certain questions is the nematodes. Some of these small, free-living worms contain only about one thousand cells (many of which are of the same types found in humans) and, as previously mentioned, have life spans of less than thirty days. Another very important advantage of using nonhuman animal systems is that experiments can be performed under relatively defined conditions

Table 10.1   Influences of age on mouse duodenal crypt cell division

Age groups	DNA synthetic index	Generation cycle (hours)
Infant (10 da)	63.3	11.4
Young adult (30-70 da)	57.9	12.4
Adult (380-399 da)	53.4	14.0
Senescent (579-638 da)	50.2	15.0

SOURCE: Adapted from Thrasher and Gruelich, 1965.

and proper controls can be maintained. A development which has been invaluable to the study of aging mechanisms has been the production of syngenetic mice. Through repeated sibling matings and stringent selection criteria, mouse strains have been developed in which intrastrain tissue transplants can be made without eliciting the usual immunological tissue rejection reactions. With these animals, cellular aging can be examined under continuing conditions which are optimal for growth and development, and the relative effects of intrinsic and extrinsic factors can be evaluated.

An extensive analysis has been provided by experiments of C. W. Daniel and his coworkers (1968, 1972, 1975) with mouse mammary gland cells. Normally the mammary gland begins as an invagination of cells from the abdominal skin layer. These cells form tubules and through the process of cell division make a highly branched network, infiltrating the abdominal fat pad. The available space within the pad is usually occupied by six to eight weeks and growth by cell proliferation ceases. If the initial bud of invaginating cells is surgically removed, glandular tissue does not form, indicating that neither the fat pad nor the over-lying skin layers have the ability to regenerate the gland. On the other hand, if mammary gland cells from another mouse of the same syngenetic strain are implanted at this site, normal growth and development begins and goes to completion in the usual length of time. Therefore by serial transplantations, one can ask if mammary gland cells can repeat this cell proliferation cycle indefinitely or if there is a limited growth potential. In order to discount the effects of host aging, the cells may be retransplanted into young female mice each time. When the mammary gland cells were serially transplanted at regular intervals, the amount of proliferation declined steadily as measured by the percentage of available fat pad filled by the transplant. Growth eventually ceased, and the maximum number of passages seen in any of these experiments has been eight. Furthermore, several different syngenetic mouse strains have been tested and all have given similar results, suggesting that this is a general phenomenon. It was somewhat surprising, however, that when the growth potential of young (three weeks) and old (twenty-six months) mouse mammary gland tissues were compared side by side on three-week-old hosts, there was no significant difference. These results suggested that some factor other than the passage of time was limiting the proliferative response. To test this, a comparison was made between colonies of mammary gland cells which were serially transplanted at three- or twelve-month intervals. Under these experimental conditions the transplants made at three-month intervals displayed a continuous growth phase whereas the twelve-month intervals allowed for long periods of nongrowth due to space limitations once the fat pad was filled. The results of these experiments are quite clear, showing that cells which were transplanted on the short-interval schedule had a greatly reduced temporal life span. Even cells which were begun on the long-interval schedule and were then shifted to the short, showed an immediate decline in proliferative capacity, indicating that there was nothing inherently different in the long-term colony cells. The most likely interpretation of these findings is that the potential for cellular proliferation is indeed limited and that the *major contributing factor is the number of times cells have divided and not the amount of time which has passed.*

A second series of experiments explored this further by attempting to rule out possible variation introduced by the difference in number of times the cells were transplanted on the three- and twelve-month schedules. Based on the observation that growth and branching within the developing gland takes place primarily at the tips of the ducts, it follows that cells at the periphery of the gland undergo almost continuous proliferation while those at the center divide only during the early growth phase. Therefore, separate colonies were started from cells of the central and peripheral mammary gland regions of young mice and serially transplanted at similar time intervals. The pattern of donor cell selection in each subsequent transplant was consistent with the original donor site so that the distinction between continuous and intermittent proliferation was maintained throughout. As with the previously reported series of experiments, the continuously proliferating cells showed a more rapid decline in capacity, providing additional support for the concept of a limited proliferative potential.

Studies with other systems also suggest that there may be a limited potential for cell proliferation. Serial transplants of skin appear to show a limited viability (Krohn, 1962) as do transplants of bone marrow used to "rescue" mice lethally irradiated to inactivate the endogenous cells (Cudkowicz et al., 1964). A particularly clear case of a limited cell proliferation was demonstrated in experiments in which a single clone (E9) of spleen cells was propagated through successive transplants in irradiated syngenetic mice (Williamson and Askonas, 1972). The clone of cells was first identified and subsequently followed by a characteristic antibody that it made against DNP (dinitrophenol). Based upon amount of antibody secreted, the relative size of the cell population could be estimated, even though the specific cells were not distinguishable from other spleen cells. It was found that cell proliferation remained high throughout the first four transplant generations, then began to decline, eventually disappearing from the remaining spleen cell population. That the E9 cells no longer existed was 'demonstrated when the remaining spleen cells were stimulated to make more antibodies against DNP, and the E9 characteristic antibody failed to appear even though other anti-DNP molecules were formed. It was estimated that the E9 clone cells underwent something less than ninety cell divisions, beginning with the first definitive progenitor E9 cell and ending when the clone was lost. These findings should be interpreted at two levels. First, in general, the principle of limited proliferative potentials for mammalian dividing cell populations is strongly supported. Secondly, the ninety cell division figure should not be equated to organismic longevity but rather to a finite growth potential which is imposed on the cells as they differentiate toward their specialized function. This says nothing of the stem cells from which the progenitor antibody producing cells arose or the embryonic cells from which the stem cells were derived. The relation of these findings to longevity will be discussed in a later section.

Cell Replicative Potentials *In Vitro*

It is of considerable interest that the number of cell doublings observed in the E9 clone *in vivo* was on the same order as the number of doublings observed in cultures of human fetal cells *in vitro*. These experiments employ tissue culture techniques and were initially performed by L. Hayflick and his colleagues (1961, 1965, 1972). In these experiments, cell suspensions derived from human fetal tissues by mild trypsin treatment were added to bottles containing a synthetic growth medium and incubated at 37°C. The cells first settle and attach on the bottom where they undergo divisions until all the available surface area is covered by a single layer (confluency). When confluency is reached, cell division ceases. The next step is to subculture the cells by first loosening them from the vessel, again by mild trypsin treatment. Then, before they are reintroduced into fresh culture bottles they are diluted to an extent that on settling, the bottom density will be one-half confluency. Therefore, each time confluency is reached it represents a population doubling. A plot of the proliferative ability of a culture of cells derived from human fetal lung tissue is shown in Figure 10.6. This plot is based upon the

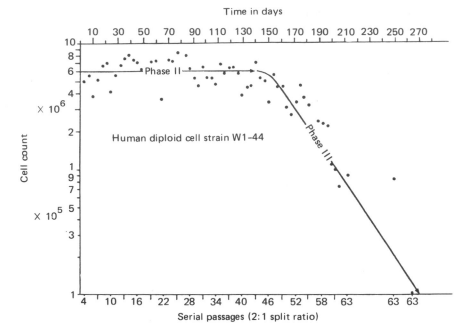

Figure 10.6. Cell counts determined at each passage of strain WI 44. The figure results in a curve suggestive of multiple-hit or multiple-target inactivation phenomena as an explanation for the mechanism of the occurence of Phase III. The initial plateau during Phase II, with no apparent loss of biological function as measured by constant doubling time, is followed by Phase III, where doubling time increases exponentially. (Hayflick, et al., 1965)

doubling times and cell counts. The so-called phase II represents a period of constant doubling times which lasts for about 50 population doublings and phase III is a period during which the cell doubling time slows down exponentially until all division ceases.

The question which arises is whether the decrease in cell division rate is determined by intracellular or environmental factors such as accumulated toxins or microorganisms in the medium. To test this, male human fetal cells which had already experienced 49 doublings (old) were mixed with female human cells at passage 13 (young). Seventeen doublings later the cells were examined by chromosome analysis and found to consist entirely of cells of female origin. Since the young cells continued to proliferate while the old cells died, the findings indicated that the environmental conditions for growth had not been altered and further that neither population of cells had any effect on the other.

The number of cell doublings achieved has a high degree of consistency even when the temporal sequence is interrupted by storage at −190°C in liquid nitrogen. Regardless whether the cells of a single strain are cultured continuously or are cultured, stored frozen for up to 15 months and recultured, the population doublings in every case fall within the same range (50 ± 10). This has been taken as evidence for excluding the passage of calendar time as a factor in determining the onset of phase III. However, because it is not clear how storage at −190°C might affect time-related changes, this conclusion does not necessarily follow. Recently, by using a nutritional block to interrupt divisions, cells have shown as much as a four-month increase in viability prior to phase III without any significant increase in number of accumulated population doublings (Dell'Orco, Mertins, and Kruse, 1974). As the cells remained metabolically active throughout the period of nondivision, these findings give strong support to the concept of an intrinsically limited proliferative capacity in normal cells derived from mammalian tissues rather than a chronological effect.

Replicative Potentials, Age, and Longevity

The *in vitro* cell culture system has developed into a very important model for the study of the aging phenomenon. In addition to demonstrating a limited proliferation, the number of cell doublings may also be roughly related to the life span and age of the donor. The correlation of cell doubling numbers to life span is based on a limited number of examples. Other than human tissue, the most thoroughly studied cells have been derived from chicken embryos. Under conditions in which human fibroblast cells show approximately 50 doublings, the chick cells give an average of 25 (Hayflick, 1972). Mouse embryo cells also show a 25 doubling potential. It must be realized that since these figures are averages of data from several laboratories, they should be interpreted only as indicating a trend. However, even in the most closely comparable examples, it is not clear how to relate the human life span of approximately 100 years and 50 cell doublings to the 10-15 year life span of chickens and 25 cell doublings or to the 3-4 year life span of mice and 25 doublings.

The general concept of the growth potential as a function of the life span is strongly supported by recent studies with cells from tortoises (Goldstein, 1974). The Galapagos tortoise is a species which reportedly lives to be 150 or even possibly 200 years old. Therefore one might expect that its cells would show more doublings in culture than human cells. Of the four tortoises from which cultures were derived, two were

Table 10.2   Growth history of cultural fibroblasts from Galapagos tortoises

| | Mean population doublings[a] at which | | Calendar time (weeks)[b] at which | |
Tortoise	Growth began to decline	Growth ceased	Growth began to decline	Growth ceased
T-1[c]	114	130	56	79
T-2	92	112	50	75
T-3	87	102	50	75
T-4	72	90	47	70

[a]There are no quantitative data on how many population doublings occur during the stage of explanation; no attempt has been made to estimate this unknown number which is, therefore, not included.
[b]A total of 8 weeks comprising the 4-week interval of explantation and the same time prior to declaring cultures dead is not included.
[c]Ages: T-1, 4 years; T-2, 6 years; T-3, T-4 25–100 years.
SOURCE: Adapted from Goldstein, 1974.

young and two were estimated to be much older. In every case, the number of recorded population doublings (Table 10.2) exceeded those for human fetal tissue cells. The difference is more striking if the comparison is made between known values for adult human cells (30 doublings), and the adult tortoise cells at approximately 80 doublings. These comparisons suggest that there may be a much closer relationship of cell doubling potential to longevity span than had heretofore been indicated. However, it should be pointed out that before this point can be established, a great deal of careful, well-controlled research is required with a variety of different organisms.

Hayflick (1965) reported a very significant reduction in the number of population doublings observed prior to onset of phase III in cultures from older adult lungs as compared to fetal lungs—suggesting that there was a correlation between remaining growth potential and donor age (Table 10.3). Curiously, the tissue from the younger adults included in this data showed a growth potential no greater than the older adults. However, because of possible individual variations this cannot be considered as significant. In a more recent study (Martin, Sprague, and Epstein, 1970) of the doubling potentials of human skin cells from donors of different ages, the individual variation within age groups is very apparent, but statistical analysis suggests that there is a linear regression of potential with age. These results are to be viewed with some caution because several highly deviant cultures were from individuals with known diseases, and how this affects cell growth potentials has not been thoroughly studied and their inclusion in the data is questionable. Thus, whether the loss of cell proliferative potential is a continuous function with age or occurs in a different pattern still remains to be answered.

In the above context it is of special interest to consider those experiments using cells from patients with Werner's syndrome or progeria (Hutchinson-Gilford syndrome). Both diseases are characterized by what might be described as accelerated senescence. With progeria, a child ten years of age may show the physical signs of aging characteristic of a normal seventy-year-old person. The symptoms of Werner's syndrome usually do not become apparent until somewhat later in life, although they may begin during the teens. The average life span for Werner's syndrome is 47 years; it is characterized by the early appearance of arteriosclerosis, diabetes mellitus, osteoporosis, skeletal muscle atrophy and cancer. When compared to normal skin cell donors, the cell doublings for the two older patients (40-50 years) with Werner's syndrome was more than two standard deviations below the mean of the control cultures from that age group, and the number of doublings of cells from a younger patient (30-40 years) was more than three standard deviations below the mean for its group (Martin, Sprague, and Epstein, 1970). Goldstein (1969) reports

Table 10.3 A comparison of the passage levels at which Phase III occurred in human diploid cell strains of adult and fetal origin[a]

Fetal lung		Adult lung			
Strain	Passage level at which Phase III occurred (cell doublings)	Strain	Passage level at which Phase III occurred (cell doublings)	Age of donor	Cause of death
WI-1	51	W-1000	29	87	Heart failure
WI-3	35	W-1001	18	80	Cerebral vascular accident
WI-11	57	W-1002	21	69	Bronchial pneumonia
WI-16	44	W-1003	24	67	Dissecting aneuryism
WI-18	53	W-1004	22	61	Renal failure
WI-19	50	W-1005	16	58	Rheumatoid arthritis
WI-23	55	W-1006	14	58	Pulmonary embolus
WI-24	39	W-1007	20	26	Auto accident
WI-25	41				
WI-26	50				
WI-27	41				
WI-38	48				
WI-44	63				
Average	48		20		
Range	35–63		14–29		

[a]All strains cultivated at a 2:1 split ratio. Fetal strains derived from donors of 3–4 months' gestation obtained by surgical abortion. Adult and fetal strains derived from both male and female tissue.
SOURCE: Hayflick, 1965.

that skin cells derived from a nine-year-old boy with progeria could undergo only two cell doublings whereas control experiments using cells from young adults were capable of 20-30 doublings. A second study, utilizing three different individuals with the disease, gave a very clear indication that the growth rate of these cells in culture was greatly reduced as compared to those derived from normal tissues (Danes, 1971). However, the cultures did not show the characteristics of phase III such as increased generation time, gradual cessation of mitotic activity, accumulation of cellular debris and eventual degeneration of the culture. Thus it is not clear that it is an analogous phenomenon, but one can safely say that cells derived from patients with accelerated senescence diseases consistently reflect the reduced growth and replacement rate observed in these individuals. It is also noteworthy that the cells show a much longer latent period in culture than do normal tissues. The significance of this observation will be discussed.

Latent Period and Age

The latent period is defined as the time it takes before cells begin to migrate out from a piece of tissue placed in culture medium. These cells divide and eventually reach confluency. It is often research practice to use these cells for subsequent population doubling measurements. Studies of the length of this period in rat and chicken tissues (Soukupovà, Holečkovà, and Hnevkovsky, 1970) and human skin (Waters and Walford, 1970) have indicated that barring individual variations it is directly proportional to the age of the donor group. This proportionality also holds in tissues which have ceased active growth in size and which have achieved a low stable mitotic index (percentage of cells undergoing division at a given time). Thus it presents another example of a cellular response in tissue culture which is affected by aging. The fact that this and the cell doubling phenomenon both show donor age-related changes indicates the validity for extrapolating the interpretation of observations in these systems to the general phenomenon of aging. The first conclusions which would appear to be justified by the tissue culture work are that the limited cell doubling potential and its age-related decrease are intrinsically determined. However, to rule out possible systemic effects on the cells in the organism, we must return to tissue transplant studies.

Cell Division and Aging

As previously noted with mammary gland, there is very little difference between the proliferative capacity of old and young tissues when serially transplanted. However, since most of its history is spent under nongrowth conditions, its replicative potential is not reduced. On the other hand, with tissues undergoing near continuous growth there are indications that this capacity is diminished with age. Serial transplants of skin from old mice do not on the whole survive as long as those from young mice (Krohn, 1962). Studies with bone marrow (Harrison, 1973) and spleen transplants (Price and Makinodian, 1972a,b) also show related changes with certain cell types but not as a total population function. In the first of these experiments, bone marrow was used to cure mice of the same strain which were genetically deficient in hemopoietic (red blood cell forming) tissue and thereby anemic. Transplants of old and young mouse marrow produced equivalent normal numbers of erythrocytes (red blood cells) through four hosts and for up to 70 months, long beyond the normal donor life span. However, after three transplants the percentage of cures began to drop more rapidly with marrow from old mice than from young mice. Furthermore, the number of colony forming units, a measure of the earliest defined marrow precursor cells, was also declining at a more rapid rate. These results indicate that aging can reduce the replicative potential of certain cell types *in vivo* and suggest the possibility that the overall aging phenomenon might be due to such limitations imposed on a specific, highly important cell population.

When spleen tissue from young and old mice was used to rescue young hosts which had been lethally irradiated and then tested for the ability to carry out different immunological activities, certain cellular functions were reduced with the old spleens. The most striking effect was an 80 percent decline in the number of cells capable of mounting a localized immunological assault on foreign cells. Since the transplants were made into young hosts, the conclusion may be made that the age-related change was intrinsic within the cells themselves. What happens though, when young and old spleens are transplanted into irradiated old mice? In each case, the cell-based immunological response was one-half what it had been in young hosts; that is, young spleens into old mice was 50 percent of young into young, and old spleens into old mice was 10 percent of young into young. These observations indicated not only an intrinsic aging mechanism but also an extrinsic or systemic effect on the cellular proliferative capacity. In agreement with this are the experiments in which mammary glands from young mice were transplanted into old hosts and observed to grow very poorly. Thus we cannot say simply that aging is related exclusively to cells' intrinsically limited capacities for replication. With the introduction of the additional extrinsic factor, some of the complexity of the aging phenomenon begins to appear.

An observation which has important implications and is consistently seen in the tissue transplantation experiments is that the length of survival of the transplant tissue in young hosts can exceed the older donor animal's life-span by several times, indicating that even with old cells there is an excess of proliferative potential. Thus the decline in the *rate* of cell proliferation would appear to be a more likely factor in causing age related changes. By way of illustrating this possibility, one could propose, as in the case of the spleen transplant experiments discussed above, that a decline in the production of immunologically competent cells with age would result in a reduction of the system's ability to function in surveilance and destruction of precancerous cells, and thereby heighten the chances of contracting the disease. We might point out that in the mammary gland transplant experiments the decline in proliferative ability began almost immediately and was not an all or none phenomenon. A decrease in cellular proliferative rate *in vivo* was noted earlier with intestinal epithelium and probably occurs in most tissues (Buetow, 1971). This phenomenon could result in the reduction of a vital cell population to a level which is no longer sufficient to maintain completely a critical body function, even though the potential proliferative capacity exceeds the requirements for a "normal" life span.

Possible Limitations on Cell Division

One major advantage of the use of model systems is that various cellular functions can be monitored throughout the aging process of a single piece of tissue or cell culture. While these studies have not identified the causative factor(s), a number of age-related changes have been measured which suggest interesting possibilities. Careful light and electron microscopy examination of "old" mammary gland tissue which has stopped growing after serial transplantation failed to show any degeneration of the structural components of the cells; in fact, the tissue closely resembled young mammary glands which had ceased to grow due to space restrictions. However, experiments utilizing the radioactive precursor, ^{3}H-thymidine, clearly showed that DNA synthesis had stopped, suggesting that replication of the cellular genetic material may be one of the first processes which is affected by aging. This may be the crucial factor causing the cessation of cell division.

DNA synthesis also slows down and eventually stops in cultured cells (Cristofalo, 1972). In this case, many other processes are affected (Table 10.4) and the problem becomes one of delineating causal relationships. Analysis of the enzymes required for the conversion of glucose to precursors which can be utilized by mitochondria for the production of ATP indicate a fully functional system in "old" cells. In addition, the ability of precursors to pass into cells from the medium is for the most part unimpaired. Coupling these findings with the observations that "senescent" cells contain more protein, RNA, storage carbohydrate (glycogen), and lipid and are larger than dividing cells, one comes to the conclusion that they are fully capable of the interdivision growth process. From the available information then, the essential lack appears to be associated with the division process itself. Whether this lack of further division is based on factors affecting the synthesis of DNA or on cell division itself (cytokinesis) remains to be seen.

One of the normal constituents of cells which shows an interesting age-related change in tissue culture is the lysosomes. As mentioned previously, these organelles contain enzymes which are involved in intracellular breakdown processes. It has been shown that they increase in number and size with increasing cell doubling number. Furthermore, by measuring one of the lysosomal enzymes it has been shown that there is a concomitant increase in activity suggesting that autolytic (self-digesting) capacity within the cell might be one of the major factors in limiting cell proliferation. Again however, the question of first causes becomes important in view of the following observations. The first is that cells derived from

Table 10.4 Some metabolic properties of diploid cells studied during aging

Parameter	Variation with cell age[a]
Glycolysis	o
Glycolytic enzymes	o; −
Pentose phosphate shunt	−
Permeability to glucose	o
Glycogen content	+
Mucopolysaccharide synthesis	−
Respiration	o
Respiratory enzymes	o
Lipid content	+
Lipid synthesis	+
Protein content	+; o
Permeability to amino acids	o
Transaminases	o; −
Glutamic dehydrogenase	o
Nucleohistone content	o
Collagen synthesis	−
DNA content	o; −
RNA content	+
Nucleic acid synthesis	−
RNA turnover	+
Lysosomes and lysosomal enzymes	+
Alkaline phosphatase	o

[a](+), increase with age; (−), decrease with age; (o), no change.
SOURCE: V. J. Cristofalo, 1972. Reprinted with permission of Academic Press, Inc., New York.

old tissues do not show these properties during the initial culture phases. The second observation is that in a phase II culture the percentage of nondividers within the population increases with passage number, and it has been shown that even in the earliest passages, some cells are present which have large numbers of lysosomes and show signs of phase III-type degeneration (Brandes et al., 1972). This heterogeneity within the culture might suggest that the gradual increase of lysosomal enzymes is a reflection of the increased number of dying (necrotic) cells rather than the cause of it.

Theories of Cellular Aging

The former observations and experiments have suggested a number of different explanations for the cellular aging phenomenon (Orgel, 1973). One of the most popular is the error accumulation hypothesis whose principal tenet states that cellular reproduction is not perfect and that defective cell components may occasionally be generated due to inaccuracies within the synthesis processes. Assuming that these defective parts are stable and passed on to subsequent generations then eventual build up and impairment of function would result. Such a process could be occurring at one or many different levels within the cell. For instance, one suggestion is that of an accumulation of mutations within the DNA. The presence of increasing numbers of mutations with age would result in the synthesis of more and more functionally impaired enzymes, eventually affecting the DNA synthesis mechanism itself and bringing cell division to a halt. This so-called somatic mutation theory no longer enjoys the popularity it once had, largely because of the inability to obtain evidence in its favor. However, before it can be ruled out as a contributing factor, improvements on the current techniques are required.

On the other hand, it has been shown that the incidence of chromosome structural defects increases with the "age" of cells in culture, usually beginning sometime after the fortieth passage in human cells. These anomalies include abnormal numbers of chromosomes as well as broken and translocated pieces. Since the effects of genetically inherited chromosomal defects are well known, such as in the case of Down's syndrome (mongoloidism), it is conceivable that their appearance in cultured cells might be related to the limited life span. As mentioned previously, there is also some evidence to suggest that a similar relationship might exist with *in vivo* aging. Admittedly based upon limited observations, the eventual application of this phenomenon to a general theory of aging shows promise and should be pursued further.

The idea of an accumulation of defective components also applies to the mitochondria of older cells in culture. Whereas the mitochondria found in early passage cells tend to be oval, they are more ellipsoid in older cells and show some decline in their functional aspects. Concern for errors in the genetic material also applies to mitochondria since they contain their own DNA and protein synthesis systems and are for the most part self-replicating. Because of their central position in maintaining normal cellular metabolism, they could profoundly affect the cell's proliferative capacity.

The experiments of Holliday and Tarrant (1972) support the hypothesis that an accumulation of defective proteins may be responsible for cellular aging. Based upon the principle that the degree of resistance of an enzyme to heat denaturation (as measured by the loss of activity) is directly related to structural stability, it was shown that glucose-6-phosphate dehydrogenase from late passage cells is more unstable than that from young cells. The heat denaturation curves from older cells are best interpreted as indicating that two protein populations exist, one normal and one defective. Quantitation indicated that approximately 25 percent of the enzyme was defective in the late passage cells. A similar phenomenon has also been shown for an enzyme, aldolase, found in the liver of mice (Gershon and Gershon, 1973). The initial measurements suggested that the enzyme concentration in old mouse livers (31 months) was approximately one half that found in young adults (3 months). However, on precipitating the aldolase with a very specific antibody, approximately equivalent amounts of material were obtained from each. Subsequent kinetic studies strongly indicated that this precipitate contained two populations of enzyme molecules, one fully active and the other inactive, in approximately equal proportions. These findings provide strong evidence that inactive or defective proteins appear in the normal course of aging *in vivo* and *in vitro*. While the mechanism which produces these abnormal proteins (whether mutations or defective synthetic machinery) is still a matter for speculation, the observations of their existence provide a strong basis for an explanation of the age-related loss of functional capacity.

Other hypotheses proposed to explain the aging phenomenon incorporate ideas of programmed aging, dilution of essential components and accumulation of harmful metabolic by products. Of these, the dilution hypothesis seems the least likely on theoretical grounds simply because for a substance to persist for fifty cell divisions in culture before becoming limiting would require that the concentration within the starting cells would be well beyond that possible. This hypothesis also cannot apply to the aging of nondividing cells such as neurons or muscle cells since there is no mechanism for dilution to occur.

Programmed aging implies that there is a biological clock which keeps track of divisions or elapsed time and initiates the aging sequence when certain limits are reached. The attractiveness of this hypothesis lies in its ability to account for the apparent consistency of population doubling numbers from sample to sample in cell culture and also, at the organismic level, for the apparent maximum life span within a given species. Since both of these vary considerably with different species, one would like to think that the clock is controlled by the genetic material. Evidence for this is only circumstantial, and the concept of a preprogrammed life span in its purest sense should be considered as hypothetical at this time.

The hypothesis centering around the accumulation of harmful by-products implies that certain compounds are formed for which cells have inadequate removal mechanisms. This idea provides a reasonably satisfactory explanation for some of the observed changes in nondividing cells. However, it is difficult to apply the hypothesis to rapidly dividing cells for the reason that if a harmful material is formed at a uniform rate throughout the life span then the maximum concentration will approach only twice the amount formed during one cell cycle. To obtain an increasing rate of accumulation of a product, more complex models are needed which employ interdependent processes and products with feedback characteristics. This could provide the necessary conditions and furnish a plausible mechanism for the aging phenomenon in dividing cell populations. As yet there is no indication that toxic by-products are accumulated with aging *in vivo* or *in vitro,* but based upon the example provided by lipofuscin, the hypothesis is very attractive and is a viable approach for additional studies.

Prospectives in Cellular Aging Research

As is the case in much of biological research, the questions to be asked are not new or particularly profound but the answers are hard to achieve and often require years or tens of years of coordinated research. While many observations and experimental conclusions have been presented here, it is obvious that very few of the fundamental mechanisms of cellular aging are understood. The greatest obstacle towards achieving this knowledge is that the aged cell has not been adequately described, especially as relating to its physiological, biochemical and molecular aspects. Such questions as changes in RNA synthesis, protein synthesis and respiration are basic and often have to be reevaluated when there are advances in the understanding of the fundamental process or more precise methods become available.

An area of research which would benefit from a greater understanding of the cell is that of changes in cellular responsiveness with age. Many investigations have been made showing the effects of stress on the senescent to be more severe than on the young or mature organism, and the few which have been performed at the cellular level show a similar pattern. It is conceivable that much of what has been observed at the organismic level can be traced to limitations at the cellular level. Continued research along this line should prove to be interesting, as would investigations of the causes of the observed reductions in cellular responsiveness.

It appears that one of the phenomena central to cellular aging is the observed decline in cell divisions. The mechanism for this is not known, but perhaps a more relevant question is how this decline relates to tissue and organism aging. It would seem especially important to determine if there are causal relationships. Two interesting and very active research areas which also bear upon this question are cancer and cellular transformation. Tissue-culture cell lines which normally have a limited life span gain the potential for dividing indefinitely when infected with transforming viruses or treated with chemical carcinogens. Cells derived from cancerous tissues also have this potential. Therefore, it is possible to remove the block to cell division and while this result at our current level of understanding is highly undesirable, these systems provide models for the study of factors regulating the division process.

A major concern with the cell culture studies is to what extent the observations, limited population doublings and the latent period, can be related to organismic aging and longevity. From the results which are available it would appear that both observations, the potential cell doubling number decline with age and the correlation with longevity, are not well substantiated. Since these observations provide much of the justification for applying this research approach to the study of aging, one would like to see them more strongly supported.

The above reservations notwithstanding, the cell culture experiments continue to produce very interesting and exciting results. In current experiments by Wright and Hayflick (1975) the question of nuclear versus cytoplasmic control of the cell doubling number is being investigated. Their approach is to remove nuclei from either "young" or "old" cells and replace them with nuclei of their choice. These experiments which are very complex in both design and execution suggest that nuclear function rather than the cytoplasm controls the cell doubling number.

Table 10.5   Increase in cell doublings with continuous exposure to hydrocortisone (mother-daughter subcultivations)

Cell Type	Passage at start of experiment	Cumulative cell doublings from start of experiment		Percent increase with hydrocortisone
		Control	Hydrocortisone	
WI-38ⱼ	19	42.0	56.0	33
WI-38ₕ	18	37.0	49.0	32
WI-38ₚ	18	35.0	48.0	37
WI-26	22	46.0	60.0	30
WI-38ₓ[a]	21	18.0	26.0	44
WI-38ᵧ[a]	21	17.0	25.0	48

[a]Subcultivated once a week; others subcultured at confluency.
SOURCE: Cristofalo, 1974.

In other experiments with the cell culture system it has been conclusively demonstrated that the cell doubling potential can be extended either by hydrocortisone (Cristofalo, 1974) or vitamin E (Packer and Smith, 1974). Hydrocortisone at a dosage of 5 ug/ml of culture medium extends the doubling potential 30 percent to 50 percent (Table 10.5) primarily by keeping more cells in the proliferating pool. Vitamin E, as discussed earlier, is thought to be a membrane antioxidant and when added to cultures of human fetal lung cells (50 ± 10 doublings) extends the cell doubling potential by at least a factor of two. In fact, at the 97th passage level approximately 95% of the cells were still capable of synthesizing DNA. Vitamin E also protected these cells against stress induced by visible light or high oxygen tension. Thus in culture the cellular life span can be increased, suggesting that there may be mechanisms for extending the life span of organisms. It is obvious that research along these lines should be continued and could be highly beneficial.

References

Adelman, R. 1970. An age-dependent modification of enzyme regulation. *Journal of Biological Chemistry* 245:1032–1035.

Barrows, C.; Falzone, J.; and Shock, N. 1960. Age differences in the succinoxidase activity of homogenates and mitochondria from livers and kidneys of rats. *Journal of Gerontology* 15:130–133.

Brandes, D.; Murphy, D.; Anton, E.; and Barnard, S. 1972. Ultrastructural and cytochemical changes in cultured human lung cells. *Journal of Ultrastructure Research* 39:465–483.

Buetow, D. E. 1971. Cellular content and cellular proliferation changes in the tissues and organs of the aging mammals. *Cellular and Molecular Renewal in the Mammalian Body,* eds. I. L. Cameron and J. D. Thrasher, pp. 87–106. New York: Academic Press.

Cameron, I. L. 1971. Cell proliferation and renewal in the mammalian body. In *Cellular and Molecular Renewal in the Mammalian Body,* eds. I. L. Cameron and J. D. Thrasher, pp. 45–85. New York: Academic Press.

Cristofalo, V. 1972. Animal cell cultures as a model system for the study of aging. *Advances in Gerontological Research* 4:45–79.

Cristofalo, V. 1974. Aging. In *Concepts of Development,* eds. J. Lash and J. R. Whittaker, pp. 429–447. Stamford, Conn.: Sinauer Association, Inc.

Cudkowicz, G.; Upton, A.; Shearer, G.; and Hughs, W. 1964. Lymphocyte content and proliferative capacity of serially transplanted bone marrow. *Nature* (London) 201:165–167.

Curtis, H. J. 1963. Biological mechanisms underlying the aging process. *Science* 141:686–694.

Daniel, C. 1972. Aging of cells during serial propagation *in vivo. Advances in Gerontological Research* 4:167–198.

Daniel, C. 1975. Regulation of cell division in aging mouse mammary epithelium. In *Prospectives in Aging Research,* eds. V. Cristofalo, J. Roberts, and A. Adelman. New York: Plenum Press.

Daniel, C.; DeOme, K.; Young, J.; Blair, P.; and Faulkin, L. 1968. The *in vivo* life span of normal and preneoplastic mouse mammary glands: a serial transplantation study. *Proceedings of the National Academy of Sciences, U.S.A.* 61:53–60.

Danes, B. 1971. Progeria: A cell culture study on aging. *Journal of Clinical Investigation* 50:2000–2003.

Dell'Orco, R.; Mertins, J.; and Kruse, Jr., P. 1974. Doubling potential, calendar time, and donor age of human diploid cells in culture. *Experimental Cell Research* 84:363–366.

Finch, C.; Foster, J.; and Mirsky, A. 1969. Ageing and the regulation of cell activities during exposure to cold. *Journal of General Physiology* 54:690–712.

Epstein, J. and Gershon, D. 1972. Studies on ageing in nematodes. IV. The effect of antioxidants on cellular damage and life span. *Mechanisms of Ageing and Development* 1:257–264.

Gershon, H. and Gershon, D. 1973. Inactive enzyme molecules in aging mice: liver aldolase. *Proceedings of the National Academy of Sciences, U.S.A.* 70:909–913.

Goldstein, S. 1969. Life span of cultured cells in progeria. *Lancet* 1:424.

Goldstein, S. 1974. Aging *in vitro.* Growth of cultured cells from the Galapagos tortoise. *Experimental Cell Research* 83:297–302.

Harrison, D. E. 1973. Normal production of erythrocytes by mouse marrow continuous for 73 months. *Proceedings of the National Academy of Sciences, U.S.A.* 70:3184–3188.

Hayflick, L. 1965. The limited *in vitro* lifetime of human diploid cell strains. *Experimental Cell Research* 37:614–636.

Hayflick, L. 1972. Cell aging and cell differentiation *in vitro.* In *Aging and Development,* eds. H. Bredt and J. W. Rohen, pp. 1–15. Mainz, Germany: Mainz Academy of Science and Literature.

Hayflick, L. and Moorhead, P. 1961. The serial cultivation of human diploid cell strains. *Experimental Cell Research* 25:585–621.

Holliday, R. & Tarrant, G. 1972. Altered enzymes in ageing human fibroblasts. *Nature* (London) 238:26–30.

Krohn, P. 1962. Review lectures on senescence. II. Heterochronic transplantation in the study of aging. *Proceedings of the Royal Society of Medicine* 157:128–147.

Martin, G.; Sprague, C.; and Epstein, C. 1970. Replicative life-span of cultivated human cells. Effects of donor's age, tissue and genotype. *Laboratory Investigation* 23:86–92.

Orgel, L. 1973. Ageing in clones of mammalian cells. *Nature* (London) 243:441–445.

Packer, L. and Smith, J. 1974. Extension of the lifespan of cultured normal human diploid cells by vitamin E. *Proceedings of the National Academy of Sciences, U.S.A.* 71:4763–4767.

Price, G. B.; Modak, S.; and Makinodan, T. 1971. Age-associated changes in the DNA of mouse tissue. *Science* 171:917–920.

Price, G. B. and Makinodan, T. 1972a. Immunologic deficiencies in senescence. I. Characterization of intrinsic deficiencies. *Journal of Immunology* 108:403–412.

———— 1972b. Immunologic deficiencies in senescence. II. Characterization of extrinsic deficiencies. *Journal of Immunology* 108:413–417.

Soukupovà, M.; Holečkovà, E.; and Hnevkovsky, P. 1970. Changes of the latent period of explanted tissues during ontogenesis. In *Aging in Cell and Tissue Culture*, eds. E. Holečkovà and V. J. Cristofalo, pp. 41–56. New York: Plenum Press.

Strehler, B. L. 1962. *Time, cells and aging.* New York: Academic Press.

Strehler, B. L.; Mark, D.; Mildvan, A. S.; and Gee, M. 1959. Rate and magnitude of age pigment accumulation in the human myocardium. *Journal of Gerontology* 14:430–439.

Sulkin, V. M. and Sulkin, D. F. 1967. Age differences in response to chronic hypoxia on the fine structure of cardiac muscle and autonomic ganglion cells. *Journal of Gerontology* 22:485–501.

Thrasher, J. and Greulich, R. 1965. The duodenal progenitor population. II. Age related changes in size and distribution. *Journal of Experimental Zoology* 159:385–396.

Timiras, P. S. 1972a. Structural, biochemical and functional aging of the nervous system. *Developmental Physiology and Aging*, pp. 502–526. New York: Macmillan Co.

———— 1972b. Degenerative changes in cells and cell death. *Developmental Physiology and Aging*, pp. 429–449. New York: Macmillan Co.

Waters, H. and Walford, R. L. 1970. Latent period for outgrowth of human skin explants as a function of age. *Journal of Gerontology* 25:381–383.

Williamson, A. R. and Askonas, B. A. 1972. Senescence of an antibody-forming cell clone. *Nature* (London) 238:337–339.

Wünscher, W. and Küstner, R. 1967. Untersuehungenüber die mengenmäßige Verterlung von Lipofuszen und Vitamin-E-Mangel-Pigment in Nervenzellen von Ratten verschiedener Altersstufen. *Gerontologia* 13:153–164.

Wright, W. E. and Hayflick, L. 1975. The regulation of cellular aging by nuclear events in cultured normal human fibroblasts (WI 38). In *Prospectives in Aging Research*, ed. V. Cristofalo, J. Roberts, and R. Adelman. New York: Plenum Press.

11

Changing Physiology of Aging: Normal and Pathological

RUTH B. WEG

During a recent political campaign, the mystery of longevity was addressed by an old man sitting on a park bench in San Diego. He refused to shake the hand of a politician. "Why not?" asked the nonplussed congressman. The old man said, "I'm 105 years old. I've never touched or been touched by a politician in my whole life, and I think I owe my longevity to that."

While that remark lacks the sanction of scientific evidence, a definitive statement on prolongevity awaits the continuing search into the processes of aging. The human family has always lived with the conflict between two concepts: the acceptance of old age as the inevitable, debilitated, end of life; and the powerful drive to longevity, and even immortality. In Chapter 2 of this volume Birren and Clayton trace historical concerns with aging and immortality; therefore, only a few examples of the age-old search will be presented here.

In Greek mythology, the Goddess Aurora and her husband Tithonus paid a tragic price for the lack of resolution of the conflict between aging and immortality. Zeus finally granted the immortality to Tithonus that Aurora had asked (Guillerme, 1963). However, as her husband grew old, became disabled, and prayed for the freedom of death, Aurora realized in despair that she had failed to request eternal youth for him as well.

In the first century B.C. Cicero in his essay "On Old Age" accepted the notion of aging as natural and inevitable, "that it is not old age that is at fault but rather our attitude toward it." He did not see aging as disease.

Ancient philosophers and poets, such as Hippocrates, Xenophon, Seneca, and Plutarch, wrote of "aging great men," lauded and honored them, and included special recipes for long life. Aristotle, one of the world's earliest careful observers and classifiers of all living systems, wrote that "aging is not disease, because it is not contrary to nature." Galen, a renowned Greek physician of the second century, built on early Greco-Roman medical thought and pronounced aging as "beginning at the very moment of conception." (Guillerme, 1963).

Ancient Babylonian cuneiform tablets and Chinese pharmacopeoias described aphrodisiacs and preparations with tiger's testes for achieving sexual vitality and thus youth and longevity (Trimmer, 1970). At the turn of this century the poet Yeats in "The Land of Heart's Desire" cries out for a yet unrealized place where youth lasts forever.

Continued search for youth and immortality is part of the history of magic and sorcery—of potions, alchemist's elixirs, plant and animal tissue tonics, and folk remedies. Today the search goes on, some efforts as serious industry in scientific laboratories everywhere and some as the "fountain of youth" industry which continues to grow the world over.

One of the more recent treatments for aging to receive considerable attention is the "procaine and vitamin therapy," Gerovital, of Dr. Ana Aslan of Bucharest. In 1959 she claimed her "KH₃" injections resulted in significant retardation, even reversal, of aging; these claims are somewhat modulated now. Gerovital, she has written, is also effective in combating a large group of diseases generally associated with old age. Dr. Aslan admits to having had no controls in the early studies with old people she treated in the hospital/home where she held a major post. She has since attempted more careful, reproducible studies which are still in progress (Aslan, 1972, 1974). The Federal Food and Drug Administration has authorized limited research on Gerovital in the United States to examine only its efficacy (it has demonstrable euphoric effects) in the treatment of depression.

The other treatment that appears to gather increasing believers is embryonic cell therapy begun 44 years ago in Switzerland by Dr. Paul Niehans, who died in 1971 at the age of 89. His approach came out of an episode in which he used legitimate replacement therapy as a recommended regimen for hormone dysfunction. In 1931 Dr. Niehans was called in to help a female post-thyroidectomy patient. The parathyroids had also been accidentally removed. He injected the patient with fragments of the parathyroid from a freshly killed calf and she recovered.

Dr. Niehans moved from that incident to the working theory that specific embryonic cells could be used effectively to combat specific disease, and further that these injections could maintain youthful health and vigor and delay or prevent disease. The cell-therapy technique and derivatives thereof are now used in many "clinics" in England, Switzerland, Germany, and the Bahamas. Many apparently grateful, satisfied beneficiaries can be counted among the notables of the world, in the clergy, the arts, and politics. Since in this instance, as with Gerovital, experimental controls are difficult if not impossible, the success or failure of the technique has been based largely on the claims of the clinics and patients that use it.

"Does this procedure work?" is soon followed by the question, "How does it work?" On the face of it, its reputed success is doubtful because of the body's immunological defenses which break down foreign protein. Perhaps if the embryonic cells migrate to damaged organs and are there modified by macrophagy and combination with antibodies, it is conceivable that the broken-down cell constituents might be useful as a source of metabolites and energy. Otherwise "cell therapy" seems like "sympathetic magic," such as Achilles eating bone marrow to give him strength, and is in keeping with Paracelsus' sixteenth-century concept of "like cures like."

Physiology of Aging, What We Do Know

Not so long ago, at least up to the middle 1950s, the only available data about functional changes with age were a result of the biased comparison between healthy, young college adults and ill, institutionalized elderly. Predictably, the older persons were found to possess only marginal percentages of the capacities of youth.

A more accurate and ongoing evaluation of changes in physiology with age has developed from longitudinal studies. In 1958 Dr. Nathan Shock of the Gerontology Research Center began a study of age changes in 600 healthy males between 20 and 96 living in the community (Shock, 1962, 1968). Another study at the National Institutes of Health (Birren et al., 1963, 1971) of healthy elderly men began at about the same time. A third important longitudinal study was undertaken at the Duke Center for the Study of Aging in 1955 with persons 60–90 years of age and was completed in 1973. The Duke Center in 1973 carried out final examinations in another longitudinal study begun in 1968 with persons 46–70 years of age (Palmore 1970, 1974). All of these have led to validation and incorporation of several generalized concepts of aging and the aged into the study of gerontology.

Generalized Age Changes in Physiology

Gradual changes.   Physiological changes through adulthood into old age are gradual. Therefore, during the greater part of adult life, in the absence of overt pathology, there is most often a slow decrement in function. Homeostasis is maintained moderately well, albeit at lowered levels. This is a reasonable observation. An individual can survive (under particular conditions) with less than 49 percent of the liver, fractions of stomach and intestines, one lung, and one kidney (Shock, 1974). It is possible that the observable gradual rate of decline may be explainable, at least in part, by the enormous reserve of and redundancy in tissue and organ system capacity.

Complex function, more decline.   Decrements are greater in the performance of coordinated activities involving a number of connections between nerve and nerve, nerve and muscle, nerve and gland. Important differences between young and old exist at the level of intracting systems. For example, the decline in velocity of nerve conduction is less than the decrease in maximum breathing capacity. A single physiological system is involved with the former, while the latter relates to the coordination of numerous nerve and muscle activities.

Individual differences.   Individuals age at different rates, and different tissues and systems within one person demonstrate differences in rates of aging as well. Older people are less alike than they have ever been, as they have lived through a long life in a particular life style with a unique heredity. Therefore, while it is useful to indicate the average declines of functions, it is equally important to keep in mind that any one individual may not fit that picture.

Vulnerability to disease.   Older persons do become more vulnerable to disease; they are twice as likely to be physically disabled and to require hospitalization as younger people. There is an increase in morbidity and mortality with age. Cardiovascular disease, cancer, and cerebral accidents, the nation's three major chronic diseases and killers, have their greatest impact in severity and number among older persons. Those causes of illness and death that have come to be associated with old age undoubtedly have their etiology in young adult years, and frequently are diagnosed in the middle years.

Homeostasis.   Perhaps the single most critical and salient age-related difference is in diminishing ability to respond to stress (physical and emo-

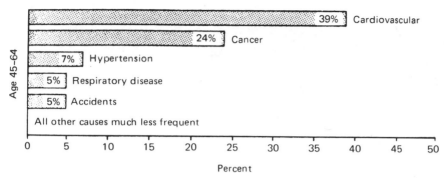

Figure 11.1. Common causes of death in middle age, as percent of total deaths between ages 45 and 64. (From Smith and Bierman, 1973)

tional) and return to the pre-stress level, that is, a decrease in homeostatic capacity (Shock, 1974; Seyle, 1970). This decrease is most marked in neuroendocrine interaction and exists as well in the systemic alteration in responsivity of the nervous and endocrine systems separately. Various physiological parameters, such as blood pH and volume and blood glucose, appear relatively constant over the years. In a number of older individuals blood pressure and heart rate may be comparable to that of younger persons, but only at rest. Stress reveals the declining capacity to achieve responses equivalent in extent and intensity to those of younger years. Characteristically, increased time is needed to return to pre-stress levels. Demands can no longer be adequately met, the reduction in reserve capacity is finally deleterious, and pathology may result. With stress—whether physical, as in exercise, or emotional, as in excitement or fear—the magnitude of displacement is greater, and the rate of recovery is slower with increasing age.

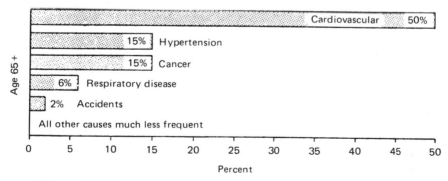

Figure 11.2. Common causes of death in old age (above age 65) as percent of the total. (From Smith and Bierman, 1973)

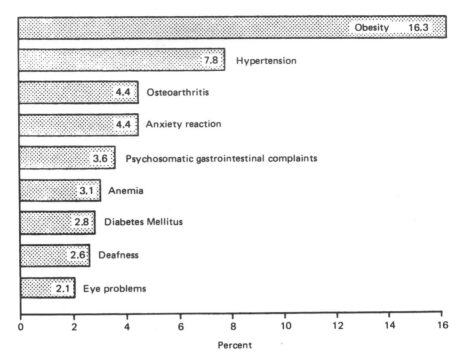

Figure 11.3. Disorders of middle age. (From Sharpe and Keen, 1968)

Quantitation of certain hormones in the urine makes possible the identification of the changing capacity for stress response. One of the measurable hormonal responses to stress is the trophic hormone of the anterior pituitary, ACTH; this in turn stimulates the adrenal cortex to secrete corticoids which elicit, among other biochemical changes, an increase in the liver's production of glucose, an important metabolite in the provision of energy. With stress there is also an initial increase in the urine concentration of adrenaline and noradrenaline secreted from the adrenal medulla.

Further evidence of a breakdown in homeostatic efficiency is found in adjustment to environmental temperature change. Exposure of young and old subjects to 5° to 15° C. for 45 to 120 minutes resulted in a fall of 0.5° to 1° C. among the old, but insignificant rectal temperature changes among the young. Other experiments provide evidence that adaptation to heat stress is also more difficult for older persons. Measurement of heat loss in calories/unit volume from the hand under standard conditions was approximately 33 percent lower at age 70 than at age 24 (Pickering, 1936). Water loss from finger tips and toes also measured significantly less in older subjects. Decreased heat and water loss both contribute to the reduction of the body's ability to cool itself by means of evaporation (Burch, et al., 1942). In a statistical overview, it was clear that the death rate from heat stroke rose sharply after the age of 60: 8/100,000 deaths between 70–79 to 80/100,000 deaths between 90–100 years (Shattuck and Hilferty, 1932).

Molecular and Cellular Changes

The gross physiological changes to be described below may have their origin in some of the molecular and cellular changes that have recently been explored (Hayflick, 1970, 1965, and Chapter 10 in this volume).

Not all cells and tissues age in the same way; some body cells retain the ability to reproduce all through life: skin, lining of the gut, liver, and bone marrow cells. Even in these tissues the capacity for regeneration does slow down. Some cells lose this capacity before birth or shortly thereafter: neurons, muscle and kidney cells. With the death of these cells, fewer functional units remain for body processes; this loss could theoretically result in a less than minimal body mass necessary to maintain life. A third substance, intercellular connective tissue, made up of collagen and elastin fibers, also changes with time and probably contributes to the potential pathology of the cardiovascular system. As cross linkages of collagen increase, there may be interference with intercellular exchanges.

It may be, therefore, that in those systems whose cells still retain capacity for division, the slowed rate of repair and any accompanying chromosomal errors could result in dysfunctional enzymes or faulty structural proteins. As a consequence, aberrant liver reactions, ineffective protein synthesis, and inappropriate hormonal responses may be measurable. The very large number of biochemical reactions that are a function of these processes take place in virtually every tissue and organ system of the body. One small error in the structure of a single enzyme, and its catalytic action is thereby multiplied by the failure in a number of subsequent, dependent or coupled reactions. It is known that the activity of a number of enzymes decreases, while a few specific activities increase with age (Timiras, 1972).

An irreplaceable loss of cells in tissues that no longer have a regenerative capacity could be responsible for some of the changes in function associated with age in brain, and kidney, and heart, and other muscle tissue. The older kidney has fewer nephrons; skeletal muscle loss with age is obvious; the older brain may have fewer neurons. Redundancy in these organs needs to be considered, and no doubt explains the relatively good health and behavior through most of the middle and early older years, as well as the possibility of retaining functional capacities even with age. But the loss in some older individuals could be excessive and damaging to adequate homeostatic function and good health.

Functional Changes with Time

Unfortunate stereotypes about "the old" are well entrenched and fairly widespread. Some of the more obvious age-related changes have contributed to the negative image. The skin grows thinner; the wrinkles accumulate; pigmentation (so-called "liver spots") is more widespread; the hair thins out and grays; the walk slows down; the frame settles and becomes shorter, less flexible, more brittle; the eyes appear grayer and cataracts may form. These are the visible results of changes on an organic and systemic level, as well as of underlying molecular changes.

Gerontologists agree there is a steady decline with time (about one percent per year in adult life) in functional capacities in most organ systems (Shock, 1962). However, it has been successfully demonstrated that not all the functional changes we see in older persons are due to aging; some are pathological, some due to misuse or disease (Butler, 1975; de Vries, 1970, 1974).

Changes resulting in decreasing work capacity, among the earliest to be investigated, are associated with bone, muscle, and nervous tissues. (Shock, 1960, 1974; Smith and Bierman, 1973; Birren, 1964, 1971).

Tissue Changes

Bone.   There appears to be fairly widespread decrease in bone mass, frequently resulting in increased stress in weight-bearing areas that become predisposed to fracture. There may be some thinning or even collapse of intervertebral discs. On the other hand, calcification within cartilage and ligaments is observed to some degree in a majority of older individuals (Smith and Bierman, 1973). There is a loss of elasticity in particular joints, and some pre-osteoarthritic degeneration in joint cartilage.

Muscle.   Muscle size and strength both diminish with age. Muscle tone and strength appear to peak between 20 and 30 years and then decline. Although regeneration of muscle is still possible in the older person, muscle mass does decrease, gradually but steadily. This loss may be secondary to the decrease in activity, as well as to changes in the connective and circulatory tissues so intimately connected with muscle. There appears to be an increase in interstitial fat and lipid within the muscle fibers. The age decrement in muscle strength, as evaluated by the cranking of an ergometer (Shock and Norris, 1970), is greater than the decrease in static strength of the same muscle groups.

Nervous, sensory. There is a decrease in efficient function in all the senses with time. Diminution in smell and taste affect appetite and finally nutrition. Proprioception (the perception of one's position and relatedness in and to space) also appears to be impaired (Smith and Bierman, 1973) and may relate to balance and coordination. Most older people expect vision and audition to diminish with time—and they do. The gradual loss of visual acuity necessitates the use of glasses for many middle-aged and older persons. Loss in audition, particularly of the higher frequencies, typically begins at adolescence and appears to peak between

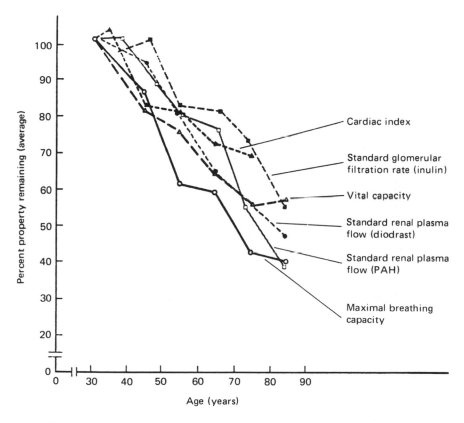

Figure 11.4. Efficiency of human physiological mechanisms as a function of age. Level at 3 years is assigned a value of 100%. (Modified from Shock, 1962)

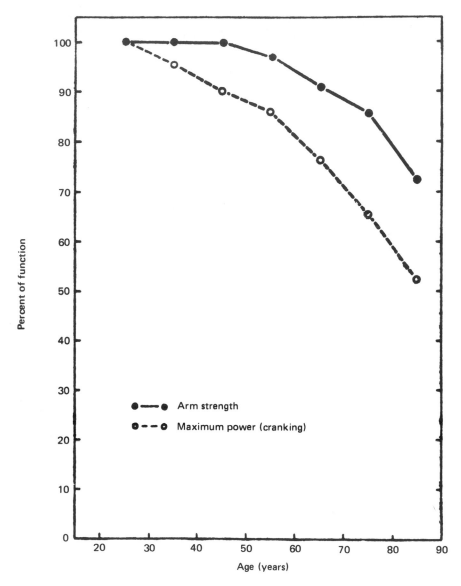

Figure 11.5. Age decrements in muscle strength compared with decrements in maximum powers developed in a coordinated movement (cranking) utilizing the same muscle groups. (Adapted from Shock and Norris, 1970)

40 and 50 years. The decline in touch sensitivity and therefore response does not appear to be very critical to well-being and behavior. Nevertheless, the sensation of touch is part of the individual's capacity for adaptation to the environment. Other changes include the decrease in perception of vibration and temperature, and an increased pain threshold. In general, then, there is a declining capacity in awareness and internalization of environmental stimuli and, therefore, a concomitant decrease in responsivity and adaptation.

Systemic Changes and Consequences

Pulmonary system. With increasing age, there is a measurable reduction in breathing efficiency. The decreases in maximum breathing capacity, residual lung volume, total capacity and basal oxygen consumption bring about a diminished metabolic rate. The building blocks (amino acids, glucose, fatty acids) and energy required for synthesis and all intermediary reactions, are derived from the combination of oxygen with food in the processes of digestion, cell respiration, and assimilation. When the oxygen level is lowered and nutrition falls off as well, there is a decrease in the reserves for all body functions. Optimum health is achieved through protective and repair mechanisms. These are in turn dependent on sources of materials for synthesis and energy to keep the reactions going. Thus lowered reserves present a greater challenge to health maintenance.

Digestive system and nutrition. Recent studies indicate there is more malnutrition among the elderly than was previously thought. Some early data suggest that there may be some critical deficiencies in mineral, protein, and vitamin intake which may be involved with blood and cardiac and psychologic dysfunctions (Bender, 1971; Caster, 1971). Potassium, calcium, iron, and vitamin B_{12} deficiencies are among those most frequently cited and relate to bone, thyroid, and heart muscle function. Excesses especially in fat-soluble vitamins (vitamin A, E) may also represent a serious assault on homeostatic balance. It is also true, however, that very little systematic inquiry and observation have been pursued in nutritional deficiencies and requirements among middle-aged and older persons.

Still, some age-related decrements seem to be related to nutrition. Periodontitis rather than caries appears to be responsible for the loss of teeth. Periodontal disease, in turn, may be a function of malnutrition rather than solely of mouth neglect (Kaplan, 1971; Friedman, 1968). Problematic dentition, the declining senses of smell, taste, and vision, inadequate funds, and loneliness may all play a part in the limited appetite and consequent malnutrition. There are changes in the digestive tract: lowered levels of changes in the digestive juices, reduction in peristalsis, and probable constipation. Sweets often become a major dietary constituent, an apparent substitute for the shrinking life space and loss of other satisfactions, and may compound an already skewed food intake. Much research remains to be done in nutrition, not only related to analyses of diets for general health and illness, but in the relationship of diet to age, ethnicity, income, drugs, personal interactions with the human and physical environments, past eating habits, current level of energy needs, and stress.

Cardiovascular/renal.   These systems also undergo changes leading to lowered efficiency and servicing of the body's requirements. The heart pump works harder to achieve less. Peripheral resistance, circulation time, as well as diastolic and systolic blood pressure increase with age in many older persons. This is especially so in those individuals whose blood vessels have narrowed with atherosclerosis and arteriosclerosis. Renal blood flow, glomerular filtration, and tubular excretion rates decrease. There are expectations of a 55 percent decrease in blood plasma flow between the ages of 30 and 80 (Shock, 1970, 1974).

Nervous system.   Perhaps the most significant alteration of neurological function for overall physiological efficiency is reflected in the coordinator-integrator role of the nervous system for the body's interacting muscular, neuronal, glandular, and circulatory systems (Birren, 1964; Shock, 1962). Simple neurological function (simple reflex time) remains relatively unimpaired from 20 to 80 years (Hügin et al., 1960). This response, which involves the spinal cord primarily, represents the transmission of nerve impulses through few synapses.

On the other hand, reaction time shows significant decline with the years and involves a complex of factors in the central nervous system as well as a number of synapses. Speed of conduction of the nerve impulse is measurably decreased with aging, but is a relatively low-level loss, 10 to 15 percent. Measurements of separate components of the locomotor system—muscular, neural, glandular, and circulatory—do not add up to the apparent overall loss of speed, flexibility, reserve, and coordination. This reinforces the integration function of the nervous system. The decline in the overall function of the nervous system has generally been blamed on the apparent loss of the posmitotic neurons. These conclusions about drastic neuronal loss may have resulted from autopsies on brain tissue with some massive accidental trauma or other pathology. More recently it has been suggested that the most rapid loss occurs between birth and maturity, with only very low level loss after maturity (Brody, 1970). Current data are insufficient and inconclusive. Diminishing neuronal capacity may also be secondary to dysfunction of the vascular system (arteriosclerosis) and resulting decreased blood flow; to changes in tissue permeability; to alterations of the connective tissue; or to changes in responsivity of receptor organs.

Immune and endocrine behavior.   Hormones promoting immunity responses decrease, and those remaining do not effect the same degree of response. For example, thymosin from the thymus gland decreases with age. It may be more important than earlier realized, since it appears to stimulate the proliferation of those cells that participate in the synthesis of antibodies. Goldstein (1972) suggests it may be possible by injection of this hormone in humans to retard or even prevent a number of age-associated chronic diseases.

Current research suggests that the decreased responsiveness of the hormonal receptors is of primary importance. For example, the kidneys

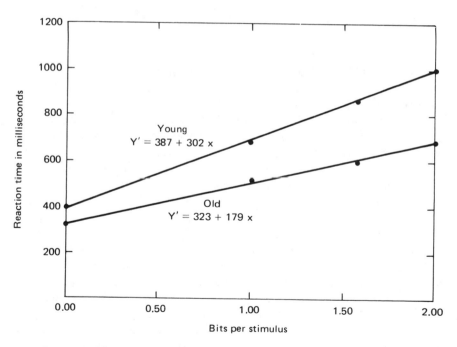

Figure 11.6. Reaction time as a function of stimulus information and age. (From Suci, Davidoff, and Surwillo, 1960).

of aged subjects respond at a lower level than those of younger individuals to a standard amount of the antidiuretic hormone pitressin.

Age-associated decline in glucose tolerance, fairly universal with age, begins as early as the fourth decade of life (Andres, 1967; Shock, 1974). This may be due to the reduction in sensitivity of the pancreatic beta cells to levels of blood glucose. There is no age difference in peripheral utility of glucose (Andres et al., 1969).

In another set of experiments, the administration of thyrotropic-stimulating-hormone elicited the same elevation of oxygen consumption, increase in radioactive iodine uptake by the thyroid gland, and an increase in protein-bound iodine in the blood of young and old persons (Baker et al., 1959). In the experiments of Clemens et al. (1969), reactivation of ovarian cycles in post-estrus female rats (23 months) was achieved by electrical stimulation of the preoptic area of the hypothalamus. This is persuasive evidence that the functional aging of the ovary may be determined not by the ovary alone but by some age-related change in an integrating central nervous system tissue, the hypothalamus (Finch, 1973). There is then considerable evidence that the major deficit in physiological response to hormone stimulation is the changing sensitivity of the target organ. There is also the documentation of remaining responsive capacity in the target organs if adequate stimulus is provided.

Sexual changes. Gonadal hormones also decrease over time in men and women. This decline produces slow, involutionary changes in genital tissue, a reduction and finally total loss of fertility, but no consequential or inevitable loss of libido.

Sexual hormones stimulate sexual attractiveness and activity and are responsible for the growth and development of reproductive structure and function from conception through old age. There is, in menopausal and postmenopausal women, gradual atrophy of ovarian, uterine, and vaginal tissues and a decreased level of lubrication. In men, there is also a steady decrease of the gonadal hormone. However, the decline in testosterone starts later than sexual decline in most women and continues at a modest level into old age. This decline is accompanied by a lower rate of spermatogenesis, a decrease in viable sperm, smaller and firmer testes, and an enlarged prostate. The volume and viscosity of the seminal fluid decreases so that there is also a reduction in the force of the ejaculation. Although no one of the described changes are major, in concert they are responsible for some of the real and apparent changes in sexual behavior.

The significance of the changes is more readily measured in men and women as sexual partners. Frequency of intercourse, intensity of sensation, speed of attaining erection, and force of ejaculation are all reduced in men. In women, thinning vaginal walls may provoke some pain upon intromission of the penis. Increased time is necessary for lubrication of vulval and vaginal areas and for heightened clitoral response. There is, nevertheless, little age difference among appropriately stimulated women in the capacity for orgasm. Nipples and breasts are still responsive to all kinds of stimulation even in the 80- or 90-year-old woman.

The increased time for reaching erection in the older male is accompanied by the ability to maintain the erection longer. This results in providing the increased time needed by the older female to reach the excitement level necessary for orgasm. The climax is as effective as in younger years, because the same muscles, nerves, and circulation are involved as before, albeit in a somewhat differently timed sequence (Kinsey, 1948, 1953; Butler, 1975; Masters and Johnson, 1966, 1970). Most of the studies provide data that make it quickly apparent that past experiences—enjoyment, frequency, and pleasure—are important predictors for sexual activity in the last half of life. Many old women today have the additional need for a sanctioned partner (Pfeiffer and Davis, 1972). While interest and capacity persist through old age, activity declines most frequently due to illness or unavailability of a suitable mate. Cultural mores and morality, which assign older men and women to the "sexless" years and sees only young lovers as suitable, are equally responsible for the inhibitions and prohibitions from which older people suffer. Society's stereotypes have contributed to a negative, powerless self-image which is surely responsible for the unlovable, invisible labels that older persons have accepted for too long (Weg, 1975).

Drugs and Changing Physiology

Enough information is available to state that there are age-dependent differences in mechanisms of drug action. Drug therapy in the elderly requires an understanding and incorporation of changing functional levels particularly in absorption, detoxication, and excretion of drugs.

With fewer functional units, and demonstrated decreased capacities of the many units that remain, absorption of drugs may be significantly reduced because of several factors: the number of intestinal absorbing cells may have decreased; altered gastric pH may affect drug solubility; intestinal blood flow may be reduced; and specific transport mechanisms may not be as available because of faulty or reduced protein synthesis.

Detoxication and excretion of drugs are frequently slower than in younger individuals. In part this may be due to decreased renal capacity which results from the impairment of glomerular and tubular function, augmented by lost nephrons.

An overall decrease in metabolism may contribute further to the delay of elimination. The decrease in the major detoxication function of the liver may inhibit other liver functions as a result of the accumulation of toxic substances. An increased proportion of body fat in body weight delays total metabolism of drugs such as barbiturates that tend to localize in adipose tissues.

Increased circulation time, decrease in regional blood flow, and decreased cardiac reserve also appear to be involved in the delayed distribution and elimination of drugs.

The already lowered capacity for homeostatic control increases the possibility of undesirable side effects. A hypotensive drug, frequently important in the treatment of hypertension, may, in lowering the blood pressure, result in a pressure too low to deliver adequate blood to all parts of the body, especially the brain. Generally speaking, most drugs may be more active in older people even at reduced dosage levels. In view of the overall decrease of functional capacities, the greater individual differences, and the drug interaction with particular organ systems, the choice of drugs is complex and at best must be made with regard for making the most of whatever potential and capacities that do remain.

Life Changes and Health

We have seen that functional decline is measurable in a number of physiological capacities among older persons. What is significant is not that these gradual diminutions occur, but that the majority of older persons accommodate well to these changes, and that approximately 86 percent of people over 65 remain in their communities and demonstrate more than adequate coping behavior in meeting the challenge of everyday living (Brotman, 1974). Nevertheless, the lowered efficiency of a number of organ systems leads to increased susceptibility to disease. The occasionally imperceptible line between altered sensitivities and frank pathology has made it possible for a *Newsweek* article (16 April 1973) to use the headline "Can Aging be Cured?"

Nevertheless, disease is not an inevitable companion of aging. Since 1967 a number of studies have suggested that life change alone may be an important factor contributing to the rate of age changes and illness among older persons. Death of a spouse, marriage, retirement, divorce, residential move, job change—enough of these in one year could lead to illness. On a "Social Readjustment Rating Scale" a 75 percent correlation has been demonstrated between the number of life-change units and the severity of illness (Rahe et al., 1970). This correlation has been validated among pregnant women, leukemia patient families, and retirees. There has been a highly significant correlation between life-change scores and chronic diseases: leukemia, cancer, heart attack, schizophrenia, menstrual difficulties, and warts.

The aged in contemporary society experience a great many changes, perhaps more than other groups: change in living arrangements, loss of job, decrease in income, loss of status, loss of friends and relatives, loss of identity, and often a decline of former physical capacities. It appears conceivable then that these multiple changes represent mounting stress that finally taxes homeostasis and coping abilities to the limit, leading to the breakdown of adaptability and to disease. In addition, other independent studies provide support for the notion of a psychosomatic base to disease. A recent report in the *World Health Organization Chronicle* (24:4) documented an example of the strong psychosocial base for cardiovascular disease in the way of life in advanced societies. The town of Roseta, Pennsylvania was originally settled in 1887 by Italians from Roseto Valley in Southern Italy. A study of this town, extending over a 12-year period, found the death rate from myocardial infarction was less than one-half of the neighboring community or that of the U.S.A. as a whole. Yet relatives of the 1,700 inhabitants of Roseta who lived in New York and Philadelphia were characterized by death rates close to the national average. All the usual risk factors associated with affluence, that is, obesity, smoking, and drinking, were present. It was concluded that the significant variables were based in the way of life (societal mores, attitudes) and the individual psyche. As with the societal structures of the vigorous, long-lived peoples, there was a cohesive social structure that had developed and remained in this community without poverty or crime. Men have remained as unchallenged heads of households, and the elderly are not only revered but retain their community and family influence.

Pathology

Although there are physiological (and anatomical), psychological, and sociological changes with time, aging is not disease. Nevertheless, it is irrefutable that morbidity and mortality do go up with age. One of the major characteristic pathological changes with age is the shift from acute to chronic disease. Additional research is sorely needed to establish "norms" for levels of systemic function in middle-aged and older persons. For example, in many (though not all) older persons there is an apparently normal increase with age in diastolic and systolic blood pressure. Some, not all, of them will develop pathological hypertension. Similarly, the decrease in glucose tolerance which is measurable in a number of older persons may not necessarily be a prelude to diabetes. Continued study of the physiology of change with time could help identify more subtle clues in the pattern of these early nonpathological changes that would discriminate those at risk and likely to develop hypertension or diabetes. A course for intervention could then be undertaken. A brief overview of the more common diseases and serious dysfunctions will help to describe more adequately the population under consideration.

Obesity. Nutritional and metabolic dysfunctions—obesity, gall-bladder disease, and anemia—frequently become apparent in the middle years and are carried over into old age. It is important to correct these dysfunctions not only to alleviate the symptoms of discomfort and decreased efficiency, but also because of their interaction with other dysfunctions such as diabetes mellitus, arteriosclerosis, varicose veins, hernia, osteoarthritis, cardiovascular disease, peptic ulcer, and hypertension. This is particularly obvious when the individual's overweight coexists with hypertension to cause an increased mortality risk. Overweight patients are also high risks for respiratory difficulties, heightened frequency of thromboembolism, infection and wound breakdown from surgery (Smith and Bierman, 1973).

Stress-related illness.   Coronary heart disease, hypertension, and peptic ulcer also appear to be time dependent and to increase in the middle years. The mortality risk from heart disease over 45 doubles for males and triples for females from one decade to the next, but males have a higher incidence in earlier middle age. Risk factors that increase susceptibility toward coronary diseases include hypertension, cigarette smoking, and elevated blood levels of cholesterol and triglycerides. Associated, but not necessarily causally related, are such behavioral and personality characteristics as aggression, perfectionism, heightened sense of responsibility, high dietary fat and sucrose intake, and low or absent physical activity.

According to insurance company statistics (Metropolitan Life, 1959) about 10 percent of the American population between the ages of 40 and 50 have blood pressures greater than 140mm Hg systolic and 90mm Hg diastolic (Bierman and Hazzard, 1973). Although some of these individuals go on to develop "hypertensive vascular disease and arteriosclerosis of the smallest arteries of the kidney, retina and brain and in large vessels" (Bierman and Hazzard, 1973, p. 166), many never experience significant ischemia or other easily observable symptoms.

Peptic ulcer is another disease that demonstrates a high correlation with the stress factors of a highly competitive, industrialized, tension-ridden society (Stamler and Epstein, 1972). Although duodenal ulcer is more common, all of the upper digestive tract is sensitive to the factors that disturb the balance between the mucosal resistance and secretion of hydrochloric acid and the digestive enzyme pepsin. Both coronary disease and peptic ulcer appear to exhibit genetic predisposition, yet unquestionably the environmental factors are importantly involved.

A marked increase of cerebrovascular accidents (stroke) among older persons may be the result of the years of arterial changes from arteriosclerotic and hypertensive disease. There are 200,000 deaths from strokes per year in the United States; 80 percent among persons over 65. Those who survive frequently have disabilities in speech and movement. Atherosclerotic lesions—atherosclerosis in the large arteries of the kidney, heart, and brain—are considered the most common cause of death among older people of Western societies.

Pulmonary disease.   Chronic bronchitis, fibrosis, and emphysema are all manifestations of chronic obstructive pulmonary disease, increase with age, and may lead to disability and death in old age. Four times as many men as women succumb to these diseases, probably because of a combination of age changes in the lung connective tissue and the continued assaults from cigarette smoking and air pollution in the community and at work. Should these pathological tissue changes continue unchecked, death may come from the additional insult from infections, right ventricular heart failure, and severe hypoxia (Bierman and Hazzard, 1973).

Allergic responses appear to increase with age, and hypersensitivity to bacterial products and pollutants often begins during the middle years and may become a cause of disability. Asthma, if persistent, may contribute to pulmonary emphysema and respiratory insufficiency. Drug allergies in particular show greater incidence with age. These may be, in part, a function of the decrements in physiological capacies, but they are no doubt also related to the growing use and frequent abuse of multiple drug agents, especially sedatives, tranquilizers, depressants, and antibiotics. The realization that there is an interaction between drug action and declining physiological capacities, together with the rise in allergic reactions, should stimulate care in the prescription and administration of drugs to older persons.

Immunity.   Immune capacity does appear to break down with age and is reflected in the decreased prevalence of an immune response to the tuberculin skin test in older persons (Smith and Bierman, 1973). Most cancers increase in frequency with age, and about one-half of all cancer deaths are in the over 65 group. Sex differences in malignancies may be seen in the greater incidence of lung cancer and neoplasia of the prostate among men, and the sex-related breast and uterine cancer among women. There are some researchers (Walford, 1967; Makinodan et al., 1971) who suggest that with the declining immune capacity, cancerous cells which were earlier eliminated from the body by an efficient immune system are able to prosper in the later years when the lymphocytes may fail to recognize cancerous cells as non-self.

Autoimmunity.   On the other hand, there is growing evidence that the autoimmune response increases with age (Walford, 1967). The related pathologies include pernicious anemia, Addison's diseases, and chronic thyroiditis. Possibly DNA gene aberration and/or the resultant RNA and enzymatic alteration may produce cells and tissues recognized as non-self, which may be destroyed by normal antibodies. Or, as has also been suggested, inaccurate mutated DNA may direct the synthesis of altered RNA and therefore lead to faulty protein synthesis such as the production of antibodies. These immune bodies remain attached to cells and conceivably lead to the destruction of healthy tissues. A possible etiological relationship between faulty immunity and disease entities of aging has been explored by others (Burch, 1969; Burnet, 1970; Walford, 1967).

Arthritis.   While the frequency of joint disease increases with age, there is no definitive pathogenesis of these disorders. Arthritis of all kinds has been described as a problem of significant proportion in adult medicine today (Smith and Bierman, 1973). It affects approximately 14 percent of males and 23 percent of females beyond 45 and is second only to heart disease as a cause of limited activity.

Osteoporosis.   This painful disease, also described as osteopenia— a loss in total bone mass—frequently results in late middle and old age in diminished height, instability in maintenance of normal posture, ease of fracture, and often acute pain. This disorder may be found in as many as 30 percent of people of age 65 and is four times more common in women than in men.

The etiology of osteoporosis is unclear and the results of studies are not definitive. Although at one time it was thought to be estrogen dependent (with increasing incidence in the postmenopausal woman), some estrogen-treated women and men are stabilized while others are not (Bartter, 1973). There is some research which suggests that lifelong dietary habits may be more important than estrogen in maintenance of bone structure (Lutwak, 1969). Good results have been reported with increased dietary calcium which promotes protein retention and activation of osteoblasts. There may be another genetic factor that determines the porosity of the bone. Those with more porous bones may be more suscept-ible to any estrogen-primed alteration in calcium metabolism.

Normal Aging

The promise that greater numbers of persons will grow old with little or no pathology is suggested by the presence of active, moderately healthy older persons in this society, and by the existence of even small pockets of long-lived, working peoples of the world. With the victory over infec-tious diseases and infant mortality in the past century, the elimination of the chronic diseases associated with old age would appear to be the next major task for biomedical and governmental personnel.

Longevity Predictor and Long-Lived Peoples

The common predictors for increased longevity (and they would appear related as well to the improved quality of life) were summarized by two independent researchers, Chebotarev in the U.S.S.R. and Palmore in the U.S. (Chebotarev, 1971; Sachuk, 1970; Palmore and Jeffers, 1971). These predictors were not related to heredity (as in choosing long-lived parents and grandparents) nor in a major way dependent on absence of disease. There were four: (1) maintain a role in the society; (2) hold a positive view of life and positive self-concept; (3) have moderately good physical function; (4) and be a nonsmoker. These criteria fit in well with the information that has been gathered and examined concerned with the long-lived populations in Abkhasia of the Georgian Soviet Republic (Benet, 1971; Leaf, 1973a, 1973b) in the land of the Hunza of the Karkoram Range in Kashmir (Leaf, 1973a, 1973b) and in the Andean Vil-lage of Vilcabamba in Ecuador (Davies, 1973).

The life style of these peoples is predictable. Each person has a task and is expected to work at something all during his life span, with a reduction in hours as age advances. There is no rocking-chair philosophy in Abkhasia. Work is rigorous and out of doors in the high elevation, mountainous terrain.

The low-calorie diet is, by and large, simple, low in saturated animal fat and meat, and high in fruit and vegetables with no or small amounts of alcoholic beverages and nicotine. Little pathology has been recorded. When it does exist, disease has seldom been incapacitating or necessitated hospitalization.

Many American researchers correctly suggest that an absence of long-term record keeping, inaccurate birth records, and some exaggeration in claims should lead to caution in the evaluation of these reports. Even with the admission of error and exaggeration, these peoples are visibly old, yet vital and healthy. Perhaps they are 100 instead of 128, 110 instead of 148. There would still seem to be useful clues about successful aging that could be harvested from the data that are now being gathered.

What Can Be Done

Manipulation of the environment.   If anything is to be learned from the long-lived peoples of the world, and from those older persons of this country who age "successfully," it would seem possible and desirable to alter those factors in the environment that appear to contribute to the kind and degree of functional changes that have been discussed. In a number of the organ systems, a percentage of the loss appears to be due to disuse or misuse, and thus susceptible to control or at least retardation.

A careful examination of functional capacities emphasizes the continuum of life. The level of capacity available at 70 and 80 is a consequence of all that has gone before—one's heredity, the interaction with the human and physical environments, nutrition and exercise, intellectual and affective pursuits—in the total life style to date.

Recent studies on aging and the aged suggest at least the association, if not causal relationships, between physiological dysfunction, psychology, frank pathology, and particular aspects of the environment. They include many factors already mentioned in the foregoing pages and attest to the interdependent nature of the quality of life:

arteriosclerosis atherosclerosis coronary disease hypertension	and	high fat, high carbohydrate diet; sedentary life style; tension; cigarette smoking.
cerebral accidents	and	atherosclerotic and arteriosclerotic changes
chronic pulmonary disease	and	cigarette smoking; air pollution
obesity	and	high caloric intake; lack of exercise
osteoporosis	and	inadequate calcium and protein intake
periodontal disease	and	malnutrition
"senility"	and	malnutrition; social isolation
sexual dysfunction	and	ignorance; societal stereotypic attitudes

A review of the information available related to these environmental variables evokes a number of possibilities for change.

Exercise. A shift from the inactive middle-aged/aging existence to a more active life, making regular exercise an integral part of everyday living, would seem prudent. Studies have documented that continued use and exercise of many physiological capacities prolong retention of those capacities (de Vries, 1970, 1974; Bierman and Hazzard, 1973; Freeman, 1965). Dr. de Vries has demonstrated that an exercise regimen of 6-8 weeks regains some of the muscle strength and tone among older men aged 60-90 years (see Chapter 12).

There are suggestions that even the rate of atheromatous plaque formation is slowed down by exercise and the risk factor of sedentary life style for coronary artery disease is reduced significantly (Stamler and Epstein, 1972). Cardiovascular efficiency may also increase and maximize the limited capacity of individuals who are already at risk with coronary disease. A measurable improvement in aerobic ventilation and usable ogygen is another benefit of exercise.

Diet, nutrition. Changes in diet toward a low to moderate caloric intake and an increase in minerals, proteins, and vitamins may have multiple benefits in prevention or modulation of a number of the age-associated disorders.

Decreased cholesterol and total fat intake may diminish the risk of atherosclerosis and the coronary disease sequence (Dayton et al., 1970; Brown and Ritzmann, 1967). Increased dietary calcium and protein have been demonstrated to be effective in abating the loss of bone in osteoporosis.

There have been demonstrations that careful protein and vitamin therapy may reverse the confusion, fatigue, irritability, insomnia, and even "senility," all heretofore considered inevitable with aging (Brody, 1970; Anonymous, 1969; Meindok and Dvorsky, 1970). The morbidity related to gallstones, hepatic dysfunction, and osteoarthritis that is frequently consequent to obesity could be moderated by diet control and loss of weight.

It is possible that the loss of teeth and periodontal disease so marked in the elderly are not inevitable. Although there is a suggestion (Slavkin, 1974) that some individuals may have a predisposition to periodontitis, there is also the indication that prevention may be realized with adequate professional dental care and balanced nutrition.

Nutrition alone cannot determine length of the life span. But there would appear to be enough suggestive evidence that nutrition surely influences the life span and quality of life (Shock, 1970; Bender, 1971). Adequate and appropriate nutrition will depend not only on education of the helping professions who serve the older population, but consumer education of the aged themselves (Leong, 1970; Piper and Smith, 1970).

Since it is apparent that malnutrition may have serious consequences for numerous physiological processes, it may be a responsibility for the society to make good nutrition possible and probable for all older persons. This is difficult and complicated by the loneliness that depresses appetite and the subversive effects of existence near poverty level.

Cigarette smoking.   The decrease and, finally, cessation of cigarette smoking could reverse the now well-documented excess morbidity and mortality related to lung and oral cancer, pulmonary diseases, and cardiovascular disease. Reduction and cessation of smoking have been shown to effectively decrease disease and death (Bierman and Hazzard, 1973). There is a twofold increase in the overall death rate of smokers to nonsmokers which is at its height from ages 45 to 55. Smoking is often cited as culprit with not only respiratory tissue, but the cardiovascular system as well. There appears to be a positive correlation of smoking with the increased rate of ather development as a direct effect of nicotine on the peripheral blood vessels.

Stress.   A move to the modification of life styles tied to compulsion, achievement, and deadlines is very difficult in the work and dollar orientation of the culture. Stress, especially that stress of psychological and emotional origin associated with work and home, has been increasingly identified as a major and predisposing factor in cardiovascular dysfunction; specifically these disturbances include atherosclerosis, coronary heart disease, and hypertension. The changes in hormones—adrenaline, noradrenaline, corticords—all have both generalized metabolic effects as well as specific toxic effects on heart muscle and blood vessels. The noticeable absence of this kind of stress among the long-lived peoples and the absence or low level of organic disturbances are suggestive of the serious consequences of the pace of most American life styles.

Conclusion

"Normal aging" is admittedly still a notion difficult to incorporate into the thinking of society at large. Yet the numerous recognizable interrelationships among psyche, society, and physiology signal the importance of societal attitudes and support for older persons.

Admittedly, there are decrements in physiological function with time. Yet these changes are gradual and there is more than enough capacity left for independent living. The data demonstrate that to the degree that people use, nourish, and extend the remaining capacities, the body and spirit will benefit and the whole person prosper.

The negative image of the aged person as an invalid, a legacy of long ago, was not created without evidence in our imaginations. There have been and still are individuals who may conform to part or even all of that image. However, many cohorts and techniques later, there are greater numbers of older persons who live longer, are in better health, are better educated, and are determined to remain involved with living.

Human aging, with all the fact and fiction that surrounds it, is comprehensible, but not if we look only at the physiology, or at the psyche, or at the social forces; it becomes knowable only on examination of the interaction of all of these in older men and women.

It is conceivable, with societal commitment and with continued progress in the biomedical revolution, that those chronic diseases which too often accompany age will in the near future fall away, as did the infectious diseases in the early 1900s. Then perhaps it will, as Isaiah imagined, be "a new heaven and new earth" where living to 100 is expected, and at that age the individual will be considered "a mere child."

References

Andres, R.; Swerdloff, R.; and Tobin J. D. 1969. In *Proceedings of the 8th International Congress of Gerontology* I:36–39. Bethesda, Md.: FASEB.

Andres, R. 1967. Relation of physiologic changes in aging to medical change of disease in the aged. *Mayo Clinic Proceedings* 42:413–674.

Anon. 1969. Editorial. Old age, nutrition, and mental confusion. *British Medical Journal* 3:608.

Aslan, A. 1974. Theoretical and practical aspects of chemotherapeutic techniques in the retardation of aging process. In *Theoretical aspects of aging,* eds. M. Rockstein, M. Sussman, and J. Chesky, pp. 145–156. New York. Academic Press.

Aslan, A. 1972. Principles of drug therapy. *Proceedings of the 9th International Congress of Gerontology Symposia Reports* 2:115–118.

Baker, S. P.; Gaffney, G. W.; Shock, N. W.; and Landowne, M. 1959. Physiological responses of middle-aged and elderly—administration of thyroid-stimulating hormone. *Journal of Gerontology* 14:37–47.

Bartter, F. C. 1973. Bone as a target organ; toward a better definition of osteoporosis. *Perspectives in Biology and Medicine* 16:215–231.

Bender, A. E. 1971. Nutrition of the elderly. *Royal Society Health Journal* 91:115–121, passim.

Benet, S. 1971. Why they live to be 100 or even older in Abkhasia. *New York Times Magazine,* 26 December.

Bierman, E. L. and Hazzard, W. R. 1973. Old age, including death and dying.

In *The biologic ages of man,* eds. Smith and Bierman, Chapter 10. Philadelphia: W. B. Saunders Co.

Birren, J. 1964. *The psychology of aging.* Englewood Cliffs, N.J.: Prentice Hall.

Birren, J. E.; Butler, R. N.; Greenhouse, S. W.; Sokoloff, L.; Yarrow, M. R. 1963 (1971). *Human aging: a biological and behavioral study.* Washington, D.C.: Government Printing Office.

Brody, H. 1970. Structural changes in the aging nervous system. In *Interdisciplinary Topics in Gerontology* 7:9–21.

Brotman, H. B. 1974. *Every tenth American.* Statement to U.S. Senate Special Committee of Aging, Spring 1974.

Brown, R. D. and Ritzmann, L. 1967. Some factors associated with absence of coronary heart disease in persons aged 65 or older. *Journal of the American Geriatrics Society* 15:239.

Burch, G. E.; Cohn, A. E.; and Neumann, C. 1942. A study of the rate of water loss from the surfaces of the fingertips and toe tips of normal and senile subjects and patients with arterial hypertension. *American Heart Journal* 23:185–196.

Burch, P. R. 1969. *Growth, disease and aging.* Toronto: University of Toronto Press.

Burnet, S. 1970. An immunological approach to aging. *Lancet* 2:358–360.

Butler, R. 1975. Sex after sixty. In *The later years,* eds. L. Brown and E. Ellis, pp. 129–143. Acton, Mass.: Publishing Sciences.

Caster, W. O. 1971. *The nutritional problems of the aged.* Athens, Georgia: University of Georgia.

Chebotarev, D. 1971. Fight against old age. *Gerontologist* 11:359–361.

Clemens, J. A.; Amenoamori, Y.; Jenkins, T.; and Meites, J. 1969. Effects of hypothalamic stimulation, hormones and drugs on ovarian function in old female rats. *Society of Experimental Biological Medicine* 132:561–563.

Cicero. 1967. *De Senectute (on old age),* trans. F. Copley. Ann Arbor: U. of Michigan.

Davies, D. 1973. A shangri-la in Ecuador. *New Scientist,* 1 February 1973, pp. 236–238.

Dayton, S.; Chapman, J. M.; Pearce, M. L., et al. 1970. Cholesterol, atherosclerosis, ischemic heart disease, and stroke. *Annals of Internal Medicine* 72:97–110.

de Vries, H. A. 1974. *Vigor regained.* Englewood Cliffs, N.J.: Prentice Hall.

de Vries, H. A. 1970. Physiological effects of an exercise training regimen upon men aged 52–88. *Journal of Gerontology* 24:325–336.

Finch, C. E. 1973. Monamine metabolism in the aging male mouse. In *Development and aging of the nervous system,* eds. M. Rickstein, and M. L. Sussman, pp. 199–213. New York: Academic Press.

Freeman, J. T. 1965. *Clinical features of the older patient.* Springfield, Illinois: Charles C. Thomas.

Friedman, J. W. 1968. Dentistry in the geriatric patient: mutilation by consensus. *Geriatrics* 23:98.

Goldstein, A. 1972. Purification and biological activity of thymosene, a hormone of the thymus gland. *Proceedings of the National Academy of Science* 69:1800–1803.

Granick, S.; Patterson, R. D., eds. 1971. *Human aging II: an eleven-year biomedical and behavior study.* Washington, D.C.: Government Printing Office.

Gruman, G. J. 1966. History of ideas about the prolongation of life. *Transactions, American Philosophical Society.* 56 (part 9).

Guillerme, J. 1963. *Longevity.* New York: Walker and Co.

Hayflick, L. 1965. The limited *in vitro* lifetime of human diploid cell strains. *Experimental Cell Research* 37:614–636.

Hayflick, L. 1970. Aging under glass. *Experimental Gerontology* 5:291–303.

Hügin, F.; Norris, A.; and Shock, N. W. 1960. Skin reflex and voluntary reaction time in young and old males. *Journal of Gerontology* 14:338–391.

Kaplan H. 1971. The oral cavity in geriatrics. *Geriatrics* 26:96–102.

Kinsey, A. C.; Pomeroy, W.; and Martin, C. E. 1948. *Sexual behavior in the human male.* Philadelphia: W. B. Saunders Co.

———. 1953. *Sexual behavior in the human female.* Philadelphia: W. B. Saunders Co.

Krehl, W. 1974. The influence of nutritional environment on aging. *Geriatrics* 29:65–78.

Leaf, A. 1973a. Every day is a gift when you are over 100. *National Geographic.* 143(1):93–118.

———. 1973b. Growing old. *Scientific American* 229(3):44–53.

Leong, Y. 1970. Nutrition education for the aged and chronically ill. *Journal of Nutrition Education* 8.

Lutwak, L. 1969. Nutritional aspects of osteroporosis. *Journal of American Geriatrics Society* 17:115.

Makinodan, Y.; Perkins, E. H.; and Chen, M. G. 1971. Immunologic activity of the aged. *Advances in Gerontological Research* 3:171–198.

Masters, W. H. and Johnson, V. E. 1966. *Human sexual response.* Boston: Little Brown and Co.

———. 1970. *Human sexual inadequacy.* Boston: Little Brown and Co.

Meindok, H. and Dvorsky, R. 1970. Serum folate and vitamin B12 levels in the elderly. *Journal of the American Geriatrics Society* 18:317.

Palmore, E., ed. 1970. *Normal aging: report from the Duke longitudinal study, 1955–1969.* Durham, N.C.: Duke University Press.

———. 1974. *Normal aging II: reports from the Duke longitudinal studies, 1970–1973.* Durham, N.C.: Duke University Press.

Palmore, E. and Jeffers, F. C., eds. 1971. *Prediction of life span, recent findings.* Lexington, Mass.: D. C. Heath and Co.

Pfeiffer, E. and Davis, G. 1972. Determinants of sexual behavior in the elderly. *Journal of the American Geriatrics Society* 20:4:151–158.

Pickering, G. W. 1936. The peripheral resistance in persistent arterial hypertension. *Clinical Science* 2:209–235.

Piper, G. M. and Smith, E. M. 1970. Geriatric nutrition. In *Working with older people: a guide to practice. The Aging Person: Needs and Services* 3:15. Rockville, Maryland: U.S. Department HEW.

Rahe, H.; Mahan, J., and Arthur, R. J. 1970. Prediction of near future health; change from subjects preceding life change. *Journal of Psychosomatic Research* 14:401–406.

Sachuk, N. 1970. Population longevity study: sources and indices. *Journal of Gerontology* 25(3):262–264.

Seyle, H. A. 1970. Stress and aging. *Journal of American Geriatrics Society* 18:9:669–690.

Sharp, C. and Keen, H. 1968. *Presymptomatic detection and early diagnosis.* London: Pitman Medical Publication, Ltd.

Shattuck, G. C. and Hilferty, M. M. 1932. Sun stroke and allied conditions in the United States of America. *American Journal of Tropical Medicine* 12:223–245.

Shock, N. W. 1962. The physiology of aging. *Science American* 206:100.

————. 1970. Physiologic aspects of aging. *Journal of the American Dietetic Association* 56:491.

————. 1974. Physiological theories of aging. In *Theoretical aspects of aging,* eds. Rockstein, et al., pp. 119–136. New York: Academic Press.

Shock, N. W. and Adres, R. 1968. In *Adaptive capacities of an aging organism,* ed. D. F. Chebotarev, pp. 235–254. Kiev, USSR: Academic Science.

Shock, N. W. and Norris, A. H. 1970. Neuromuscular coordinating as a factor in age changes in muscular exercise. In *Medicine and sport, Vol. 4: physical inactivity and aging,* eds. D. Brunner, and E. Jokl, pp. 92–99.

Slavkin, H. 1974. Personal communication at a colloquium, Andrus Gerontology Center, October, 1974.

Smith, D. W. and Bierman, E. L., eds. 1973. *The biologic ages of man.* Philadelphia: W. B. Saunders Co.

————. 1973. Adulthood, especially the middle years. In *The biologic ages of man,* eds. D. W. Smith and E. L. Bierman, Chapter 9. Philadelphia: W. B. Saunders Co.

Stamler, J. and Epstein, F. M. 1972. Coronary heart disease: risk factors as guides to preventive action. *Preventive Medicine* 1:27–48.

Suci, G. J.; Davidoff, M. D.; and Surwillo, W. W. 1960. Reaction time as a function of stimulus information and age. *Journal of Experimental Psychology* 60:242–244.

Timiras, P. S. 1972. *Developmental physiology and aging.* New York: Macmillan Co.

Trimmer, E. J. 1970. *Rejuvenation.* New York: A. S. Barnes and Company.

Walford, R. L. 1967. Autoimmune phenomena in the aging process. *Symposium of the Society for Experimental Biology* 21:351–373.

Weg, R. B. 1973. Interaction with the changing physiology of the aged: practice and potential. In *Drugs and the elderly,* ed. R. Davis. Los Angeles: Andrus Gerontology Center.

————. 1975. Normal aging in the reproductive system; sexuality of age. In *Nursing and the aged,* ed. I. Burnside. New York: McGraw-Hill.

Wright, W. E. and Hayflick, L. 1975. Contributions of cytoplasmic factors to in vitro cellular senescence. *Federation Proceedings* 34(1):76–80.

Zisserman, L. 1969. Diabetes in the aged. *Geriatrics* 24:140.

12

Physiology of Exercise and Aging

HERBERT A. DE VRIES

As we grow older there appear to be losses in functional capacity at the cellular level, the tissue level, the organ level, and the system level of organization. However, as pointed out by Shock, the decrements in physiological functions that take place with increasing age become most readily apparent in the responses of the whole organism to stress (Shock, 1961b). As an exercise physiologist my raison d'être lies in the measurement of the human organism's responses to the most physiological of stressors, physical activity, exercise, or the stress of increased energy demands from whatever source. We are most concerned with the various functional capacities of the human individual: how they may be lost through aging or other processes; how they may be improved through such modalities as physical conditioning, improved nutrition, and better relaxation.

Since functional losses are greatest when the whole organism is under stress, we like to think of exercise physiology as the vernier on the scale of general physiology. That is to say, the methods of exercise physiology provide us with a rather sensitive tool for evaluation of physiological decline in aging. Thus, for example, if some of the metabolic capacity is lost at the cellular level, this would not be easily observed or measured under resting conditions, but the measurement of maximal oxygen consumption in the exercise laboratory would display losses in metabolic capacity dramatically. A man of 75, for example, has on the average only about 50 percent of his oxygen consumption value at age 20, while his resting oxygen intake has only declined by 20 to 25 percent over the same period of time (Robinson, 1938). In recent years it has also become apparent to cardiologists that in some cases early ischemic heart disease, which shows no electrocardiogram (EKG) changes at rest, may be successfully diagnosed if the individual's EKG is observed during the stress of a treadmill run or bicycle ergometer ride such as we use daily in the exercise physiology laboratory.

Thus, we are looking at the physiological changes which *accompany* the aging process from the rather circumscribed vantage point of the exercise physiologist interested not in disease processes but primarily in the gross losses of functional capacity which the aging individual himself experiences as a creeping loss in "vigor." This is not to deny the interest of the exercise physiologist in the entire spectrum of physiological changes, but only to suggest a focus upon those systems which in the "normal" older individual are most likely to be limiting with respect to physical working capacity (PWC) and which are most likely to be amenable to improvement by physical conditioning. Excellent reviews are available for the reader desiring a more comprehensive treatment of physiological age changes than our treatment in this chapter allows. (See, for example, Robinson, 1938; Shock, 1961a; Chapter 11, this volume.)

Physiological Changes Involved in the Age-Related Loss of Vigor

In evaluating the effects of the aging process on human performance several problems arise. First, it is difficult to separate the effects of aging per se from those of concomitant disease processes (particularly cardiovascular and respiratory problems) which become more prevalent with age. Secondly, the sedentary nature of adult life in the United States makes it very difficult to find "old" populations to compare with "young" populations at equal activity levels. Lastly, very little work has been done involving longitudinal studies of the same population over a period of time. Conclusions drawn from cross-sectional studies in which various age groups of different people are compared must be accepted with reservations because the "weaker biological specimens" are not likely to be represented in as great numbers in the older populations tested as in the younger, due to a higher mortality rate. Thus we must be careful to realize that the age changes described are at best only representative of the average losses and that even these mean values may be derived in some cases from very small samplings.

It must also be realized that just as various individuals within the human species age at different rates, so various physiological functions within the individual seem to have their own rates of decline with increasing age. Indeed, some functions do not seem to degenerate with age

(Shock, 1961b). Under resting conditions there seem to be no changes in blood sugar level, blood pH, or total blood volume, for example. In general, the functions which involve the coordinated activity of more than one organ system, such as aerobic capacity and physical work capacity (PWC), decline most with age. Changes due to the aging process are most readily observed when the organism is stressed. Homeostatic readjustment is considerably slower with increasing age. (See chapter 11 for a discussion of aging and homeostasis.)

The Cardiovascular System

Assuming appropriate levels of muscle strength and endurance, oxygen transport has been widely accepted as the major factor determining the limits of physical working capacity (PWC) in the young, if the activity lasts more than a minute or two. Oxygen transport as defined by the Fick equation (Oxygen consumption in milliliters/minute = cardiac output in liters/minute × arteriovenous difference in milliliters/liter blood) depends upon cardiac output and the arteriovenous difference in oxygen. Cardiac output is in turn determined by heart rate and the volume of blood per beat (stroke volume).

Studies of age differences in cardiac output are scarce, but enough work has been done to provide suggestive evidence. With respect to cardiac output at rest, data are available from the work of Brandfonbrener, Landowne, and Shock (1955) on 67 healthy males ranging in age from 19-86. They found a significant age-related decrease of about one percent per year. Their measurements of cardiac output are supported by the ballistocardiographic data of Starr (1964), who estimated a loss in strength of the myocardium (the heart muscle) which was about 0.85 percent per year after the age of 20. This constitutes fairly close agreement from two very different methodological approaches as to the changes in function of the heart at rest.

Of the several studies available regarding age changes in cardiac output at submaximal exercise, only two were found in which cardiac output was measured during exercise and in which the subjects and exercise loads were sufficiently similar to allow any meaningful comparisons. Becklake et al. (1965) found cardiac output to increase by small amounts with increasing age while Granath, Jonsson, and Strandell (1964) found a small but constant difference in the other direction. Since even in these two studies the methods differed and physical fitness levels were not ruled out among the different age levels, age changes in cardiac output during submaximal exercise must still be considered an open research question.

Most important to our discussion here, however, is the question of what happens to the functional *capacity* of the heart in terms of cardiac output. This means, of course, measurement (or estimation) of *maximal cardiac output*. Only one study was found, but these data from the work of Julius et al. (1967) appear to allow valid age group comparisons and cautious conclusions. They used the indicator-dilution technique to measure cardiac output in 54 subjects in three age groups: I (18–34), II (35–49), and III (50–69). The three groups appear to have been roughly equated in body surface area and physical activity levels. The cardiac outputs at maximum tolerated exercise on a bicycle ergometer were found to be 16.19, 14.96, and 11.98 liters/minute for groups I, II, and III respectively. The age data probably represent a reasonable estimate of the loss in maximum cardiac output with age in a relatively sedentary population. Thus, from the third decade to the sixth and seventh decades we may postulate a loss of some 26 percent. Taking an assumed mean age of 26 for group I and 59 for group III (individual age data were not provided) results in an approximation of the yearly loss at about 0.80 percent per year, a figure roughly similar to the loss rates found for resting cardiac output and myocardial strength.

It has been known that maximum heart rate goes down with age since the classic study by Robinson in 1938. There is also evidence that stroke volume declines with age (Strandell, 1964), so that on these bases we might expect maximum cardiac output to decline at a greater rate than maximum heart rate, which declines almost linearly from 190-195 beats/minute at age 20 to about 160 at age 70 (Robinson, 1938). Assuming a resting rate of 70, this would then result in a lowered capacity for heart-rate response of approximately 0.56 percent per year, over the age range of 20 to 70. Thus the loss of 0.80 percent per year in maximum cardiac output found by Julius et al. (1967) is in the range of what might have been predicted.

The Respiratory System

It has long been known that maximal ventilation attained during exhausting work shows a gradual decline of about 60 percent from the late teens to the eighth decade (Robinson, 1938). It has also been firmly established that vital capacity (the volume of air that can be expelled by the strongest possible expiration after the deepest possible inspiration) declines with age (Norris et al., 1956; Norris, Shock, and Falzone, 1962; Pemberton and Flanagan, 1956). There appears to be no very good evidence for any change in total lung capacity. Therefore since vital capacity and residual volume (the volume of air remaining in the lungs after the strongest possible expiration) are reciprocally related, residual lung volume increases with age (Norris et al., 1956; Norris, Shock, and Falzone, 1962).

Aging therefore increases the ratio of residual volume to total lung capacity, and anatomic dead space also increases with age (Comroe et al., 1962).

The available evidence suggests that lung compliance increases with age (Turner, Mead, and Wohl, 1968), resulting in less elastic recoil to aid in the expiratory process; but even more importantly, thoracic wall compliance decreases in that the elastic stretch and recoil is reduced (Mittman et al., 1965; Rizzato, 1970; Turner, Mead, and Wohl, 1968). Thus the older individual may do as much as 20 percent more elastic work at a given level of ventilation than the young, and most of the additional work will be performed in moving the chest wall (Turner, Mead, and Wohl, 1968).

Changes in Muscle Function

The many studies which have been reported on muscular strength changes with age have been reviewed by Fisher and Birren (1947), and there seems to be good agreement that for most muscle groups maximal strength is achieved between the ages of 25 and 30. Strength decreases slowly during maturity but seems to decrease at a somewhat faster rate after the fifth decade. However, even at age 60 the total loss does not usually exceed 10-20 percent of the maximum (see Chapter 11).

With respect to muscular endurance or fatigue rate, Evans (1971) has shown that fatigue rate is significantly greater in the old than the young when holding isometric contractions of 20, 25, 30, 35, 40, and 45 percent of maximal voluntary contraction.

Physical Working Capacity (PWC)

The best single measure of physical working capacity (PWC) is the maximal oxygen consumption, sometimes referred to as aerobic capacity. Two excellent studies have related this variable to age in men (Robinson, 1938) and women (Astrand, 1960). After a maximum value in early adulthood, there is a gradual decline for both sexes. For men, the maximal values were found at mean age of 17.4 years, and they declined to less than half those values at mean age 75. For women, the maximal values were found in the age group 20-29, and they fell off by 29 percent in the age group 50-65, the oldest tested.

Body Composition

It is typical (though not desirable) for humans to increase their weight with age. Brozek (1952) has provided interesting data on the composition of the human body as it ages, which clearly show that the weight gain in his sample represented a mean increase of 27 pounds of fat from age 20 to age 55, while the fat-free body weight had actually decreased.

Shock et al. (1963), using estimates of intracellular water as an index of the amount of metabolizing tissue, found losses of active protoplasm (which is protein tissue mass as compared against fat tissue) to average about 0.44 percent per year after age 25. Measurements using total body potassium (Allen, Anderson, and Hangham, 1960) are in relatively good agreement.

Thus we can see that even if we maintained body weight at our young adult value, we would nevertheless be getting fatter since we are losing active protoplasm at approximately 3-5 percent per decade after age 20-25.

Aging Processes versus Hypokinetic Disease

It is easy to see how the age-related losses in function described above can individually and in concert result in the relatively large losses in PWC which *accompany* the aging process and which are interpreted by the aging individual as a loss in vigor. However, we must be cautious with respect to attributing all of this functional decline to the aging process per se. Indeed, the entire body of knowledge regarding the loss of function with increasing age must be viewed with caution, since in very few cases has the effect of habitual physical activity been controlled or ruled out. Wessel and Van Huss (1969) have shown that physical activity decreases significantly with increasing age. This is not surprising news, but it does provide scientific validation of the need for consideration of this variable in all investigations directed toward aging changes in performance. To support this contention further, Wessel and Van Huss showed that age-related losses in physiological variables important to human performance *were more highly related to the decreased habitual activity level than they were to age itself.*

It would seem that "Hypokinetic Disease," a term coined by Kraus and Raab (1961) to describe the whole spectrum of somatic and mental derangements induced by inactivity, may be of considerable importance as one factor involved in bringing about an age-related decrement in functional capacities.

For example, most of the age-related changes described in previous sections can also be brought about in young, well-conditioned men in as little as three weeks by the simple expedient of enforced bed rest. In one of the outstanding studies in this area, it was found that in three weeks of bed rest, the maximal cardiac output decreased by 26 percent, the maximal ventilatory capacity by 30 percent, oxygen consumption by 30 percent, and even the amount of active tissue declined by 1.5 percent (Saltin et al., 1968). Thus we see that inactivity can produce losses in function entirely similar to those brought about more slowly in the average individual when he grows more sedentary as he grows older (Wessel and Van Huss, 1969). These observations lead us to question how much of the observed losses in function as people grow older are functions of aging and how much may be brought about by the long-term deconditioning of the increasingly sedentary life we usually lead as we grow older. It seems abundantly clear that the physiological changes which accompany the aging process may not be the result of aging alone. Indeed, there is at least one other process which could conceivably account for some of the changes observed. Incipient disease processes, undiagnosible and unrecognized in their early state, could also contribute to the losses in function. For example, the coronary arteries, whose occlusion by fatty deposits ultimately results in a heart attack, may show early changes even in the teenager. Autopsies on 200 battle casualties of the Korean war (mean age 22.1 years) indicated that 77.3 percent of the hearts showed some gross evidence of coronary arteriosclerosis. Some of these casualties were in their teens (Enos et al., 1953).

To summarize, we may hypothesize that the functional losses which have been observed and reported in the medical and physiological literature as age changes must be considered as resulting from at least three composite factors, only one of which is truly an aging phenomenon. Of the other two factors, unrecognized incipient disease processes may or may not be causally related to aging. The third factor, disuse phenomena or "Hypokinetic Disease," is the only one of the three factors which can be easily reversed. The remainder of this chapter is directed toward the physiological and methodological considerations involved in achieving and maintaining physical fitness in middle and old age.

Trainability of the Older Organism

Only a few years ago, the trainability of older people was still in question. In Germany, it had been concluded that commencement of physical training in a person unaccustomed to sport causes only slight effects of adaptation after the age of 40, while after 60 there is practically no observable effect (Hollman, 1964; Nöcker, 1965). An article from Japan also stated that marked improvement of physical ability by training could not be expected in older people (Katsuki and Masuda, 1969).

On the other hand, Czechoslovakian physiologists had reported better physical performance and functional capacities in a sample of physically active older men than in a comparable sample of sedentary older men (Fischer, Pariskova, and Roth, 1965). Two other investigations had shown significant improvement in physical working capacity and cardiac function by conditioning older people, although the sample size was very small in both—eight in one (Barry et al., 1966) and thirteen in the other (Benestad, 1965). An excellent series of investigations from Stockholm clearly demonstrated the trainability of men in the 34-50 age bracket (Hartley et al., 1969; Kilbom et al., 1969; Saltin et al., 1969). This work demonstrated a 14 per cent improvement in aerobic capacity, a 13 percent increase in cardiac output, and some suggestion of decreased numbers of EKG abnormalities. However, it is difficult to consider even the upper end of this age bracket as old, although the investigators did refer to their subjects as "middle-aged and older" men.

We have entered into a series of experiments regarding the trainability and training methodology for older men and women. This work was done at the Laguna Hills retirement community under the sponsorship of the Administration on Aging (H.E.W.).

In the first experiment (deVries, 1970), 112 older Caucasian males aged 52 to 87 (mean = 69.5) volunteered for participation in a vigorous exercise training regimen. They exercised at calisthenics, jogging, and either stretching exercises or aquatics at each workout for approximately one hour, three times per week under supervision. All subjects were pretested and 66 were retested at 6 weeks, 26 at 18 weeks, and 8 at 42 weeks on the following parameters: (a) blood pressure, (b) percentage of body fat, (c) resting neuromuscular activation (relaxation) by electromyogram (EMG), (d) arm muscle strength and girth, (e) maximal oxygen consumption, (f) oxygen pulse at heart rate = 145, (g) pulmonary function, and (h) physical work capacity on the bicycle ergometer. A subgroup of 35 was also tested before and after 6 weeks of training for (a) cardiac output, (b) stroke volume, (c) total peripheral resistance, and (d) work of the heart, at a workload of 75 watts on the bicycle.

The most significant findings were related to oxygen transport capacity. Oxygen pulse and minute ventilation at heart rate 145 improved by 29.4 percent and 35.2 percent respectively. Vital capacity improved by 19.6 percent.

Significant improvement was also found in percentage of body fat, physical work capacity, and both systolic and diastolic blood pressure for the large six-week group (N=66), but with the smaller group which exercised for 42 weeks (N=8) statistical significance was not achieved, although the same trends were observed. Controls did not improve upon any of the above measures. No significant changes were seen in any of the hemodynamic variables tested.

A group of seven men was placed in a modified exercise program because of various cardiovascular problems. This group exercised in the same manner except that they substituted a progressive walking program for the jogging and were restricted to a maximum heart rate of 120 instead of 145 which obtained with the normal group. This group was exercised for six weeks, at which time their improvement showed a similar pattern to that of the harder working normal subjects at six weeks.

Life history of physical activity was evaluated in a subgroup of 53. Neither the mean of high and low years of activity nor the peak level of activity engaged in for a period of six weeks or more correlated positively with physiological improvement found.

It was concluded that the trainability of older men with respect to physical work capacity is probably considerably greater than had been suspected and does not depend upon having trained vigorously in youth.

Since not a single untoward incident occurred during the 18-month tenure of our exercise program, and in view of the improvements in function demonstrated, it was concluded that the exercise regimen as developed was both safe and effective for a normal population of older men in the presence of medical and physiological monitoring.

In a subsequent study, 17 older women (age 52-79) from the same community participated in a vigorous three-month exercise program and again physical fitness was significantly improved, although the women did not show the large improvement in the respiratory system shown by the men (Adams and deVries, 1973).

On the basis of these studies, we conclude that the older organism is definitely trainable. Indeed the percentage of improvement is entirely similar to that of the young.

Improvement of Health Factors

Since we had earlier found in our electromyographic investigations that vigorous exercise has a well-defined tranquilizer effect (both immediate and long term) upon young and middle-aged men (deVries, 1968), we decided to evaluate this effect of exercise in our older population. Toward this end, the tranquilizer effect of single doses of exercise and meprobamate (a commonly used tranquilizer pill supplied on prescription as either "Miltown" or "Equanil") were compared with respect to reduction of muscle action potentials in ten elderly, anxious subjects (deVries and Adams, 1972). Thirty-six observations were made of each subject before and after (immediately, 30 minutes and one hour after) each of the five following treatment conditions: (1) meprobamate, 400 mg, (2) placebo, 400 mg lactose, (3) 15 minutes of walking-type exercise at a heart rate of 100, (4) 15 minutes of walking-type exercise at heart rate of 120, and (5) resting control. Conditions 1 and 2 were administered double blind (the investigators did not know which subjects received the drug or placebo). It was found that exercise at a heart rate of 100 lowered electrical activity in the musculature by 20, 23, and 20 percent at the first, second, and third post tests respectively. These changes were significantly different from controls at the one percent confidence level. Neither meprobamate nor placebo treatment was significantly different from control. Exercise at the higher heart rate was only slightly less effective, but the data were more variable and approached but did not achieve significance.

Our data suggest that the exercise modality should not be overlooked when a tranquilizer effect is desired, since in single doses, at least, exercise has a significantly greater effect, *without any undesirable side effects,* than does meprobamate, one of the most frequently prescribed tranquilizers. This is especially important for the older individual in that this approach can avoid the further impairment of motor coordination, reaction time, and driving performance, which may occur with any of the tranquilizer drugs. A 15-minute walk at a moderate rate (sufficient to raise heart rate to 100 beats per minute) is a sufficient stimulus to bring about the desired effect which persists for at least one hour afterward.

Many investigators have found decreases in arterial blood pressure resulting from the physical conditioning process. One of the best-controlled studies is that of Boyer and Kasch (1970) who found highly significant decreases of 12 mm Hg in diastolic and 13 mm Hg in systolic pressures in 23 hypertensive subjects who exercised for six months. The subjects with normal blood pressure showed only small and nonsignificant decreases as expected. It seems likely that this normalization of hypertension may be related to the tranquilizer effect discussed above.

With respect to body composition, Greene (1939), who studied 350 cases of obesity, found that inactivity was associated with the onset of obesity in 67.5 percent of the cases and that a history of increased food intake was present in only 3.2 percent. Pariskova (1964), who analyzed the body composition of 1,460 individuals of all ages, concluded: "One of the most important factors influencing body composition is the intensity of physical activity, and this is true in youth, adulthood, and old age." Many other investigations, too numerous to cite, provide indirect support for the belief that lack of physical activity is the most common cause of obesity. Thus, a clear-cut case can be made for the importance of habitual, lifelong, vigorous physical activity as a preventive measure against obesity.

Furthermore, if we consider the functional capacity of the cardio-respiratory system as an important factor in the health of the older individual, then it is of interest to note that two longitudinal studies have shown that typical loss with age in aerobic capacity can be slowed down (Dehn and Bruce, 1972) or even reversed (Nunneley, Finkelstein, and Luft, 1972) by the physical conditioning process.

It seems then that vigorous physical conditioning of the healthy older organism can bring about significant improvements in: (1) the cardiovascular system, (2) the respiratory system (at least in the male), (3) the musculature, (4) body composition, and in general the result is a more vigorous individual who can also relax better. Other health benefits are likely to include a lower blood pressure and lower percent body fat with the concomitant lessening of "risk factors" for development of coronary heart disease that these factors entail.

Prescription of Exercise: Dose-Response Data

Precautions

Because the older organism has lost much of its capacity to respond to homeostatic displacements and also because degenerative diseases of the cardiovascular and pulmonary systems progress with age, it seems important to base the use of vigorous exercise for the older individual upon experimentally derived "dose-response" data.

Indeed, our experience over the last six years with older men and women in a series of exercise physiology investigations leads us to believe that the physician-patient relationship should be a close one. This is necessary to maximize benefit and minimize hazard. For at least three "normal" subjects in our experiments, our standard exercise program was found at six-week retest to have overloaded them. It would seem that "prescription" of exercise is almost as necessary as the prescription of drugs.

Leadership by professionally trained physical educators with a strong background in physiology of exercise and physical fitness work is needed to produce the maximum in benefits with a minimum of hazard for the older age group if the exercise program is to be vigorous. I will define the term "vigorous" as any activity which raises the heart rate more than 40 percent of the way from resting to maximal. Any exercise of less intensity is unlikely to bring about benefits to the cardio-respiratory systems (deVries, 1971a). Although it is possible that some significant physiological benefits to muscles and joints may occur at lower intensity exercise, these are not as yet defined by scientific research.

"How Much Is Enough?"

In order to provide objective levels of stress for our subjects to govern their workouts, we furnish each subject with three reference heart rates for guiding his personal progress: (1) minimum rate for cardio-respiratory improvement, (2) target rate for optimal improvement, and (3) maximum or "do not exceed" heart rate. These values are calculated from % Heart Rate Range (HRR) as follows:

$$\% \text{ HRR} = \frac{\text{EHR} - \text{RHR}}{\text{MHR} - \text{RHR}} \times 100$$

where EHR = exercise heart rate
RHR = resting heart rate in standing position
MHR = maximum heart rate predicted from age by use of Table 12.1.

Minimum heart rate is set at 40% HRR, *Target heart rate* at 60% HRR, and Maximum "do not exceed" heart rate is set at 75% HRR.

Thus, for example, an individual of 73 years of age with a resting heart rate of 70 beats/min. would be given the following values:

HRR = MHR − RHR
= 153 − 70 = 83 beats/min.

Minimum HR = RHR + 40% HRR
= 70 + (.40 × 83) = 70 + 33 = 103 beats/min.
Target HR = RHR + 60% HRR
= 70 + (.60 × 83) = 120 beats/min.
Maximum HR = RHR + 75% HRR
= 70 + (.75 × 83) = 132 beats/min.

Table 12.1   Maximal heart rates in older men

Age	Heart rate	Age	Heart rate	Age	Heart rate	Age	Heart rate
50	174	60	166	70	156	80	147
51	173	61	165	71	155	81	146
52	172	62	164	72	154	82	145
53	172	63	163	73	153	83	145
54	171	64	162	74	152	84	144
55	170	65	161	75	152	85	143
56	169	66	160	76	151	86	143
57	168	67	159	77	150	87	142
58	168	68	158	78	149	88	141
59	167	69	157	79	148	89	141

SOURCE: Robinson, 1938.

This approach is based on one of our studies in which 52 asymptomatic male volunteers from the Laguna Hills retirement community participated in a six-week jogging program which constituted a varying level of stress for the participants, depending upon their physical fitness level. They were tested before and after the exercise regimen with the Astrand bicycle ergometer test (Astrand and Rhyming, 1954) for prediction of their maximal oxygen consumption. During the six-week exercise regimen, they kept daily records of the heart rate elicited by each of the five to ten run phases, and the daily peak heart rate was used in calculating the mean exercise heart rate for the six-week period. This mean peak heart rate was then used in calculating the percentage of heart-rate range at which each subject worked.

It was found that:

(1) Improvement in cardiovascular-respiratory function (aerobic capacity) varied directly with the percentage of heart-rate range at which the subject worked.

(2) Improvement in aerobic capacity varied inversely with the physical fitness level (Astrand score) at the start of the program.

(3) The exercise-intensity threshold for older men appears to be about 40 percent of heart-rate range compared with about 60 percent found by others for young men.

(4) Normalizing the percent heart-rate range (%HRR) for physical fitness level furnishes the best estimate of the exercise-intensity threshold. On this basis, men in this age bracket need to raise their heart rate slightly above that %HRR represented by their aerobic capacity in milliliters per kilogram per minute to achieve the intensity threshold necessary for a training effect.

(5) On the basis of the data, men in the 60s and 70s of average physical fitness need only raise their heart rates above 98 and 95, respectively, to provide a training stimulus to the cardiovascular system. Even well-conditioned men in these age brackets need only exceed 106 and 103, respectively (when heart rate is taken immediately *after* exercise).

(6) It was concluded that for all but highly conditioned older men, vigorous walking which raises heart rate to 100 to 120 beats per minute for 30 to 60 minutes daily constitutes a sufficient stimulus to bring about some, though possibly not optimal, improvement in cardiovascular-respiratory function.

Table 12.1 provides the data on maximal exercise heart rates for men based on the data of Robinson (1938). Similar data for women are as yet not available, but our experience in the laboratory suggests that these data may also be used for the older women, until more specific data are developed.

Figure 12.1 shows the relationship of the improvement from training (Δ Astrand score = estimated maximum oxygen consumption) to the intensity of the training stimulus (percentage of HRR normalized for pretraining fitness level).

Figure 12.2 provides a nomogram developed from telemetered heart rates of healthy men aged 60-79 during various combination of run-walk (deVries, 1971b). The broken line illustrates its application in the prescription of a jogging program for a man with an aerobic capacity of 30 ml/kg/min. Going upward on the 30 ml ordinate to its intersection with the 50 run-50 walk line shows its intersection to lie at a heart-rate value of 118, which is the predicted response for this individual based on our data. The standard error of prediction is 8 to 10 beats per minute for all of the 5 regression lines. We may, therefore, predict that approximately five-sixths of the men in this age bracket with an aerobic capacity of 30 ml/kg/min. would not exceed a heart rate of 118 ± 10 or 128 beats per minute in performance of 5 sets of 50 steps run-50 steps walk.

Importance of Type of Exercise

So far we have talked about exercise in very general terms, and what has been said applies only to rhythmic exercise of large body segments such as found in walking, jogging, running, or swimming.

For any given workload that the body as a whole is subjected to, the

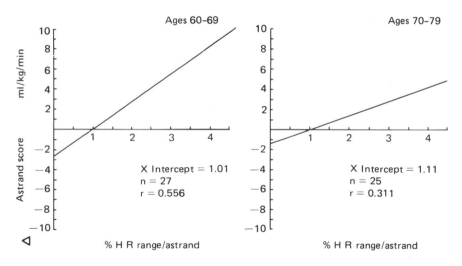

Figure 12.1. Change in Astrand Test score after six weeks of training as a function of percentage of HR range/pre-Astrand. (From deVries, 1971a. Used by permission.)

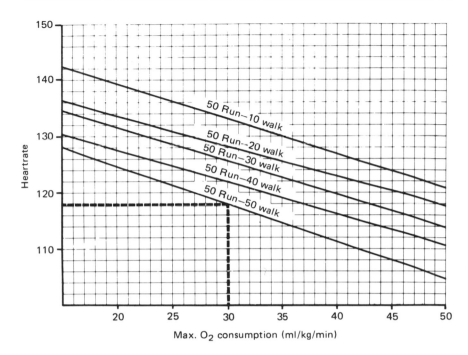

Figure 12.2. Nomogram for the estimation of heart rate response to a given "dose" of jog-walk for men aged 60-79. Example: for a man in this age bracket with a measured (or estimated from Astrand test) maximal O_2 consumption of 30 ml/kg/min., go vertically from 30 on the horizontal axis to the intersection with the 50 run-50 walk regression line. Now go horizontally to the heart rate axis to read 118 which represents the mean response to this dose. The standard error for the 5 regression lines is 8 to 10 beats/min. (From deVries, 1971b. Used by permission.)

work of the heart is greater under conditions of (1) static (isometric) muscular contraction or (2) high activation levels of small muscle masses (Astrand, Guharay, and Wahren, 1968; Lind and McNicol, 1968). This is so because the blood-pressure response to exercise loading is set not by the total body work accomplished but by the arterial blood pressure required to perfuse that muscle which requires the greatest perfusion pressure. Thus, even a small muscle working at 90-100 percent of its maximum strength occludes muscle blood flow and can raise the systemic blood pressure very significantly (Lind and McNicol, 1967a, 1967b). Isometric exercise would be undesirable, because not only are high levels of muscle contraction attained, but they are maintained without the relaxation pauses provided by rhythmic activity during which blood flow is unresisted. Thus we may conclude that exercise programs for older people should maximize the rhythmic activity of large muscle masses and minimize (1) high activation levels of small muscle masses and (2) static (or isometric) contractions. The natural activities of walking, jogging, running, and swimming seem to be best suited to this purpose. If properly designed to conform to these principles, calisthenics can also be very beneficial.

Summary

(1) With respect to the age-related losses in functional capacity of the human organism, it is important to recognize that the observed and reported decrements do not represent the true aging process alone, but may also reflect the functional decline resulting from losses in physical fitness (the "Hypokinetic Disease" of Kraus and Raab) and incipient, undiagnosed degenerative disease processes as well.

(2) The loss in vigor experienced by older people is undoubtedly the result of the well-documented losses in aerobic capacity which are reflected in lessened physical working capacity. The losses in aerobic capacity are to be expected on the basis of the reported decrements in function in the cardiovascular system, the respiratory system, the skeletal musculature, and changes in body composition. The extent to which changes in each of these factors contributes requires further elucidation.

(3) The importance of the Hypokinetic Disease factor in contributing to the loss in aerobic capacity and to the systemic physiological decrements which may act as determinants, is suggested by the results of many "bed rest" studies which have produced physiological changes in a matter of weeks in young, well-conditioned individuals which approximate the long-term aging effects. Indeed, evidence has been presented that apparent age-related losses in physiologic variables important to human performance were more related to decreased habitual activity than to age itself!

(4) Evidence has been presented which suggests that both middle-aged and older healthy men and women are relatively as trainable as are young people. That is to say that their percentage improvement from the conditioning process is roughly equivalent to that of the young, although they start from lower achievement levels. The author has found no reason to believe that this trainability depends in any way upon a previous history of physical conditioning.

(5) It has been shown that training effects in the middle-aged and older individual are demonstrable in the cardiovascular and respiratory systems and in the musculature and that important health benefits such as decreased percentage of body fat, lowered blood pressure, and a better ability to achieve neuromuscular relaxation may result as well.

(6) Since the older organism has lost much of its capacity for response to homeostatic displacements and also because degenerative diseases of the cardiovascular and respiratory systems progress with age, certain precautions are necessary in the use of vigorous physical conditioning for the elderly. A preliminary medical examination is, of course, a "must" and for group exercise, well-trained professional leadership is highly desirable.

(7) Rudimentary dose-response data have been presented to allow the beginnings of a "prescription" approach to the vigorous activity of jogging (alternate jog-walk). In general, improvement from training varies directly with the intensity of the exercise (within limits) and inversely with the pretraining aerobic capacity. The author's data suggest that a minimum exercise intensity (intensity threshold) of 40 percent of the individual's heart rate range (HRR) is required for a training effect in the 60–79 age bracket when workouts are taken three times per week. Sixty percent of HRR is used as the "target heart rate" and 75 percent is the "maximum (do not exceed) heart rate." Every participant in a vigorous exercise program (defined as requiring more than a 40 percent HRR response) should be carefully instructed in taking his own pulse rate, after which he is provided with the minimum, target, and "do not exceed" heart rate values on the basis of his observed resting heart rate and his age-predicted maximum.

(8) For poorly conditioned elderly male (age 60–79), brisk walking constitutes a sufficient stimulus to bring about some training effect, though this may not provide the optimal effect. A nomogram is provided to allow estimation of heart rate response to varying levels of training stimulus in the jog-walk regimen.

(9) The type of exercise is almost equally as important as the intensity level. Exercise programs for older people should maximize the rhythmic activity of large muscle masses and minimize: (1) high activation levels of small muscle masses, and (2) static (or isometric) contractions. The natural activities of walking, jogging, running, and swimming are best suited to this purpose.

References

Adams, G. M., and deVries, H. A. 1973. Physiological effects of an exercise training regimen upon women aged 52–79. *Journal of Gerontology* 28:50–55.

Allen, T. H.; Anderson, E. C.; and Langham, W. H. 1960. Total body potassium and gross body composition in relation to age. *Journal of Gerontology* 15:348–357.

Astrand, I. 1960. Aerobic work capacity in men and women with special reference to age. *Acta Physiologia Scandanavica* 49:suppl. 169.

Astrand, I.; Guharay, A.; and Wahren, J. 1968. Circulatory responses to arm exercise with different arm positions. *Journal of Applied Physiology* 25:528–532.

Astrand, P. O. and Rhyming, I. 1954. A nomogram for calculation of aerobic capacity (physical fitness) from pulse rate during submaximal work. *Journal of Applied Physiology* 7:218–221.

Barry, A. J.; Daly, J. W.; Pruett, E. D. R.; Steinmetz, J. R.; Page, H. F.; Birkhead, N. C.; and Rodahl, K. 1966. The effects of physical conditioning on older individuals. *Journal of Gerontology* 21:182–191.

Becklake, M. R.; Frank, H.; Dagenais, G. R.; Ostiguy, G. L.; and Guzman, C. A. 1965. Influence of age and sex on exercise cardiac output. *Journal of Applied Physiology* 20:938–947.

Benestad, A. M. 1965. Trainability of old men. *Acta Medica Scandinavica* 178:321–327.

Boyer, J. L. and Kasch, F. W. 1970. Exercise therapy in hypertensive men. *Journal of the American Medical Association* 211:1668–1671.

Brandfonbrener, M.; Landowne, M.; and Shock, N. W. 1955. Changes in cardiac output with age. *Circulation* 12:557–566.

Brozek, J. 1952. Changes of body composition in man during maturity and their nutritional implications. *Federation Proceedings* 11:784–793.

Comroe, J. H.; R. E. Forster; A. G. Dubois; W. A. Briscoe; and E. Carlsen. 1962. *The lung*. Chicago, Illinois: The Yearbook Publishers, Inc.

Dehn, M. M. and Bruce, R. A. 1972. Longitudinal variations in maximal O_2 intake with age and activity. *Journal of Applied Physiology* 33:805–807.

deVries, H. A. 1968. Immediate and long-term effects of exercise upon resting muscle action potential level. *Journal of Sports Medicine and Physical Fitness* 8:1–11.

deVries, H. A. 1970. Physiological effects of an exercise training regimen upon men aged 52–88. *Journal of Gerontology* 25:325–336.

deVries, H. A. 1971a. Exercise intensity threshold for improvement of cardiovascular-respiratory function in older men. *Geriatrics* 26:94–101.

deVries, H. A. 1971b. Prescription of exercise for older men from telemetered exercise heart rate data. *Geriatrics* 26:102–111.

deVries, H. A. and Adams, G. M. 1972. Electromyographic comparison of single doses of exercise and meprobamate as to effects on muscular relaxation. *American Journal of Physical Medicine* 51:130–141.

Enos, W. F.; Holmes, R. H. and Beyer, J. 1953. Coronary disease among United States soldiers killed in action in Korea. *Journal of the American Medical Association* 152:1090–1093.

Evans, S. J. 1971. An electromyographic analysis of skeletal neuromuscular fatigue with special reference to age. Doctoral Dissertation. University of Southern California.

Fischer, A.; Pariskova, J.; and Roth, Z. 1965. The effect of systematic physical activity on maximal performance and functional capacity in senescent men. *Internationale Zeitschrift Fuer Angewandte Physiologie Einschliesslich Arbeitsphysiologie* 21:269–304.

Fisher, M. B. and Birren, J. E. 1947. Age and strength. *Journal of Applied Psychology* 31:490–497.

Granath, A.; Jonsson, B.; and Strandell, T. 1964. Circulation in healthy old men, studied by right heart catheterization at rest and during exercise in supine and sitting position. *Acta Medica Scandinavica* 176:425–446.

Greene, J. A. 1939. Clinical study of the etiology of obesity. *Annals of Internal Medicine* 12:1797–1803.

Hartley, L. H.; Grimby, G.; Kilbom, A.; Nilsson, N.J.; Astrand, I.; Bjure, J.; Ekblom, B.; and Saltin, B. 1969. Physical training in sedentary middle aged and older men: 111 cardiac output and gas exchange at submaximal and maximal exercise. *Scandinavian Journal of Clinical and Laboratory Investigation* 24:335–344.

Hollman, W. 1964. Changes in the capacity for maximal and continuous effort in relation to age. In *International Research in Sport and Physical Education*, eds. E. Jokl and E. Simon, pp. 369–371. Springfield, Illinois: Charles C. Thomas.

Julius, S.; Amery, A.; Whitlock, L. S.; and Conway, J. 1967. Influence of age on the hemodynamic response to exercise. *Circulation* 36:222–230.

Katsuki, S. and Masuda, M. 1969. Physical exercise for persons of middle and elder age in relation to their physical ability. *Journal of Sports Medicine* 9:193–199.

Kilbom, A.; Hartley, L. H.; Saltin, B.; Bjure, J.; Grimby, G.; and Astrand, I. 1969. Physical training in sedentary middle-aged and older men I. Medical Evaluation. *Scandinavian Journal of Clinical and Laboratory Investigation* 24:315–322.

Kraus, H. and Raab, W. 1961. *Hypokinetic disease*. Springfield, Illinois: Charles C. Thomas.

Lind, A. R. and McNicol, G. W. 1967a. Muscular factors which determine the cardiovascular responses to sustained rhythmic exercise. *Canadian Medical Association Journal* 96:706–713.

Lind, A. R. and McNicol, G. W. 1967b. Circulatory responses to sustained hand-grip contractions performed during other exercise, both rhythmic and static. *Journal of Physiology* 192:595–607.

Lind, A. R. and McNicol, G. W. 1968. Cardiovascular responses to holding and carrying weights by hand and by shoulder harness. *Journal of Applied Physiology* 25:261–267.

Mittman, C.; Edelman, N. H.; Norris, A. H.; and Shock, N. W. 1965. Relationship between chest wall and pulmonary compliance and age. *Journal of Applied Physiology* 20:1211–1216.

Nöcker, J. 1965. Die Bedeutung des Sportes den Alten Menschen. In *Handbuch der Praktischen Geriatrie*, eds. Hittmair, R. Nissen, & F. H. Schulz, pp. 176–198. Stuttgart: F. Enke.

Norris, A. H.; Shock, N. W.; Landowne, M.; and Falzone, J. A. 1956. Pulmonary function studies: age differences in lung volume and bellows function. *Journal of Gerontology* 11:379–387.

Norris, A. H.; Shock, N. W.; and Falzone, Jr., J. A. 1962. Relation of lung volumes and maximal breathing capacity to age and socio-economic status. In *Medical and clinical aspects of aging*, ed. H. T. Blumenthal, pp. 163–171. New York: Columbia University Press.

Nunneley, S. A.; Finkelstein, S.; and Luft, U. C. 1972. Longitudinal study on physical performance of ten pilots over a ten year period. *Aerospace Medicine* 43:541–544.

Pariskova, J. 1964. Impact of age, diet and exercise on man's body composition. In *International research in sport and physical education,* ed. E. Jokl and E. Simon, pp. 238–253. Springfield, Illinois: Charles C. Thomas.

Pemberton, J. and Flanagan, E. G. 1956. Vital capacity and timed vital capacity in normal men over forty. *Journal of Applied Physiology* 9:291–296.

Rizzato, G. and Marazzini, L. 1970. Thoracoabdominal mechanics in elderly men. *Journal of Applied Physiology* 28:457–460.

Robinson, S. 1938. Experimental studies of physical fitness in relation to age. *Arbeitsphysiologie* 10:251–323.

Saltin, B.; Blomquist, G.; Mitchell, J. H.; Johnson, R. L.; Wildenthal, K.; and Chapman, C. B. 1968. Response to exercise after bed rest and after training. *American Heart Association Monograph #23.* New York: The American Heart Association.

Saltin, B.; Hartley, L. H.; Kilbom, A.; and Astrand, I. 1969. Physical training in sedentary, middle aged and older men: II oxygen uptake, heart rate, and blood lactate concentration at submaximal and maximal exercise. *Scandinavian Journal of Clinical and Laboratory Investigation* 24:323–334.

Shock, N. W. 1961a. Physiological aspects of aging in man. *Annual Review of Physiology* 23:97–122.

Shock, N. W. 1961b. Current concepts of the aging process. *Journal of the American Medical Association* 175:654–656.

Shock, N. W. 1970. Physiologic aspects of aging. *Journal of the American Diet Association* 56:491–96.

Shock, N. W.; Watkin, D. M.; Yiengst, M. J.; Norris, A. H.; Gaffney, G. W.; Gregerman, R. I.; and Falzone, J. A. 1963. Age differences in the water content of the body as related to basal oxygen consumption in males. *Journal of Gerontology* 18:1–8.

Starr, I. 1964. An essay on the strength of the heart and on the effect of aging upon it. *American Journal of Cardiology* 14:771–783.

Strandell, T. 1964. Circulatory studies of healthy old men. *Acta Medica Scandinavica* suppl. 414.

Turner, J. M.; Mead, J.; and Wohl, M. E. 1968. Elasticity of human lungs in relation to age. *Journal of Applied Physiology* 25:664–671.

Wessel, J. A. and Van Huss, W. D. 1969. The influence of physical activity and age on exercise adaptation of women aged 20–69 years. *Journal of Sport Medicine* 9:173–180.

Issues in the Physical Environment

13

Planning Micro-Environments for the Aged

ARTHUR N. SCHWARTZ

Any environment can and does produce effective responses; more often than not the environment elicits intense emotional response. This basic principle is especially relevant to older people because of the unequivocally higher incidence of organically induced perceptual deprivation among the elderly. If, indeed, sensory losses in the later years of life produce invisible yet nonetheless very real barriers to the informational input which is necessary for the maintenance of competent behavior, then it clearly follows that understanding the relationship of the aged to environmental elements is crucial to better understanding the behavior of the aged, as well as for devising intervention strategies to assist them.

Environmental Influence

The concept of environmental influence and impact upon human behavior and well-being is now well entrenched in the study of man. Yet curiously enough, much of the assessment of the circumstances and behavior of mature persons, especially those in the later decades of life, appears to pay little more than lip-service to the kind of person/environment transactional process which provides essential clues to understanding much of the behavior of aged persons. Kurt Lewin (1936) has described this transactional process in detail in elaborating his notion of "life space." His notions of the barriers existing between environmental events, of how these barriers become permeable, and of the continuous interaction between the internal environment of the human organism and the external environment, provide one of the earliest and richest formulations of what is now referred to broadly as person/environment transactions. Roger Barker (1963) pioneered in finding many of the operational components of the person/environment transaction. He devised a systematic methodology for quantifying and recording behavioral and environmental events *in vivo* within specific time frames. In his two landmark monographs (1959, 1969) E. T. Hall fleshed out the skeleton of Lewin's conceptual and theoretical framework with behavioral applications. Hall's descriptive reports of culturally derived differences in the uses of social space (including but not limited to territoriality, personal space, and intimate space) as a meaningful dimension of person/environment transactions have been followed up with substantial empirical data in the same area by Robert Sommer (1969), among others, on the behavioral basis of environmental design. Drawing on Lewin and Hall and using Barker's methodology, Sommer has shown how differential behaviors in daily living are elicited from or "coerced" by environmental designs or spatial arrangements in a variety of settings, such as the library, hospital ward, defense shelter, or campus student union. Unquestionably the most comprehensive compilation of recent work done in this area of concern is that completed by Harold Proshansky, William Ittelson, and Leanne Rivlin (1970) of the Environmental Psychology Program of CUNY.

Investigations such as the ones just cited clearly indicate interest in the general problem of how and to what extent environment is colored by and in turn influences behavior. But only within the last half-dozen or so years have gerontologists begun to extend these basic concepts and apply them to people in their later decades of life. Although only the surface has as yet been scratched, both in terms of research and application, it is encouraging to note that approaches to this multifaceted, multidimensional problem are rich and varied. O. R. Lindsley (1964), basing his experimental work on the postulate that human behavior is a functional relationship between the individual and a specific social or mechanical environment, has very well detailed the utility of developing geriatric prosthetic environments as a free-operant conditioning mode. He draws attention to the ways in which manipulation or modification of the physical environment can compensate for deficits in old age and produce the positive reinforcements necessary to improve unproductive behaviors (or behavioral deficits) when they occur in old age. His major point, shared by all others writing on micro-environments for the aged, is that we have not even begun to exhaust the vast possibilities for developing prosthetic devices for the aged which will prevent them from being penalized as a consequence of multiple loss.

A. Ciucă (1967) has investigated in his native Romania the role of environmental conditions in relation to longevity. He and his colleagues examined such factors as geographical characteristics, dietary regimen, alcoholic consumption, incidence of smoking, and specific occupational activity. Margaret Blenker (1967) has reviewed a series of studies of environmental change, that is, relationship of survival of elderly to relocation. Some of her data do suggest that psychological factors may play a significant role in determining the survival of elderly persons following relocation.

Frances Carp (1967) in her now classic study of Victoria Plaza asked whether old people can be changed by altering the environments in which they live. She compared residential status groups of elderly who had just moved into newly-built Senior Center high rise apartments and found dramatic evidence of improved outlook and life style among the resident group which were attributed to improved housing.

Schwartz and Proppe (1969) in an earlier investigation of the institutionalized aged found that the desire for privacy among them correlated highly with length of time in the institutional setting and not at all with such demographic variables as education or marital status. They later (1970) postulated that person/environment transactional variables are significantly related to levels of positive self-regard in the elderly. This was further investigated with empirical study by Aloia (1973), who examined the relationship of perceived privacy options, feeling of control over one's own life, and self-esteem in institutionalized and noninstitutionalized older adults. Schwartz (1974) has further elaborated this conceptualization of the interaction between person/environment transactions and self-esteem in the elderly and the possible modes of intervention. Kermit Schooler (1969) in similar fashion has addressed himself to the even-recurring question: does environment make a difference to the elderly and if so, in what way? His investigation of the relation of social interaction to morale in the elderly underscores the complex nature of these variables and the necessity of assessing them within the environmental fabric. A parallel theme is echoed by M. Powell Lawton (1970, 1974) who describes a framework for suitable integration of the older person and his environment. Lawton's schema of behavioral indices, ranging from simple to complex, offers an approach to matching the person to the appropriate environment, thus opening a broader range of alternatives for residence selection. All of which is to point out that those who study aging are gradually coming to understand that the environment is not simply the backdrop, the "scenery" against which the lives of older persons are lived. If, indeed, such were the case, then planning the micro-environment for older persons could be construed (as it often used to be) as merely repainting or rearranging the environmental scenery, in effect, an architectural exercise.

We are rapidly discovering that quite the opposite is true. The beha-

viors of aged persons no less than those of their cohorts do not occur
in a vacuum. Behavioral responses of the elderly, which are a direct consequence of the interaction between the person and the environment, can
only be understood in their contexts. Furthermore, environmental modifications are a most pragmatic and immediate intervention strategy. As we
study environmental manipulations carefully and systematically, we increase
our ability to predict behavior and thus to control the consequences of
such interactions. The knowledge of consequences implies prior options
and choices; we do, in fact, have such choices and we will subsequently be able to observe differential kinds of behaviors as a result of
those choices.

Institutions

As we learn more and understand better which consequences follow which
particular environmental manipulations then, it appears, we will learn
how to produce particular positive results. At least from such information
we shall be better able to design micro-environments than we could from
random manipulations or random designs. What comes most readily to
mind relative to older people is the long-term care environment. Most
readers will be aware that a very small proportion of the elderly in our
society actually live in an institutional or quasi-institutional setting. The
figure usually cited is something like five percent or a little less. However,
it is more important for us to be acutely aware that whether or not older
persons live in a setting formally identified as "institutional," they are
embedded within environmental influences and behave in response to
person/environmental transactions. We also need to give credence to
the notion that the goodness or badness of an older person's environment
is not necessarily a function of whether the environment is "institutional."
It is certainly a well-documented fact that many institutions are "bad,"
attested to by many health professionals and students of the sociology
of institutions who cite such factors as the lack of options, the sterile
and dreary environment, routines which primarily serve staff needs and
are deadening to initiative on the part of the residents (read inmates),
monotonous food, and the like. But the assumption that such a sterile,
"filtered" environment is a function of the setting's being "institutional"
is at best problematic. One can easily document the existence of such
environmental conditions in the context of a private home or dwelling.

All of which leads to the assertion that it serves no useful purpose
to characterize institutions as being "bad" by definition; rather a more
accurate and meaningful assessment is that bad institutions are bad. Con-

versely, good institutions can and do provide good environmental settings and thus fulfill necessary and useful societal needs. This relates to a second issue which planning micro-environments for the elderly raises, and that is what particular environmental designs or components of the design mean in terms of their daily experience to the individuals interacting with that environment. We have already recognized that man can alter his environment in ways which will lead to favorable or unfavorable consequences or outcomes to himself. Whether the outcome is judged favorable or not is a subjective judgment; this means that the subjective perspective or frame of reference is critical. That is to say, there is no such thing as an "ideal," a "model," or an "optimal" environmental setting per se. We are used to hearing that "man is the measure"; the individual's point of view and interaction with any given environmental inputs must be taken into account. Here, of course, is where this issue (the perception of environment) overlaps the issue raised before, namely, person/environment transactions. In any attempt to plan micro-environments we need to recognize the human response to the environment, not in terms of an objective "way it is" but in terms of the way it is experienced, a notion first expressed by Koffka's concept of the "behavioral environment" (1935) and later elaborated in the Lewinian field theory of the life space (1936). Behavior derives not from the objective dimensions of the stimulus world "out there," but rather from that stimulus world transformed and translated into a subjective world or psychological environment.

If our attempts to design micro-environments for the elderly are to have any validity at all, then I would argue with Proshansky that we must always take into account the relationship between the older person's physical world and the world he "constructs" from it. Take, for example, the idea of aesthetics. Fitch (1970) makes the important point that a fundamental weakness in most discussions of aesthetics is our usual failure to relate it to experiential reality; it is simply unrealistic to discuss aesthetics as if it were an abstract problem in logic. It is still true that "beauty is in the eye of the beholder," thus the "beauty" of a building is not a discrete and unvarying property of the building. Rather the word describes the particular beholder's response to the building's impact upon him at a particular time.

Another example of this is the oft-observed phenomenon of the businessman exhibiting two sets of behavior, two personalities as it were, one his "office behavior" and the other his "home behavior," each a function of interaction with a differently perceived setting or behavioral context. Still another example has to do with the individual's need to be properly oriented in space (both physical and emotional space). This need runs deep and according to E. T. Hall is ultimately linked to survival and sanity. To be disoriented in space, physical and/or emotional space, is to be or act psychotic. Thus, in considering micro-environments for the elderly, we must carefully consider what positive or negative behaviors that environment is likely to foster or produce.

Stress and the Environment

A series of studies recently reported by Stewart Kiritz and Rudolf Moos (1974) examines the physiological effects of social environments. Their work cites experimental evidence suggesting that cohesion or affiliation reduces susceptibility to physiological stress responses. Their experimental evidence suggests that a cohesive group is less susceptible to stress, and also that a group member may experience stress responses if he deviates from the norms of his cohesive group. Subjects exhibit greater galvanic skin response when interacting than when they have "neutral attitudes" (are uninvolved with each other). Other evidence indicates covariation in elevation of free fatty acid and heart rate in pairs of subjects, one of whom listened passively while the other answered personal questions; subjects in high interaction had higher diastolic blood pressure than subjects in low interaction interviews, even though the actual content of both interviews was found to be about the same. The study reports similar findings with respect to a significantly greater rise in free fatty acid during involvement of subjects in "important" versus "unimportant" tasks. Additional evidence supports the hypothesis that "responsibility is a dimension of the social environment which is associated with physiological changes in its members" (namely, greater corti-costeroid responses, 17 percent to 20 percent higher heart rates, greater incidence of coronary atherosclerosis, excretion of adrenalin, and the like). These physiological changes are related most persuasively by experimental evidence to such environmental elements as personal responsibility, involvement and interaction, work pressures, and uncertainty, that is, the clarity or ambiguity of the setting, of one's roles, or of the amount and degree of environmental change.

From these considerations, Kiritz and Moos conclude that environments, like people, may be said to have unique "personalities," differentiable and measurable. They propose three basic categories of such differentiation and measurement, namely

1. relationship dimensions (support, cohesion, reduction of stress, involvement)
2. personal development dimensions (responsibility, importance)
3. system maintenance and system change dimensions (work pressure, clarity, ambiguity, change).

We can create the bridge from these findings to the design of micro-environments for older people by producing environments, for example, which minimize to the greatest extent possible ambiguous, enclosed space. This is easily and economically accomplished by providing environmental cues, such as signs, which help the elderly find their way around and through the designed space. Color, light, and texture clues also can assist the aged in easily finding their way through various areas of the environment, and provide ready identification of the functions of spatial components. Such identifying cues should tell the ambulating person at the entrance of a long maze of corridors which are cul-de-sacs and so help him to conserve energy; they should tell the elderly person in a wheel chair which corridors end at a staircase or a locked door. As another example, the findings of engineers (exemplified by the work done in airline cockpit design and also specified to some extent by Lindsley) show us how we might design elevator controls which not only provide visual cues (the almost universal mode in current usage) but also provide, by differential shapes for push buttons, tactile cues for those with impaired vision who need to tell which button to push by "feel" alone. Such permanent cues not only provide initial orientation and reduce ambiguity but also provide continuous reminders and warnings for persons who forget.

In all such instances it is crucial to the basic concept involved here to insist that the cues and clues themselves be unambiguous, be large enough, appropriately placed, and clear enough to be easily and quickly noticed and readily comprehended. Tiny room numbers or similar designations made up of inch-high letters or numbers and placed over a seven-foot door, for instance, are ostensible compliances with the principle but turn out to be worse than useless.

The findings of Kiritz and Moos may also be directly applied to the circumstances of the aged in terms of support, personal involvement, and change. Thus design of the micro-environment must take into strict account the need for maximum environmental stimulation; visual and auditory stimulation are especially important, but other sense modalities are also necessary and important. In this connection it is important to keep in mind that most elderly with moderate to severe loss experiences, whether economic or physical, tend to remain indoors most, if not all, the time, even when not residing in an institution. The significance and importance of such factors as variety, change, sense of adventure, and overall stimulation as a function of the interim environmental setting become all the more apparent.

Some of the elements of these three dimensions—environmental clues, stimulation, and support—of the micro-environment are categorized in the tables which follow. I would caution the reader that this schema is intended only as an illustration and is not meant to cover all possibilities or contingencies, a task which is better left to further research and more formal elaboration of such applications, with respect to which Pastalan (1970) has already produced some excellent work and provocative leads.

Table 13.1 indicates some of the general elements relevant to design of micro-environments for the aged under each of three environmental rubrics. Table 13.2 suggests specific ways in which the elements of Table 13.1 can be implemented. Again, I would caution that these are only illustrative and should be used as points of departure within the context of design.

Suffice it to say here that the intended outcomes of such environmental modifications as suggested in these two tables should not be construed as merely decorative, enriching, or pleasant. The meaning of Kiritz and Moos' work, as applied to the aged, strongly suggests that such applications to micro-environmental design for the aged will make the crucial difference between sick or well, competent or incompetent, oriented or confused, satisfied or miserable older persons.

All of this builds upon the careful and extensive work of Hans Selye which documents the basic principle that stress is the nonspecific response of the body to any demand made upon it (1973). The present emphasis of this discussion, therefore, is that the person/environment transaction principle in designing micro-environments for the aged is not to be construed, either, as mere academic speculation. On the contrary, designs for aged persons, whether appropriate or inappropriate, have immediate as well as long-range effects upon the behavior and physiological functioning of the elderly; they can and often do contribute directly to the difference between adequate, good, or ill health of an elderly population.

It is unfortunately true, as Joseph Koncelik, a teacher and architect involved in the design of long-term care facilities for the elderly, has pointed out, that the design of environments for the aged has up to now not benefited from this kind of focus or attention. Builders, planners, architects, or engineers, for whatever reasons (usually ranging from the limiting constraints of mortgaging programs to lack of time, interest, or competence) have rarely, if ever, taken the time to evaluate the space which they have designed and built after its completion. None of the professionals characteristically goes back to his project to ask if space is being utilized as it was intended, and if it is, why, and if not, why not. Nor do these professionals evaluate the effects of the design upon the user. This lack of follow-up implies the need for a new professional group who will undertake this essential work of evaluation (see Koncelik, 1972).

Table 13.1 Design elements for (prosthetic) micro-environments for aged

Enviromental clues to	Environmental stimulation	Environmental support
Identify spaces a. personal or private b. public or shared	Use all senses Enhance new learning behavior	Provide real choices Age-appropriate design of furnishings
Find way to different areas	Maintain appropriate degree of variety	Congruent life-style orientation
Find way through space	Appropriately "challenge" a. activities which have intrinsic value b. activities with meaningful outcomes	a. appropriate kinds, amounts of food b. familiar setting c. congenial schedules
Anticipate unseen hazards a. hidden stairwells b. changes in floor level or slope c. areas exposed to undue heat, cold, weather d. slippery surfaces	Provide sufficient "success" experiences Maximum "associative" inputs	Individualization
Locate needed persons		Abundant prosthetic devices a. for easy manipulation b. compensating for deficits
Locate static service areas		Privacy options
Locate utilities		Noninfantilizing
Adequately use utilities		Communication aids

Table 13.2 Implementation modes for design elements

Environmental cues	Environmental stimulation	Environmental support
Signs with letters or recognizable symbols (cf. traffic signs), good contrast, easily read from walking or wheelchair eye-level	Use bright, intense colors; maximum contrast for both color and music	Clearly communicate expectations of as much self-management as possible, even where some "risk" exists; provide options
For traversing large spaces, additional reinforcing signs at frequent intervals	Employ sounds (e.g., train or cricket sounds), varying levels of music to create or enhance moods	Chairs, sofas designed for age-compatible use; seats with lift-tilt device; chairs with arms
Differentiating entry ways or functional use by brightly painted doors, plus symbols	Pictures, plant life, flowers which can be changed	Oversize knobs, handles; controls with extensions that allow control by arm or leg pressure
Color cue stripes on walls, floors, to match color of "target" space	Mobiles (changeable) and mural for visual enrichment on bare walls and ceiling areas	Detachable head, shoulder, or arm supports for wheelchairs, sitting chairs
Color-themed suites or complex of areas to identify location or function of space	TV, radio, tape-recordings, records provide basis of entertainment, information, discussion	In-house phone system to reach other residents, staff, beauty shops, etc.
Differential use of lighting to enhance "quiet" or "noisy" areas	Sound levels and quality must be compatible with elderly listeners	Maximum encouragement to personalize rooms
Texture or texture effects to provide cues (e.g., for hazard zones)	Make variety of large-print books and newspapers available	Some personal items throughout living areas
Shape (tactile) cues for utility controls; use of multiple cues (both tactile and visual)	Oversize clocks and calendars which can be read at minimum of 10 feet	Entering a room only when invited; provision for locked door privacy
Auditory cues: chimes to signal events (e.g., meals, baths)	Emphasize use of nonbland foods, wines, spices	Maximum flexibility to accommodate individual eating tastes, habits, and "rhythm"
Automatic devices wherever possible (slide doors)	Variety of textured surfaces, objects in place	Ready access to bright reading lights, large print, magnifying glasses, radio-TV earphones
	Ready availability (for those who wish) of pets for observing, stroking, or care-taking (dogs, cats, birds, aquaria, etc.)	For congregate living, full-face pictures of residents at each room entry, of staff at usual work areas
	Everyday living activities: meal planning, preparation, serving, cleaning, shopping record keeping, income producing, activity planning, as options	Personal ID (decals, name tags) for staff, residents, volunteers, visitors, etc.
	Frequent contact options with babies, children, young adults (on site nursery school, e.g.)	

Quality of Life

Quality of life, imprecise term though it may be, ultimately comes down to the issue of positive self-regard, the self-esteem of the aged. The issue has been detailed by Schwartz (1974), but the essential concept is that design of micro-environments for the aged must be aimed not only at ameliorating stresses, minimizing the effects of losses, and compensating for deficits but must do so in ways which enhance the individuals' effectiveness, support their competence, and thus help them maintain self-esteem. Design modifications and concepts which omit or underestimate these outcomes, especially for the aged, may be seen as irrelevant, if not pernicious, in their consequences. Design concepts, construction, and modifications, when effectively implemented, on the other hand, constitute the kind of prosthetic environment which compensates the elderly in large measure for their losses, and helps them maintain functional competence to a significant degree. Such designs can be said to sustain self-esteem which is what the design of micro-environments for the elderly is really all about.

Other students and investigators of person/environment transactions have articulated congruent formulations which are readily adaptable to designing environments for the aged. Raymond Studer, for example, in his analysis of behavior-contingent physical systems (1970) is obviously leaning heavily upon Skinnerian operant behavioral analysis when he views a designed environment as a "learning system." Such a system requires that environmental variables are arranged so as to bring about the desired state of behavioral outcomes.

The impression one gets from a great many environments in which aged persons live as well as from that which is written to describe such environments suggests the existence of a simplistic notion that man is infinitely adaptable. This is surely an erroneous view of man. Both common sense and very good empirical data persuasively demonstrate that human adaptability is finite. Given the fact that our experience repeatedly shows the limits of adaptability with respect to certain modes and intensities of environmental dissonance, it is curious, even surprising, to find relatively little attention being paid to environments specifically designed to adapt to the special needs and requirements of the aged.

Designers of micro-environments for the aged should know that ambiguous space, difficult enough to negotiate under ordinary circumstances, can become at times the source of intolerable stress for the elderly person with poor vision or hearing, or one who has suffered minor strokes. Designers must, therefore, attend to and evaluate the space they design in terms of its ultimate utility to such elderly persons. The needs of elderly persons, in utilizing environmental space without penalty, must be associated by designers with such demonstrably important factors as the need for familiarity, ease of manipulation, safety, clarity, sensory signals and cues, supportive and prosthetic systems, comfort, ease of mobility, and sensory stimulation, to name some of the most important factors. All such design strategies move in the direction of making the various deficits of aging less relevant with respect to function and thus tend to maintain individual competence for daily self-sufficiency with its attendant self-esteem. We shall come back to this point later.

The Nonpenalizing Environment

The whole category of furniture nicely illustrates the continuing problem. Chairs, tables, shelves, storage bins, blackboards, doorknobs, and all the accoutrements of a nursery or other school environment, are almost without exeception specifically designed for children so as not to impair or penalize them with respect to their functioning in that environment. Also special so-called "orthopedic" designs are utilized for persons with special motoric disabilities or deficits. Yet, in general, those who choose furniture utilized in settings for older persons tend to ignore the penalties imposed by chairs or sofas too low or too soft or without arms on those who by virtue of arthritis or restricted mobility or stiffness or other deficits find it enormously difficult to get in and out of such chairs. The same criteria can readily be applied to other aspects of the environment which presume to serve the aged: poorly designed beds; storage space so low or so high as to be virtually inaccessible to the elderly; tables of unsuitable height or dimensions; visual and other orienting cues virtually indistinguishable or nonexistent; windows, elevators, water faucets, and heat controls almost impossible to manipulate by stiff fingers or aged joints; wheelchairs which are unstable or allow discomforting and even unsafe slumping by the elderly occupant; heavy doors and "blind" entry and exit portals; eating and cooking utensils and stoves, medicine cabinets, storage bottles and stairs which often range from the inconvenient and unsuitable for the aged to the unsafe and positively dangerous. All of these instances suggest the desirability of developing a diagnostic approach to designing the micro-environment for the elderly; the converse of negative elements will help us to establish criteria for relevant and adequate design concepts.

A special cautionary note is in order at this point. In our attempt to proceed on the principle of designing micro-environments which do not penalize the older person and thus impair or minimize whatever functional capacities are available, we must bear in mind at the same time that a very fine line often exists between the supportive, compensating, prosthetic environment and environmental inputs which either subtly or blatantly tend to preempt the functional capacities of the aged individual and, therefore, to infantilize such persons. Designers and behavioral scientists who presume to contribute to environmental design must also recognize and respond to the principle that it is neither possible nor wise to eliminate all risks for the older person. Nor is it wise to try to do any more than will facilitate self-sufficiency. In person/environment transactional terms, any environment which tends to infantilize the older person will subvert his sense of self-worth and self-esteem, and will ultimately defeat many of the positive effects which can be envisioned for an environmental design program for older people.

Beatrice Wright's thesis (1958) is quite relevant and applicable in this regard. She persuasively documents her conclusion that there is a fine but very necessary distinction to be made between the disabled person and the person with a disability. The application of this to the later years of life is self-evident. The extension of life across the years in itself allows a greater accumulation of disabilities and/or decrements across a range of functional capacities. It is not surprising, therefore, to observe the clinical evidence of multiple losses to a greater or lesser degree (allowing for individual differences) in most if not every instance within an aged population. The older person truly is not the same as the young or middle-aged person, only older (any more than children are "minature" adults). There are indeed very real differences. In recognizing such clinical losses, however, the assumption unfortunately is often made that "older" is synonymous with "disabled." This conclusion, according to Wright, is neither warranted nor accurate. Where compensatory or prosthetic interventions are sensible, early, and effectively instituted, the probability is very great that the older person can function quite effectively in spite of deficits right up to the end. The blind repairman or pianist is not a "disabled" person because competent function in such an instance is not contingent upon sightedness.

This principle is one of the keys to the appropriate design of micro-environments for the aged. To the list of items-to-be-avoided developed earlier we must add those positive environmental aspects which enable the aged person with disabilities to continue to function reasonably competently. The environment must not "penalize" the aged person for his deficits, to be sure; it must also be reasonably barrier-free. But more than that, the environment must be designed not only to make life "possible" but also to make life worthwhile. The environment must maintain beauty (or bring beauty back if it has been missing); it must overcome the filtering effects of possibly increasingly defective senses (vision, hearing, taste, touch, smell) by increasing the amount and intensity of environmental stimulation and impact; it must provide real options and thus the possibility of real choice (not the least of which is the privacy option); it must provide for relatively easy negotiation of space through clarity of space and extensive use of "readable" environmental cues; it must help maintain at least a modicum of familiar life style and provide some incentives for modification and growth; it must provide continuing opportunities and mechanisms for activity which can be both taken seriously and found personally rewarding by the individual; it must make involvement in the ebb and flow of daily living gratifying and reassuring rather than anxiety arousing; finally, it must offer variety and adventure within limits that are satisfying to the individual.

Conclusion

It is obvious from even a brief catalogue such as the above that designing the micro-environment for the aged as defined in this context goes well beyond the mere arrangement or allocation of space or even beyond basically architectural concerns. The design problems to be solved include all dimensions of the life space. Based upon the person/environment transactional premise, considerations must include the requirement of adapting the environment to the aged individual as much as expecting the aged individual to adapt to the environment. It is not even likely, to say nothing of possible, that we can design a single suitable environment which will meet the aforementioned criteria for any and all aged persons. We must, therefore, begin to think in terms of designing different environments for different populations of older persons.

It is not simplistic to point this out in the face of the long-practiced tendency to design one environment to which a diverse population of older persons, with a variety of backgrounds, life styles, needs, tastes, capacities, and interests, are expected to adapt. At best this has produced very limited success. The classic example of this, of course, is the long-term care facility (nursing home) which has been proliferating throughout our society and which has somehow expected a very heterogenous population of older persons to adapt successfully to one particular kind of environment, namely the medical model. It should now be all too obvious that such an approach in general tends to exacerbate the most serious problems of the aged, from a clinical, pragmatic, and esthetic point of view. This is precisely what Harold Proshansky means when he refers (1973) to the "environmental crisis in human dignity."

The environmental crisis in human dignity lies not just in the overuse, the misuse, and the decay of physical settings, but far more significantly in how we conceive of the individual in relation to any such existing setting, including the newest ones and those still on the drawing board.

He goes on to label this a crisis because spaces and places are improperly designed not only in physical terms but because designs also overlook human needs for privacy, territoriality, and freedom of choice, and often conceive the individual as a simple machine man. Unintended consequences are often ignored and no attempt is made to evaluate just how well the setting actually works. The danger is that the person will adjust at the price of continuing erosion of the properties that make him distinctly human.

Speaking to this very issue, Bayne (1970) suggests that in large measure the dependency, apathy, and withdrawal so frequently observed in elderly residents may be a function of their accommodation to an environment that purports to promote health but actually encourages the sick role, that provides treatment but does so through regulation and control. The very effectiveness of such a program can literally endanger the patient's will to self-determination.

Abraham Heschel of the Jewish Theological Seminary put it even more dramatically: "Enabling us to reach old age, medical science may think it gave us a blessing; however, we continue to act as if it were a disease" (Address to the 1961 White House Conference on Aging).

Person/environment transactions, life space, self-esteem, and functional competence: these are the essential concepts for designing micro-environments for the aged. Without these, environmental design will provide small service and contribute even less to the well-being of the aged and thus fail to realize the full potential of the role which it deserves.

References

Aloia, A. 1973. *Privacy options, locus of control, and self-esteem in the aged.* Doctoral dissertation. California School of Professional Psychology, Los Angeles.

Barker, R. G. 1963. *The stream of behavior.* New York: Appleton-Century-Crofts.

Bayne, J. R. 1970. Environmental modification for the older person. *The Gerontologist* 10:1.

Blenker, M. 1967. Environmental change and the aging individual. *The Gerontologist* 7:2, Part I.

Carp, F. 1967. The impact of environment on old people. *The Gerontologist* 7:2, Part I.

Ciucǎ, A. 1967. Longevity and environmental factors. *The Gerontologist* 7:4.

Fitch, J. M. 1970. *Experiential bases for aesthetic decision.* In *Environmental Psychology,* eds. H. Proshansky, W. Ittelson, and L. Rivlin. New York: Holt, Rinehart and Winston, Inc.

Hall, E. T. 1959. *The silent language.* Greenwich, Conn.: Fawcett Publications, Inc.

————. 1969. *The hidden dimension.* New York: Doubleday and Co., Inc.

Koffka, K. 1935. *Principles of gestalt psychology.* New York: Harcourt, Brace.

Kiritz, S. and Moos, R. 1974. Physiological effects of social environments. *Psychosomatic Medicine* 36:2.

Koncelik, J. 1972. Design to meet patient needs and enhance longevity of the long term care facility. *Empire State Architect,* March 1972.

Lawton, M. P. 1970. Assessment, integration and environments for older people. *The Gerontologist* 10:1.

————. 1974. Coping behavior and the environment of older people. In *Professional obligations and approaches to the aged,* eds. A. Schwartz and I. Mensh. Springfield, Ill.: Charles C. Thomas.

Lewin, K. 1936. Principles of topological and vector psychology. New York: McGraw-Hill.

Lindsley, O. R. 1964. Geriatric behavioral prosthetics. In *New thoughts on old age,* ed. R. Kastenbaum. New York: Springer Publishing Co.

Pastalan, L. n.d. *The simulation of age related sensory losses: a new approach to the study of environmental barriers,* unpublished manuscript.

Pastalan, L., and Carson, D., eds. 1970. *Spatial behavior of older people.* Ann Arbor, Michigan: Wayne State University.

Proshansky, H.; Ittelson, W.; and Rivlin, L. 1970. *Environmental psychology: man and his physical setting.* New York: Holt, Rinehart and Winston, Inc.

Proshansky, H. 1973. The environmental crisis in human dignity. *The Journal of Social Issues* 29:4.

Schooler, K. 1969. The relationship between social interaction and morale of the elderly as a function of environmental characteristics. *The Gerontologist* 9:1.

Schwartz, A. and Proppe, H. 1970. Toward person/environment transactional research in aging. *The Gerontologist* 10:3, Autumn.

Schwartz, A. 1969. Perception of privacy among institutionalized aged. *Proceedings, 77th American Psychological Association Meeting.* Washington, D.C.

Schwartz, A. 1974. A transactional view of the aging process. In *Professional obligations and approaches to the aged,* eds. A. Schwartz and I. Mensh. Springfield, Ill.: Charles C. Thomas.

Selye, H. 1973. The evolution of the stress concept. *American Scientist* 61.

Sommer, R. 1969. *Personal space.* Englewood Cliffs, New Jersey: Prentice-Hall, Inc.

Studer, R. 1970. The dynamics of behavior-contingent physical systems. In *Environmental psychology,* eds. H. Proshansky, W. Ittelson and L. Rivlin. New York: Holt, Rinehart and Winston, Inc.

Wright, B. 1958. *Physical disability: a psychological approach.* New York: Harper and Row.

14

Neighborhood Planning for the Urban Elderly

VICTOR REGNIER

When the subject of environments for the elderly is discussed, the image that usually comes to mind is of special housing types. Housing and various living arrangements have been the subject of extensive research seeking to discover ways to improve the environment for older persons. In much of the literature, housing and environment have become synonymous, because most research focused on environments for the elderly has been conducted within the particular contexts of public housing, special homes for the aged, or nursing homes. The review of residential distribution in Chapter 3 on the demography of aging underscores the need for a more comprehensive approach to the planning of urban environments, since nearly three-fourths of the older population reside in urban areas.

   This chapter discusses an approach to problem identification and solution that stresses the scale of the neighborhood. Recent trends in legislative action have reinforced the growing realization that our previous single-minded and narrowly focused approach to housing through the public sector is fiscally inadequate. In addition, it does not provide a large enough number of housing options for a diverse elderly population.

   It is clear that in order to accommodate—financially, physiologically, and psychologically—the requirements of today's elderly and plan for the needs of tomorrow we must start to think about inexpensive but effective ways of reinforcing and altering the existing urban fabric so that it will become most accessible to older persons.

Housing

We do need more housing in large quantities built in areas of the city that support the present and future life styles of our elderly population. We need housing of high quality and low cost. But more importantly we need to provide the elderly with the choice of where and in what type of housing they would like to spend their retirement.

The age-segregated public housing projects of the late 1960s and early 1970s are good examples of the public response to the need for low-cost housing. Housing projects for the elderly were very popular because of the assumption that housing per se was the critical need. Not only did housing projects for the elderly meet less resistance from neighbors than family projects, but they were also generally easy to fill and provided local politicians with a ready example of what they were doing for the elderly and the poor in their communities. Unfortunately, survey research has shown that the older community member has generally preferred to have income-enhancing supplements, rather than access to a project (Riesenfield et al., 1972).

Another assumption that stimulated the construction of age-segregated housing was that housing would be made more functional if it were designed specifically for the elderly. It was believed that environmental designers, architects, engineers, and developers could incorporate in their work physically related design features for the special needs of the elderly as presented to them by social scientists. Unfortunately, the information exchange system between behavioral scientists and designers has been disappointing because the gap between their interests and language is formidable.

Assuming the information flow to be perfect, however, the designer can only control and specify the physical environment of the housing. One of the most important products of housing research has been the realization that both housing location and managerial policies frequently are far more limiting to elderly tenants than the building design.

Housing managers exercise tremendous control over the programing and administration of a housing facility, and thus their policies greatly affect the use of the housing facility. The more dependent the housing, such as homes for the aged and nursing homes, the greater the impact of managerial policy. In dependent types of housing, administrative policies and rule structures are often expressed as repressive controls that limit the choices of residents (Bennett and Nahemow, 1965).

The neighborhood area of the housing project also exerts tremendous pressures on the freedom of elderly residents. Although the elderly may spend a majority of their lives inside their residential units, the contact they have with the outside neighborhood can provide very positive stimulation or can be a dangerous, threatening experience. The purpose of this chapter is to probe the potential of the local neighborhood as a vehicle for the delivery of reinforcing services to the elderly.

The Concept of Life Space

The notion that our control over the manipulation of space varies with age has been expressed by other researchers (Pastalan and Carson, 1970; Gelwicks, 1970). From fetus to grave, our ability to interact with the environment is controlled by social, economic, and societal policies manifested by the built environment. An individual's ability to control and manipulate the surrounding environment over time might plausibly be plotted as a simple curve. What is most apparent is the fact that at both ends of the age-spectrum curve, life space—the environment over which one has control—decreases. Some researchers have categorized this process as a loss continuum (Pastalan, 1970; National Center Housing Management, 1974).

Table 14.1 outlines the losses that generally occur in preretirement and retirement. These can include death of a spouse, loss of body image (physical strength, appearance, and performance), loss of a working role, loss of income, loss of status and position, and a lessening of the ability to make independent choices and decisions.

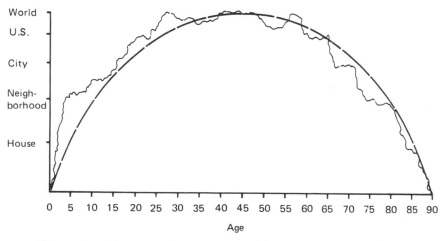

Figure 14.1. Life space change with age. Life space in this context is defined as the individual's ability to access differing plateaus of spatial use. This is a schematic diagram that represents the life-space characteristics of an imaginary individual and is not meant to represent any particular person or group of persons.

This personal loss continuum has a direct effect on every aspect of an individual's life, including the options for housing and environmental choices. Table 14.2 outlines some of the connections between the personal losses in Table 14.1 and environmental change.

It is clear that as people age their dependence on the local surrounding environment is increased; for the age cohorts between 65 and 85 in particular, the neighborhood environment takes on special significance. In other words, for children and the elderly the collection of local resources we normally think of as making up a neighborhood is very important. For this reason we must be sensitive to the environmental needs of older persons when considering the design and makeup of an overall neighborhood.

The Neighborhood and the Public Policy Arena

The individual's ability to exercise control over his own destiny in the neighborhood is much less than in the self-contained housing environment. Even in the most sterile living space individuals can augment and decorate to their own tastes and preferences. This ability to control and make personal choices is lessened in more institutional settings, but only the most unenlightened nursing-home administrators do not allow personal effects to be retained and displayed in a patient's room. However, the individual has very little control at the neighborhood level because most decisions regarding services are in the hands of the public sector. For example, the locations of public transit lines, senior citizen centers, retail stores, social services, and low-cost housing, are largely decisions reserved for the public policy arena. It is extremely difficult for most older persons to effect policy because group cohesiveness and age-consciousness is necessary to impact the political process. There are few avenues of influence open to the elderly. Advocacy and radical activist groups, such as the Gray Panthers, are providing an organized structure for the participation of the elderly in the decision-making process, but this influence is limited. The option of relocation has limited applicability because many older persons do not possess the mental, physical, and financial strength to change their environmental context voluntarily.

Table 14.1   Personal losses prompted by change in age

50–65	65–75	75–87	85+
Children leave household, begin to prepare for retirement.	Loss of job, spouse, friends, income, some body image loss.	Increased loss of sensory activity, health, strength, and independence.	Serious loss of health and independence.

SOURCE: Adapted from Pastalan and Carson, 1970, p.98.

If the elderly do relocate, they often find it difficult to adapt or adjust to the surrounding neighborhood. Involuntary relocation, in particular, can have a deleterious effect on the mental and physical well-being of older persons (Niebanck and Pope, 1965; Markus et al., 1971).

Because of this lack of power and mobility, the elderly are often left behind in neighborhoods that have deteriorated or are highly unsupportive. The inability of the elderly to exercise adequate influence on the social and environmental policies that affect their surrounding neighborhood means that planners and decision makers must, themselves, become advocates for the aged, when planning is being carried out that affects the older person's interest. For example, the locations of transit lines, social services, and even zoning for retail goods and services should be examined to identify the positive and negative effects neighborhood changes such as these will have on the life satisfaction of elderly members in the community.

Housing-Services Continuum

The loss continuum displayed in Tables 14.1 and 14.2 illustrates the problems most individuals face as they enter retirement. In order to counter these losses the elderly must have an environment that provides augmenting medical, social, and physiological supports. Lawton and Nahemow's (1973) "environmental docility hypothesis" suggests that an individual of

Table 14.2 Age-related environmental changes and personal losses

50–65	65–75	75–87	80+
Loss of relationship to younger friends and acquaintances of children. Loss of neighborhood role to schools and youth. Home is too large, but mortgage payments are low and equity high.	Loss in relation to work environment, loss of mobility due to lessened income. Dissolving of professional work associations and friendships. Move to apartment, smaller home, or struggle with increased maintenance costs of larger home.	Loss of ability to drive independently. Must rely on bus or relatives and friends. Connections with community, church associations slowly severed. Move to more supportive housing, such as apartments with meals and maid service. Maintenance costs for single-family house unmanageable.	Losses of ability to navigate in the environment. Loss of strong connection with outside neighborhood. Dependence on supportive services. Move to supportive environment necessary, such as nursing home, home for the aged, or siblings' home.

SOURCE: Adapted from National Center for Housing Management, 1974.

high competence (mental, physical, and social) is relatively free from the pressures of the environment, while an individual of low competence is often affected adversely by a taxing environmental context. As a counteractive to losses in ability to deal with the pressures of environment, some older people must be provided added support.

Supports can be provided in the form of social, physical, or psychological boosts. For example, the installation of grab-bars, handrails, and other prosthetic devices in corridors and bathrooms provides physical supports that help to compensate for loss of balance control and strength in the lower limbs. Social programs, such as friendly visitors, meals on wheels, telephone reassurance, and various crime-control services, provide physical and psychological assurances. In other words, as one becomes less able to cope with the environment, his dependence on added supports, whether from prosthetic devices or social services, increases. The manner in which this added support is provided normally takes one of two forms: (1) these support systems can be part of the larger community, or (2) they can be internally delivered within a housing environment.

The collection of supportive housing arrangements includes independent age-segregated residential units; slightly more supportive congregate housing with provided meals and transportation; the more traditional home for the aging with mandatory meals, maid service, perhaps a nurse on call, and transportation; the intermediate care facility with all of the above including a full-time nursing staff; and finally, the skilled nuring facility with the capability of providing long-term convalescent care.

We have financed the two ends of this continuum (independent public housing and nursing homes) by public expenditures, while for the most part the "home for the aged" has been sponsored by nonprofit, primarily church-sponsored groups. Public financial support has been inadequate for all the levels described except perhaps nursing homes. However, for nursing homes the job of monitoring the quality of patient care has been completely inadequate. Whether poor care is a result of inadequate state reimbursement levels or the moral bankruptcy of the provider is an issue that can be argued; regardless, the reputation of many nursing homes as hellish environments is often founded in fact (Mendelson, 1974; Townsend, 1970). It is a sad postscript to note that the majority are owned and managed as proprietorships.

The Community as a Service Provider

Title III of the Older Americans Act established subregional Area Agencies on Aging (AAA) specifically directed to provide services that would enable older persons to maintain themselves in a home environment (Hudson, 1974). The Area Agencies on Aging were created in a conscious effort to provide coordinated, comprehensive services to older Americans through the use of community supports. In part, their creation was a result of the desire to give older persons alternatives to the dependent environments of the nursing home or home for the aged.

Included within the Title was the mandate to provide information and referral services, transportation services, escort services, outreach services, and support for other social services needed by older persons which no other public or private agencies could or would provide. Included within this category are the mobile or community services that seek to help persons maintain themselves in their own homes. Social and community services include place-bound services such as senior centers, clinics, law centers, and nutrition sites; and mobile services such as visiting nurses, homemakers, home health aids, and meals on wheels.

The strongest public policy emphasis has been placed on the provision of supports encouraging the aged to remain in their own homes as long as they possibly can before seeking an institutional environment. This strategy is more desirable from an environmental choice standpoint and also less costly to the public than premature institutionalization. Furthermore, the limited amounts of money available for the creation of federally subsidized apartments for the elderly have also satisfied only a small percentage of the demand for such housing, making low-cost subsidized housing a realistic option for only a small percentage of elderly Americans.

Good neighborhoods can provide a safe, convenient environment for social interaction as well as a location for basic life supportive goods and services. The importance of the neighborhood is indicated by the fact that the elderly rarely shop for needed goods and services outside a radius of six blocks from their residential housing location (Lawton and Byerts, 1973). Because of these centralized activity patterns, the neighborhood takes on special importance as a location for the delivery of social services, including transportation. Therefore, it is important to identify areas of the city that could act as social service delivery centers for place-bound services.

Before this can be accomplished, a viable strategy for identifying neighborhoods and assessing their major strengths and weaknesses must be established. Although the definition of "neighborhood" is vague and may vary from one individual to another, some recent attempts have been made to define clearly the like characteristics of contiguous urban areas.

Neighborhood Typologies

One such study factor- and cluster-analyzed census tracts into neighborhood types for the elderly in Los Angeles (Kendig, 1975). In this study ten factors from two primary dimensions of housing and population charac-

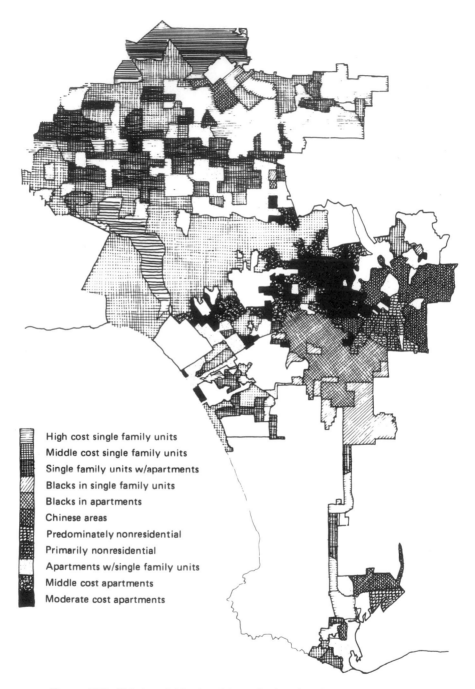

Figure 14.2. Elderly neighborhood types in the city of Los Angeles. (Compiled from information contained in H. L. Kendig, 1975.)

High cost single family units
Middle cost single family units
Single family units w/apartments
Blacks in single family units
Blacks in apartments
Chinese areas
Predominately nonresidential
Primarily nonresidential
Apartments w/single family units
Middle cost apartments
Moderate cost apartments

teristics were analyzed using a cluster-analysis approach to identify eleven neighborhood typologies (Figure 14.2). These eleven neighborhood typologies are compared with the demographic and housing variables of the aged population, neighborhood conditions of the aged, and municipal policies for the aged. The results of this analysis confirm the supposition that each neighborhood type is generally characterized by a unique percentage of elderly residents and that neighborhood conditions and municipal policies vary dramatically for each neighborhood type. The implications of this exploratory research for policy implementation and service delivery are great. If specific neighborhood areas in the city can be identified and the present condition of housing, transportation, service needs, and social problems in each neighborhood specified, then a flexible strategy can be designed to best meet the needs of older persons within each unique neighborhood type.

In order to have a better understanding of how to improve the neighborhood area, one must first identify the positive and negative elements that characterize the neighborhood. This research (Kendig, 1975) attempts to narrow the scale of target area identification from a city scale to smaller, neighborhood-size units, but even at this scale numerous problems exist. The most pervasive question is where and how should a neighborhood be altered to provide for the older persons living there a more supportive yet independent environment. The altering process, interpreted from the standpoint of urban design, could include the decision of what improvements need to be added to the neighborhood and where those improvements should be located. This could include the addition of physical structures, transit lines, or police patrols, as well as the alleviation of social problems or environmental hazards.

Needs Analysis

Through the use of social indicators, reasonably operational approaches have been developed to identify target areas of social and environmental concern (Community Analysis Bureau, 1973). However, the scale is often too large or the variables inappropriate to provide enough information for fine-grained analysis. Many attempts at needs analyses have taken place using primary survey techniques to discover information about what the elderly need. These attempts have been successful in identifying general needs or preferences but have often been unable to specify the strategies for meeting these needs (Cantor, 1973; Gelwicks, Feldman, Newcomer, 1971). Nevertheless, the needs analyses of the past have been helpful in outlining specific neighborhood issues of greatest relevance. In addition to this type of descriptive data, other researchers have sought to understand more about how older persons use neighborhood resources and how they navigate within the larger city-scale environment (Cantilli and Smeltzer, 1970).

Strategies for Neighborhood Intervention

Our major concern beyond the targeting of neighborhood typologies and the identification of needs and preferences is the question of strategy. Where and how should the attempt to fulfill needs for services and facilities take place? Two basic approaches are available.

Reinforcement by redefinition.   One approach assumes that any concentration of elderly residents within the city possesses both an obvious and underlying social and physical structure. City ecologists have known for a number of years that most concentrations of elderly residents within cities are a result of the aging process of the city. In the western third of the United States, most of our current elderly concentrations have been a result of development that took place early in the twentieth century. The housing stock has aged, and along with it so have the home owners. Areas that normally have a large aged population also have attracted retail stores and city services that are focused toward the needs of an older population. Often these neighborhoods, because of their geographical proximity to central city areas, are in need of protection from institutional and commercial business expansion. Furthermore, their crime rates, traffic problems, and fire safety needs are often much greater because of the condition of the housing stock.

Cognitive mapping methodologies measure collective patterns of neighborhood cognition (Regnier, Eribes and Hanson, 1973; Regnier, 1974a) in order to identify the key services and geographic areas within the neighborhood that older individuals regard as essential (Regnier, Eribes, and Hanson, 1973; Regnier, 1974a). These methodologies are important and useful because they establish a geographical context within which needed services can be analyzed.

In the studies cited above, respondents were asked to outline the portion of a large-scale map that constituted the neighborhood area they used or felt was familiar. Each individual response was coded, and a synagraphic computer process created an overall consensus map that outlined the neighborhood areas selected by the greatest number of respondents. The final map highlighted areas that currently are used or seem very familiar to respondents. The result of such an analysis can mean systematic improvements, such as rerouting bus lines, or incremental improvements, such as selecting the best location for a needed senior center. Figure 14.3 details a consensus neighborhood map of the Westlake district of Los Angeles.

This map was created by the responses of 107 older community residents distributed throughout the district. The Westlake area of the city contains the highest concentration of elderly residents within the city of Los Angeles and is an excellent example of an inner-city, low-income neighborhood that continues to attract elderly residents because of the low rents and excellent services it provides.

Reinforcement by selective intervention. The second approach addresses probably the most common condition, that of an unstable neighborhood which has continued to lose elderly residents from attrition and relocation. In such areas of the city, the social and physical fabric is less contiguous and the elderly are often isolated, divorced from the companionship of peers and the services of convenient retail stores. This condition has been typical in many cities where a radical change has been caused by an influx of poor family residents or the initiation of a publicly

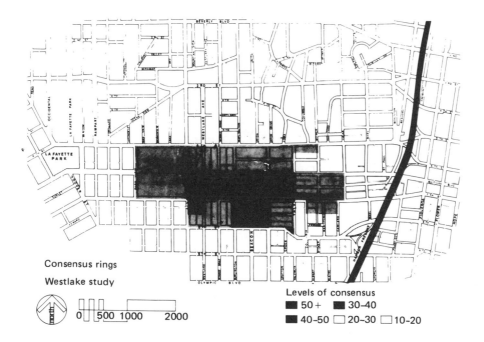

Figure 14.3. Consensus rings, Westlake study. (Lawton, Newcomer, Byerts, 1975)

sponsored, urban-renewal project has caused older neighborhoods to be recycled into commercial or high-income residential use.

The planning strategy suggested here is to intervene by placing improvements, such as housing projects or social services for the elderly, near the greatest concentration of older residents to create a more supportive context for the neighborhood. By such selective additions, strong elderly concentrations can be established in the most conducive neighborhood environment available. In neighborhoods such as these, relocation from single-family, dispersed housing to safe, easy-to-maintain, conveniently located, low-cost apartments has some very positive advantages. Older persons who still wish to live within the neighborhood they have known for years can do so more safely and with less anxiety. Unfortunately, the tremendous demand for publicly subsidized housing for the elderly has created scheduling processes such as city-wide waiting lists. Although the purpose of city-wide listing is to reduce waiting time, in many cities qualified persons wait for years and when their names surface they are often asked to relocate to unfamiliar neighborhoods in other parts of the city.

Critical Distances

The location decision for housing projects is of primary importance. Site selection aids in the form of "critical distance" formulations have been devised by numerous groups, and the resulting guidelines have provided a giant step forward for decisions about the most appropriate locations for housing projects (Noll, 1973; Newcomer, 1975; Philadelphia Planning Commission, 1968; Langford, 1962).

Figure 14.4 contains critical distance formulations resulting from responses of 117 managers of public housing designed for the elderly (Noll, 1973). This figure is the result of a reexamination of data originally compiled by the Institute for Environmental Studies, University of Pennsylvania, under the direction of Paul Niebanck. Twelve services and facilities were rated by the housing managers. The created scale categorizes responses from managers so as to create three bands of relative satisfaction. For each facility or service, the first band is the distance from the facility that registered no dissatisfaction from managers. This varied from less than one block for a bus stop location to one-half mile for a hospital, library, or movie house. The second band represents the critical distance. Within this band, managers notice both satisfaction and dissatisfaction. The third band outlines clearly unacceptable distances. These distance formulations were refined more recently by Robert Newcomer (1975).

In Newcomer's research, a questionnaire was taken directly to the housing tenant who was asked also to note the frequency of use associated with 24 goods and services. Newcomer's questionnaire was a follow-up to a more extensive survey conducted by M. Powell Lawton of the Phila-

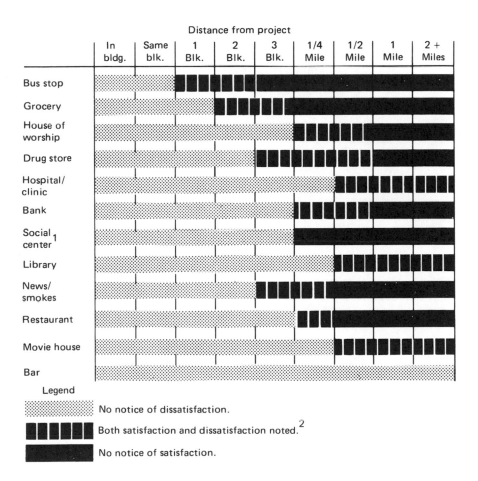

Figure 14.4. Relative satisfaction of the elderly with the distance from their building to necessary facilities. (Adapted from Noll, 1973)

delphia Geriatric Center. The responses of 600 housing residents were used to create Table 14.3.

In this formulation the general conclusions of the Niebanck study were reinforced. However, the number of services included in the survey was greatly expanded. The service importance rankings from each study did vary. While Noll ranked church and physician near the top, Newcomer dropped their importance to the bottom end of his scale. The distance criteria, however, stayed reasonably constant.

Other researchers have also dealt with the problem of describing the environmental support system of older persons in the city (Nahemow and Kogan, 1971; Regnier, 1974a). These efforts have resulted in the nearly consistent specification of a core group of services. In neighborhood terms they would seem to make up a "critical mass" that must be present within walking distance (3-6 blocks) in order for the neighborhood selected to be a viable setting for elderly housing. The literature would suggest that the following services be included in this critical mass:

bus stop	bank
grocery store/supermarket	post office
drug store/variety store	church

These few services are indeed a minimum neighborhood package and should not be construed as the optimum collection. Other important services, such as an out-patient clinic (medical), department store (clothing), and senior citizen center (social), are also necessary; however, it should be noted that these services are often visited less than once per month and are normally located further than walking distance. This finding underscores the need for accessible transportation linking the site with other areas of the city (particularly the downtown). In cities where inexpensive public transportation is not available this list of critical services must be expanded to include the following:

medical hospital	library
senior club/senior center	dry cleaners
public park	luncheonette/snack bar

Critical distances are extremely useful indicators of where housing should be placed in the neighborhood. It should be noted, however, that most critical distance formulations have been established by survey research using residents of low-income, publicly sponsored housing. Furthermore, the formulations suggest an average distance between the housing location and a service location at which patronage is curtailed. In applying this average critical distance one must note that the surrounding environmental context varies substantially. For example, a six-block distance up a steep hill, across several busy streets, into a high-crime area is much more difficult to navigate than the same six blocks on the flat, in the direction of a grocery store with several intervening benches on the route. Distance measurement is often subjective, rather than a reflection of actual cartographic distance (Rivizzigno and Golledge, 1974). Although a hypothetical six-block distance can be measured, understood, and applied, the actual six blocks under consideration is modified and distorted by a diverse set of social and physical delimiters and incentives (Regnier, 1974b).

Some of these factors are easy to identify and have a universally positive and negative affect on the older person, while other factors may be perceived as hazardous or helpful only to a few individuals. A few examples of these incentives and delimiters include:

topography	ethnic identification
street crime	traffic patterns
land-use	district designations
percentage of elderly	income/rent
bus routes/public transportation	

Table 14.3 Service importance and critical distance

Service	Importance	Critical distance	Recommended distance
Bus stop	1	1 block	adjacent to site
Park/outdoor	2	1-3 blocks	adjacent to site
Grocery store	3	1-3 blocks	1 block
Laundromat	4	on-site	on-site
Supermarket	5	4-10 blocks	3 blocks
Post office	6	4-10 blocks	3 blocks
Bank	7	1-3 blocks	3 blocks
Service center	8	1-3 blocks	on-site
Cleaners	9	4-10 blocks	3 blocks
Department store	10	4-10 blocks	3 blocks
Social centers	11	1-3 blocks	3 blocks
Senior citizen club	12	on-site	on-site
Bingo, cards	13	1-3 blocks	on-site
Arts, crafts, hobbies	14	1-3 blocks	on-site
Movies	15	indeterminate	3 blocks
Parties, socials	16	1-3 blocks	on-site
Lectures, discussion	17	indeterminate	on-site
Organized trips	18	indeterminate	indeterminate
Church	19	indeterminate	indeterminate
Physician	20	indeterminate	indeterminate
Public library	21	indeterminate	indeterminate
Dentist	22	indeterminate	indeterminate
Luncheonette/snack bar	23	indeterminate	indeterminate
Bar	23	no importance	no importance

SOURCE: Newcomer, 1973.

Each of these characteristics is part of a continuum which could potentially exert either a positive or negative force on the use of neighborhood resources. Therefore, in addition to critical distance criteria it is important to consider the actual characteristics of the environment within which these distance criteria are applied. Much of the ecological data available on a fine-grained block level can be used to evaluate the quality of a site location. Coupled with critical distance criteria, this type of analysis can guarantee a better match between the capabilities of elderly residents and the neighborhood site location most appropriate for housing these residents.

Conclusion

The problems of selecting and reinforcing neighborhoods for the elderly are indeed complex and require action at many levels. This chapter has dealt with a schematic approach for isolating target neighborhood areas and a set of strategies that can be applied at a neighborhood level to meet problems. Planners and environmental decision makers are beginning to understand that many of the problems that affect older persons cannot be alleviated by wholesale destruction and renewal. The neighborhood fabric is too important, too frail, and too salvageable to be submitted to radical surgery. Positive steps toward constructive intervention must be taken, but they should progress selectively by reinforcing positive environmental elements and providing needed community services in accessible locations.

References

Bennett, R., and Nahemow, L. 1965. Institutional totality and criteria of social adjustment in residences for the aged. *Journal of Social Issues* 21:44–78.

Cantilli, E., and Smeltzer, J. 1970. *Transportation and Aging: Selected Issues.* Washington, D.C.: Government Printing Office.

Cantor, M. H. 1973. Life space and the social support system of the inner city elderly of New York. Paper presented at the 26th annual scientific meeting of the Gerontological Society, Miami.

Community Analysis Bureau. 1974. *State of the city: priorities of need.* Los Angeles: The bureau.

Gelwicks, L. 1970. Home range and use of space by our aging population. In *Spatial behavior of older people,* eds. L. Pastalan and D. Carson, pp. 148–162. Ann Arbor: University of Michigan Press.

Gelwicks, L.; Feldman, A.; and Newcomer, R. 1971. *Report on older population: needs, resources and services.* Los Angeles: Andrus Gerontology Center.

Hudson, R. 1974. Rational planning and organizational imperatives: prospects for area planning in aging. *Annals of the American Academy of Political and Social Sciences* 415:41–54.

Kendig, H. L. 1975. An empirical study of the distribution and effect of neighborhood conditions among the aged: a municipal policy analysis. Unpublished doctoral dissertation. University of Southern California.

Langford, M. 1962. *Community aspects of housing for the aged.* Ithaca: Cornell University Press.

Lawton, M. P. and Byerts, T. 1973. *Community planning for the elderly.* Washington: U.S. Department of Housing and Urban Development.

Lawton, M. P. and Nahemow, L. 1973. Toward an ecological theory of adaptation and aging. In *Environmental design and research, volume one,* ed. W. Preiser. Stroudsburg, Pa.: Dowden, Hutchinson and Ross.

Markus, E.; Blenkner, M.; Bloom, M.; and Downs, T. 1971. The impact of relocation upon mortality rates of institutionalized aged persons. *Journal of Gerontology* 26:537–541.

Mendelson, M. A. 1974. *Tender Loving Greed.* New York: Knopf.

Nahemow, L. and Kogan, L. 1971. Reduced fare for the elderly. New York: City University of New York, Center for Social Research.

National Center for Housing Management. 1974. *The on-site housing managers resource book: housing for the elderly.* Washington: The National Center for Housing Management, Inc.

Newcomer, R. 1973. Housing services and neighborhood activities. Paper presented at the 26th annual meeting of the Gerontological Society, Miami.

Newcomer, R. 1975. Group housing for the elderly: defining neighborhood service convenience for public housing and section 202 project residents. Unpublished doctoral dissertation. University of Southern California.

Niebanck, P. L. and Pope, J. 1965. *The elderly in older urban areas.* Philadelphia: University of Pennsylvania.

Noll, P. 1973. Site selection criteria for housing for the elderly: a proposal for policy change. Paper presented at the 26th annual scientific meeting of the Gerontological Society, Miami.

Pastalan, L. 1970. Privacy as an expression of human territoriality. In *Spatial behavior of older people,* eds. L. Pastalan and D. Carson, pp. 88–102. Ann Arbor: University of Michigan Press.

Pastalan, L. and Carson, D. 1970. *Spatial behavior of older people.* Ann Arbor: University of Michigan Press.

Philadelphia City Planning Commission. 1968. *Locational criteria for housing for the elderly.* Philadelphia: The Commission.

Regnier, V. 1974a. Matching older persons' cognition with their use of neighborhood areas. In *Man-environment interactions: evaluations and applications,* ed. D. Carson. Milwaukee: Environmental Design Research Association.

Regnier, V. 1974b. The effects of environmental incentives and delineators in the use and cognition of neighborhood areas. Paper presented at the 27th annual meeting of the Gerontological Society, Portland, Oregon.

Regnier, V.; Eribes, R.; and Hanson, W. 1973. Cognitive mapping as a concept for establishing service delivery locations for older people: the use of synagraphics as methodological tools. In *Eighth annual ACM urban symposium,* ed. J. Highland. New York: ACM.

Riesenfeld, M.; Newcomer, R.; Dempsey, N.; and Berlant, P. 1972. Perceptions of public service needs: the urban aged and the public agency. *The Gerontologist* 12:185:191.

Rivizzigno, V., and Golledge, R. 1974. A method for recovering cognitive information about a city. In *Man-environment interactions: evaluations and applications,* ed. D. Carson. Milwaukee: Environmental Design Research Association.

Townsend, C. 1971. *Old age: the last segregation,* New York: Grossman.

Social Issues

15

Television Communication
and the Elderly

RICHARD H. DAVIS

Social gerontologists have not always identified mass communication as a significant issue in aging. Nevertheless, it has always been necessary to include the mass media in any discussion of uses of leisure time by the elderly. Wilbur Schramm's study of uses of media by the elderly, published in 1969, was the first to present an in-depth look at communication and the aging. Since then, various of the disciplines associated with gerontology have paid increasing attention to media use and its impact. Specifically, the content of television programs and the television viewing behaviors of selected audiences have commanded the attention of those who study behavior and social change. The child audience has received the greatest attention, but there are parallels in the captive, dependent audience status of the preschooler and of the elderly television viewer. For both audiences there are benefits and liabilities. It should be remembered that before television, radio in its infancy was regarded with some alarm as an instrument capable of causing great social change (as indeed it did). Before radio, the dime novel, and, later, comic books were considered disturbing influences. Each new technology for mass communication is in turn regarded with concern for both the good and bad results it may potentially cause.

Two social phenomena are brought together here. The changing demographics of our time force upon us a real awareness of the elderly and a recognition that people should be better prepared for being old. At the same time, television communication has become the most commonplace channel for information dissemination and the most preferred of the mass media for entertainment.

The social gerontologist's examination of media and aging can be roughly divided into two parts. The first is a consideration of the images of the aging process and of being old which are projected through television broadcasting. The second part is a concern about the uses of media by older people. Both areas of concern are not only suitable for investigation, but are relevant at a time when technological advances, both to date and in process, allow for more rapid and pervasive information dissemination through electronic methods than ever before in history.

This chapter focuses on television communication for the reasons just stated and because (as will be documented) television is the communication medium most often attended to by most of the elderly. For many older persons who must budget their money carefully, the expense of a newspaper may cause it to be eliminated as a daily information source. Nevertheless, the television is not regarded as a luxury. Once paid for, it is regarded as a "free" source of information. More importantly, television offers easier entertainment than reading which may strain the older person's eyes. Information about aging delivered via television not only reaches more people, but is also more readily believed than the same information in print media.

The two-part concern of the social gerontologist reflects two separate but related issues. The first is that of image making, of modeling for aging and for being old. This issue relates to the needs both of old persons themselves and of those who are becoming old. What information is given through television communication channels about the processes and conditions of aging? What subtle conditioning by the mass media helps to orient our value structure about age? The second issue is that of television as an environmental component for older people. What is the impact, the importance of television communication in the lives of older persons? What purposes does it fill, and what are its values for old people? These are all important questions, but they are not answered easily.

Mass Communication and the Older Population

In speaking of an older population we are implying group behaviors, and when we are dealing with group behavior we are less concerned with the process of individual, person-to-person communication, except (and this is important) as such behavior structures participation in mass communication. It might be assumed that the less opportunity for interpersonal relationships, the greater will be the reliance on mass or group communications to fill the need for that social behavior.

The older adult's structure of interpersonal relationships forms the necessary basis of communication. His available contacts are limited by circumstances, but they are not quite as limited as the popular notion may have it. The picture of the older person as a social isolate, as one disengaged from the activities of living, is being challenged by social scientists who see change developing in the role played by the elderly in today's society.

Beyond the psychological advantage of participating in human interaction through the communication process, there is a need for the transmission of certain vital information if the older adult is to retain a beneficial connection with the greater world. That is, he needs to share in a common body of knowledge regarding current affairs if he is to maintain points of contact with other people; he needs also to be the recipient of certain information necessary for his personal welfare. In short, he needs information services, and this is a communications need. The older person quite often suffers some disadvantages that prohibit easy fulfillment of this need. Lessened mobility plus the presence of fewer significant other people limit social interaction and information exchange. At the same time the older person has greater need of information support services than does the younger person. His health needs are greater; less money makes him more dependent on the social services and the subsequent interaction with the bureaucratic structure. He must, therefore, rely on mass communications for information on how to satisfy these needs more than most other members of society.

There is still more than this. In addition to a need for information, people need diversion, escape, excitement. They need entertainment. The older person usually has fewer opportunities to create those experiences for himself. The stimulation of direct experience is often unavailable and he must attempt vicarious fulfillment. The mass media can provide this in varying degrees of intensity.

The obvious communications media available for mass dissemination of information are print and broadcast facilities.

Surveys have indicated the obvious: that the use of print media for information service by those of little education, the "culturally disadvantaged," and the elderly is significantly less than for other segments of the population. The Roper National Surveys have asked for an indication of the primary sources of news "about what's going on in the world." Television consistently ranks as a first choice with the majority of the respondents who represent a cross-national sample. (See Roper reports, 1959–1972.)

What are the apparent positive aspects of broadcast communication? Radio and television are communication channels especially suited to their audiences with what Otto Kleppner (1966) calls "a sense of participation, personal access and reality which approximate face-to-face contact." In addition to this, the two media reach virtually the entire population, including groups such as the very old, the very young, and the less well educated—all of whom by virtue of their status do not have easy access to the print media. Although not empirically demonstrated, Kleppner and others assert on the basis of studies in communication that the broadcast media are the most persuasive of all the mass media.

Television as the preferred broadcast medium outranks radio by a large percentage. Radio, it might seem, is the medium of the young, music-oriented generation and the commuter who finds it companionable through his long stints on the highways. This is not to imply that radio is less effective in influencing audience behavior—far from it. Under certain conditions it is a more powerful agent than television. The radio listener is more likely to employ his imagination and thus become subjectively involved. But when the communicator wishes to imprint a visual identification in the recipient's consciousness, television is superior. Because of television's visual impact and its demonstrated popularity with the general audience, and specifically the older audience, the focus of this chapter is on television communication and its influence in the lives of the elderly and its potential for affecting attitude and behavioral changes about aging.

Television as a Channel for Education of Older Viewers

Since the Children's Television Workshop demonstrated television's potential to educate, attention has been paid to the uses of television to deliver educational experiences to other viewing audiences, including the elderly (Anderson, 1962; Davis, 1971). Much of what is happening in this area is in the formative stages and has yet to be reported in the literature. Yet current feasibility studies seem to indicate that closed circuit and cable television, for example, can provide older people with access to needed information. A description of two current projects is given here to illustrate the way television is being used as an educational tool for older people.

Under a 1972–73 government Title III grant, Cosumnes-River Community College in Northern California has produced a series of 24 videotape cassettes suitable for closed circuit use. These tapes present information deemed to be important to older people and packaged for easy access at video reception stations set up in community libraries. The list of these tapes also provides us with a fairly thorough catalog of what it was felt older viewers should know. (See pp. 320–321.)

The Mount Sinai School of Medicine of the City University of New

York is presently carrying out a research program on telecommunications technology and the aged in East Harlem, New York City. The purpose of the project is to explore the application of communication technology to the dissemination of health care to an inner-city geriatric population. It is to be conducted in a high-rise public housing building in East Harlem, with 248 apartments and 339 tenants with a median age of 69 years. The basic project plans call for the installation of a two-way cable television in each of the 248 apartments with the activation of a presently unused VHF channel for exclusive use of the facility residents and health care providers. Health- and nonhealth-related programming will be produced with the maximum involvement in the production by the residents themselves. Evaluations will be structured to determine the extent of the educational experience as it is demonstrated by increased and more beneficial health care behaviors by the elderly viewers.

These are two current projects using television as a channel for planned and evaluated educational experiences. Neither reflects commercial TV as we know it. Commercial television as a profit-making enterprise is not in the business to educate in the way we usually think of educational experiences. Over the past ten years, numbers of locally produced low-budget television series on commercial channels have been designed around the premise that television can deliver needed information to the elderly. These television series almost always exist because it is necessary to fill the station's obligation to the Federal Communications Commission to broadcast in the public interest. Nevertheless, viewer involvement by the specialized target audience is significant. Thus education continues to occur in an informal way via television.

The concept of education over the life span is increasingly attractive, both to educators and to people in middle and later life who see the experience of learning as an enrichment and a reward in itself. Birren and Woodruff (1973) discuss in depth the necessity and benefit of continuing education, and they recommend television as an ideal source of life-span education in the home setting. The National Retired Teachers Association and the American Association of Retired Persons have combined to form an Institute of Lifetime Learning. The Institute has adopted eight courses for standard radio format, and they are broadcast over more than one hundred stations across the country. It is possible to adopt the same material for television, but, as always, the cost is an inhibiting factor.

Formalized educational experiences offered on television are available in every city. The 6:30 A.M. "Sunrise Semester" series is familiar under various titles across the country. Just how many of the viewers are older persons is not known, for these programs do not elicit much attention from those interested in audience ratings. Nevertheless, the potential

Community-area Television System
Educational Programs Developed for
Cosumnes River Community College
Sacramento, California

PROGRAM 1 *The New Social Security and You.* A 28-minute program detailing who can collect Social Security. The pros and cons of early retirement.

PROGRAM 2 *Medicare, Medicaid, Medi-Cal.* This program goes into the differences between Medicare and Medi-Cal and explains Medicaid is simply the national program called Medi-Cal in California. Must viewing for anyone who wants to know more about how to receive Medicare and Medi-Cal and what is covered by them.

PROGRAM 3 *A Place to Live.* For anyone thinking of a retirement place to live. A survey of housing covers everything from owning your own home to low-cost apartment housing to mobile home living. A comparison of cost and availability.

PROGRAM 4 *A Place of Care.* Are nursing homes still places where the old go to die? This program takes you through extended care facilities, points out what to look for to find the best and what to avoid. Discussion with the Deputy Attorney General on latest regulations controlling nursing-home management.

PROGRAM 5 *Tax Benefits for Senior Adults.* Covers benefits and exemptions available both at the state and federal level. The federal level covers everything from exemption for age to retirement income credit. At the state level senior citizens' property tax assistance, homeowners' property tax exemption, and renters' refund are discussed. Included is discussion of forms—how to use, where to obtain and when to file.

PROGRAM 6 *You Have the Right.* In our complex society new rules and laws protecting us occur frequently. As a consumer and citizen, it is difficult but important to keep up with these laws and to know our rights. This program discusses the rights you have as a consumer of prescription drugs, as a credit card holder and as a tenant or landlord.

PROGRAM 7 *Legislation for Senior Adults.* Covers the Joint Legislation Committee on Aging, recent legislation of benefit to older Americans, and tells of the work of the National Senior Citizens Law Center and the National Council of Senior Citizens.

PROGRAM 8 *Estate Planning—Wills & Inheritance Taxes.* Do you have a will? Why do you need one? This program tells how to plan for the best distribution of your estate.

PROGRAM 9 *Estate Planning—Trusts & Inheritance Taxes.* Discussion of trusts— when, why, and how to use them and how they fit into your estate planning.

PROGRAM 10 *The Bunko Boys.* Millions of dollars are lost yearly by citizens of California due to bunko crime. Such bunko crimes as the pigeon drop, the bank examiner, and other bunko schemes are shown.

PROGRAM 11 *Consumer Beware!* Covers consumer fraud perpetuated against older Americans, problems with mobile homes, hearing-aid sales, and cemetery burial plots. A must for anyone considering investment in these areas.

PROGRAM 12 *Nobody's Victim.* Program especially for women telling how to avoid purse snatches, burglary, personal assault, and other crimes of force. Excellent discussion on types of locks to protect your home and personal defense habits.

PROGRAM 13 *Quackery—The False Profit.* Quackery is a 50-million-dollar-a-year business in California. This program goes into the kind of quackery prevalent today, what to watch out for to avoid being taken on health fraud schemes. Includes discussion with investigator from the Food and Drug Administration.

PROGRAM 14 *Community Resources & Services.* A survey of agencies and organizations which provide a variety of services to senior adults. Covers the areas of transportation, home health care, legal services, and social activities.

PROGRAM 15 *A Distant Drum.* This program deals with the question, what can individuals and communities do to help solve some of the problems of the elderly? Covers problems and what has been done in other communities as creative solutions. Ultimately, the program falls back upon the viewer and asks, "What are you doing with your talents?"

PROGRAM 16 *To Work or Not.* Forced retirement is occurring earlier and earlier. Some companies are even retiring employees at age 50. This program is concerned with the question, what happens to those people who are neither emotionally nor financially ready for retirement? Three retired individuals discuss the problems they have encountered in finding work after retirement.

PROGRAM 17 *What Is Old?—Myths & Realities of Growing Older—Part I.* An introduction to some of the myths and realities which have grown around the area of aging. The film "Don't Stop the Music" counters many stereotypes of age with factual research by presenting many people who do not "fit" the old-age stereotype.

PROGRAM 18 *What Is Old?—Part II.* What exactly is that mysterious process called aging? Two eminent gerontologists discuss the physical and mental aspects of aging. Via the discussion many myths are destroyed. Must viewing for anyone interested in their own aging or that of a loved one.

PROGRAM 19 *What Is Old?—Part III.* This program takes a look at what is old from the inside—from the point of view of the older person. A group of people discuss their feelings as they watch images of the elderly on film. Do they relate to the situations presented and to the image of old age?

PROGRAM 20 *Fit as a Fiddle.* How many of you feel fit as a fiddle? Do some of you begin to puff after walking a few blocks or find that last year's new suit or dress just doesn't quite make it around the middle anymore? If so, you had better watch this program. Those of you who say you're too old for all that physical activity had better watch this program twice. Excellent discussion on various physical fitness plans to improve and maintain good health.

PROGRAM 21 *Hobbies for Fun.* A survey of various hobbies available—some old, some new—which discusses the cost and time involved in the various hobbies. Also discusses how to get started in a hobby and what to consider when picking a hobby. Covers everything from model aircraft to macrame.

PROGRAM 22 *Hobbies for Profit.* This program discusses, when does a hobby become a business and what does that mean to the individual in relationship to licenses, taxes, etc.? Film segments of hobbies which have become profit-making ventures and discussion with a Management Assistance Officer of the Small Business Administration. Good information for anyone thinking of starting his own business.

PROGRAM 23 *Older Americans—A Natural Resource.* This program surveys volunteering. Takes a look at what benefit volunteer programs are to the community and to the individual volunteer.

PROGRAM 24 *Living the Life.* A look at three people, all over 60 and going like 20. Meet the world's oldest helicopter pilot, a school administrator turned song composer and a very fascinating lady known as "Lou." All of them are living their life as they see it and have some interesting things to say along the way.

for television as a channel for adult education exists, and with developing uses of multiple channel VHF reception this potential will increasingly be realized.

Television and the Image of Aging

There is a great deal less in the literature about television as an influence in providing role models for aging persons than there is about television as an environmental influence and its uses by older viewers. At the 1974 Media and Aging Conference sponsored by the Gerontological Society, the issue of current images of old people on television was identified as the number-one priority for research investigation. This indicates the current paucity of information in this area and the need to fill this gap.

Television perpetuates myths of old age through stereotypic characterizations. The "dirty old man" and "little old lady from Pasadena" both have earned places in our story-telling repertoire along with the Irish cop and farmer's daughter. These stock characters are useful in television drama because they don't have to be filled out as multidimensional personalities. In the brief time allowed to tell a story on television, stock characters are useful. The audience has already learned their characteristics, so time need not be spent fleshing them out. Little old ladies and men will be expected to behave only in a few anticipated patterns. This makes story telling simpler.

The National Council on the Aging (NCOA) has completed, although not yet published, an extensive survey of perceptions about aging. This survey sampled young, middle-aged, and old-aged groups for their values relative to certain attributes and behaviors associated with the condition of being old. Tied in to this survey is a concern with how television and radio, along with related media, are being utilized, if at all, to influence these perceptions. Preliminary indications are that negative perceptions about being old are more likely to be held by older than by younger people. The NCOA study will result in some conclusions and suggestions about the use of the media for more positive image making.

What are the opportunities for positive feedback through the image of aging as it is projected via television? What opportunities has the older viewer to see his counterpart realistically portrayed? Aronoff (1974) made an anlysis of 2,741 characters in prime-time network television drama sampled between 1969 and 1971. He found that the elderly comprise less than five percent of both sexes populating television drama. This percentage is far less than in the real population, and it reflects an apparent conviction that interesting things only happen to the young.

Much of the subject matter of prime-time programming is romance, action, violence, and some comedy. When the elderly appear in these settings, they are most often portrayed as victims or villains. Aronoff plotted curves showing "good guys" and "bad guys" as dramatic characters. His curves show that chances of male villainy increase with age; the young adult is most likely the "good guy," and as he ages he moves into the "bad guy" category. Female characters fare even worse. Aronoff says,

> In television drama, females age earlier and faster than males. Chances of male villainy increase with age . . . But while most males in prime time drama fail because they are evil, females fail just as they age. Elderly female characters actually fail more often they succeed. Aging in prime time drama is thus associated with increasing evil, failure, and unhappiness. In a world of generally positive portrayals and happy endings, only forty percent of older male and even fewer female characters are seen as successful, happy, and good. (p. 87)

The problems of older adults are not generally the problems that occupy the heroes and heroines of today's programs. But this is changing. Aging is becoming a viable subject for prime-time shows (Davis, 1975). Programming, even in situation comedies—long an adult fantasy land—now deals with real and controversial issues. Aging and the accompanying losses and adjustments, once treated as humorous, are subjects now available to writers who are allowed to treat honest human drama in a way heretofore not acceptable. Programs about older persons will find an audience as people learn to deal with reality on television and to accept not only issues about aging, but the presence of older faces as attractive faces.

The Place of Television in the Lives of the Aged

Among those concerned with the issue, there is virtually universal agreement regarding the great importance of television in the lives of older people. Glick and Levy (1962) represent a typical view. They categorize the elderly as "embracers" of television. To be an embracer signifies "a particular close identification with television, a rather undiscriminating and accepting attitude toward it, and, usually, great use of the medium" (p. 44). A whole generation of people have reached adulthood with television as commonplace in their lives. But for today's older person, television may retain a certain uniqueness. Here is a generation of people who witnessed the introduction and rapid growth of radio broadcasting as a means of mass communication; they are people who through the second World War depended upon and accepted gratefully the information coming to them from their radios. When television reception became commonplace throughout the nation, today's older person was already past the age of 50. A child of the 1970s may accept with equanimity the experience of watching man take the first step on the moon. This is not so with the older adult.

The classification of the elderly as active television viewers is well supported by research data. De Grazia (1961) questioned aged people regarding their daily activities during their recent past and found that the activity of "watching television" appeared more often than did any other activity in the things people said they did "yesterday" and again in the things they did "in the last four weeks." In a similar survey of five thousand Social Security beneficiaries in four areas of the United States, Schramm (1969) found that the most frequently named daily activity was watching television. Seventy percent of the aged reported that they watched television, and the median number of hours given daily to that activity was three. Hoar (1960) found that television viewing is not only a frequent activity among the aged but that such activity increases with age.

Past research has also shown that the importance of television viewing for old people is relatively independent of their living arrangements. Consider the findings of studies in three settings representing a range of levels of confinement and dependence. Schalinske (1968) investigated television in the lives of a small sample of institutionalized elderly. He conducted an intensive, in-depth study of a select group of institutionalized old persons and their use of television, and he concluded that personality patterns and viewing acivity in his elderly population were similar to those of the general elderly public. Zborowski (1962) studied 204 members of the Age Center of New England and reported that television viewing is seen by the majority of people there as an important recreational activity. Peterson, Hadwen, and Larson (1969) looked at a highly active, well-motivated group of older persons, in-movers into a Southern California retirement community. All but one of the respondents indicated that they watched television daily, and this particular activity had the highest reported incidence of any acivity.

Viewing Preferences of Older Persons

Although it is clear that television viewing is an important activity for older people, there is less consensus regarding program preference. The ambiguity may simply reflect the fact that the elderly are diverse in their attitudes, values, and preferences. Nevertheless, the research findings suggest some support for Meyersohn's (1961) contention that older people prefer personal, nonfiction programs rather than fictional or more abstract presentations. Meyersohn states:

The program preferences indicate that older adults have a greater interest in concrete, non-fictional entertainment, in which they or people like them play an important role (either as members of the studio audience or perhaps as "Queen for a Day"), and a lesser interest in the more abstract and perhaps less personal forms. (p. 268)

In support of that conclusion, Tennant (1965) records a greater interest in variety shows, "old-time" music, quiz programs, wrestling, religious programs,' and news and public affairs programs, with a lesser interest in detective dramas, comedies, and love stories.

The elderly have shown a preference for programs that apparently reflect the culture of their youth and their earlier active adult years. This is perhaps best demonstrated by the apparent aversion on the part of the elderly to the cultural elements of modern youth, particularly as represented by pop music. There also appears a tendency toward preference for wholesome, happy, not very intense kinds of programs. These three elements of program preferences—nonfiction human interest, old-time culture, and wholesome happiness—are well represented in the categorical descriptions of program preferences by Glick and Levy (1962).

The Function of Television for the Older Audience

The social circumstances of the aged are the most commonly cited reasons for the popularity of television viewing. Despite conflicting opinion, a predominant view in the literature seems to be that old people are somewhat disengaged from active social involvements and in a dependent status in those social relationships in which they do participate. To the extent that such characterizations are true, older people seem naturally among those most likely to be television viewers, because, as Berelson and Steiner (1964) wrote: "The people most likely to utilize the external opportunities for entertainment furnished by the largest mass medium tend to be those least able to rely on their own resources, or least used to relying on them" (p. 533).

There are other conditions besides dependency that would seem to support television viewing among the aged, as Meyersohn (1961) has said:

Three conditions of the aging person might predispose him particularly to television. First of all he grows more sedentary; second, he has more leisure time; and third, he has fewer ties to the world. These restrictions or preconditions may eliminate much of what is available to the rest of the population filling its time. (p. 264)

Of course, anecdotal evidence suggests that the aforementioned social characteristics foster television viewing among the aged. For example, Steiner (1963) quotes one of his subjects as saying, "I am an old man and all alone, and the TV brings people and music and talk into my life. Maybe without television I would be ready to die; but this TV gives me life" (p. 25–26). Marian Marshall (1970) gives similar examples, quoting an older woman: "We always have something to talk about when we call each other." Marshall's subjects expressed a fear of violence that kept them inside at night, but they all attested to the fact that they were fortunate because, "It isn't so bad. You can turn on the television and have company" (p. 22).

Perhaps because of attitudes such as those discussed above, the literature reflects a tendency to view television not as a means of improving the dependent disengaged social circumstances of the aged, but merely as a means of making such circumstances tolerable. Glick and Levy (1962) call television "a panacea for old age." Christenson and McWilliams (1967) labeled television "a tranquilizing agent" for the older viewer, calling it therefore "a Godsend for those charged with their care" (p. 60).

Many of the suggested benefits of television make it sound like little more than a vicarious life for the old person:

1. "It gives the older person the 'illusion of contact' with other human beings, thus allowing him to gain a vicarious sense of participation in human interaction" (Meyersohn, 1961).
2. "It takes your mind off yourself and provides an opportunity to become engrossed, diminishing self-concerned self-awareness" (Glick and Levy, 1962).
3. "It is always there, like a babysitter, cutting through silence and loneliness, and available at the turn of a button" (Glick and Levy, 1962).
4. "The day and the week can be organized around special and favorite programs" (Glick and Levy, 1962). Also, "the rigid time schedules of radio and television have become significant substitutes for those other schedules that characterized preretirement life, and provide a set of externally imposed routines" (Meyersohn, 1961, p. 264).

Such opportunities for a vicarious experiencing of life are, of course, important to those for whom direct contact with other human beings is minimal or unavailable.

In this review of the literature a final paragraph should be devoted to some of the findings of a recent study conducted in Canada. In this study 616 completed interviews with older people surveyed media usage and impact (Canadian Radio-Television Commission, 1973). As in other studies discussed here, television proved to be the medium of communication most depended upon by the elderly. Taken from the research report, this paragraph compares the media while explaining some of the function of television for the older audience:

> In order to evaluate the relative importance attached to each medium by the elderly audience a series of questions was addressed to the respondents "about how radio, newspapers and TV compare." . . . The all too formidable array of statistics . . . indicates that, by a healthy margin, a majority of seniors felt that of the three media television is the most entertaining (deemed so by 63%); the best source of companionship (by 58%); the most relaxing (by 51%); and best allows you to see life as others live it (by 65%). The other two media trailed far behind in each of these categories, although the radio was considered slightly more relaxing than the newspaper (23% selected the former, 16% the latter); and a somewhat better source of companionship (17% to 13%). (p. 91)

There are those who fear that the easy opportunity for vicarious involvement may entice other elderly away from the genuine human interaction that may be accessible to them. The answer to the question posed by that fear is unknown, but a more important question may be whether or not television may be used, not as a vicarious existence, but as a means for encouraging the involvement of older people in genuinely useful mental, physical, and social activities. Some researchers have emphasized enriching results of television: it may enhance self-esteem by allowing people to keep educated and informed; it may provide topics for conversation. But the extent to which television can indeed enhance rather than replace the mental, physical, and social vitality of older people, and the way in which that enhancement of life might be accomplished, remain to a great extent unexplored issues.

Research in Television and the Older Audience

It is not surprising that there has been an increase in recent years in research regarding the older person as a special television viewer. In the middle and late 1960s, many in the field of television communication were concerned about the audience behaviors of children and the effects of television on that particular age group. Since the viewing audience at the other end of the age scale might also be classified as captive and dependent, some behavioral scientists in the field of communications turned to the subject of television and the elderly. Early investigations within the television industry itself indicated that there was very little concern, if any, with broadcasting either for or about this particular segment of society. The elderly simply have not been seen as a significant consumer market. This view is shifting slowly, as it must, in reflection of changing demographies.

The rapid changes in electronic communication have led researchers into an appropriate field of inquiry regarding the potential of the new technologies. It is anticipated that in the future there will be a proliferation of channels available to the viewer, and television broadcasting as we know it today will be dramatically altered. This will enable broadcasting to a fragmented audience rather than to the mass audience now perceived by the television industry. Current research in this area is just now finding its way into the literature.

A Report on the Assessment of Television-Viewing Behavior of Older Adults

In a six-year span, covering the years from 1970 through 1975, this author has conducted a series of related studies on the relationship between the older adult and the media. The first two studies were both second party —one utilizing a questionnaire and the other an interview schedule. The third study is a direct assessment of viewing patterns accomplished by means of recording devices attached to television receivers. These studies are discussed here as examples of the current concern mentioned and as a way of providing most recent relevant data.

Study 1.   The Long Beach study.   This study (Davis, 1971) used a questionnaire dealing with viewer preference. The sample was taken from a population of 166 retired persons ranging in age from 55 to 80 and living in Long Beach, California, in December of 1969. The sample was 78 percent female. Seventy-four percent of the sample was over 66 years of age, and 28 percent was over 75 years of age. Fifty-four percent of the population lived alone and all lived in private housing. In addition, 53 percent had education beyond high school.

A major finding of this study was that 75 percent of the population indicated that they watched television five hours a week or less. Since the weekly average according to the December 1969 Nielsen National Survey was 26.52 hours for males over 50, and 33.33 for females over 50 (Nielsen, 1970), there is an obvious discrepancy, though no clear reason for it. This older population reported a viewing pattern similar to that of the national trend as reported by Nielsen. That is, viewing was lowest in early morning: it built toward the middle of the day, doubled by early evening, and reached its peak between 8:00 and 9:00 P.M.

With regard to program preferences, the sample population was asked to rank their three top preferences from among ten program types. The three program types most preferred were: (1) news and public affairs, (2) educational programs, and (3) travelogues. As a second method of determining these preferences, the respondents were also asked to list by title their favorite shows. In this latter instance the three top program types were (1) news and public affairs, (2) music, and (3) drama.

Study 2. The Los Angeles study. The second study (Davis, 1972) used the method of an in-depth interview. The sample was taken from a geographic area within the central urban area of Los Angeles. The number of completed interviews was 289. The age range of the subjects was 55–90. The sample was 62 percent female. Fifty-four percent of the population was at least 65 years old, and 15 percent was at least 76 years old. One half of these subjects were married. One third of the subjects were still in the work force. The median educational level was eighth grade.

In this study also, more than 75 percent said they watched television five hours a week or less. Here again the distribution of the older audience follows the national pattern—starting from a low in the morning, building through afternoon and evening, and peaking at night.

The program types preferred by this audience were: (1) news, (2) situation comedy, and (3) variety shows. In this study a survey of specific program preferences correlated with the indicated program type preferences.

Study 3. The institutionalized elderly. This study, a three-year project, investigated the potential of television as a therapeutic tool for the elderly living in communal facilities. Here a specialized audience of elderly viewers was surveyed. The concern in this study was with television in the lives of older people living in a variety of facilities ranging from apartment complexes through convalescent homes and health care centers. None lived at the level of independence characterized by the other two populations. The methodology for this study differed drastically from the two previously reported studies. Here, rather than using personal communications about viewing patterns, this study directly measured the actual viewing behavior of the older adult. The study population totaled 215 subjects. In this study Rustrack event recorders were built into the sets and, as in the early Nielsen studies, were constantly in operation and set to coincide with actual time. Further, the on-off button for each set was located in a handpiece along with the speaker on an extension cord from the set. The sets were programmed to turn off at intervals of 20 to 23 minutes. In this way it could be determined if attention was being paid to the program. If it was, the viewer would press the button to reactivate the set immediately. Data were collected in 15-minute increments of viewing, and each of these increments was termed a share of viewer involvement. Each subject's viewing behavior was monitored for a period of six weeks, at the end of which time a fresh subject population was given the sets. This continued throughout the calendar year 1973.

Of the total population studied during this period of one year (N–215), 138 lived in board and care facilities, while 77 lived in convalescent homes. Of those in board and care facilities, 31 were men and 107 were women; 45 men and 32 women lived in convalescent homes. The age range of the subjects was 60 through 90.

The curve relating to the level of education of this subject population is uneven and skewed in favor of the higher levels: 22.8 percent of the subjects had some college education, and 27.9 were college graduates. A high percentage also fell at the other end of the curve, with 13 percent of the subject population having less than a ninth-grade education and only 9.9 percent reported having had some high school; 26.4 percent of the population graduated from high school.

Perhaps because this particular population was somewhat older than the two previous populations and because of the environments in which they were found, most (84.2 percent) lived alone, being either widowed, divorced, or single.

The average daily viewing for this audience was 3.94 hours, or 27.58 hours per week. This average is more in keeping with the Nielsen weekly viewing averages for individuals over 50 years of age (26.52 for men and 33.33 for women) in the same geographic area and for the same time period (Nielsen, 1973).

The viewing pattern as determined by this study diverges from the national average. Both the Nielsen and the first two studies show a gradual increase of viewer numbers through the day with a sharp building in the evening and a peak between 8:00 and 9:00 at night. In this sample there were three discernible peaks: one in the morning between 11:00 and 12:00, one in the afternoon between 1:00 and 2:00, and one at night between 6:00 and 7:00. A curve, then, showing the availability of this older audience would show viewing to peak two hours earlier than the Nielsen audience.

The content of programs viewed was not completely consistent with the findings of the first two studies. The major program type preferences were news and public affairs; the next three in very close order of preference were game shows, comedies, and dramas, in that order. (The biggest single attraction for all three of the study populations was the Lawrence Welk musical program.)

Implications of the Research

These three studies polled three diverse segments of the older viewing audience: (1) self-maintaining, mobile, independent older viewers living in a metropolitan suburb; (2) a similar population, but financially disadvantaged and in great part an ethnic subculture (black) living in a central metropolitan area; and (3) a population of mixed income, education, and mobility living in communal or care facilities. One of the major differences in the findings of these three studies is the amount of day viewing. In the two self-reported studies, the report of hours spent viewing is significantly lower than either the third study or the Nielsen estimates. The third study relies on physical measurements of actual television sets in operation. Other major variations in the studies are the differences in daily viewing patterns and in program preferences. It is possible, of course, that these differences are a function of the varying samples rather than of the data-collecting methods. However, if demographics affect the reports of viewing patterns, one would expect to find this in the first two samples where there was a high degree of similarity in the findings despite the huge disparities in demographics. The basic demographics of the third study were somewhat like an average of the first two studies. Represented within the sample were subjects with higher education and some with low education, some suburban dwellers and some urban residents, etc. Lastly, in terms of sample variance it might be argued that living in such facilities as has been described for Study 3 means that there is less to occupy the time of these elderly. On the contrary, the opportunity to socialize is no less than that for the retired urban elderly of Study 1 or the poor urban elderly of Study 2. In congregate facilities there is always company right next door.

The implication for studies of this type is that self-reporting television habits are unreliable when the dependent variable is one of physical viewing patterns, rather than content or preference statements. It is possible that the level of attention is less than total, so that in self-reports the subject is unaware or does not consider that he has "watched television" for 28 hours during the week. It should also be noted that the preferences of content are for the most part invariant over the methods of assessment. This suggests that conscious preference statements override viewing selection patterns; thus the viewer, whether the attention level is high or low, will at least adjust his selection of viewing material to that which most closely approximates his schedule of preference.

Of course, these three studies and the others mentioned in this chapter have generated a large amount of data not all detailed here. There are reasons for seeking such information as is revealed in these studies. Generally, the research is an attempt to learn more about the dimensions of television as an environmental factor in the lives of an elderly population. In the process of measuring viewer behaviors, it is possible to learn more about the total impact of television on the lives of the elderly.

Perhaps the verbalized evaluative statements and the conversational "case-history" data collection in combination with the quantified data from the studies of the older population allow for some significant conclusions.

Some Conclusions

It is always dangerous to talk about the older population as though it were a homogeneous group. Of course it is not. Perceptions of the television experience will be influenced by individual differences among elderly viewers as well as by age-related properties held in common. Although in any audience study a mass of people is being discussed, the mass is always composed of many separate and individual components. An elderly audience may span 30 or more years of age. There will be differences in the attitudes of 55- or 60-year-old viewers and 75- and 80-year-old viewers. Audience behavior will differ subtly according to these differences. Audience behavior is further dependent on differences within the separate age categories. These are differences such as sex, race, marital status, work status, mobility, health, income, interpersonal relationships—and the list goes on. Each individual responding to a survey is characterized by a status in each of these areas which is unique to him. Many responses and designations may be similar and even identical to others within the broad group of older viewers, and this similarity is what gives validity to the findings. However, it is obvious that each of the members of a sample is not to be described exactly like each of the other members of a sample. Television audience behavior will reflect a group age status, i.e., old, but with subtle variations dependent upon where they are in the over thirty year span of old age.

By and large television viewing is felt by the elderly audience to be an important and necessary experience that provides positive benefits in the forms of information and entertainment. Two other functions which also seem to be important to the older viewer are television's ability to provide companionship and to help pass the time. The older audience seems to relate strongly to what it views consistently. Involvement with the dramatic material as well as with the personality of favored entertainers, talk-show hosts, and performers is strong. It is interesting to note that despite the apparent lack in numbers of elderly persons as role models seen on the television screen, older viewers are inclined to identify with both the people and story situations that, simply by virtue of appearing on television, are given high status.

When attitudes about television are examined over an age span of 30 years or more, represented by the various survey populations, it is seen that strong attitudes toward the experience diminish and are not held by as many persons in the older age brackets as in the younger age brackets. As the viewer ages, he becomes less concerned about the television experience, even though he may continue in his television viewing habits.

The importance of television viewing to the elderly is relative to the other opportunities for interaction in their lives. It is true that television viewing may function as a compensating mechanism for the older population. That is, when they do not have frequent and close relationships with family and/or friends, the elderly may tend to spend more time viewing and perhaps will value much more highly the television experience. When interaction with others is limited, television viewing helps to pass the time. When older people live alone, they indicate that they seek more general information from television than do those who may acquire this general information through social contacts.

When studying the audience behavior of any group, it is important to consider not only what the group is doing with television (that is, what are its choices, how much time is spent in television viewing, and what is its impact), but also what are the other options for activities open to that particular group. The elderly are unique as a television audience because there may not be so many other options for them. Nevertheless, the collected data should not be accepted simply at face value. For example, information about program preferences may lead one to assume certain conclusions about the viewers based on the programs they prefer. One should not lose sight of the principle of the least objectionable program; a choice sometimes must be made not of the best-liked program, but of that program which is the least objectionable. So one must consider choices the viewer is able to make at the time of his viewing experience.

These are some of the many factors that must be taken into account when making an analysis of television and the older audience. Nevertheless, the potential exists for television to be an ever greater force for good in the lives of elderly persons. For older viewers TV is a dependable, trusted medium of communication. Therefore, information delivered via the television channel is more likely to be accepted. The elderly can gather new information; they can be given appropriate knowledge of benefits and services available to them. Although the elderly have few role models readily available, well-chosen television personalities, newscasters, analysts, and a host of older citizens can be made visible to the elderly, to those approaching that status, and even to the young. Here is the place where models for successful aging may be made available. Television thus offers an opportunity to influence attitudes of the entire population about aging and about being old. Perhaps this is one of the most important values inherent in the television-viewing experience. This may be the most appropriate reason for attending still more closely to television communications and the elderly.

References

Anderson, J. E., Jr. 1962. Aging and educational television: a preliminary survey. *Journal of Gerontology* 17:447–449.

Aronoff, C. 1974. Old age in prime time. *Journal of Communication* 24:4.

Berelson, B. 1948. Communication and public opinion. In *Communication in modern society,* ed. W. Schram. Urbana: University of Illinois Press.

Berelson, B. and Steiner, G. 1964. Mass communications. In *Human behavior,* ed. B. Berelson. New York: Harcourt, Brace and World.

Birren, J. E. and Woodruff, D. S. Human development over the life span through education. In *Life span developmental psychology: personality and socialization,* eds. P. B. Baltes and K. W. Schaie. New York: Academic Press.

Canadian Radio-Television Commission. 1973. *Reaching the retired.* Ottawa: Information Canada.

Christenson, R. M. and McWilliams, R. D. 1967. *Voice of the people: readings in public opinion and propaganda.* New York: McGraw-Hill.

Davis, R. H. 1971. Television and the older adult. *Journal of Broadcasting* 14.

Davis, R. H. 1972. A descriptive study of television in the lives of an elderly population. Unpublished doctoral dissertation. University of Southern California.

Davis, R. H. 1975. Television and the image of aging. *Television Quarterly* 13:2.

De Grazia, S. 1961. The uses of time. In *Aging and leisure,* ed. R. W. Kleemeier. New York: Oxford University Press.

Glick, I. O. and Levy, S. J. 1962. *Living with television.* Chicago: Aldine Publishers.

Hoar, J. R. 1960. Reading, listening and viewing behavior of the aged: an inventory of the mass communication habits and preferences of 200 aged persons in Oxford, Mississippi. Unpublished doctoral dissertation. State University of Iowa.

Kleppner, O. 1966. *Advertising procedure.* Englewood Cliffs, New Jersey: Prentice-Hall.

Marshall, M. G. 1970. Living a lifetime. A proposed television series for older adults. Unpublished Master's thesis. California State College, Los Angeles.

Meyersohn, R. 1961. An examination of commercial entertainment. In *Aging and leisure,* ed. R. W. Kleemeier. New York: Oxford University Press.

Nielsen Television '69. 1970. *A review of audience trend.* Chicago: A. C. Nielsen Company Media Research Division.

Nielsen Television '73. 1973. *A review of audience trend.* Chicago: A. C. Nielsen Company Media Research Division.

Peterson, J. A.; Hadwen, T.; and Larson, A. E. 1969. *A time for work, a time for leisure.* Los Angeles: University of Southern California Gerontology Center.

Roper Organization, Inc. 1973. *What people think of television and other mass media, 1959–1972.* Television Information Office.

Schalinske, T. F. 1968. The role of television in the life of the aged person. Unpublished doctoral dissertation. Ohio State University.

Schramn, W. 1969. Aging and mass communication. In *aging and society. Volume 1: aging and the professions,* eds. Riley, Johnson, Foher, and Hess, New York: Russel Sage Foundation.

Steiner, G. A. 1963. *The people look at television.* New York: Alfred A. Knopf.

Tennant, F. B. Jr. 1965. A descriptive estimate of the adequacy of network television service to older viewers. Unpublished Master's thesis. University of Southern California.

Zborowski, M. 1962. Aging and recreation. *Journal of Gerontology.*

16

Economics and the Older Population

ROBIN JANE WALTHER

In the United States there is general agreement that no person, no matter how old, should be forced to suffer economic distress. This is the "humanitarian" objective on which much of current social and economic policy is based (Musgrave, 1968). There is, however, general disagreement as to how to achieve this goal.

In previous generations family and voluntary community efforts were primarily responsible for providing for the economic needs of individuals in distress. During the Great Depression of the 1930s the inadequacy of individual and voluntary efforts was recognized. Slowly government was awarded the primary responsibility of providing for the economic needs of the population. Various separate programs have been instituted such as Social Security, Supplemental Security Income, Food Stamps, and Medicare with the objective of alleviating economic distress. These efforts have been criticized as being both inequitable and inefficient partly because of the confusion resulting from the variety of programs (United States Congress, 1974b, Chapter 17). Of greater importance than the criticism of the specific programs is the extent to which society has been able to achieve the humanitarian objective of eliminating economic distress in the population.

The problem of how to provide for those in economic distress is of special concern to those interested in the economic welfare of the elderly population. Through various approaches economists are continually contributing to understanding and solving this problem. Economists have assisted in defining the specific goals of society. Part of this role has involved explaining how some of society's goals, such as individual freedom, conflict with the goal of alleviating economic distress and how any acceptable solution to the problem of inadequate incomes requires compromise. Economists have also worked on defining who the needy are and who benefits from government programs intended to help the needy. Too often a problem such as inadequate housing is recognized; a solution such as property tax relief for elderly, low-income home owners is devised; and only after the program is instituted is it recognized that those who benefit most from this program are not the needy, but instead the individuals with low current income and large homes (Aaron, 1973). In addition to specifying goals and determining needs, economists also try to predict how people as a group will react to a particular policy. In the case of property tax relief for home owners over age 65, the expectation is that fewer home owners approaching age 65 will sell their large, partially lived-in homes and move to smaller homes or apartments. As a result, although the program does help some in the elderly population, it also encourages an excess consumption of housing services.

As suggested by the above example, economists, by defining goals, determining needs, and understanding the economic behavior of groups, can contribute to solving the problem of how to provide for the needs of the older population. This chapter describes some of the contributions of economists to solving the problems of the older population. The first section discusses some of the issues involved with designing policies intended to benefit the older population. The second section discusses some of the problems in determining who are the needy in the elderly population. This section also includes a survey of the current status of the older population. The third section considers the retirement decision and how changes in tastes and attitudes, retirement incomes, and market wages influence the decision.

Issues and Concerns

There are a number of policies and programs which either directly or indirectly influence the economic position of the older population as well as that of other age groups in the population. A major concern of both policy makers and economists is whether these programs and policies are equitable and efficient. An equitable program is one which treats individuals and families in similar circumstances equally. An efficient program is one which allocates available resources in such a way as to achieve the maximum possible benefit from the program. Both equitability and efficiency are important issues in evaluating the actions of government and the operation of a complete economic system.

However, defining and, moreover, designing an equitable program is extremely difficult. One interpretation of "similar circumstances" includes families with similar demographic characteristics who have similar sets of resources available for providing for their needs. For example, for some programs "similar circumstances" is determined by geographical location, sex of family head, age of family head and of family members, and size of family. In other cases, "similar circumstances" is interpreted as similar work effort on the part of the individual. Thus, some programs exist which treat the retired and unemployed equally. They assume that similar work efforts produce similar results, which is not necessarily the case given the existence of race, sex, and age discrimination in the labor market. In both interpretations of "similar circumstances" the time period over which the comparisons are to be made must be specified. Some argue that individuals with the same sets of resources available to them over their life times should be treated equally. While this may be somewhat unrealistic for determining the resources available to elderly individuals, a comparison of incomes over a year instead of for a month might not be unreasonable.

The choice of the relevant demographic characteristics for determining "similar circumstances" is based on several considerations. To some extent, demographic characteristics such as age, sex, and size of family do determine the nutritional needs of the family. In addition, demographic characteristics are also related to health and to labor-force experience. Since age is related to a deterioration of physical ability and to discriminatory treatment in the labor market, the argument can be made that individuals in the same age groups should be treated similarly. Additional arguments favoring the use of demographic characteristics to define "similar circumstances" are based on social and political norms. For example, it can be argued that age is a relevant characteristic since all people deserve some leisure time in their "later" years. In addition, sex has been used to define "similar circumstances" based on judgments that widows should be provided for by their departed husbands and that mothers are more important to their children in single parent families than are fathers. Both of these norms are now being challenged (U.S. Department of Health, Education, and Welfare, 1975; Mathews, 1975).

As well as determining the demographic characteristics which define "similar circumstances," the designers of social and economic policies should also be concerned with the criteria used to define similar resources. One somewhat idealistic approach is to compare the consumption potential of various individuals over their life times. However, with present knowledge concerning the relationship between innate ability, education, and potential consumption this criterion is not practical. Policy makers should, however, consider making comparisons based on future consumption potential. Using this criterion the value of one's home, the monetary value of savings and other financial assets, and the value of one's leisure time should be included in comparisons of available resources of families. Current income and current income after taxes are both inadequate measures. The extent to which adjustments in the measure of reported income result in differences in consumption potential will be considered in the following section.

In addition to designing equitable programs, policy makers are also concerned with designing efficient programs. In order to determine whether a program is efficient, that is, whether it provides maximum benefit at least cost, the purpose of the program must be defined. The definition of the purpose is closely related to the question of efficiency. In addition, some programs have several purposes which also makes a determination of efficiency difficult.

The Social Security program in the United States is a case of a program with at least two purposes (Pechman et al., 1968; Musgrave, 1968; Schulz, 1971). The first purpose is to replace the income of families whose major earner has died, retired, or become disabled. The second purpose is to provide a minimum floor to the income of families covered by the program. The Social Security program is generally judged as technically efficient. However, since the program does not differentiate individuals who have other sources of income from those who do not, the program is not particularly efficient if the purpose is to provide a minimum floor. But if the purpose of the program is to replace income of retired workers who have contributed to the program, then possibly the program should be judged as efficient.

Efficiency and equity are just two standards by which a particular policy or an economic system should be judged. Other factors to be considered are whether the policy or economic system is "adequate," preserves individual incentives to work and save, and is financially sound. In all cases, the determination of whether a particular program meets these general standards of equity, efficiency, maintenance of individual incentives, and financially stability is difficult. First, the objectives are conflicting. A program which provides a minimum standard of living for all will influence work incentives. Second, the specification of objectives, such as equity, is not particularly straightforward. Nevertheless, these are issues which one must consider in designing and implementing particular economic policies, including those directed at helping the elderly.

Who are the Needy?

Despite the agreement that no individual or family should be forced to suffer economic distress, the questions of who the needy are and what are their particular needs have not been adequately answered. In designing social and economic policies this information is of major importance, and various attempts have been made to answer what at first appears to be a straight-forward question. In this section, the emphasis is on the needs of the older population, although some information on the needs of other age groups will be considered.

One of the more popular approaches to determining who the needy are is based on the comparison of the income of a particular family to a subsistence income. The determination of what constitutes a subsistence income is based on a somewhat arbitrary approach. Families are divided by size and composition, by sex and age of family head, and by farm-nonfarm residence. Based on the nutritional requirements of family members the cost of a minimum food budget is determined. This cost is then multiplied by a fixed factor in order to determine the subsistence income of a family with a particular set of characteristics. For comparisons between two years the cost of the food budget has been adjusted either for changes in the cost of food or for changes in the cost of living (Orshansky, 1968; United States Bureau of the Census, 1974).

Before this low-income or poverty index is used to compare the welfare of the population of the United States, it should be emphasized that the index was meant to be used to assess the extent of poverty in the United States. It was not meant to be used to consider the level of welfare of two individuals. A comparison of the needs of two individuals should include measurements of the states of health at the very least.

By using this index, changes in the percent of the older population in poverty can be considered (see Chapter 3). As noted in Table 16.1, the percent of persons 65 and over with incomes below the subsistence income level has decreased between 1966 and 1973. In absolute percentage terms the decline has been greater for the nonwhite population than for the white population. However, the number of nonwhite individuals in poverty is double the number of white individuals in poverty in the 65 and over population. The comparison of the percent with incomes below the subsistence level for the 65-and-over population to the total population indicates the extent to which the concentration of poverty differs between the older population and the total population. This measure of relative concentration indicates that poverty is more concentrated in the 65-and-over population than in the total population. The decrease in the measure of relative concentration between 1966 and 1973 for both the white and nonwhite populations does suggest that the relative position of the 65-and-over population is improving. The comparison of the measures of relative concentration for the two racial groups also indicates that the relative position of the older white population to the total white population is inferior to the relative position of the nonwhite older population to the total nonwhite population. Using this somewhat arbitrary measure of subsistence income it has been possible to compare the relative positions of the older population to the total population and of the white population to the nonwhite. These comparisons have suggested (1) that the position of the older population is improving relative to the total population, (2) that the need for assistance of the nonwhite population is greater than that of the white population, and (3) that the relative differences between the older population and the total population are less among the nonwhites than among the whites.

The usefulness of these comparisons depends on the extent to which the arbitrary measure of subsistence income corresponds to a measure of "adequacy." There are a number of reasons why they do not, in fact, correspond. Some of the criticisms of this index have concentrated on the absolute nature of the measure, while other criticisms have concentrated on the imperfect relationship between reported income and resources available for consumption.

As part of the first set of criticisms, the argument has been made that the concept of "adequacy" is a relative concept and that a set of fixed subsistence incomes cannot be used to approximate the concept. More specifically, the argument is that the "need" of a family or individual is related to the gap between their income and that of other individuals in the society. Based on this view one economist has suggested that the low-

Table 16.1   Persons below the low-income level by age and race for selected years: 1966 to 1973

Percent of group below low-income level	1973	1971	1969[a]	1966[b]
All persons				
Total	11.1	12.5	12.2	14.7
65 years and over	16.3	21.6	25.3	28.5
Rel. conc.[c]	1.47	1.73	2.07	1.94
White				
Total	8.4	9.9	9.5	11.3
65 years and over	14.4	19.9	23.3	26.4
Rel. conc.	1.71	2.01	2.45	2.34
Negro and other races				
Total	29.6	30.9	31.1	39.8
65 years and over	35.5	38.4	48.1	53.4
Rel. conc.	1.20	1.24	1.55	1.34

[a]Data for 1973 and 1971 is not directly comparable to data for 1969.
[b]Data for 1969 is not directly comparable to 1966.
[c]Relative Concentration is the ratio of percent of 65 and over group to percent for all persons.
SOURCE: U.S. Bureau of the Census, *Current Population Reports,* Series P-60, No. 94, July 1974, "Characteristics of the Low-Income Population: 1973," Table 1.

income level should be defined as a fixed percent of the median income of persons in the society (Fuchs, 1969). Others have argued that the "low-income" level should be related to both the monetary and psychological needs of the family. Thus, the "adequacy" of pension income should be related to previous income while working (Schulz, 1974). This position regarding the definition of "adequacy" could result in higher "low-income" levels being specified for retired engineers than for retired laborers (Bok, 1965). Some consider this a ridiculous suggestion, but there is some precedent for such a notion.

The second set of criticisms of the low-income index are based on the view that in assessing the welfare and needs of the population, policy makers are not interested in how many dollars a family has relative to a subsistence income level but instead in the extent to which the needs of the family are satisfied. This suggests that the "adequacy" standard should be based on the concept of potential consumption and not on current income. As a consequence, a low-income index which relies solely on a comparison of current income to a subsistence income measure is generally considered inferior to measures which approximate potential consumption (Morgan, 1965, 1975; Havighurst, 1975).

In order to assess the needs of the population using the criterion of potential consumption, the factors which determine consumption must first be considered; then reported measures of income must be adjusted to approximate the concept of potential consumption. The possession of owned assets, such as a house, and of monetary assets, such as savings and other financial assets, although not directly affecting income does, in fact, contribute the value of consumption (Chen, 1965; Weisbrod and Hansen, 1968). In addition, potential consumption also depends on the potential earnings of family members employed in the labor market (Becker, 1965; Taussig, 1973). In addition to potential earnings and owned assets, potential consumption depends on the cost of living in the local area, the reduction in earnings due to taxes, and the benefits received from family and friends and from government services. The implication is that the determination of an "adequate" standard which will be used both to assess the welfare of the total population and to design relevant eligibility requirements for programs directed at the needy should not be based solely on current income. Other factors such as the value of assets and savings, potential income from work and work-related expenses, taxes deducted from earnings, benefits from government expenditures, and regional differences in the cost of living should also be considered in assessing needs and determining eligibility requirements.

The importance of considering these factors in determining "need," of course, depends on the contribution of these factors to potential consumption. Efforts have been made by various economists to make these assessments (Weisbrod and Hansen, 1968; Taussig, 1973; Institute of Social Research 1974; Havighurst, 1975). A conclusion of these studies is that the proportion of the older population in poverty as compared to other age groups is overstated given the current income-based measure. An additional result is that the use of current income overstates the extent to which the levels of economic welfare differ within the older age groups. These results, of course, depend on specific assumptions and on the accuracy of particular sets of survey data.

The purpose of this section has not been to provide extensive details on the current status of the older population. Instead the intention has been to provide some insights into interpretations of particular measures of "adequacy" and "economic welfare." (See Chapter 3 for additional details on income distribution.)

Is Retirement a Problem?

In the previous section it was noted that a number of families in the older population have incomes below what has been termed the subsistence level of income. Although this measure has been thoroughly criticized as an inaccurate measure of "adequacy," it remains a useful measure for comparing differences in reported incomes within the older population. In this section one of the major determinants of reported income—the timing of reitrement—is considered.

The issue of whether retirement is a problem will be considered somewhat indirectly. First, the relationship between reported income, work experience, education, and the labor-force participation will be considered. Second, some of the changes in labor-force participation over time will be described. And third, some of the factors which influence the timing of retirement by the individual will be considered. By considering the factors which control the timing of retirement, the question of whether retirement is a problem can be considered.

As suggested above, income in the older population is closely related to work status. The most complete information on this question is found in survey data collected in the late 1960s. In Table 16.2, the relationship between income and work experience is presented for aged units 65 and over surveyed in 1967. The reported median incomes are higher and the percent with incomes below $3,000 are lower for those aged units in which some income was reported from work.

In Table 16.3, similar results for a sample of men between the ages of 58 and 63, for data collected in 1969, are reported. Although the

Table 16.2   Statistics on income by work for aged units over 65: 1967

Work and marital status	Median income	Percent with income below $3000
Married couples		
With work, total	4,691	24
Neither worked	2,621	60
Nonmarried persons, men		
Worked	2,518	59
Did not work	1,516	89
Nonmarried persons, women		
Worked	2,200	71
Did not work	1,162`	93

SOURCE: Bixby, 1970.

median incomes for all but single men without work are considerably higher than those reported for the aged units in Table 16.2, the same positive relationship between work status and income is apparent. From these two tables the differences in reported income between married and single men can also be noted. For both sets of data, the percent of single men with incomes below an arbitrarily chosen income level is much larger than the comparable percentages reported for married men. Thus, for both the sample of aged units and the sample of men between age 58 and 63, reported income is related both to work status and to marital status. For the sample of men aged 58 to 63 it is also possible to compare work status with previous work experience and education. As noted in Table 16.4, the men with less education and work experience in generally lower-status jobs were more likely to have withdrawn from the labor force than the other groups of men. The information provided by this survey of men aged 58 to 63 provides additional support for observations that the men most likely to retire are those men with more limited job opportunities (J. Abbott, 1974; Kreps, 1971).

Table 16.3   Statistics on income of men aged 58-63 by work experience and marital status: 1969

Work and marital status	Median income	Percent with income below $5000
Men, spouse present		
With work	8,555	19
Without work	4,610	55
Men, no spouse present		
With work	5,555	44
Without work	1,530	86

SOURCE: Schwab, 1974, p. 10.

Table 16.4 Percent out of labor force by occupation of longest job and by education, men aged 58-63: 1969

	Percent out of labor force
Occupation of longest job	
Professional	10
Farmer	12
Manager	13
Clerical	17
Sales	11
Craftsmen	16
Operative	21
Service	21
Farm laborer	24
Nonfarm laborer	27
Years of school	
0–8	21
9–11	17
12	11
13 or more	12

SOURCE: Schwab, 1974, p. 10.

There are, of course, various explanations for these relationships between the decision to retire and the characteristics of the individual. Following the discussion of some of the trends in retirement in the United States, some possible explanations will be considered.

The age at which an individual decides to withdraw from the labor force is important both to society and to the individual. For the individual, retirement generally leads to a reduction in current income and, of course, an increase in "leisure." For society, the withdrawal from the labor force results in a decrease in taxes collected from earnings and an increase in pension benefits paid to retired workers (Schulz, 1974; United States Department of Health, Education, and Welfare, 1975). Thus, the trends in retirement in the United States are important both for the understanding of the economic needs of individuals and for the estimates of the predicted costs of private and public pension programs.

In this section, for statistical reasons, retirement will be defined as complete withdrawal from the labor force. Thus, a person is retired if he or she is neither working nor looking for work. The reduction in the percent of individuals in a given population either working or looking for work is by this definition equivalent to increases in the retirement rates.

Rates of labor-force participation are collected from the decennial United States Census for a number of different age groups. In comparing labor-force participation rates over time, one should be aware that the procedures used by the Bureau of the Census have changed and that the rates are not always directly comparable. As a result, small changes in labor-force participation rates should not be considered particularly significant (for an example see Bowen and Finegan, 1969, p. 52).

When comparing data for 1940, 1950, 1960, and 1970, one finds the expected inverse relationship between age and labor-force participation which has been pointed out by a number of previous researchers (Bowen and Finegan, 1969). The workers of the United States do not abruptly leave the labor force at some fixed age, such as 65. Instead, individual workers withdraw at a number of different ages and, as a consequence, the labor-force participation rates gradually decline with age. In 1970, for males age 55 the rate of labor-force participation was 88.9 percent; age 62, 72.7 percent; age 65, 47.1 percent; age 70, 11.1 percent. The comparable rates for women were: age 55, 49.6 percent; age 62, 35.9 percent; age 65, 22.0 percent; age 70, 11.1 percent. At age 75+, the rate for men had declined to 12.1 percent, and for women, to 4.7 percent.

In all the years for which we considered data, the male labor-force participation rates begin to decline at around age 55. This usually gradual decline in labor-force participation is, however, characterized by a large drop in rates for males between age 64 and age 65, and in 1970 by a smaller but noticeable drop between age 61 and age 62. One possible explanation for the latter break is the provisions in the Social Security programs which now allow men to collect the maximum retirement benefit at age 62. For women, the increase in retirement has also begun by age 55 in the period beginning with 1940. However, the decline in labor-force participation rates for women between age 64 and 65 is not as dramatic as the decline observed for the male labor force.

In addition to the inverse relationship between age and labor-force participation, we can also observe the changes which have taken place in the timing of retirement over time. The labor-force participation rates of males over age 60 have been declining since 1950. According to the data reported, there has been no rapid decline among workers under age 60. The entrance of women into the labor force has resulted in increases in labor-force participation rates for all female age groups, but especially for those under age 65. Labor-force participation rates of women have been increasing since 1940. Since 1960 these increases in rates of labor-force participation have been almost exclusively limited to the under age 65 group. By comparing the rates of labor-force participation for male and female workers, two trends in the timing of retirement have been suggested: (1) men after age 60 are tending to withdraw completely from the labor force more frequently than was the case previously; (2) although women in the younger age groups are tending to participate in the labor market more frequently than previously, they also tend to withdraw from the labor market around age 65.

In the above discussion, decreases in the age of retirement and relationships between retirement and education, occupation and marital status have been suggested. At this point some of the factors which influence the retirement decision and determine the observed trends and relationships will be considered. At present, policy makers are most interested in the results of this type of inquiry (United States Congress, 1974a, 1974b). They need exact estimates of the impact a given increase in retirement benefits or a given change in market wages will have on the retirement decisions of the population. However, economists, despite extensive recent effort, are not yet able to supply these exact estimates with much confidence.

The retirement decisions which are made by individuals every day are extremely complex. The decisions are made under conditions of uncertainty, and they are influenced by subjective attitudes of family and by constraints imposed by limits on time and work opportunities. The subjective attitudes which enter the decision include society's attitudes toward work and leisure, the individual's satisfaction with work, the attitudes of other family members towards the individual's retirement, and the family's preferences for activities which are time intensive and those which are market goods intensive. Examples of time intensive activities are long walks near home and quiet evenings reading at home. Examples of activities which are termed market goods intensive are evenings at the theater and skiing vacations in Switzerland.

In addition to these subjective factors, there are other factors which limit the range of a family's decisions and, as a consequence, also influence the retirement decisions of family members. These constraints include the physical limitations on time and the monetary constraints on the purchase of market goods. Since the number of hours in a day are given, the time available for market work and household activities is limited. An additional limitation on time results from time lost because of illness. A change in the constraint on time available for allocation between market work and household activities is expected to influence the retirement decision. The actual impact is generally a decrease in time allocated to market work.

The monetary constraints on the purchase of market goods in any one time period are the result of previous savings decisions, government transfers, and potential earnings of all family members in the labor market. Mandatory retirement rules limit the potential market earnings of older family members. In 1971, a survey of over twenty thousand workers covered by some type of pension program found that over fifty percent of the workers were covered by plans with mandatory retirement provisions (Davis, 1973). In addition, more indirect forms of age discrimination resulting from employer attitudes that older workers are less flexible in adjusting to new employment situations, more prone to accidents, and more likely to lose time due to illness will also limit the potential income of the older family member (Sobel and Folk, 1965; Sheppard, 1971; Brennan et al., 1967). Additional constraints result from the expected value of family-owned assets and monetary assets and from the potential market income of other family members.

Other factors entering into the retirement decision are those which influence the family's ability to combine the time of family members and market goods purchased with monetary assets to produce "activities" or "commodities." This process, which is sometimes referred to as household production, is most likely influenced by the formal education of family members and by information which can be used in making decisions. For example, information obtained from preretirement preparation courses possibly assists the family in reallocating market goods to produce desired housing services more efficiently (Michael, 1972; Grossman, 1972; Schulz, 1971).

As an example of how these factors control the retirement decision, we consider the case of an older, unemployed worker. When the worker loses his job for whatever reason—age discrimination, mandatory retirement provisions, or the closing of the local plant—he has two alternatives. The first alternative is to invest his time and effort in finding another job. The second alternative is to quit looking for a job and to devote all of his time to household activities. The choice which the individual makes is based on a subjective comparison of the value of his time in the two activities (Reder, 1969; McCall, 1970).

The value of time spent searching for work is related to the wages he expects, the number of years which he intends to continue working, and the demand for market goods by the family. The value of his time spent in household activities depends on his efficiency in household work and the inputs of time and market goods by the family. If the unemployed worker expects to find a high-paying job, he will be more likely to continue searching for work, all other things equal, than if he expects to find only low-paying jobs. Thus, the earlier observation that workers in less skilled occupations are more likely to withdraw from the labor force is not surprising (Table 16.4). If the purchasing power of the family has decreased, the unemployed worker is probably more likely to continue looking for work than if purchasing power has not decreased. This is because of the decrease in the value of his time in household activities relative to the value of his time in searching for work. Thus, recent data which suggest that increased rates of unemployment for all workers in 1975 will retard the retirement decisions of both the employed and unemployed older workers can be explained by the decrease in purchasing power of the family due to the decrease in work opportunities for other family members (J. P. Smith, 1975; R. E. Smith, 1974).

At the beginning of this section, the retirement decision of the individual was looked upon as a problem. Observations of the decreased purchasing power of retirees outside the labor force also suggest that retirement is a problem (Schulz, 1974). However, from the above discussion the problem does not appear to be retirement but instead the constraints which limit the family's decisions on how to allocate time of members between market and nonmarket activities. Certainly high unemployment rates should not be maintained in order to discourage retirement among older members of the labor force. But possibly work opportunities should be increased through the elimination of mandatory retirement rules and less blatant age discrimination.

Conclusion

In addition to considering some of the issues involved with designing policies to improve the economic status of the older population, the intention of the chapter is to suggest three separate ways in which economists are continuing to contribute to efforts to improve the economic position of the elderly: (1) the specification of goals and objectives, (2) the measurement of needs, and (3) the understanding of the impact of economic factors on behavior. In each case, the insights provided by political scientists, sociologists, and psychologists can and do contribute to the current efforts of economists. In none of these areas is the work completed.

References

Aaron, Henry. 1973. What do circuit-breaker laws accomplish? In *Property tax reform*, ed., George E. Peterson. Washington, D.C.: The John C. Lincoln Institute and the Urban Institute.

Abbott, Julian. 1974. Covered employment and the age men claim retirement benefits. *Social Security Bulletin* 37:12:3–16.

Becker, Gary S. 1965. A theory of the allocation of time. *Economic Journal* 75:299:493–517.

Bixby, Lenore E. 1970. Income of people aged 65 and older: Overview from 1968 survey of the aged. *Social Security Bulletin* 33:4:3–34.

Bok, Derek C. 1967. Emerging issues in social legislation: Social Security. *Harvard Law Review* 80:4:717–764.

Bowen, W. G. and Finegan, J. A. 1969. *The economics of labor force participation.* New Jersey: Princeton University Press.

Brennan, Michael J.; Taft, Phillip; and Schupack, Mark B. 1967. *The economics of age.* New York: W. W. Norton and Company, Inc.

Chen, Yung-Ping. 1965. Economic poverty: the special case of the aged. *The Gerontologist.* 6:1:39–45.

Davis, Harry. E. 1973. Pension provisions affecting the employment of older workers. *Monthly Labor Review* 96:4:41–45.

Fuchs, Victor R. 1969. Comment. In *Six papers on the size distribution of wealth and income,* ed. Lee Soltow. *Studies in Income and Wealth* 33. New York: National Bureau of Economic Research.

Grossman, Michael. 1972. *The demand for health: a theoretical and empirical investigation.* NBER Occasional Paper No. 119. New York and London: Columbia University Press for the NBER.

Havighurst, Robert J. 1975. The future aged: the use of time and money. *The Gerontologist,* 15:1:10–15.

Institute of Social Research. 1974. *Five thousand families.* Ann Arbor: University of Michigan.

Kreps, Juanita M. 1971. *Lifetime allocation of work and income: essays in the economics of aging.* Durham, North Carolina: Duke University Press.

Mathews, Linda. 1975. Justices grant equal benefits to widowers: Social Security law denying aid to men with children voided. *Los Angeles Times,* XCIV (20 March 1975), p. 1, col. 4.

McCall, John J. 1970. Economics of information and job search. *Quarterly Journal of Economics* 84:113–126.

Michael, Robert. 1972. *The effect of education on efficiency in consumption.* New York: National Bureau of Economic Research.

Morgan, James N. 1975. Economic problems of the aging and their policy implications. Paper for the conference on Public Policy Assessment of the Condition and Status of the Elderly, Santa Barbara, California, 14–15 February 1975.

Morgan, James N. 1965. Measuring the economic status of the aged. *International Economic Review* 6:1:1–17.

Musgrave, Richard A. 1968. The role of social insurance in an overall program. In *The American system of social insurance: its philosophy, impact, and future development,* eds. William G. Bowen et al. New York: McGraw-Hill Book Company.

Orshansky, Mollie. 1968. The shape of poverty in 1966. *Social Security Bulletin* 31:3–32.

Pechman, Joseph A.; Aaron, Henry J.; Taussig, Michael K. 1968. *Social Security—perspectives for reform.* Washington, D.C.: The Brookings Institution.

Reder, M. 1969. Theory of frictional unemployment. *Economica* 36:141:1–28.

Schulz, James, et. al. 1974. *Providing adequate retirement income in the United States and abroad.* Hanover, New Hampshire: University Press of New England.

Schulz, James. 1971. *Retirement: background and issues.* 1971 White House Conference on Aging. Washington, D.C.: Government Printing Office.

Schwab, Karen. 1974. Early labor-force withdrawal of men: participants and nonparticipants aged 58–63. *Social Security Bulletin* 37:8:24–38.

Sheppard, Harold L. 1971. *New perspectives on older workers.* Kalamazoo, Michigan: Upjohn Institute.

Smith, James P. 1975. On the labor-supply effects of age-related income-maintenance programs. *Journal of Human Resources* 10:1:25–43.

Smith, Ralph E.; Vanski, Jean E.; and Holt, Charles C. 1974. Recession and the employment of demographic groups. *Brookings Papers on Economic Activity,* eds. Arthur M. Okun and George L. Perry, 3:737–760. Washington, D.C.: The Brookings Institution.

Sobel, Irvin, and Folk, Hugh. 1965. Labor market adjustments by unemployed older workers. In *Employment policy and the labor market,* ed. Arthur M. Ross. Berkeley and Los Angeles: University of California Press.

Taussig, Michael K. 1973. *Alternative measures of the distribution of economic welfare.* Research Report Series No. 116, Industrial Relations Section, Department of Economics, Princeton University.

United States Bureau of the Census. 1974. Characteristics of the low-income population, 1973. *Current Population Reports, Consumer Income,* Series P-60, No. 94.

United States Congress. 1974a. Joint Economic Committee. How income supplements can affect work behavior. *Studies in Public Welfare,* Paper No. 13. Washington, D.C.: Government Printing Office.

United States Congress. 1974b. Joint Economic Committee. *Income security for Americans: recommendations of the public welfare study.* Washington, D.C.: Government Printing Office.

United States Department of Health Education and Welfare. 1975. *Reports of the advisory council on Social Security.* Washington, D.C.: Government Printing Office.

Weisbrod, Burton A. and Hansen, W. Lee. 1968. An income-net worth approach to measuring economic welfare. *American Economic Review* 58:5:1317–1329.

17

Public Policy and Aging: Analytic Approaches

PAUL A. KERSCHNER · IRA S. HIRSCHFIELD

In this chapter we will look at the premises upon which legislation involving America's elderly is based, and then analyze the relationship of this framework to delivery systems and public policy outcomes. It will be posited that policy outcomes, whether positive or negative, are a direct result of four prevailing approaches to the legislative process.

Traditionally, when public policy failures occur, Americans rely on the restructuring of internal organizational processes as a means of improving public service programs. When problems arise in the operation or delivery of public programs, we typically look to their organizational context for relief. Wilcox (1969) documents this pattern and states that the alteration of agency structure has become the vehicle for change in the minds of many authorities in the field of organizational theory and analysis.

This major approach to and philosophy of changing public policy stems from a "sickness model," which assumes that any pathology lies at the end of the policy train—in the operationalizing agency—rather than at the beginning within the offices of the legislator and his policy development staff. Although there is little supportive evidence for the notion that reorganization of public agencies brings about public policy effectiveness, many organizational models still recommend the "curative" approach. Major surgery or administrative transplants in the form of systems reorganization and structural gerrymandering remain the typical suggestions.

We are now learning the hard way that if legislation is written with insufficient data concerning the nature of the problem or, even worse, with inaccurate data, no amount of structural manipulation will result in clear and accurate policy outcomes. In contrast to the structural manipulation approach is the strategy to be presented in this chapter. We will begin by examining the genesis of the problem, namely, the basis upon which policy makers enact legislation in the field of aging.

There are four model dichotomies from which legislation often is formulated: *Categorical versus Generic; Holistic versus Segmented; Crisis versus Rational;* and *Political Context versus Future Planning*. After explaining these model dichotomies, we will examine each of them in juxtaposition to the major legislative enactments for older Americans: Health Care, Housing, and Income Maintenance. In addition to the information provided from this legislative analysis, we will present alternative approaches to public policy investigation.

The traditional methods of exploring public policy have focused on the bureaucratic process, the organizational structure, or the service delivery system. Hopefully, the perspective provided in this chapter will be of use to those wishing to influence legislative procedure.

Model Public Policy Dichotomies

Categorical Versus Generic

Legislation in aging traditionally has suffered from a lack of understanding of the clientele it intends to assist. The proverbial question is whether the aged should be singled out categorically for purposive and specific age-oriented action, or whether they should be only one segment of a larger generic grouping and thus forced to compete for attention, programs, and funds. Any discussion of service programs for the elderly in the United States inevitably turns to the issue of categorical versus noncategorical programs. How do we best serve the elderly: by improving services for all groups, including the elderly, or by singling out the pressing and sometimes unique problems of the elderly for intensive action in hopes that some day such individual programs can become part of a more comprehensive system? The debate between these two groups continues to rage within legislative, as well as gerontological circles, indicating the need for a clear philosophy from which to design public policy.

The same discussion also occurs within federal agencies. Here it centers on the placement of resources within an autonomous bureau controlling its own network of delivery systems. The prevailing situation, however, is the proliferation of resources and responsibilities in and among a variety of agencies and departments, with a minimum of responsibility or autonomy. The issue of nutrition and aging exemplifies this proliferation of resources and responsibilities. The Department of Agriculture and Labor and the Administration on Aging each handle varying components of the nutrition issue. No single agency coordinates these efforts and the consequences are inefficiency, repetition, and competition. As the aged disappear into and suffer from the morass created by this system, there is compelling evidence that a *categorical* stance is vitally needed.

This conflict in "strategy" strikes at the heart of the policy initiation process. Accepting the *generic* approach, whereby the aged are one among many groups to be affected by legislation, public policy makers can use a more general data base than would be necessary if they were solely applying a categorical approach. For example, in the development of a mass transit system serving a total (*generic*) population, there is a need to know the specific preferences of the aged (routes, times, costs, accessibility). Given the limitations in available resources, however, these preferences may be disregarded in an effort to serve the larger population.

If, on the other hand, one utilizes the *categorical* approach, whereby legislation and programs are tailored exclusively to the requisities of older adults, then the data base must be absolutely accurate as well as focused, or it may well be destructive to the well-being of the user population. For example, a mass feeding program designed for the elderly should be structured around a detailed knowledge of age-related issues such as diet, eating periods, and group versus individual preferences.

Legislation affecting the aged has been neither wholly categorical nor wholly generic in approach. What has occurred is a continual shifting between the two approaches, resulting in chaos within the public policy process. It would not be inappropriate to use the analogy of an individual who constantly is having to shift between cooking for one person and cooking for a family of ten. It should be easily recognized that he would be dealing with two distinct types of data bases with varying needs for specificity and accuracy. The Social Security Administration, like the alternating chef, once served primarily the aged, but now has expanded its scope to also include the blind, poor, disabled, and dependent survivors. It, like many organizations, has had to reorient itself to serving a more comprehensive population. Such a reorientation often results in greater inefficiency and inadequate delivery of services to its recipients.

In summarizing the categorical versus generic approach, it is useful to quote from the British experience:

> Services for the elderly, whether medical services or social services, may be integrated with services for other age groups or developed separately. Proponents of integrated services argue that unless special provisions are made for the elderly, the low status of this group among professional workers and the general public will result in their being ignored in program planning and resource allocation. (U.S. Senate, 1971, p. 5)

The Holistic Versus The Segmented

In addition to the categorical issue, those initiating policy in the aging field appear to have had difficulty addressing the older adult in anything but a segmented manner. For too many years we have divided the aged individual into segments separated in much the same manner that a butcher sorts out cuts of beef. Essentially, we have categorized the aged into selective needs, and then passed legislation and designed programs to address those specific needs. Thus, as we peruse the national and state aging scene, we discover a landscape dotted with specialized divisions: Institutional Care, Home Health Care, Supplemental Security Income, Nutrition and Recreation.

The result of this segmentation has been a twofold dilemma. First, legislative formulation, already suffering from the categorical versus generic difficulty, has not reflected the integration of data resulting from other aged programs and legislation, but rather has been contrived within a vacuum of isolated and unrelated information. Secondly, the older adults who have attempted to utilize those segmented services have been required to visit a number of agencies, most often geographically distant from one another. They not only have been forced to assemble their own constellation of services, but also have had to struggle with the difficult task of securing access to them.

The structure of social service agencies in this country has contributed greatly to the exacerbation of the segmented versus holistic approach. Few departments of social services have created a protective services unit for older adults. The lack of such units is all the more puzzling given the success of protective services for children. Indeed, it could be argued that since children have many surrogate parents available to them (such as courts, adoption agencies, foster parents, big brothers) existing resources should be spent on the aged, who are largely without protectors.

Taking a holistic approach has been one of the most difficult tasks for policy makers, for our natural inclination is to "hone in" on those problems which are most visible and amenable to solution. Thus, the segmented, divide-and-conquer approach appears to be both humane and productive, although it could be argued that it further divides and dehumanizes the older adult.

Political Context Versus Future Planning

Social legislation, at the time of its enactment, reflects the values of the society it represents. In other words, public policy is a reflection of what the times, or better yet, the market will bear. Legislation consistently is based on prevailing social standards and conditions of the present, and rarely on the anticipated needs of the future. Public policy, therefore, is usually reactive and seldom proactive (initiatory).

The political context approach requires the ability to sense society's readiness to accept certain new policies or legislation. One example is the passage of the Workmen's Compensation Act. Political folklore presents Franklin Roosevelt as being prepared, in the 1930s, to introduce a form of National Health Insurance to Congress and the nation. His secretary of labor, Francis Perkins, convinced him that Congress would accept this idea at any time and advised him to defer its introduction in order to devote full attention to passing the then controversial issue of Workmen's Compensation. We will never be able to determine if the American society would have accepted National Health Insurance at that time, but the example of Perkins's assessment of Congress, based on its "buying" mood, is a classic example of operating within a political context rather than future planning (Lansdale, 1972).

Similarly, given the bitter climate which evolved around the Medicare issue, it would have been impossible for Lyndon Johnson's Congress to have written a bill focusing on outpatient and preventive medicine rather than on curative and institutional care. Even in 1965, a year of sky-rocketing health costs, society was far too distant from the concept of national health insurance even to consider it. Instead, it opted for the more conservative approach of Medicare.

The tragic elements of this approach, from a public policy perspective, are that most legislation in aging evolves not from a group of policy scientists drafting programs for the future, but rather from some pragmatic assumptions about what will be tolerated by the dominant forces in the society.

Crisis Versus Rational Approach

It has long been known that a vast percentage of public policy has been derived from the onset of a crisis. The Social Security Act, for example, did not grow out of a long-planned move to insert the federal government into the economy on a massive scale. Rather, the Social Security Act was a direct outgrowth of the crisis of the Depression. Once the initial shock hit and people began to lose their jobs, it became apparent that older workers were being deprived of occupations, incomes and savings.

The three major health programs serving the elderly, as well as other age groups, also resulted from the onset of a crisis. The Medical Assistance for the Aged Program, Title XIX of the Social Security Act (Medicaid—for the medically indigent), and Title XVIII of the Social Security Act (Medicare—those for the 65 and over) grew from the health care cost crisis sweeping the nation in the 1960s. An additional example is the Supplemental Security Income Program (Title XVI of the Social Security Act) which provided federal control of the state-operated payment programs for the aged, blind and disabled. The Supplemental program was hastily enacted in part to calm the dismay resulting from the failure to enact the far broader Family Assistance Proposal (HRI).

This demonstration of the "crisis reaction" process contradicts the administrative purists who deny the crisis theme and yet continue to rail against the poor conceptual framework of public policy. They somehow are convinced that public policy emerges out of a rational examination of the available facts and pertinent data. We posit this to be far from accurate, since experts cannot even agree on what is considered to be a sound conceptual framework. In analyzing a series of issues like the economy, the anti-ballistic system, and age-related topics, we immediately can line up experts on each side of the debates, who all claim patents on the key to rational planning. Scientific data is useful but not the magic word to opening the door to rational policy making. We can listen to economic experts like Schultz, Samuelson, Friedman, and Galbraith. We can examine pages of statistical facts verifying the overwhelming numbers of older Americans suffering from malnutrition, and we can read about the mortality rates in the Sudan. Yet the hard core facts are not simply the statistics or the deaths. Facts can reveal crisis situations daily, but change cannot occur unless this information gets into the right hands, and is subsequently communicated to and accepted by the general public.

We are suggesting here that given the resultant stalemates of the dilemmas created by categorical versus generic approaches, holistic versus segmented programming, current political context versus future planning designs, and crisis versus rational planning, aging legislation has been caught in a morass of conflicting and competing interests and issues. The result of these fragmented approaches is that in most cases involving major aging legislation, policy makers have abdicated moral responsibility by passing laws based on flimsy and often inaccurate data. At the same time, researchers in the field of gerontology have all but ceased to provide any current data useful for drafting legislation. They have often despaired over being able to influence the policy process.

To illustrate the problems of these four approaches to political decision making, let us examine the recent major pieces of legislation for the aged. It will become apparent that our public policy makers have opted, primarily, for the categorical, segmented, politically acceptable and crisis-oriented approach to political decision making.

Health Care (Medicare and Medicaid)

The basic goal of Title XVIII of the Social Security Act (Medicare) has been to provide America's older adults with financial protection against the heavy costs associated with hospital, nursing home, and physician care. The President's and Congress' choice of aged as the population category to be served was based not so much on an overwhelming concern for the older person but rather on a compromise hammered out with the organized medical profession which had vehemently opposed most public policy in the medical care field.

Once the political decision had been made and the program designed categorically, an immediate search should have begun to uncover and validate the specific health problems of the aging. The development of a health program based on the needs of older adults required accurate research data in the areas of utilization patterns of older persons, types and incidence of disease prevalent in older adults, percentage of illnesses resulting in restricted mobility, and health spending patterns of older persons including funds spent on preventive care. What occurred, however, was an initial policy decision to "go categorical" with a subsequent legislative and administrative move to ignore the data needed to create a categorical program.

The decision on a categorical emphasis with little knowledge or use of a sophisticated data base has had long-term and tragic implications for the older person. The discussion in recent years of the need for alternatives to institutionalization, and the demand that we get those 25 percent of all inappropriately placed nursing home residents back into their homes (Kerschner, 1973) is a result of that ill-planned categorical decision. There was little investigation of the use older persons would make of services such as day hospitals or outpatient clinics. As it became clear that there were few reimburseable outpatient services available, older adults had no choice but to go into institutions, thus increasing the total Medicare bill and adding to the notion that what was needed were more institutional services (namely beds). While many citizens have become aware of the vicious circle being created, public policy has yet to alter significantly its original direction or scope.

As the legislative process in 1965 moved to develop and clarify the Medicare Act, it became obvious to many in the health care field that not only was the categoric system being subjected to generic-like manipulation, but also that Congress was opting for a fragmented rather than comprehensive approach. The legislators had an opportunity to devise legislation and put into operation a program which would have addressed the total health needs of the total person. They lost the opportunity to provide coverage for varying types and levels of care, which would have ensured that only a minimum of health care needs went unaddressed and unfinanced.

Research conducted at Brandeis University, the University of Southern California, and by the Senate Special Committee on Aging indicates the overwhelming need for preventive and home-based medical care for older adults. Even with these numerous studies indicating that older adults require services beyond those which are offered within health care institutions, the Medicare Act concentrates almost exclusively upon inpatient care.

The passage of Medicare represented a major departure in the financing of health care in this nation; it did not, however, represent a radical shift in health care quality, quantity, or mode of delivery. Partly as a result of the segmented and categorical approach discussed earlier, health care for the aged, poor, and disabled has gone in the direction of less coverage and higher costs. In 1972, the average person 65 and over paid $42 more out of pocket expenses for his medical care than he did in 1964, one year prior to passage of the Medicare Act (Glasser, 1974). Even with staggering inflation, a plan which is touted as being low cost, categorical, and comprehensive should more than "hold-the-line" in its coverage of personal expenditures.

This continual increase in personal cost is due, in large part, to the acceptance of a basic "myth" put forth at the time of the Act's passage and reinforced by later segmental decisions. Because factual data was overlooked or disregarded, the assumption was that the elderly primarily would utilize inpatient care, the coverage of which was relatively extensive under Medicare. What transpired, however, was that the aged increasingly required, or desired, preventive outpatient services, the costs of which were usually personally borne. Glasser's Senate testimony is instructive in this regard: in 1973, Medicare covered less than 50 percent of the personal health costs of the individuals in the aged and poor and disabled class. Almost 50 percent of the aged in 1973 did not have supplemental insurance coverage in addition to Medicare, leaving a substantial portion unable to meet their share of the medical bills (Glasser, 1974). A more damaging figure is one quoted by former Health, Education and Welfare Secretary, Wilbur J. Cohen. He revealed that in 1967 only about 10 percent of persons 60 years and over visited private physicians for general medical examinations. If, as Cohen continues, ". . . no fewer than 86 percent of all persons 65 years and over have one or more abnormalities" (Cohen, 1968, p. 14), then surely the basic tenets of the Medicare Act contain some rather glaring deficiencies.

It is obvious that the inconsistencies are great. Only 10 percent of the elderly visited private physicians, yet at least 86 percent have one or more abnormalities. People are spending more time utilizing outpatient care and yet money continues to be poured into inpatient services. Medicare has not satisfactorily addressed the needs of the older person and a major share of the blame lies with its original philosophy. Those early decisions, which were categorically and segmentally based, forced the scope and direction of the program towards a bias of institutionalization (inpatient care).

A recitation of the financial figures produces a litany reinforcing the belief that the decision to make Medicare basically an inpatient service 1) was not based on any "real" data as to older patient utilization and 2) has resulted in a movement over the years which has reinforced and increased rather than evened-out the institutional bias. The Special Committee on Aging of the United States Senate reported 1971 Medicare reimbursement figures as follows:

Inpatient hospital	$5,026,025
Extended care	$ 167,834
Home health	$ 40,771
Outpatient hospital	$ 104,778
Physicians	$1,748,270

(U.S. Senate, July 1973, p.54)

The discrepancy among the figures clearly shows that either outpatient and physician care is not required or desired by older adults, or that the system forces inpatient utilization. We suggest that the latter is the predominant case. The same source reports bed disability days of the over 65 population as 1.29 days of bed disability per person per year (1969). In 1969 only 1.3 percent of Medicare beneficiaries were hospitalized 61 days or more. These figures suggest a need for an immediate reordering of health care services to older adults. A study under the auspices of the State of Maryland found that many older adults indicated that a major unmet need was that of easily accessible and reimburseable outpatient services. In an open-ended discussion with the same group, a majority indicated that they would allow themselves to be placed in a hospital or nursing home for reasons of payment rather than for the facility's ability to meet their specific health requirements (Kerschner, 1973).

In the area of health care, it has become increasingly clear that policy makers at the federal level have responded to pragmatic political realities instead of to clear indications of the type of services desired and required by the older adult. (The recent proposals of National Health Insurance appear to acknowledge this past flaw, for the majority of them reflect a movement toward the preventive side of the health delivery system.) Although there should have been extensive inquiry into and use of age-related data, we know that due to the political pressures in the environment, the program did not reflect the critical needs of the elderly. Instead, Medicare reflected what the politicans could safely legislate at the time.

Many significant activities were occurring in 1965. Bills for health care were requiring astronomical sums and the Older American Act and the War on Poverty were beginning their legislative lives. It was obvious that the poor, disadvantaged, and elderly would require a specific and comprehensive focus. Some form of health insurance would have to be passed if we were to protect the health of our older citizens. The current political atmosphere appears to have been the critical factor in deciding the final form of legislation. In view of John Kennedy's death, Lyndon Johnson's legislative power, the vast sums of money being channelled into the battle by the American Medical Association, and the conservative's fear of socialized medicine, it appears that legislators considered the prevailing political climate and built a system they hoped would be open to incremental changes during subsequent years.

We posit that the final Medicare Bill, as well as the regulations which preceded it, did not reflect the accumulated data available regarding the health needs of older adults. Rather, it was based on the prevailing environmental constraints, opposing political pressures and growing crisis-like atmosphere. Thus, the realities of constructing public policy in 1965 precluded the possibility of a revolutionary piece of health care legislation.

We have stated that in order to devise a health plan for older Americans, we first must become knowledgeable about their health needs. Then a system must be developed which utilizes this data in a comprehensive delivery scheme. Medicare was a major breakthrough in the battle to ensure older adults access to health care. Yet, it has been built upon a shaky philosophical foundation unbuttressed by solid data.

Now it is up to the researchers and public policy makers to cooperate in insuring that the next phase is constructed upon a more solid foundation. We must move to a point where health care legislation has a knowledge, rather than a political-mood, base. The solution appears readily accessible, yet in reality, its application is exceedingly difficult. For in order to actually succeed, statistically sound scientific data will have to take precedence over the fierce lobbying powers and intense political pressures that bear down upon our legislators.

Housing

Another area in which legislation for the elderly currently exists is housing. There is a close association between the need for legislation on housing for the elderly and for legislation on medical care. Both involve the need for alternatives to institutionalization. Health officials have difficulty deciding to discharge elderly patients from mental hospitals and nursing homes if sufficient and appropriate housing suitable for these displaced individuals does not exist.

In an attempt to ameliorate the housing problem there has been substantial national legislation providing for the planning, development, and construction of housing specifically designed for occupancy by elderly persons. We will present the most significant of these housing acts followed by commentary linking this legislation to the four models previously discussed. (Also see the Annual Reports of the U.S. Senate Special Committee on Aging, U.S. Senate, published annually by the Committee since its inception in 1959).

The 1956 Amendments to the National Housing Act. These Amendments authorized mortgage-insurance financing of cooperative housing and nonprofit housing for the aged. In addition, they required local public housing authorities to give first priority to the aged in their admission policies, and removed the then legal prohibition to housing of single elderly widows and widowers in federally subsidized housing projects.

It is apparent that prior to the 1956 amendments, the categorical versus generic issue had been a critical one. Because no specific quota of elderly was specified they were forced to compete for public housing with the general population, many of whom could argue greater need because of their dependent children. This same rationale based on dependent children was used to disallow single elderly access to public housing. It was argued that providing housing for single elderly was poor use of limited housing resources.

The 1959 Amendments to the National Housing Act. These Amendments also authorized housing programs for the aging. Section 202 provided a direct, long-term, low-cost loan program designed for those with moderate incomes. Section 231 was a mortgage insurance program designed for those with above average incomes as well as for strengthening and expanding low-rent public housing for the elderly.

The enactment of these Amendments is representative of the holistic versus segmented issue as well as of the political context versus future planning approach. It was assumed that through the provision of low-cost monies, the needs of older citizens could be met. What was ignored, however, is that the mere provision of a roof and walls addresses only one of the many needs of older adults. Missing, for example, were the needed provisions for both health and social services. Yet once again, as in the case of Title XVIII (Medicare), it was believed that legislation with an incremental approach, the expansion and alteration of which could take place over time, stood the best chance for passage and implementation.

The Amendments to the Housing Act of 1964, P.L. 88–560. These Amendments further expanded the low-rent public housing program and included specific provisions for relocation assistance, relocation rental assistance, and rehabilitation loans. In addition, they extended the rural mortgage insurance program of housing for the elderly.

The 1964 Amendments expanded the incremental improvements begun earlier, but remained anchored within a segmented base, using monetary reimbursement as the panacea for improving the general standard of living. The assumption appears to have been that money would or could be translated into services by the recipient, a thesis unsupported by both past and present data.

The Housing and Urban Development Act of 1965. This act extended the existing federally-assisted housing programs for the elderly and authorized grants for home rehabilitation and neighborhood facilities in addition to rental supplements. This was the first time that the Housing Act included provisions for neighborhood facilities, thus appearing to reflect a change to a slightly more holistic philosophy. However, there was little if any integration of the housing and service components except on a very isolated, demonstration-project basis.

The Housing and Urban Development Act of 1968. This act called for a further extension of a number of existing federal housing programs including rent supplements and Model City Programs. Section 236 of this act provided interest subsidies for moderate-income housing programs sponsored by nonprofit organizations.

It was Section 236 which finally began to move the federal government from the posture of reactor to that of a proactive catalyst. It was hoped that the growth of Section 236 would attract segments of the private building market in numbers sufficient enough to make a dent in the documented need for moderate income elderly housing. The exciting aspect of this housing act was that nonprofit organizations were tuned in to the categorical as well as holistic approach.

The 1969 National Housing Act.   This act included such provisions as increased authorization for the Section 202 direct loan program, and limited rents fixed by public housing agencies to no more than 25 percent of a tenant's income. It mandated that in instances of urban renewal, for every housing unit razed a new, low-income unit would have to be built in the city or county involved.

In the housing arena, this act reflected little deviation from the existing philosophy of the federal government. HUD was still operating from a "segmented" base and with an apparently limited perception of the existing "social climate."

In any discussion of a framework underlying housing programs for the aged, one must relate the reason for the framework to the larger social trends existing in the country at the time. Although it is true that during the late 1950s and the 1960s the Department of Housing and Urban Development moved to fund and develop large-scale, high-rise facilities for the aged poor, it must be acknowledged that the emphasis was upon high-rise dwellings for low income persons in general. This emphasis upon the generic approach assured that assumptions which proved invalid for the poor were equally inaccurate for the aged. Seemingly, the final results of the large high-rise developments were generally increased crime, greater social disorganization and the breakup of family and community ties.

We have previously mentioned that much of this housing was not built solely for older people. However, a few thoughts on the ramification of these high-rise dwellings for the elderly are in order. Studies, beginning with those in Boston (Fried, 1963), have indicated that when the elderly are subjected to relocation, subsequent moving traumas and isolation occur. Regardless of the improvement in their environments/conditions, their death rates rise precipitously. Once living in these high-rise apartments, many older people found themselves far removed from their families and friends. The large buildings, long corridors, numerous elevators, and masses of people added to their isolation. The friendliness, familiarity, and closeness of their past dwelling experience had been completely removed from them. Instead of the familiar, albeit unclean, horizontally located ghettos, the elderly found themselves in lonely, unadaptable vertical ghettos.

In addition, private developers and builders have not aided the impoverished elderly in any significant manner. For many years the construction of new housing for low income and elderly persons has been by and large an unprofitable venture. Section 236 started to attract a lot of private developers, but since it has ended, very little private money has been freed for "low cost" housing.

Generally, in the area of public housing, decisions have been made "in spite" of the elderly and not because of them. It is likely that the recent housing act occurred in part as a result of the heavy lobbying of private real estate interests.

Perhaps the assumption most difficult to destroy is that public housing could make a dramatic impact upon the general housing situation. It might be posited that public housing is a drop in the bucket, with its major attribute being that of allowing the general public to collectively state, "see, we are doing something." Obviously, when 50 percent of single family households over 65 are living below the poverty level, a massive and comprehensive assistance program is needed. We would need billions of dollars actually to help people find or afford decent housing.

Rather than dwell on a point which should now be clear, namely, that housing for the elderly was derived from some rather questionable assumptions, we can sum up the housing program by providing a discussion of some major issues which are in need of attention by those designing future housing programs:

1. Immediate attention must be given to the rising incidence of crimes committed against the elderly living in deteriorated neighborhoods and public housing projects. The deterioration of the housing projects may very well be a direct result of the segmented approach, wherein housing has been seen as a self-standing, non-integrated solution separate from social and health needs.
2. Despite legislation which is trying to address increased rates, the elderly homeowner faces the continuing problem and burden of rising property taxes. The flurry of activity on this issue around election time is a good example of the crisis versus rational approach to planning for the elderly.

Existing housing programs are not meeting the need for specially designed housing for low and moderate income older people. Although there are existing laws which require all buildings funded with federal money to be barrier free (by eliminating such physical barriers as stoops) the provisions are either not sharply drawn or no one is willing to enforce the regulations. This is a good example of the importance of implementing existing legislation. If federal funds were cut off on projects not including barrier-free access, it is most probable that the projects would be designed to include features such as ramps, lower curbs, wider doors and accessible bath facilities. (In this regard see Chapter 13).

Income Maintenance

The majority of the elderly in this country are dependent upon some type of retirement income to pay for their basic needs. Their standard of living is determined largely by the adequacy of civilian and military pensions, Social Security and for the poorest of poor, public assistance. Thus, the elderly are primarily dependent on the efforts and paternalism of others. Herman Brotman, formerly with the Administration on Aging, has very aptly described the posture of the aged in this regard:

> When someone retires, he does not have a basement stuffed with goods and services he will need for the rest of his life. For him, as for everyone else, practically everything consumed comes out of the current production of goods and services. The owners, the managers and the members of the labor force exercise first claim. The non-producers, including the aged, get a share based mostly on the producers' willingness to share. The size of the aged's share is determined by how much purchasing power is transferred to them. Methods of financing and the like are important, but incidental. It comes down to the younger group's willingness to share—in other words, on the ordering of our national priorities. (Brotman, 1973, Vol. 11, No. 1)

In short, there is no program of adequate, standardized care for our aged. Social Security and Old Age Assistance (now SSI) do not provide incomes that meet even officially-defined poverty levels. In fact, 16 percent of the elderly in our country live below this income line. Sixteen percent translates into well over three million old people who live a poverty stricken existence. Income is only one aspect of the problem. It is closely related, for example, to the issue of long-term care, when a person is in need of continued medical and personal care assistance. Without adequate finances, however, it is impossible to pay for that care, let alone receive the nutrition necessary to maintain an adequate diet.

The natural inclination has been to focus on the need for increased funds. This emphasis, however, is a good example of the segmented approach as it relates to program design for income maintenance. Even though 70 percent of the elderly are living above the government's poverty income level, and even though there is an emphasis on upgrading those below the poverty line, our approach still is a segmented one focusing solely on the economic aspects and thus refusing to concentrate on the total human being. To provide only enough money to pay for basic essentials while ignoring accompanying life support requirements is to ignore the overall needs of the person, in favor of placing bandaids on a few of his critical wounds. If one analyzes the major financial programs provided for older adults, it becomes clear that each is representative of one of the policy models or approaches presented throughout this chapter.

Private Retirement Plans

Today private retirement plans are an important economic mechanism for providing income for old age. These plans have shown significant growth since 1950, when pension plans first became accepted as a proper issue for collective bargaining. This was a result of the Supreme Court's decision in the 1949 Inland Steel case. As retirement coverage has grown, so have the number of beneficiaries—450,000 in 1950, 1.8 million in 1960, and 3.8 million in 1968. Benefit payments likewise have increased over the years, rising from $370 million in 1950 to $1.8 billion in 1960 and up to more than $5 billion in 1968 (Yung-ping, 1971).

The above statistics convey the impression that private retirement plans have gained considerable ground in terms of their support for the aged. In 1967, however, only 19 percent of married couples, 13 percent of nonmarried men and 5 percent of nonmarried women received private pension payments. It is obvious that there is a gap between the large number of employees covered (28.2 million in 1968) and the relatively small number of pensioners.

A number of factors have contributed to this discrepancy. First, companies go out of business and the pension plan is dissolved, leaving the workers with little or none of the retirement investment they had earned. Another circumstance may be the failure of the retirement plan itself through financial mismanagement or even corruption and misuse of assets. The long absence of vesting provisions is another explanation for the proportionately small number of pension plan beneficiaries. Vesting is the right of a participant in a pension plan to receive his accrued benefits if he discontinues his employment. Plans to provide vesting have been on the increase in recent years, but it is estimated that currently about a quarter of the private pension plans have no vesting provision. Closely related to vesting is the portability of pension investment. If, as is now generally conceded, the employer's contribution to an employee's pension fund is part of his renumeration and is a charge of his ongoing business, the employee clearly has a right to his accrued pension credits when he leaves his employment, whether voluntarily or involuntarily. While both vesting and portability have been receiving increased attention in the Congress and to a more limited extent from the present administration, constructive measures to protect the rights and financial investments of workers in private employment are essential.

Although recent reform legislation has significantly tightened the pension system, it is the basic approach which we question. The reforms do not reflect concerted long-term planning. Rather they are indicative of those incremental changes acceptable to both the Congress and the general public.

Retirement Benefits under Social Security

These benefits are the single most important source of income for the retired aged. As of December 1971, 853 persons of every 1,000 persons aged 65+ were receiving cash benefits. The Social Security Administration reports that as of January 1973, of the population 65 and over, 91 percent were eligible for Social Security retirement benefits, 4 percent were eligible for benefits under other federal retirement systems, and 5 percent were not eligible under any federal retirement system. By 1985, it is estimated that these proportions will be 94 percent, 4 percent and 2 percent respectively.

The average monthly cash benefit paid by Social Security for the month of November 1972, and the average cash benefit awarded in that month can be seen in Table 17.1. It should be obvious that Social Security payments are not sufficient to match an individual's preretirement standard of living.

The total number of Retirement Insurance beneficiaries 62+, the number by sex, and the average monthly payment for September, 1972 are seen in Table 17.2.

It is difficult to attack an institution as venerated as the Social Security Administration. Yet, as perhaps the single most visible age-related program, we must seek to purge it of any misconceptions originally included in its legislation or inherently acquired over the years.

Social Security was, and is, intended to be a postretirement income *supplement*. As such, it assumes that:

1. the individual is able to save for retirement;
2. pensions provide for *decent primary* retirement income;
3. older people require less and thus can afford to live on less.

We think that the above statistics and the annual congressional scramble to raise Social Security payments indicate the inadquacy of this program as an income supplement. Attempts by the Ford administration to hold Social Security payments down as an inflation fighting device indicate that public policy tools can be a two-edged sword. Although we might argue in favor of the categorical approach as an advocacy device insuring

Table 17.1 Average monthly cash benefits from Social Security, November 1972

	Average benefit Nov. 1972	Average award Nov. 1972	Monthly benefits Nov. 1972 (thousands)
Retired workers 62+	162.00	169.50	$2,341,628
Wives and husbands	83.95	80.30	229,066
Special age, 72 benefits	57.19	57.35	28,831

SOURCE: *Social Security Bulletin,* March 1973, pp. 13–22.

further aid for the aged, it can also be used to select the aged out of support programs necessary for retaining a decent standard of living.

Supplemental Security Income Program

Under the Social Security Amendments of 1972, the combined fed-
eral-state programs of Old Age Assistance, Aid to the Blind, and Aid to
the Totally Disabled were repealed. A new federal program known as
Supplemental Security Income, administered by the Social Security Administration, became operative on January 1, 1973. Individuals or couples are
eligible for assistance if their monthly income is less than the standard
payment (for basic living costs) of $146 a month per person and $219 for
an individual with an eligible spouse.

This program, then, provides funds for those elderly in abject poverty
or who are blind or disabled. While SSI is a major first step towards a
comprehensive program to provide an income floor for older adults, its
philosophy, rules and regulations perpetuate many of the inadequacies
contained in the former state-operated welfare programs. First, it is assumed that federally-based, means-tested (recipient must prove poverty)
programs are less acceptable to the elderly than to the poor in general.
This is true, it is argued, due in large part to their relatively recent entry
into the poverty category. Secondly, the SSI program appears to legitamize
the invalid assumption that lump sum payments are sufficient tools for
raising one's standard of living. Professionals in the field continue to be
concerned about the deterioration in services required over and above
the availability of cash.

The SSI program has exacerbated rather than ameliorated the trend
towards service denigration and elimination. In this regard, the following
comments in an administrative memorandum by Robert Ball, the former
Commissioner of Social Security, are significant:

> Social Security has always resisted becoming a center for the provision
> of social services, but it has willingly accepted the responsibility for
> knowing about community resources, for participating in their develop-

Table 17.2   Retirement insurance beneficiaries 62+, September 1972

	Number	Average monthly benefits
Male	8,164,514	$178.32
Female	6,229,987	139.34
Total	14,394,501	$161.45

SOURCE: *Social Security Bulletin,* March 1973, pp. 13–22.

ment, and for the operation of a referral service. This function has now been assigned to SSA by the President. A considerable upgrading of the service has already taken place, but it will not be possible to fully implement an advertised, in-depth service until after the implementation of the recent social security amendments (H.R. 1); the new legislation puts just too many additional demands on SSA offices to make this feasible. (Ball, February 8, 1973)

Not only is the SSA unwilling to provide its own service, but also it has made it extremely difficult for the aged individual to link up with services provided by outside agencies. This provision of income without service reflects the classic segmented model. Once again, we reiterate that programs providing only money cannot help to solve the multi-faceted needs and problems of the elderly. Even if the Social Security Administration successfully survived the onerous burdens thrust upon it beginning in 1965, the problems it has in administering the SSI program are greater than Medicare and the other post-1965 changes.

SSI is a revolutionary way of dealing with old problems. It has shifted older people from established institutions (state welfare agencies) to a vast and untried operation within an agency already carrying a heavy load of related (Title II and Disability) but dissimilar activities. At some point we may come upon a crisis of such magnitude that it might destroy the Social Security operation. Although it would be a costly way of forcing change, this might lead to an appraisal of the federal government's role in providing financial support to poor, elderly and disabled adults.

Re-appraisal of the Federal Role

Some 28.5 million dollars in payments are being made from federal funds for retirement or disability benefits. The Supplemental Security Income program will add another five to six million dollars in payments. Moreover, it is anticipated that over the next few years, there will be a substantial rise in Military Retirement payments and in Veterans Compensation and Pensions.

Currently there is no high-level public policy body with sufficient clout to re-evaluate the federal role of providing financial aid to retired and disabled adults. No continuing examination is made of the financing of these programs. In addition, no critical analysis has been made of overlapping payments to individuals.

With the welfare of millions of elderly at stake, and in full recognition of the responsibility borne by younger workers, it would be highly desirable to analyze and appraise current federal programs for retired and disabled adults, as well as the retirement plans of private industry. We must develop policy recommendations to correct present inequities and to provide creative and responsible direction for future action.

Current statistics have revealed the need for a complete examination of possible new avenues of revenue for the SAA. According to present figures, Social Security payments are greatly exceeding the intake of taxed income. A Presidential Commission might serve to examine the whole area of the economics of aging in the United States in an effort to reform and perhaps reconstitute the system.

The relief for the problems described above may come about only from an overwhelmingly negative, crisis-oriented response. As the aged poor enter into critical situations in the areas of health, counseling, transportation and nutrition, our policy makers will have to realize that money is not a substitute for services, but rather a supplement. The services crisis may then result in new legislation seeking to integrate these two vital needs. Should a holistic approach be utilized, we then can move away from the notion of income floors *or* social services to a posture wherein the two are combined in a systematic manner.

Conclusion

Policy making is at best a complex and at worst an irrational and idiosyncratic process. It is a difficult procedure to explain, it is even more difficult to comprehend, and it is most difficult to undertake.

We have attempted to describe specific aspects of the policy process and their relationship to the design and operation of programs for the aged. It is appropriate that we provide the reader with some thoughts about the types of improvements and new directions that would be both possible and desirable.

Categorical versus Generic.   Pluralism in this nation is a viable system when all parties have an equal ability to enter the process. Given the plethora of interest groups dotting the landscape, successful competition requires that a group gather the power to bubble to and over the surface. It is our contention that until the aged caucus and organize themselves into a competitive power base capable of participating in pluralistic competition, the larger society will address their needs and problems in a categoric rather than generic manner. Once the aged have gained the necessary clout (through the efforts of groups such as the Grey Panthers or the American Association of Retired Persons and the National Retired Teacher Association), then we can reintroduce them into the policy "pot" and allow the fight for limited resources to continue. One example representing a categorical commitment to aging research is the newly formed National Institute on Aging.

Holistic versus Segmented.   There is yet another issue to face once policy makers have made the decision to deal with the aged as a specialized enclave. Through chronological tyranny the older person is subject to segmented deprivation. Year by year he loses his individuality, income, housing, health, friends and general sense of self esteem. The least the policy formulators can do is to design ameliorative programs in as holistic a manner as is possible.

Crisis versus Rational.   In a nation that appears bored during periods of non-crisis, the plea for rational planning may fall upon deaf ears. Those working in the field of service delivery must continually point out that the aged, as a group constantly "at risk," cannot afford to be subject to the whims and variations of crisis-based programs. Indeed, it might be better to consider launching fewer programs than to begin consistently from a crisis position which usually fails to retain its level of energy and commitment.

Political Context versus Future Planning.   There is an optimistic note in relation to policy making and the prevailing political atmosphere. The unanticipated consequences of our ill-planned policy of the past decade has given new life to the "art" of long-range planning. We may now move beyond the enactment of legislation which would antagonize the fewest people towards a futuristic stance designed to anticipate the needs of an ever increasing population of aging and aged peoples.

References

Ball, R. 1973. Administrative memorandum to social security employees. 8 February 1973.

Brotman, H. B. 1973. The aging: who and where. *Perspectives on aging,* 2:1 (Jan-Feb). Washington, D.C.: The National Council on Aging.

Cohen, W. J. 1968. HEW feasibility study on preventive services and health education for medicare recipients, a report to the Congress. December 1968.

Fried, M. 1963. Grieving for a lost home. In *The Urban Condition,* ed. L. J. Duhl. New York: Basic Books, Inc.

Glasser, M. A. 1974. Testimony regarding effects of administration comprehensive health insurance proposals on the elderly. United States Senate Special Committee on Aging, Sub-committee on Health of the Elderly.

Kerschner, P. A., ed. 1973. Report of the Governor's commission on nursing homes. State of Maryland.

Lansdale, R. T. 1972. From a private interview with P. A. Kerschner, Fall 1972.

U.S. Senate Special Committee on Aging. 1971. Making services for the elderly work: some lessons from the British experience.

————. 1971. Some health services in the U.S.: a working paper on current status.

————. Various. U.S. Senate Annual Report, published annually by the Committee since its inception in 1959.

Wilcox, H. G. 1969. Hierarchy, human nature, and the participative panacea. *Public Administration Review* 7:46–53.

18

Age and Political Behavior

NEAL E. CUTLER · JOHN R. SCHMIDHAUSER

Political scientists who are interested in the relationship between age and political behavior seek answers to a variety of questions. For example, since they are generally interested in explanations of why people vote, why they participate in other kinds of political actions, and why they hold certain patterns of political attitudes, they often analyze the political orientations of various groups within society. Groups of people categorized on the basis of age are an important element of this kind of search for explanations of political behavior. Since social gerontologists have learned that many different psychological and sociological orientations are affected by the age of a person, it follows that explanations of political attitudes and behavior will also be enhanced by analyses concerning age.

At a more global level political scientists are interested in the stability and change of political systems over time. Questions concerning people's attitudes toward the political system in general as well as their attitudes toward specific issues are important in understanding how political institutions manage simultaneously to remain relatively stable and to change and respond to the flow of historical events. The political system at any point in time contains individuals of different ages, and the interaction among age groups produces patterns of both continuity and change. Younger persons are new members of the system and may make certain political demands stimulated by the events of the day or the era. Older members of the system have more years of political experience and skill, and thus might be in a position to make better political decisions. Or, since older members of the political system were reared and obtained their experience in an earlier era, they might be out of date with contemporary politics and thus make poorer political decisions than younger people. Of course, there is no simple answer to this kind of question, but it does serve to indicate the importance of age in the study of politics.

And at a quite practical level of analysis, students of politics may be interested to know if political issues are likely to become centered on questions of age. Furthermore, if age issues become a substantial element of politics, is it likely that all old people will stick together in their attitudes and voting patterns? Will politics become young versus old, or will the question of age become merged with the longer-standing bases of political conflict, such as ethnic and socioeconomic status?

The subject of political attitudes and behavior is only recently emerging as a substantial concern of gerontologists. Consequently, the available evidence is fragmentary and incomplete on two levels. First, there are many topics of concern to political analysts which have not been subjected to any formal age analysis. Second, even for those subjects for which some evidence is available, the research is only in preliminary stages, and new evidence and/or improvements in conceptual and methodological strategies may alter the generalizations. Nonetheless, there has been a fair amount of attention paid to the relationship between age and political behavior which will form the substance of this discussion.

Age, Political Participation, and Political Attitudes

Political Participation and Age

Trends in voting participation over the life cycle have been studied by several political analysts. A generalized sequence has been identified in which new voters at the youngest end of the life cycle have a relatively low rate of voter participation, with participation gradually increasing and reaching a peak in the 40s and 50s, and then dropping off in the 60s and beyond—a generalization which Milbrath (1965) makes on the basis of his review of eight separate voting studies.

Milbrath cites three factors which "intervene" between chronological age and voting behavior in accounting for this pattern: (1) integration with the community—younger persons are typically not as integrated into their communities as are older adults who have families, own homes, have children in the local school system, pay local as well as federal taxes; (2) the availability of blocks of free time—as children grow up and eventually leave home, parents have more available time to be involved in politics; (3) good health—toward the end of the life cycle a deterioration in mental and physical health may yield a lower rate of participation (sometimes referred to as "disengagement" as discussed in Chapter 3) in many forms of social behavior, including politics.

There are, of course, factors other than age which affect a person's voting participation. Some would argue that sex and education, viewed across the whole society, are more important predictors of participation than age. If we take the 1964 presidential election as an example, Table 18.1 demonstrates the combined effects of age, education, and sex.

The "total" column on the right-hand side of this table does conform to the general pattern mentioned above. In the youngest age group a little more than half of those eligible actually voted. The proportion increases through the early sixties, and then drops off. Yet when we examine the various columns of the table, each representing a different level of education, we see within each of the age groups larger educational differences in voting participation than between the age groups. Thus, for example, only 14 percent of the youngest age group with just an elementary education voted, while 80 percent of the youngest group with four years of college or more voted. At the oldest end of the life cycle these education differences are also found. Furthermore, comparison of the top and bottom halves of Table 18.1 indicates certain sex differences in patterns of voter participation: males participate more than females, and the old-age drop-off is greater for females than for males.

Voter participation in politics, therefore, is modestly associated with age. Younger persons appear to vote less, and there sometimes appears to be a drop in participation toward the end of the life cycle. This latter observation, however, must be modified in light of the sex and education influences which, as Table 18.1 illustrates, are in most cases stronger than age effects. Indeed, one recent analysis, based upon a set of quite sophisti-

Table 18.1   Voter participation, sex, age, and education, United States, November 1964 (percent voting)

| Sex and age | Years of education | | | | | | |
| | Elementary | | High school | | College | | |
	0–7 years	8 years	1–3 years	4 years	1–3 years	4 years or more	Total
Males							
21–24	14	30	34	56	70	80	53
25–44	43	58	65	76	82	87	71
45–64	63	79	81	88	88	93	79
65+	66	79	80	88	91	88	74
Total 21+	58	73	69	80	82	88	73
Females							
21–24	22	21	33	55	69	78	52
25–44	34	52	58	76	85	87	68
45–64	52	69	75	84	87	92	74
65+	46	63	72	76	82	93	61
Total 21+	45	63	63	76	83	89	68

SOURCE: Foner (1972), as adapted from *Current Population Reports,* 1965, P-20, No. 143, pp. 16–19.

cated analytic techniques, concluded that when appropriate corrections are used, there is actually a slight increase in voter participation with age (Verba and Nie, 1972).

Political Attitudes and Age

When we turn to the subject of political attitudes, there are a number of conflicting hypotheses concerning the impact of age. The range of attitudes studied by political scientists is certainly great; an inventory of them would be well beyond the purpose of this chapter (for general reviews see Key, 1963; McClosky, 1967; Flanigan, 1972). Any discussion of political attitudes could focus on broad ideologies, such as liberalism and conservatism, or on citizens' evaluations of a specific policy-relevant issue, such as the issue of the government provision of medical aid. Similarly, students of political behavior have looked at general orientations toward participation, such as political alienation and cynicism, and at attitudes which are more immediately relevant to voting, such as a person's partisan affiliation. Any and all of these could be the focus of an age-based analysis; a few of them have, in fact, been studied.

At the level of general ideology, the most popular image of the connection between age and political attitudes in American politics is that people in general get more conservative as they get older. Indeed, there is some evidence that older persons often take a more conservative position on such contemporary issues as school busing, abortion, legalization of marijuana, activism, women's rights, and protest politics (Cutler, 1974). There is also evidence that older persons are somewhat more conservative on such longer-standing political issues as federal aid to education and federal activity in civil rights (Campbell, 1971). Another analysis employed party affiliation as a rough indicator of conservatism or liberalism, and concluded that aging brought about a conversion to the Republican party (Crittenden, 1962). Older persons have also been found to be more "militaristic" or "hard line" in matters of foreign policy (Almond, 1960; Back and Gergen, 1963).

Yet in all of these examples, it is important to note that the specific issue, and the specific way in which the attitude is measured in a given attitude survey or public opinion poll, has an influence on the response and outcome. The particular nature of the civil rights or equality-of-opportunity issue, or the particular aspect of foreign policy which is under consideration, will affect the response of all respondents in an opinion survey, and, hence, the generalizations which one draws concerning the role of age in these attitudes are also subject to modification.

In addition to the measurement, or "methodological," considerations which one must take into account, there are four additional parts of the puzzle which deserve special attention.

First, while there are often differences in political attitudes along an age gradient, seldom is it the case that all young people (however "young" or "old" is defined) are on one side of the issue and all old people on the other side. Age is but one of several characteristics of an individual which are relevant to attitudes—as we have seen, for example, in the data on voter participation. These other factors combine either to smooth out lines of conflict in political controversy or to provide bases of conflict other than age per se, although at times age differences have been so great as to be considered "generation gaps" (Bengtson, 1970).

Second, the relationship between age and political attitudes may be selectively modified by various political agencies and institutions. The political party has been identified in much political science research (for example, Campbell et al., 1960) as being of great importance in organizing an individual's different political attitudes. Yet political party identification may only selectively combine with age in the association with attitudes. One analyst has argued that for issues which are relatively outside of the individual's own experience—such as issues of foreign policy or system-level economic policy—the political party, its candidates, and its platforms will have a stronger influence on attitudes than on issues with which the individual has more direct experience and personal interest—such as taxation, conscription, and social welfare issues (Foner, 1972). The nature of maturational age changes, as this argument continues, is likely to be quite different for these two general types of issues. Evidence germane to this argument was obtained in a research project which investigated age patterns in political attitudes at the family, community, and national levels. It was found that "the farther removed the political issue from the individual, the less age will have a significant effect upon his attitude toward that issue" (Douglass et al., 1974).

Third, the meaning of "age" in any description of the relationship between age and political attitudes must be clearly understood. In social research it has traditionally been the case that chronological age differences are used to indicate maturational or developmental differences (or changes) between old and young. Yet individuals of different chronological age do not simply represent individuals at different developmental stages in the life cycle; they also represent individuals born and raised in different historical contexts. Similarly, individuals of the same chronological age are not necessarily homogeneous with respect to the degree that age is salient to them as far as their political outlooks are concerned. Both of these examples illustrate the proposition that chronological age itself does not provide an automatic interpretation of patterns found in apparently age-concerned attitudes and behavior.

Fourth, it should not be concluded that the conservatism of the aged on such issues as the federal government's involvement in the economy and society is an inevitable consequence of the aging process. On the contrary, in some instances it may be to the specific advantage of older persons to favor such federal activity. In a classic analysis of political behavior in the United States, a research team at the University of Michigan classified all voters as to the kind of issue orientation which the voters implicitly expressed in their attitudes. Four general categories were employed: ideology, group benefits, nature of the times, and no issue content at all (Campbell et al., 1960). The modal category for the electorate was group benefits into which 45 percent of all voters were classified.

While the analysis did not present any information on age patterns in issue orientations, it would be reasonable to assume that older voters are just as group-benefits oriented as the rest of the electorate. More direct evidence of this is seen in a number of studies which have examined age patterns in attitudes toward a range of issues concerning federal involvement in social and economic programs. Analysis of data from the 1960 election (Campbell, 1962) indicated that there was little difference between old and young on issues of federal aid for school construction, federal involvement in guaranteeing fair treatment of blacks in jobs and housing, and the question of whether electricity and housing should be left totally to private enterprise. However, on two other issues in this general conservative-liberal cluster—governmental guarantees of full employment and government financial involvement in medical care programs—the old were substantially less conservative than the young.

A more complete analysis of this medical care issue has examined the age distribution of attitudes toward governmental support of medical care programs in four national surveys taken in conjunction with the presidential elections of 1956 to 1968; these data are presented in Table 18.2. The age distributions indicate quite clearly that "in all four studies, people age 65 and over were the most likely of the four age groupings to favor a government program of medical aid" (Schreiber and Marsden, 1972, p. 98).

When considering generalizations about age and political attitudes, therefore, there are several processes which must be taken into consideration. For some issues, age may be quite irrelevant to attitudes, or at least secondary to factors which are more salient. For other issues, the individual's attitude might be a reflection of a more general ideology, and this ideology, in turn, may be related to maturation and to such political factors as political party identification. For still other issues, the connection between age and attitudes may hinge on the fact that a particular age group may receive the benefits to be bestowed by a particular program or policy.

Table 18.2   Attitudes toward governmental medical aid program[a] **(percent in favor)**

Age group	1956	1960	1964	1968
21–34	49	57	48	45
35–49	54	52	46	51
50–64	55	67	52	54
65+	63	74	58	59

[a]See Table 18.4 for the text of the questions asked each year.
SOURCE: Adapted from Schreiber and Marsden (1972), Table 2, p. 98.

Alternative Meanings of "Age" for Political Analysis

In several places in the discussion we have noted that chronological age can have different meanings as far as analysis of political attitudes and behavior is concerned. This section presents two important alternatives to the meaning of age, that is, alternatives to the traditional approach in which chronological age is employed as an index of maturational or develop mental change. The first approach presents age as an indicator of birth cohort membership; the second examines the implications of differences between individual's chronological age and his subjective age identification.

Cohort Analysis

Knowing that a person is, for example, twenty years old, we can assume to know two different clusters of data about the person: *maturational facts* and *generational facts*. Maturationally, we know that a person who is twenty years old has lived for two decades of what is an approximately six- or seven-decade life span. This person is at a more-or-less identifiable stage in his life cycle and has probably undergone certain experiences (family socialization experiences, high school, dating, some planning for the future) and probably has not undergone others (completion of college, marriage, parenthood, retirement). Of course, chronological age is an imperfect indicator of these social, life-stage events, and there is great variability across the population as to when any individual will experience one of the life events. Nevertheless, across the whole society, chronological age gives us a general idea of the developmental stage of the individual. To the degree that social and political attitudes are known to vary in terms of life stage or maturational age, knowing a person's age may give us clues about his attitudes.

At the same time, chronological age can be used to calculate when the individual was born and to know, in general, the social and political milieu in which he was socialized. Thus in 1975, a person who is twenty years old was born in 1955 and experienced his political socialization in a particular slice of national and world history. To the degree that direct exposure to political events and circumstances, experienced during the early and important years of political socialization, has an effect upon attitudes, the individual's generational location can be quite important (Inglehart, 1967; Jennings and Niemi, 1974; Cutler, 1975).

The analytic problem in most studies which discuss age in chronological terms is that the person's age has both maturational meaning and generational meaning simultaneously. Both sets of factors can have an impact upon political attitudes, and thus it is important to be able to separate the two effects. Unfortunately, when a pattern of behavioral or attitudinal characteristics is presented along an age gradient, it is usually impossible to separate the maturational from the generational explanation.

To illustrate this ambiguity, consider a hypothetical age distribution which we will assume is based on data collected in 1970 (see Table 18.3). These hypothetical data represent the way in which age patterns in political orientations are often presented. Since the percentages are arrayed by age, the usual description would be: as age increases, the particular characteristic increases or decreases. Description, however, is not the same as interpretation, and often the interpretation is the more important contribution of the analysis. For example, if in these hypothetical data the characteristic was agreement with the policy of legalizing marijuana use, then the typical interpretation of the data might be: the older a person gets the less he is likely to support the legalization of marijuana.

The problem with this example is that while the description is accurate (the characteristic indeed does decrease as age increases), the interpretation implies that the data demonstrate a maturational change occurring over the life cycle with causal implications about attitudes toward the legalization of marijuana. There are at least two possible fallacies in this interpretation (Riley, 1973). First, since the hypothetical data are from a single year (a poll taken in 1970), there can be no evidence of maturational change over the life cycle. Second, the groups defined in terms of

Table 18.3 Hypothetical age distribution

Group	Chronological age	Characteristic
A	18–25	80%
B	26–45	60%
C	46–65	45%
D	66+	30%

their chronological age represent different birth cohorts, each of which was born in a different historical period and, consequently, reared and socialized in a different set of political circumstances. Thus, group A was born in 1945–1952, group B in 1925–1944, group C in 1905–1924, and group D before 1905. Certainly we might expect that people reared in the first decade of this century will have different attitudes toward the legalization of marijuana than those born after World War II; and their different attitudes might be more related to the particular experiences of their cohort rather than to maturation per se.

What we have suggested and attempted to illustrate here is that the cohort or generational interpretation of age differences in characteristics is a plausible alternative hypothesis to maturational or developmental explanations of age differences. In a word, age differences do not always imply age changes (Schaie, 1965, and Chapter 6).

This argument can perhaps be made clearer by returning to our hypothetical data, but considering a different characteristic. This time let us assume that the characteristic under consideration is the educational attainment of the individual and that the percentages describe the proportion of each age group that has "high education"—at least a completed high school education. (In fact, the hypothetical percentages given above are the real approximate percentages of each age group, in 1970, that has at least completed twelve years of schooling.) In this new view of the percentage distribution, the description would state that 80 percent of group A has achieved this educational level, but that only 30 percent of group D has achieved this level. The same summary description made for the data when they represented attitudes toward marijuana can be made here: as age increases, the characteristic decreases.

While the description is the same (of course, it must be since we are dealing with the same data, only giving different hypothetical labels), the interpretation must be quite different. Consider how foolish it would be to argue, using the maturational interpretation, that as the person gets older his level of education decreases! While an aging individual may appear to become less intelligent, his level of attained formal education cannot change: it is, for each individual, a personal historical fact. The interpretation which clearly is most valid would be based on the idea of birth cohort in which each age group represents individuals born and raised in different historical periods; those born before 1905 did not have the same opportunity for educational attainment as those born after World War II.

The example of educational attainment, therefore, demonstrates that an age distribution of a characteristic does not always imply age changes produced by developmental or maturational processes. While the maturational hypothesis may be quite appropriate for certain biological or physiological characteristics which may deteriorate or otherwise change with age, for a variety of psychological and sociological characteristics the generational or birth-cohort hypothesis may be the more plausible explanation. Furthermore, this may be particularly true for political orientations, since attitudes toward elements of the political system typically represent the joint contribution of the individual's psychological predispositions and the "objective" nature of political affairs (Greenstein, 1969; Renshon, 1974).

We have continued at length in describing the plausibility of the generational explanation for two reasons: first, because too often age differences in published studies and polls are automatically interpreted as maturational or developmental differences; and second, because the impact of the political environment on individual attitudes implies that people who are a part of different generations ought to be expected to hold different orientations toward various issues. Another way to make this important point is to present actual examples of possible differences in interpretation of age distributions of political orientations.

We noted earlier that one of the more popular images (or myths) of political aging is that people get more conservative as they get older. In the United States this proposition has been tested by using identification or affiliation with the Republican party as the behavioral measure of individual conservatism. Crittenden (1962) examined the age distribution of Republican party identification in a series of national Gallup polls, 1946–1958. Looking at the vertical age distributions (ignoring the diagonal lines for now) presented in Table 18.4, Crittenden observed that in each year the younger age groups had lower percentages of Republicans, and the older age groups had higher percentages of Republicans; it was further observed that this pattern was found in each of the national surveys.

It should be noted that the structure of the age distribution given for each of the annual polls is similar to the hypothetical data presented previously. Crittenden found support in these data for the proposition that maturational processes bring about a conversion to Republicanism or conservatism as a function of aging. The alternative hypothesis—that of generational or birth cohort differences—should also be considered as a plausible explanation.

The conclusion that aging brings a conversion to Republicanism was challenged in a reanalysis of the Crittenden data which employed the techniques of cohort analysis. The diagonal lines in Table 18.4 were added in this cohort analysis to facilitate an evaluation of the data in a different way (Cutler, 1969). The logic of cohort analysis is that a

Table 18.4   Age and party identification (percent Republican)

Age intervals	Cohort labels	1946	1950	1954	1958
	A				
21–24	B	46	41	42	43
25–28	C	54	43	45	51
29–32	D	51	44	39	49
33–36	E	59	50	47	49
37–40	F	59	53	51	42
41–44	G	70	58	56	44
45–48	H	58	58	52	34
49–52	I	58	50	89	62
53–56		60	60	66	47
57–60		65	75	58	63
61–64		58	86	75	55
65–68		70	60	90	66
Total		57	51	50	48

SOURCE: These data are adapted from Cutler (1969, Table 1) which reanalyzed the data representing the high education group in Crittenden's (1962) analysis.

given birth cohort can be traced over a series of national samples by simply looking at the appropriate age groups. Thus, for example, people who are 21 years old in 1946 represent the same generational birth cohort (born in 1925) as the 25 year olds four years later in a 1950 survey and the 29 year olds in a 1954 survey. In short, cohort analysis is a technique (or set of techniques) by which a political analyst can see the degree to which the maturational hypothesis and the generational hypothesis of an age distribution of behavioral characteristics are useful in explaining a particular set of age data (Evan, 1959; Hyman, 1972).

The diagonal lines in Table 18.4 direct the observer's attention to the changes, across the 1946–1958 period, within the different cohorts, whereas the original investigation looked up and down the separate columns. In looking at the cohorts within the diagonals, it cannot be concluded that as a cohort of individual's age there is strong evidence of a "conversion" to conservatism or to the Republican party. While there are indeed fluctuations, these seem to be reflections of the general political environment, and not the consequence of any "aging effect." While older people in 1946 or 1958 may in fact be more Republican than younger people in those years, the answer is not in a maturational conversion but rather in the differences between generational birth cohorts— much like the explanation given above for the differences in educational attainment.

The Crittenden-Cutler cohort controversy, although interesting, did not provide the last word on this topic. Crittenden provided the initial data, Cutler published a reanalysis, Crittenden published a "Reply," and Cutler a "Rejoinder." The whole debate, in which neither analyst changed his mind, is reprinted in Kirkpatrick (1974) for the interested reader. It was not until a later analysis by Glenn and Hefner (1972) that more definitive evidence was presented. Using a data base spanning 1945 through 1969, these authors concluded:

> Therefore, the thesis that cohorts experience an absolute increase in Republicanism as a consequence of aging receives no support from our data. . . . the positive association of Republicanism with age, consistently revealed by the cross-sectional data gathered at various times during the past 30 years or so, reflects intercohort (or "generational") differences rather than the effects of aging (p. 35). . . .
> This study should rather conclusively lay to rest the once prevalent belief that the aging process has been an important influence for Republicanism in the United States (p. 47).

A second example of the utility of applying cohort analysis to age distributions of political orientations can be taken from analyses of public attitudes toward governmental programs of medical care. It will be recalled from our discussion of the group-benefits orientation in American politics that older persons were more in favor of governmental involvement in medical aid programs than were young persons. The data in Table 18.2 presented a series of results from each of four national surveys, each taken in a presidential election year. And in each case, the older respondents were more in favor of the medical aid policy than were the younger respondents in the interview surveys.

The evidence in Table 18.2, however, does not answer the question of the maturational versus generational genesis of the age distribution of attitudes. Are older people more in favor of this policy because the processes of aging created a favorable orientation, or are older persons representative of generational cohorts which have been supportive of this policy throughout their lifetimes? A cohort analysis of this attitude (Bengtson and Cutler, 1975), reprinted in Table 18.5, presents at least preliminary evidence on this issue. In Table 18.5, changes at the young end of the life cycle and at the old end of the life cycle are given. The change from 21–24 to 25–28 is given for those cohorts which were 21–24 years of age in four successive presidential election surveys. Similarly, the change from 61–64 to 65–68 is given for four cohorts, each of which was 61–64 years of age in one of the presidential surveys. Table 18.5 indicates the percentage of those in each cohort who support federal governmental programs of medical care, and also indicates the changes that are associated with aging for each cohort.

Table 18.5   Attitudes toward federal government medical aid programs[a] (percent in favor)

Age group	1956	1960	1964	1968	1972
21–24	70	77	67	67	
25–28		69	62	56	56
Change		−1	−15	−12	−11
61–64	69	84	64	72	
65–68		85	73	76	69
Change		+16	−11	+12	−4
Total sample	70	77	65	67	61
Change		+7	−12	+2	−6

[a]The question read, for 1956 and 1960: "The government ought to help people get doctors and hospital care at low cost." For 1964 and 1968: "Some people say the government in Washington ought to help people get doctors and hospital care at low cost; others say the government should not get into this. Have you been interested enough in this to favor one side or the other?" For 1972: "There is much concern about the rapid rise in medical and hospital costs. Some feel there should be a government insurance plan which would cover all medical expenses. Others feel that medical expenses should be paid by individuals through private insurance like the Blue Cross. Which side do you favor?"
SOURCE: The data were made available by the Inter-University Consortium for Political Research. The data were originally collected by the Center for Political Studies, Institute for Social Research, University of Michigan, with partial support from a grant from the National Science Foundation. Neither the original collectors of the data nor the Consortium bear any responsibility for the analysis or interpretation presented here.

There are, of course, ebbs and flows in the nation's attitudes toward this issue over the 1956–1972 period. Support for government involvement in medical aid programs reached its peak in 1960 in conjunction with the Kennedy victory and just prior to the passage of Medicare. Yet even within the national pattern of changes, four generalizations describing support for federal medical care programs emerge from Table 18.5: (1) older people are more supportive than the nation as a whole; (2) older people are more supportive than younger people; (3) the increase in positive support at the older end of the life cycle is greater than the increase in support of the nation as a whole; and (4) the changes in support by the older people are by far more supportive than the changes at the younger end of the life cycle. Therefore, we may conclude that this particular attitude does appear to be strongly influenced by the aging process, by the effects of becoming old. While the data of Table 18.2 suggested that such was the case, it is only in light of the cohort-based analysis presented in Table 18.5 that we have substantial evidence of the impact of the aging process. Thus, while in the case of Republican party identifications cohort analysis supported a generational interpretation, in the case of attitudes toward governmental medical aid programs, the cohort analysis tends to support the maturational explanation.

Subjective Age Identification

The second alternative to the meaning of age—as contrasted to "simple" chronological age—is that of subjective age or self-identification with age. Everyone has a chronological age, just as everyone, objectively, has a social class. But not everyone is aware or "conscious" of his social class; it is only in certain circumstances that class consciousness may arise. Similarly, not everyone is age conscious; some people do identify themselves with an age group, while others do not think in age terms as far as their social and political attitudes are concerned.

Two interlinked questions for social scientific analysis flow from this distinction between chronological age and subjective age or age consciousness. First, what are the conditions which produce age consciousness? Second, what are the consequences, in political and social terms, of age consciousness? The answer to the first question is a difficult one, but it might be answered, at least for contemporary society, in terms of analogy. Just as individuals have become conscious of their racial, ethnic, and sexual statuses, they have also become conscious of their age. Of course, it is not simply by analogy that people are becoming aware and conscious of their age and of the social and political power which collective action on the part of the aged might have. There are both governmental agencies (such as the Administration on Aging and the National Institute on Aging) as well as private associations (such as the American Association of Retired Persons and the Gray Panthers) which serve in various ways to increase age consciousness.

The second of the two questions is, perhaps, more germane to this chapter: what are the political consequences of age consciousness? We have argued that simple chronological age is not, in and of itself, a sufficient explanation for many age distributions of behavioral characteristics. The previous discussion of the generational cohort interpretation of age implied that individuals of different ages at a given point in time do not necessarily manifest differences due to the maturational effects of the aging process. When we speak of age consciousness the question is turned around: are individuals of the same chronological age necessarily similar insofar as political orientations are concerned?

In an important essay on this issue, Professor Matilda White Riley (1971) draws an analogy between age consciousness and class consciousness. In certain periods of history, social class differences in a society give rise to class consciousness and in some circumstances to class conflict. Just as there is historical variation in class consciousness at the level of the whole society, so there is variation at the individual level: in any particular period, some individuals will be conscious of class differences and for others class will not be a salient component of their orientation toward the world. All of these elements of the dynamics of class and class consciousness, Riley contends, are germane to the issue of age consciousness. In some historical periods and for some individuals, age identification and age consciousness are salient elements in social interaction and political debate.

For some analysts the issue is whether the elderly have the characteristics of a "minority group"—identifiable to the rest of society, discriminated against in economic and social interaction, with common group-based needs and wants (Streib, 1965; Rose, 1965). Gerontologists and other students of the aging process have examined quite a number of factors which may lead to age consciousness of one form or another (as reviewed, for example, in Peterson, 1971; McTavish, 1971). While there is some understanding of the genesis and social psychological attributes of age consciousness, there has been little research on the political consequences of such age identification.

Politically, age consciousness is potentially extremely important. As is indicated in greater detail in Chapter 3, there will be larger numbers of older persons in the near future with a potential for substantial political activity. Given this fact, a key question is whether such a group of older persons will, in fact, be involved politically as old people. Will people be conscious of their age status or position in society, and will there be political consequences of such consciousness?

We cannot, of course, make firm predictions about the political attitudes of tomorrow's older population. Yet we do have at least preliminary evidence of the political consequences of age identification. A national sample survey taken in conjunction with the 1972 presidential election included a series of questions by which each respondent in the survey could be classified as subjectively identified with "youth" or "old age." Using these attitudinal measures of youth and old age, we can classify every individual in the sample according to two characteristics: the person's subjective age identification and the same person's chronological age (Cutler, 1974).

For purposes of the present discussion the important question is this: do older people who subjectively identify themselves as old have similar or different political attitudes from those older people who subjectively identify themselves as not old? Suggested answers to this important question can be seen in the context of three sets of political attitudes.

The data in Table 18.6 portray the chronologically old people (age 60+) in the 1972 national sample as subdivided into those who expressed a subjective age identification as old and those who did not express such an old age identification. These two subgroups are then compared in terms of traditional conservative-liberal issues (Issues 1-4), expectations as to the financial future (Issues 5-6), and what might be called contemporary issues of social conservatism-liberalism (Issues 7-8). The results of this research indicate that subjective age does indeed make a difference.

On the traditional issues the subjectively old are more liberal than are the other older respondents; this is most dramatically seen on the issue of federal medical aid programs which are much more strongly supported by the subjectively old (this, incidentally, is an interesting complement to the data presented in Tables 18.2 and 18.5 concerning this same issue). It is also the case that the subjectively old are somewhat more pessimistic with respect to their personal financial future. A smaller number of the subjectively old felt that financial conditions were better at the time of the interview than the previous year, and a similar pattern is seen when the present is compared with the immediate future. The last pair of items, however, indicates that the subjectively old are not always

Table 18.6   Subjective age identification among older persons on selected social, political, and economic issues: 1972

Issue	Subjective age identification	
	As old	As not old
1. Government action on inflation		
Percent should act	97.9	89.5
2. Federal medical programs		
Percent in favor	71.7	51.9
3. Cuts in federal military spending		
Percent in favor	41.5	26.4
4. Self-identification as liberal or conservative		
Percent liberal	21.2	16.4
5. Personal financial condition, now vs. year ago		
Percent better now	44.0	59.6
6. Personal financial condition, now vs. next year		
Percent better next year	46.2	50.0
7. Abortion allowable under certain circumstances		
Percent agree	22.0	33.6
8. Government action against industrial pollution		
Percent in favor	67.6	73.0
All respondents aged 60+	38.1%[a]	54.5%

[a]Not included here are the 7.4 percent of the 60+ group which identified as young.
SOURCE: Data represent the responses of those respondents aged 60 and over in the University of Michigan Center for Political Studies national survey of the 1972 presidential election. The election survey was made available by the Inter-University Consortium for Political Research; the age items were made available by Professor Gerald Gurin, Institute for Social Research, University of Michigan. Total N for the 1972 survey is 2700. More complete analysis of these data may be found in Cutler (1974).

more liberal than those who do not subjectively identify themselves as old. The subjectively old are less in favor of abortion and are less in favor of government solutions or action in the area of industrial pollution.

While the specifics of these and other issues which can be used to estimate the impact of subjective age identification (see Cutler, 1974) are themselves interesting, the important point is that subjective age identification does distinguish among those who are chronologically old. Age clearly has a different meaning to different individuals who share the same general position in the life cycle—as indicated by the fact that 38 percent of those age 60+ do identify themselves as old while 55 percent do not. When considering the meaning of age differences in social and political attitudes, consequently, it will be important to recognize the important interaction between the chronological age and such other meanings or interpretations of age as those suggested by the cohort analysis approach and consideration of subjective age identification.

Age and Political Leadership

In contrast to what is known about the relationship between age and political behavior and attitudes at the public or "mass" level, useful and properly classified data describing this kind of relationship with respect to political leaders are relatively sparse. Although social scientists have been concerned with the role of elites in society and politics for many years, relatively little scientific attention has been directed toward the ages of political leaders and elites.

The observation that older persons are likely to be active in politics has been generally documented in previous sections of this chapter. Data extending this kind of conclusion may be found, for example, in studies of the highly politically active citizenry. Rosenau (1974), for example, studied the political activity of members of the Americans for Democratic Action in the 1960s. The basic nature of this group is itself an indicator that this sample represents persons who are more interested in politics than is the general population. Rosenau further identified two subgroups in his sample—the "attentive public," those who maintained an awareness of political issues during nonelection periods; and the "mobilizable public," those who are not only attentive, but who are responsive to requests for actual participation between elections.

Of relevance to the present discussion is the comparison Rosenau makes among the age distributions of the attentives, the mobilizables, and the general electorate. These data are reproduced here as Table 18.7. As is demonstrated by these data, the general electorate is substantially younger than either of the two groups of active participants. The proportion of persons under 35 in Rosenau's study is about half the proportion in the general electorate. At the older end of the life cycle, the 55+ age group represents almost 40 percent of the activists, but only 25 percent of the general electorate.

The Rosenau data provide an interesting transition between our prior discussion of age patterns in the mass public and the issue of political leadership. The activist samples in the Rosenau study represent "elites" in the sense of individuals who pay particular attention to political affairs, who belong to a visible political organization, and who are available for political mobilization. While this level of participation certainly represents the elite within the context of mass public politics, these individuals are still more a part of the public than they are part of the official, legal political leadership of the society.

Unfortunately, social scientists lack comprehensive and systematic data describing the age structure of formal political leadership. Yet both the Rosenau data and some of our common-sense daily observations might tell us that older people represent a substantial component of the formal political leadership of many countries. Indeed, when social gerontologists discuss the degree to which older persons do not necessarily disengage from social activity, they often point to the political arena as the main example of an area in which no formal criteria for retirement exist, and in which, consequently, many older persons continue their careers into advanced age.

If it is the case, therefore, that politics is one area of social activity in which age does not produce necessary and automatic age-connected retirement, it is of special importance to understand systematically the

Table 18.7 Age distributions of mobilizables, attentives, and the general electorate

Age groups	Mobilizables	Attentives	Michigan SRC sample of the 1956 presidential election
Under 35	17	17	30
35–44	20	21	26
45–54	19	18	19
55+	39	38	25
Age unknown	5	6	—
Total	100	100	100
(n =)	(1,704)	(1,658)	(1,762)

SOURCE: Adapted from Rosenau, 1974, p. 253.

age composition of political leadership. From the point of view of political science, furthermore, one would want to know if age changes in the society in general—such as in the relative demographic proportions of various age groups—has any relationship to the age structure of political leadership. Indeed, the fact that certain political institutions have memberships which include noticeable numbers of older persons (for example, the Congress or the Courts)—often emotionally criticized as "Gerontocracies"—may be the simple reflection of the fact that the society itself is undergoing a transition toward an older population.

Chapter 3 presented a descriptive discussion of the demographic changes which are affecting the age structure of many societies. In a political context, Cowgill (1974) has labeled the connection between demographic processes and changes in the age structure of a population as "transition theory." Transition theory postulates that as the technologies of birth control and death control develop and become widely available in a society, that society will undergo an "aging" of its population. This "aging" (that is, an increase in the average age of the population) will take place because birth control will decrease the number and proportion of younger persons entering the population, while death control will increase the number and relative proportion of persons who survive into old age.

More directly germane to the present discussion of age and political leadership, however, are several postulates of Cowgill's "transition theory" which note that the aging of the population will initially be found in the upper socioeconomic and urban sectors of society. A political corollary of transition theory, therefore, is that the aging of society will produce a larger pool of older persons in precisely those sectors of society from which political leaders are typically drawn.

At this point, therefore, it becomes necessary to consider the age structure of political leadership. In returning to this issue, however, we are reminded of the absence of comprehensive information on the subject. This situation, consequently, has prompted the authors to sketch out the design of a data bank which would include the necessary information (Schmidhauser and Cutler, 1975). The goal of the construction of such a data bank is to collect national, international, and cross-national data on the career patterns of major executive, legislative, judicial, and bureaucratic officials in various political institutions.

Career patterns, or biographical data, on political leaders would include important age data on a number of significant stages in the life history of the political leader. In turn, when these data are collected and assembled, political scientists will be in a position to compare the age data across various political roles (for example, legislators versus members of the executive branch), and to compare the age structure of the political leadership with the age structure of the population of a given political unit. For example, to what degree are there similarities between the age structure of the Florida state legislature and the population of Florida (which has had a dramatically increasing older population), as compared with the similarly collected data for California (which has had a considerably smaller proportional growth in its older population)?

The age and political leadership data bank which we envision would include such information as the age of the leader when he or she first entered the political role, the length of time served in that role, the age at retirement of service, and the nature of that retirement (death, loss of election, resignation, or whatever). While all of these data would be collected at the national level, similar data could be collected at the intranational or subnational level for states, municipalities, and counties. In addition, such information could be collected cross-nationally in order to see if nations at different stages in the processes of demographic transition have different age patterns of political leadership.

From the descriptive information which this kind of data bank would provide, several theories relevant to the social and political system could be tested. Recent discussions of the degree of institutionalization of the U.S. House of Representatives, for example, have focused on a number of formal criteria by which an institution may be said to be stable and mature (Polsby, 1968). In turn, among the indicators of these formal criteria which have been studied by political scientists, the question of the age of the Members of the House has been investigated to see the degree to which the ages of selection, of service, and of termination affect the operation of the institution (Witmer, 1964).

We have discussed these plans for the building of a data bank because they illustrate a number of the important connections between age, politics, and the political system. While most of this information remains to be systematically collected, a small amount of such data is already available. In particular, Lehman's *Age and Achievement* (1953) provides some interesting information concerning chronological age and political leadership. Lehman systematically compiled age data on both American and foreign political leaders. Arranging these data in time series, he found, contrary to other studies (for example, Hall, 1923), that modern political leaders are older than their predecessors. In particular, Lehman found that there is "an *upward* shift in the ages of political leaders" which is in contrast to a downward shift in the age of achievement of other "scientific and creative contributions."

Lehman's data base was very diverse. He identified the ages at which offices were attained for "chief ministers" of Great Britain from 902 to

1720 and for prime ministers from 1721 to modern times. His American data base comprised similar information on (1) all American presidents, (2) all unsuccessful presidential candidates, (3) 932 governors of American states (since the American revolution), (4) 248 members of presidential cabinets, (5) justices of the U.S. Supreme Court, and (6) members of the U.S. Congress. He included some additional foreign data such as (1) Canadian Governors-General (1861–1938), (2) French hereditary rulers, and (3) 133 presidents of various republics other than the United States (1890–1938).

Lehman's findings indicated that median age of most of these categories of leaders (all from what he called "knowledge-based societies of the present") varied considerably during the periods which he investigated. The median age of members of the U.S. House of Representatives was 43.5 years in 1799 and 53.46 years in 1925. The ages of Commanders of the U.S. Army during periods of war have also varied considerably. Lehman found that 23 top-ranking American generals in the Revolutionary War and the War of 1812 averaged 39.7 years of age, their counterparts in the Civil War (143 in number) averaged 49 years of age, while the 32 top commanders in World War II averaged 58.8 years of age. Lehman (1947) suggested that while much of his evidence indicated an upward shift in the ages of political leaders, social unrest is associated with the

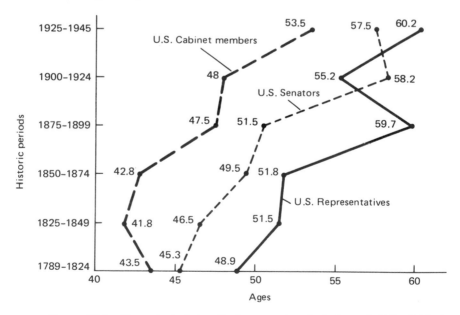

Figure 18.1 Chronological (median) ages at oath taking of U.S. Cabinet, House, and Senate members by historic periods, 1789–1945. (From Lehman, 1947)

emergence of younger leaders. A graphic reproduction of Lehman's findings is presented in Figure 18.1.

In the area of the judicial branch of government, analyses of the chronological ages of oath-taking of the justices of the Supreme Courts of Iowa, Ohio, and Wisconsin (documented respectively by Ewers, 1959; Hoopes, 1949; and Higgins, 1949) confirm Lehman's upward-trend hypothesis. On the other hand, Schmidhauser's (1962) analysis of the chronological ages of oath-taking of U.S. Supreme Court Justices and U.S. Court of Appeals Judges found a moderate downward trend in such ages since around 1920 (see Figure 18.2). Neither Lehman nor the other analysts of these chronological age variations have as yet attempted to relate age of initial office-taking and age of termination of service data to the basic systemic transition data assessed by Cowgill and other demographers.

Any discussion of age and political leadership should also consider the relationship of age to other professional or "elite" positions within society. There are two main reasons for studying other professional elites in the context of age and politics. First, historical changes in the pattern of aging in political leadership might simply reflect an overall pattern of aging in a variety of professional occupations. It would therefore be unwise to conclude that an increase in the ages of political leaders is a unique

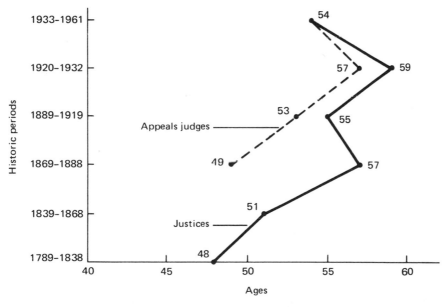

Figure 18.2. Chronological ages at oath taking of U.S. Supreme Court justices and Court of Appeals judges by historic periods, 1789–1961. (Schmidhauser, 1962)

phenomenon when additional data describing other professions would put the political pattern into its proper perspective.

Second, studies of aging in other professions could provide interesting insights and hypotheses concerning the interconnections between aging and society. Such insights may be more obvious and more easily uncovered in studies of nonpolitical elites, but may be quite germane to the discussion of aging and politics. Such other elites might include business executives, medical doctors, teachers, clergymen, and university administrators.

One notable study which demonstrates both of the factors just discussed is that of 8,300 top business executives in the United States in 1952 (Warner and Abegglen, 1955). Of even greater importance than the significantly large data base of this study is the fact that it replicated in most respects a seminal study undertaken by Taussig and Joslyn (1932), thus permitting comparisons of the characteristics of business leaders in two generations.

A comparison of the business executive data with the political data collected by Lehman is made possible since both studies employed roughly similar historical periods for their twentieth-century comparisons. Interestingly enough, the average age of business executives increased as did that of political leaders. Where Lehman found an increase in the average age of newly appointed Cabinet officers from 55.2 to 60.2 in the years between 1925 and 1945, the average age at which business leaderships was assumed rose from 35.5 to 44.7 in the years between 1928 and 1945.

This generational increase in the average age of business leaders is thus more dramatic than that of cabinet officers, even though the age levels attained are much higher for these political leaders. Unfortunately, Lehman did not investigate the possible influence of demographic and other variables upon the connection between chronological age and political office holding. Warner and Abegglen's investigation is, consequently, much more complete. In their comparison of the 1928 and 1952 data, they noted there was a substantial decrease in the proportion of 1952 business leaders under 45 years of age and a substantial increase in those between 45 and 65 years of age (from 61 percent to 74 percent). The structural or institutional factor which prevented a substantial percent increase after age 65 is the general corporate policy of compulsory retirement at that age. This structural or institutional variable does not apply in most instances to political office-holding, such as elective executive or legislative offices, or appointive political office-holding such as cabinet positions. The policy of compulsory retirement has been adopted in many jurisdictions with respect to judicial offices (Warner and Abegglen, 1955, pp. 128–137).

Warner and Abegglen's investigation also dealt thoroughly with the influence of the factors which had the greatest impact upon the "time frame characteristics" of the career ladders of business executives. Occupational background, education, and geographic mobility were most important. For example, the sons of major business executives, although entering business at a more advanced age than the sons of laborers or clerks, achieved a position of business leadership in fewer years and at a lower chronological age than any other occupational category. Similarly, differences in levels of educational attainment (categorized from "less than high school" through "post graduate work") were significant; indeed, education had the most important impact on chronological age ranges of all the variables investigated by Warner and Abegglen. Executives with the highest level of educational background entered business at a more advanced age (23.4) than others with less educational attainment but took fewer years to achieve a high executive position (19.9) and were the youngest category of executives (49.8). The distributions are consistent and most striking in contrast to those with the lowest educational attainment ("less than high school") who entered business at an average age of 15.3 but took 31 years to achieve an executive position and averaged 60.5 years of age.

In sum, an important aspect of the relationship between politics and age concerns the changing age structure of political leadership. When the appropriate collections of data are created, such as we have suggested in this discussion, it will be possible to map trends in age changes, and to correlate such changes with changes in the population in general. Such comparisons, furthermore, will profit from a comparative framework, in which comparisons can be made across subnational political units within a single country, across different countries, and across different kinds of societal and political elites.

The Future of Age in Politics

The final question for consideration in this chapter concerns the future role which age will play, or is likely to play, in the politics of the United States. We cannot predict with absolute certainty the degree to which older persons are likely to play a part in the politics of the future, or the specific issues around which political conflicts will emerge. Yet we can point to a number of factors which, when taken together, at least allow us to make a tentative estimate. And the estimate, or educated guess, which we make is that age is likely to play an increasingly significant role in the political future.

In particular, five kinds of evidence collectively support the conclusion that age will be a salient factor in the politics of the not-too-distant future. However, an important qualifying note needs to be stated. When it is argued that age will be important in the future of politics, we are not suggesting that all older people will, for example, behave as a single voting bloc, with a single mind and an agreed-upon set of social, economic, and political goals. Some analysts have dismissed the age factor in future politics too easily by noting that older persons will continue to be divided on ethnic, social class, partisan, and other traditional lines of political cleavage (Campbell, 1971; Binstock, 1974). That such division among older persons is likely to continue into the future is a position with which we generally agree. The point made here, however, is a different one: it is, rather, that for a variety of factors (described below) age will be an important fact of political life. Not all blacks and not all women agree on all issues which are important to their positions in the society and the economy, yet questions of race and gender are quite salient aspects of contemporary politics. Similarly, we are predicting that age is destined to be a salient aspect of future politics, even if all older persons do not speak with a single political voice.

Demographic factors.   Chapter 3 in this volume is concerned with the demography of aging, and the pertinent facts need not be repeated in detail here. The basic demographic data relevant to gerontologists indicate that the size and proportion of the older population will continue to increase. By the year 2020, for example, the number of persons over the age of 65 will be in excess of forty million, more than double the number of older persons in 1970. The percentage of older persons will continue to rise as well; by 2020 people over 65 will represent over 13 percent of the national population.

Chapter 3 also described the "dependency ratio"—a single number which represents the proportional relationship between the size of the working population and the size of the dependent old-age population. The dependency ratio has distinct political implications, since the question of the allocation of scarce economic resources, as in the case of Social Security and other retirement benefits systems, is, ultimately, a political question. In 1970 the old-age dependency ratio (those age 65+ divided by those age 18-64) was .177; the projected old-age dependency ratio for the year 2020 is .213. The increase in this ratio indicates that a larger number of older persons will have to be economically supported by a relatively decreasing number of workers. The political implications of the dependency ratio are exacerbated by the fact that while the figures just presented use age 65 as the average retirement age, in fact the age of retirement is becoming lower.

Political problems of retirement and related pension and economic programs arise because at any single point in time, the current worker is largely paying the bill for current payments to the retired worker. Economists have referred to this situation in such terms as the "economics of intergenerational relationship" (Kreps, 1965) and the "intergenerational social contract" (Morgan, 1975). These terms imply a situation in which the worker of today contributes to the society's pension system on the expectation that future generations of workers will pay for his pension tomorrow.

Yet tomorrow's labor force, as indicated by the dependency ratio, will be relatively smaller as compared to the dependent, pension-receiving population. The political issue becomes magnified when we consider that the age of retirement is decreasing. This situation is made clearer if we compute the dependency ratio using age 60 rather than age 65 as the definition of the dependent older population. For 1970, using this younger average age of retirement, the dependency ratio would increase from .177 to .273—already greater than the .213 predicted for the year 2020 using the age 65. It should be clear, therefore, that the mere facts of demographic change, in which the older population is increasing in both absolute and relative terms, will make age a salient factor of the politics of the future.

Participation vs. disengagement. Demographic issues by themselves predict that age will, in general, be a major issue in future politics. But we must still consider the issue of whether the aged themselves will be substantially involved in political affairs. Some theories investigated by gerontologists have suggested that as people age they naturally or inherently disengage from a variety of social activities—including political participation. Yet the evidence presented in this chapter indicates otherwise. The drop-off in voting and other forms of political participation among older persons have been seen to be the consequence of the relatively low socioeconomic status of many older persons. It is simply a translation of the fact that poor persons participate less, and that a disproportionately large number of old people are poor. But when the appropriate statistical controls for socioeconomic status are employed (Verba and Nie, 1972), it is found that, on the average, older persons do not necessarily disengage from political activity.

Furthermore, among older persons in recent years there is a substantial amount of interest in political affairs—in contrast to what theories of old-age disengagement might predict. Table 18.8 presents data from an analysis of a 1960 Gallup Poll in which each person was asked to indicate his or her interest in politics. The percentages in this table—which are given by age, sex, and level of education—represent those who answered that they had a "great deal" of interest in politics. As the authors of this analysis conclude, "the highest reported interest is consistently at age 60 and higher, and the difference between the middle-aged and the elderly is pronounced at most educational levels for both sexes" (Glenn and Grimes, 1968, p. 570).

Education: a precondition for political participation.   While the data just described indicate that older persons are not necessarily disengaged from political activity, such information describes current or past groups of old people, while our present discussion is concerned with the politics of age in the future. A major component of this chapter has concerned the concept of the birth cohort as a major interpretational tool for variations in age-linked political behavior. In this context, we may briefly examine the educational composition of the future cohorts within the electorate as part of a consideration of the possible and probable participation of to-morrow's older people.

A number of studies, many of which are summarized in Milbrath's inventory of research findings (Milbrath, 1965), have indicated that level

Table 18.8   Self-reported interest in politics[a] (percent reporting "great deal" of interest)

Years of school completed	Ages		
	21–39	40–59	60 & up
Males			
8	18.2 (33)[b]	15.2 (112)	26.8 (97)
9–11	20.8 (72)	21.2 (99)	31.1 (45)
12	23.1 (173)	26.6 (139)	28.6 (42)
All educational levels	27.4 (456)	24.9 (502)	29.5 (298)
Females			
8	5.3 (38)	14.4 (111)	21.2 (104)
9–11	18.5 (130)	21.1 (90)	26.2 (42)
12	16.1 (192)	25.5 (165)	48.2 (56)
All educational levels	19.0 (496)	22.7 (520)	34.5 (330)

[a]The data are from Gallup Survey 637 (1960); data are for white respondents.
[b]The sample is inflated by about 100 percent by a weighting procedure used to increase representativeness. Therefore, the reported N's (in parentheses) are about twice the number of respondents represented.
SOURCE: Glenn and Grimes, 1968, Table 3, p. 570.

of formal education is a major predictor of the degree to which an individual is likely to be involved in politics. Thus, an important question for consideration concerns the educational composition of the older portion of the electorate. Based on a sequence of presidential election surveys, each of which was national in scope, Table 18.9 presents the educational distribution of the electorate from 1952 through 1972. Each year is divided into "high" and "low" education, with completion of at least a high school education being defined as "high" education.

We know that because of changes in the opportunity for education, the electorate has, in general, become more highly educated. This can be seen in the "total" row of the table. In 1952 only 38 percent of the electorate had a high education, while 62 percent had a high education in 1972. Our attention in the present discussion, however, is focused on those in the electorate over age 65. These individuals were born and educated in an earlier era when mass, free public education was not as widespread as it is today. While in 1952 only 19 percent of the 65+ group had a high education, by 1972 this had increased to 30 percent.

The important point for the future, however, is given by the data which describe the future cohorts of older members of the political system. The youngest group in the 1972 election survey will all be at least age 65 by the year 2016. Therefore, by the year 2020, the 65+ age group will be represented by a cohort which we already know to be highly educated. Where the 65+ group in 1952 was divided 19 percent/81 percent in terms of high-low educational attainment, the 65+ group by 2020 will be divided 86 percent/14 percent—a rather substantial reversal. From the vantage point of political participation, then, it is clear that tomorrow's older population will be better equipped for political participation and involvement than older people have been in the past.

Table 18.9   Age composition in education

Age group	1952 Lo[a]	Hi	1956 Lo	Hi	1960 Lo	Hi	1964 Lo	Hi	1968 Lo	Hi	1972 Lo	Hi
21–24	45	55	33	67	39	61	30	70	19	81	14	86
25–34	47	53	34	66	36	64	29	71	21	79	22	78
35–44	58	42	48	52	36	64	34	66	34	66	26	74
45–54	67	33	59	42	47	53	50	50	39	61	40	60
55–64	76	24	65	35	68	32	62	38	55	45	55	45
65+	81	19	78	22	71	29	67	33	71	29	70	30
Total	62	38	51	49	48	52	45	55	41	59	38	62

[a]"Lo" Education is defined as no education through incomplete high school; "Hi" Education is complete high school (or equivalency) and higher.
SOURCE: Each year was taken from the University of Michigan Center for Political Studies presidential election national survey. The data were made available through the Interuniversity Consortium for Political Research.

Additional forms of political activity.   An additional example of the political participation of tomorrow's cohort of older persons concerns "nonconventional" forms of political activity. Many of the studies of youth and political protest of the 1960s documented that new forms of political action became widespread and accepted as legitimate by substantial numbers of the younger cohort. It cannot, of course, be predicted with certainty that the forms of political activity supported by these younger people will continue to be supported when these same people become older. Yet we can at least know that the future cohort of older persons will include persons who, as part of their own political biographies, have participated in or approved of such activity. Illustrating this point are the data in Table 18.10, which portray the percentages among old and young in 1972 who approved of three forms of "nonconventional" political activity: protest politics in general, sit-ins, and civil disobedience.

The data in this table clearly indicate that the cohort which represents tomorrow's older persons is substantially more approving of these three modes of political activity than contemporary older persons. Indeed, tomorrow's older persons are from two to three times more supportive of protest politics, sit-ins, and civil disobedience. While these data represent age differences between young and old in 1972 and cannot prove a continuity between the young responses of 1972 and the responses of the same cohort in future years, the substantial differences between old and young might be symptomatic of a large "gap" between the generations on this issue of political participation. To the degree that the approving attitudes of the young are even partially adhered to when these individuals mature, we can expect older persons in the future to be quite politically active.

Age consciousness.   The final factor to consider in evaluating the future role which age may play in politics is the question of age consciousness. This chapter has demonstrated that the subjective age consciousness of the individual does, in fact, have an influence upon the individual's

Table 18.10   Attitudes toward "non-conventional" political participation (percent "approve")

	Age	
	18–35	*60+*
Protest politics	26.4%	10.2%
Civil disobedience	22.0%	9.3%
Sit-ins	10.8%	3.2%

SOURCE: Data are from the University of Michigan Center for Political Studies 1972 national presidential election survey. Data were made available through the Inter-university Consortium for Political Research.

social, economic, and political orientations. Therefore, it may be concluded that to the degree that older persons in the future become aware or conscious of their status as old persons, to such a degree age will become a salient focal point of political activity.

As mentioned earlier, while the question of subjective age identification is certainly not new to gerontologists, it has only recently been applied to the question of political orientations. The conclusion is one which recognizes that an individual's subjective identification with age does have identifiable political ramifications. If future generations of older persons also have such personally held subjective age identifications, we might predict that age will be a salient element of political debate and conflict. Indeed, as was pointed out previously, some gerontologists have conceptualized age identification in terms similar to that of minority-group identification. Thus, to the degree that the aged share some characteristics of minority groups, we might expect an increased consciousness followed by political action.

While the data in this chapter have demonstrated that subjective age consciousness does indeed predispose to certain patterns of political response, the question is whether we can expect such age consciousness to continue to develop in the future. One answer to such a question would focus on the development of a number of old-age organizations, each of which is attempting to raise the consciousness of older persons. In fact, the maturity of a political movement may well be indexed by the fact that a large number and a wide ideological range of organizations have emerged to serve the needs of the members of that movement. Thus, such organizations as the Gray Panthers, the National Council of Senior Citizens, the National Caucus of the Black Aged, and the American Association of Retired Persons are each purposely attempting to raise the consciousness of the aged in the context of political activity and political programs (Trela, 1968; Pratt, 1974; Jackson, 1974). And as we have argued elsewhere (Bengtson and Cutler, 1975), the kinds of age and generational consciousness which have characterized the young in previous years are likely to become characteristic of the elderly in the near future.

In summary, this chapter has suggested that a sequence of factors predicts that age will become an increasingly salient element of the national political debate. As a greater proportion of the national population is represented by the aged, as future cohorts of older persons have the educational resources and political experiences for participation in politics, as age consciousness and subjective age identification among the elderly increase, and as political leadership mirrors the demographic change in the population, we may expect that age will play an increasingly important role in political affairs.

References

Almond, G. 1960. *The American people and foreign policy,* Second edition. New York: Praeger.

Back, K. W. and Gergen, K. G. 1963. Apocalyptic and serial time orientations and the structure of opinions. *Public Opinion Quarterly* 27:427–442.

Bengtson, V. L. 1970. The generation gap: a review and typology of social-psychological perspectives. *Youth and Society* 2:7–31.

Bengtson, V. L. and Cutler, N. E. 1975. Generations and inter-generational relations in contemporary society. In *Handbook of Aging and the Social Sciences,* eds. E. Shanas and R. Binstock. New York: Van Nostrand, in press.

Binstock, R. H. 1974. Aging and the future of American politics. *Annals of the American Academy of Political and Social Science* 415:199–212.

Campbell, A. 1962. Social and psychological determinants of voting behavior. In *Politics of Age,* eds. W. Donahue and C. Tibbits, pp. 87–100. Ann Arbor: University of Michigan Press.

Campbell, A. 1971. Politics through the life cycle. *The Gerontologist* 11: 112–117.

Campbell, A.; Converse, P. E.; Miller, W. E.; and Stokes, D. E. 1960. *The American voter.* New York: Wiley.

Cowgill, D. O. 1974. The aging populations and societies. *The Annals of the American Academy of Political and Social Science* 415:1–18.

Crittenden, J. A. 1962. Aging and party affiliation. *Public Opinion Quarterly* 26:648–657.

Cutler, N. E. 1969. Generation, maturation, and party affiliation: a cohort analysis. *Public Opinion Quarterly* 33:583–588.

Cutler, N. E. 1974. The impact of subjective age identification on social and political attitudes. Paper prepared for the 27th Annual Meeting of the Gerontological Society, Portland, Oregon.

Cutler, N. E. 1975. Toward a political generations conception of political socialization. In *New Directions in Political Socialization,* eds. D. C. Schwartz and S. K. Schwartz, pp. 363–409. New York: The Free Press.

Douglass, E. B.; Cleveland, W. P.; and Maddox, G. L. 1974. Political attitudes, age, and aging: a cohort analysis of archival data. *Journal of Gerontology* 29:666–675.

Easton, D. 1965. *A systems analysis of political life.* New York: John Wiley and Sons, Inc.

Evan, W. M. 1959. Cohort analysis of survey data: a procedure for studying long-term opinion change. *Public Opinion Quarterly* 23:63–72.

Ewers, T. A. 1959. A study of the backgrounds of the successful and unsuccessful candidates for the Iowa supreme court. Unpublished Masters thesis. University of Iowa.

Flanigan, W. H. 1972 *Political behavior of the American electorate,* Second edition. Boston: Allyn and Bacon, Inc.

Foner, A. 1972. The polity. In *Aging and society, volume III: a sociology of age stratification,* eds. M. W. Riley, M. Johnson, and A. Foner, pp. 118–132. New York: Russell Sage.

Glenn, N. D. and Grimes, M. 1968. Aging, voting, and political interest. *American Sociological Review* 33:563–575.

Glenn, N. D. and Hefner, T. 1972. Further evidence on aging and party identification. *Public Opinion Quarterly* 36:31–47.

Greenstein, F. I. 1969. *Personality and politics.* Chicago: Markham Publishing Company.

Hall, G. S. 1923. *Senecence: the last half of life.* New York: D. Appleton and Company.

Higgins, T. S. 1949. The justices on the Wisconsin supreme court. *Wisconsin Law Review,* 1949, pp. 738–760.

Hoopes, T. 1949. An experiment in the measurement of judicial qualifications in the supreme court of Ohio. *University of Cincinnati Law Review* 18.

Hyman, H. H. 1972. Cohort analysis. In *Secondary analysis of sample surveys: principles, procedures, and potentialities,* ed. H. H. Hyman, pp. 274–290. New York: John Wiley and Sons, Inc.

Inglehart, R. 1967. An end to European integration? *American Political Science Review* 61:91–105.

Jackson, J. J. 1974. NCBA, black aged and politics. *Annals of the American Academy of Political and Social Science* 415:138–159.

Jennings, M. K. and Niemi, R. G. 1974. *The political character of adolescence: the influence of families and schools.* Princeton: Princeton University Press.

Key, V. O., Jr. 1963. *Public opinion and American democracy.* New York: Alfred A. Knopf.

Kirkpatrick, S. A. 1974. *Quantitative analysis of political data.* Columbus, Ohio: Charles E. Merrill Publishing Company.

Kreps, J. 1965. The economics of intergenerational relationship. In *Social structure and the family: generational relations,* eds. E. Shanas and G. Streib. Englewood Cliffs: Prentice Hall.

Lehman, H. C. 1947. The age of eminent leaders: then and now. *American Journal of Sociology* 52:342–351.

Lehman, H. C. 1953. *Age and achievement.* Princeton: Princeton University Press.

McClosky, H. 1967. Survey research in political science. In *Survey research in the social sciences,* ed. C. Y. Glock, pp. 63–143. New York: Russell Sage Foundation.

McTavish, D. G. 1971. Perceptions of old people: a review of research methodologies and fiindings. *The Gerontologist* 11:90–101.

Milbrath, L. W. 1965. *Political participation.* Chicago: Rand McNally.

Morgan, J. N. 1975. Economic problems of the aging and their policy implications. Paper presented for the Gerontological Society Conference on Public Assessment of the Conditions and Status of the Elderly, Santa Barbara, California, February 1975.

Peterson, W. A. 1971. Research priorities on perceptions and orientations toward aging and toward older people. *The Gerontologist* 11:60–63.

Polsby, N. 1968. The institutionalization of the U.S. House of Representatives. *American Political Science Review* 62:144–168.

Pratt, H. J. 1974. Old age associations in national politics. *Annals of the American Academy of Political and Social Science* 415:106–119.

Renshon, S. A. 1974. *Psychological needs and political behavior: a theory of personality and political efficacy.* New York: The Free Press.

Riley, M. W. 1973. Aging and cohort succession: interpretations and misinterpretations. *Public Opinion Quarterly* 37:35–49.

Rose, A. 1965. The subculture of the aging: a framework for research in social gerontology. In *Older people and their social world,* eds. A. Rose and W. Peterson, pp. 3–16. Philadelphia: F. A. Davis.

Rosenau, J. N. 1974. *Citizenship between elections: an inquiry into the mobilizable American.* New York: The Free Press.

Schaie, K. W. 1965. A general model for the study of developmental problems. *Psychological Bulletin* 64:92–107.

Schmidhauser, J. R. 1962. Age and judicial behavior: American higher appellate judges. In *Politics of age,* eds. W. Donahue and C. Tibbits, pp. 101–116. Ann Arbor: University of Michigan Press.

Schmidhauser, J. R. and Cutler, N. E. 1975. The comparative analysis of age and politics: specifications for a research archive of data on political elites. Unpublished manuscript. University of Southern California.

Schreiber, E. M. and Marsden, L. R. 1972. Age and opinions on a government program of medical aid. *Journal of Gerontology* 27:95–101.

Streib, G. F. 1965. Are the aged a minority group? In *Applied sociology,* eds. A. W. Gouldner and S. M. Miller. New York: Free Press.

Taussig, F. W. and Joslyn, C. S. 1932. *American business leaders.* New York: Macmillan.

Trela, J. E. 1972. Age structure of voluntary associations and political self-interest among the aged. *The Sociological Quarterly* 13:244–252.

Verba, S. and Nie, N. H. 1972. *Participation in America.* New York: Harper and Row.

Warner, W. L. and Abegglen, J. C. 1955. *Occupational mobility in American business and industry, 1928–1952.* Minneapolis: University of Minnesota Press.

Witmer, T. R. 1964. The aging of the House. *Political Science Quarterly* 79: 526–541.

Name Index

Subject Index

Adaptability: cell age and, 207–8; in elderly 190; to external events, 244–5; in relocation, 299

Administration on Aging (H. E. W.), 4, 264, 353, 366

Adrenaline, 170, 234

Adrenocorticotropic hormone (ACTH), 170–1, 234

Adult development, 114–8

Adult socialization, 76

Adults, intelligence testing of, 112–23

Aerobic capacity, 261, 264, 269, 272

After Many a Summer Dies the Swan (Huxley), 16

Age and Achievement (Lehman), 393

Age changes (*see also* Aging; Aging process): age differences and, 382; functional, in time, 236; intelligence and, 112–7; learning performance and, 125–30; in memory, 130–46; personal losses and, 298–300; in physiological functions, 258–62; in test response speed, 127–8

Age consciousness (*see also* Subjective age identification), and politics, 402–3

Age groups (*see also* Birth cohorts; Generations; Life cycles; Maturational age): activity concepts of, 87–8; biological factors in, 73; as birth cohorts, 53; educational attainments by, 64; intelligence differences, 113, 116–7; numbers, by dates, 80; residential mobility by, 58; sex ratios by, 49, 51; and status, 73

Age-segregated housing, 296

Age-sex population pyramid, 35–6

Age-sex role changes, 102

Age 65 and over (*see* Elderly persons)

Age-specific death rates, 41

Age-specific sex ratio, 51

Age-specific survival rate, 33

Age status: conflicts, 72; expectations, 76; norms, 75–7; systems, 74–7

Aging (*see also* Aging process): behavioral changes and, 160; causes of, 21–3; in cell replication studies, 218–20; chronological, 70–1, 378; creativity and, 81, 83; and intellectual growth, 121–2; interventions against, 9–14, 250–3; normalized, 249–53; and politi-

cal activity, 374–7; sociological aspects of, 70–6

Aging process (*see also* Aging; Gerontology; Life expectancy): animal studies of, 153–172; behavioral changes in, 155–60, 165; biological-decremental model of, 179; brain changes and, 165–71; in cells, 204–8; exploratory behavior slowdown, 155–60, 165; hypokinetic disease and, 262; identity transformation, 74; performance effects of, 258; physiological aspects, 22, 232–6, 258–62; in pigmentation, 204; psychological aspects, 171–3, 181, 257–8; social problems, 82–8; television image of, 316, 322–3

Aging population ratio, 65–6

Aging reversibility, 182, 185

Alpha rhythms, 182–8

American Ass'n of Retired Persons, 25, 319, 403

American Chemical Society, 22

American Gerontological Society, 83

American Orthopsychiatric Ass'n, 22

Americans for Democratic Action, 390

Andrus Gerontological Center, 3

Animal experimentation in aging: behavioral changes, 153–65, 171–2, 211–2; brain function recovery, 162–5; learning and memory, 155–8, 160; manipulation of environment in, 160–2; sexual decrement, 154–5

Anxiety, 129, 190–1

Area Agencies on Aging, 300–1

Army Alpha intelligence tests, 112

Arousal level, 190–3

Arteriosclerosis, 21–2, 172, 240–1, 247, 263

Arteriosclerosis: A Survey of the Problem (Cowdry, ed.), 22

Associationism, 125–7, 133

Attitudes: to aging on TV, 316; on intergenerational relations, 95–6; on late remarriages, 104–5; on late sexuality, 243; on longevity, 249; on political activity, 377–80; toward television, 332–4

Autonomic arousal hypotesis, 128–9

Autonomic nervous system (ANS), 128, 191–2